PAPAL POWER

Jean-Guy Vaillancourt

PAPAL POWER

A Study of Vatican Control over Lay Catholic Elites

UNIVERSITY OF CALIFORNIA PRESS

Berkeley · Los Angeles · London

University of California Press
Berkeley and Los Angeles, California

University of California Press, Ltd.
London, England

© 1980 by
The Regents of the University of California

Printed in the United States of America

1 2 3 4 5 6 7 8 9

Library of Congress Cataloging in Publication Data

Vaillancourt, Jean-Guy.
    Papal power. A study of Vatican control over lay
    Catholic elites
    Bibliography: p.
    Includes index.
    1. Papacy—History. 2. Laity—Catholic Church.
3. Catholic Church—Teaching office. I. Title.
BX957.V36   306'.6   78-59443
ISBN 0-520-03733-2

IN MEMORIAM

IVAN VALLIER (1927–1974)

Contents

List of Tables

Preface

This book attempts to deal sociologically with some aspects of the phenomenon of power and control as they have been exercised in the Roman Catholic Church in recent times. It is mostly a study of Paul VI's exercise of power over the lay movement, although it started out as a survey of the third World Congress for the Lay Apostolate (held in Rome in October 1967) and gradually evolved into a study of papal control over the laity and the challenges to papal and hierarchical authority by both priests and laymen before, during, and after that congress. Hence it ultimately concentrates mainly on the rise and fall of the Montini papacy.

The research, specifically the survey and field work which served as the basis for this study, was undertaken with the assistance of a pre-doctoral fellowship from Le Conseil des Arts du Canada and a comparative-international grant from the Institute of International Studies at the University of California, Berkeley. The work was first undertaken as a Ph.D. dissertation under the direction of the late Professor Ivan Vallier, and was finished under the direction of Professor Charles Y. Glock. I would like to express my sincere gratitude to Professor Glock, the chairman of my dissertation committee, and to Professors Franz Schurmann and Philip Selznick, who served with him on that committee. I am also indebted to the organizers of and participants in the third World Congress for the Lay Apostolate whose kind cooperation made the questionnaire survey possible, and to many experts who have helped me understand better what makes the Vatican organization run.

Patricia Fournier and Manon Lalumière did a superb job in typing the manuscript. Jesse Phillips and Sylvia Wees made a great contribution as the editors and critics of various drafts of my chapters. Grant Barnes and others at the University of California Press have greatly helped me in my efforts to transform a doctoral dissertation into what I hope is now a more readable book.

Finally, Pauline and Véronique, my wife and my daughter, must be thanked for their patience during the many years that it took to finish this book.

1

Introduction

1. THE VATICAN AND THE LAITY
IN THE ROMAN CATHOLIC CHURCH

During the years since the mid-1950s, a crisis of authority has hit the whole of the Roman Catholic Church. The brief but revolutionary pontificate of John XXIII (1958–1963), the second Vatican Council (1962–1965), which he convened, and public reaction to the policies of his successor, Paul VI (1963–1978), have revealed the existence of strong conflicting tendencies inside a church looked upon for centuries as the prototype of a firmly based, conservative religious organization. Many transformations that were deemed unthinkable only a short time ago are now considered to be normal occurrences or imminent possibilities, both by those who welcome and by those who oppose them. Deep changes have been occurring at various levels of the Church's organizational structure, as well as in the attitudes, opinions, and behavior of clergy and laity alike. Pressures for reform have even struck at the traditional center of Catholicism itself, the institution of the papacy and its far-flung, proverbially effective apparatus of religious control. Numerous authors, journalists, historians, theologians, and sociologists have in recent years examined and discussed this new and in some ways unprecedented crisis.[1]

True, protest movements for change, even quite drastic change, had surfaced within the Catholic Church in previous centuries. A few of these even met with some limited success, but radical reform had nearly always been forced to take its course outside the Catholic fold, and pressure for change within the Church had nearly always been suppressed by ecclesiastical officials. Now, however, with the new fluidity of Church boundaries, and increasing pluralism and secularization, it has become increasingly difficult to enforce unpopular decisions through coercion and exclusion. Consequently, the Vatican must now try to exercise its control over Catholics through normative and manipulative means (e.g., through socialization and co-optation) rather than through coercive and repressive power.

During the Middle Ages and under feudalism, when the Catholic Church was a dominant institution in society, papal power grew in importance, relying often on force to attain its ends, which were political as much as they were religious. The Crusades and, later on, the Inquisition stand as the two most notorious of these violent papal ventures. But with the decline of the Portuguese and Spanish empires, with the advent of the Reformation and of the intellectual, democratic, and industrial revolutions, the Catholic hierarchy lost much of its influence and power. Unable to continue using physical coercion, the papacy was led to strengthen its organizational structure and to perfect a wide range of normative means of control. The declaration of papal infallability by the first Vatican Council (Vatican I), in 1870, was an important milestone in that direction. The stress on the absolute authority of the pope in questions of faith and morals helped turn the Church into a unified and powerful bureaucratic organization, and paved the way for the establishment of the papacy-laity relationship as we know it today.

Faced with cultural and institutional threats which were undermining traditional forms of authority, the modern papacy has found it difficult to cope with the new problems that have been emerging during the last hundred years or so. Knowing very well that the autocratic methods of the past had little chance of success, the papacy devised new and more sophisticated methods, adding to an already impressive arsenal, in order to meet the challenges to its authority. Like some political and business leaders, it has found it necessary (if not always advantageous) to loosen the reins of its power.

The present crisis goes much deeper than the issues that the two Vatican Councils officially tried to resolve. Erosion of the centuries-old social model of the institutional church, of the even older division between laity and clergy, and of the centralized hierarchical authority is taking place with surprising rapidity. Church leaders are faced with a generalized anti-authority protest that is world-wide and that even includes a few members of the hierarchy among its spokesmen. In meeting this process of challenge and change the Vatican has made efforts to use time-tested formulas of social control as well as some newer techniques.

For a comprehensive understanding of change in the Catholic Church at this point, many studies of various aspects of those control mechanisms are needed. In the limited context of the top administrative levels of the Church and its relations with a supradiocesan lay elite, it should be possible to put a sociological approach to work in order to begin an investigation of an authoritarian leadership's responses to growing threats and pressures from its grass-roots constituency.

Sociology has neglected the study of religious bureaucracies, their leaders, and the control mechanisms that they use to protect their authority. As far as the papacy and the Vatican are concerned, we can find certain interesting elements of analysis in the writings of Karl Marx, Friedrich Engels, Max Weber, Ernst Troeltsch, Antonio Gramsci, and a few other, more contemporary, authors,[2] but by and large, very little work has been done in this area. Many of the theoretically useful tools of the sociology of religion, such as the church-sect dichotomy, the dimensionalization of religious behavior, and the secularization hypothesis, are not very well suited for the kind of analysis envisaged here. Since I want to examine the problem of religious control, some theoretical instruments from political sociology and from organizational analysis may prove to be more useful than many of the standard tools of the sociology of religion.

Power is not only actual participation in a decision-making process. It is also a more generalized capacity to influence or to affect social activities, or, as Amitai Etzioni puts it, "a capacity to overcome part or all of the resistance, to introduce changes in the face of opposition."[3] Power is not necessarily coercive (i.e. based on the use of force). It can also be persuasive (in which case it is quite similar to influence) or utilitarian (i.e. economic).

The concept of authority is somewhat akin to that of power, with the added connotation of legitimacy. "Authority," says Etzioni, "is defined as legitimate power."[4] Authority is not competence or personal influence or leadership. It has to do with legitimate, institutionalized, officially sanctioned power. It is the right to make decisions.

Control is another related concept, but its meaning is more fluid than that of power or authority. It can refer to the internalization of norms and values, but it can also refer to coercive, remunerative, or normative power used by a social agent to compel or convince another social agent to abide by certain rules, or to stay in line. Social control can be imposed by external force, accepted for economic reasons, or internalized in one's conscience by socialization and by manipulative techniques. Etzioni has built an interesting typology of organizations and deduced a number of generalizations, using the above tripartite distinction between the kinds of power that social agents utilize to maintain social control. Organizations, according to Etzioni, can use coercive, remunerative, or normative power, or a combination of these. In religious organizations like the Catholic Church, normative power is usually predominant, even if the two other kinds are some-times used also.[5]

Etzioni's discussions of these matters owe a lot to Max Weber, who defines a church essentially as a user of a combination of norma-tive and coercive power:

> An imperatively co-ordinated corporate group will be called a hiero-cratic group (*hierokratischer Verband*) if and in so far as for the enforce-ment of its order it employs "psychic" coercion through the distri-bution or denial of religious benefits ("hierocratic" coercion). A compulsory hierocratic association with continuous organization will be called a "church" if and in so far as its administrative staff claims a monopoly of the legitimate use of hierocratic coercion.[6]

My own analysis of the means of control used by the Vatican to assure the obedience or conformity of the laity focuses on what Etzioni calls normative controls, and on what Weber calls psychic coercion, although it takes into account the other methods used. It also takes into consideration Weber's well-known types of legitimate authority (traditional, charismatic, legal-rational), along with other contribu-tions to the debate on power, authority, and control by social scien-tists like Etzioni, French and Raven, and certain Neo-Marxists. The conceptual tools developed by these people are useful, because they permit us to identify the particular types of measures that Church offi-cials are using at present to maintain their authority.

While Weber was inclined to stress the coercive aspect of the means used by the Church, he noted also the increasing use of more "modern" kinds of control:

> Certainly, the goal of the Catholic Church is to salvage its ecclesias-tical power interests, which have increasingly become objectified into

a doctrine of the fundamental interests of the church, by the employ-
ment of the same modern instruments of power employed by secular
institutions.[7]

It could also be said that many of the "modern instruments of
power employed by secular institutions" were first developed by the
Church. The word "propaganda," after all, has its origins in the
name of a Vatican bureau, De Propaganda Fide, charged with the pro-
pagation of the Catholic faith—a name which has been changed to the
Congregation for the Evangelization of Peoples, probably because of
the pejorative connotations the word "propaganda" has taken on.

Everett C. Hughes once said that sociologically everything has happened in the Catholic Church. Certainly the Church has, at different
times and in different contexts, used the whole range of means of control. But what is important here is not so much to try to classify the
means used in a particular instance under one of Etzioni's three categories, but rather to identify the major ones used by various popes and
the changes and trends that may be discernible.

In an article on religious ideology and social organization, Charles
Y. Glock uses a typology similar to that of Etzioni but more general in
scope, distinguishing between ideology, sanctions, and compensations
as means of maintaining social control. Glock notes that compensations
and especially sanctions (particularly those of the oppressive type) are
usually employed in cases where ideology is not powerful enough to
contain dissent.[8] It could be added that sometimes the use of physical
compensations and sanctions is practically excluded. This is increasingly
the case for religious organizations operating in a secular pluralistic
society. Consequently, ideological rationalizations and spiritual compensations and sanctions (i.e. psychic coercion) are more commonly
relied upon.

My study examines some of the techniques of control used by a beleaguered papacy in recent years. The major effort will be one of concrete description and analysis rather than an abstract attempt at
theorizing. On the basis of the historical and sociological data I have
assembled, I endeavor to build a new classification model of means of
control that could prove useful for the empirical study of religious and
other normative organizations. I feel that at this stage in the development of sociology the lowly job of assembling useful classificatory
models is too often eschewed for the more glorious task of construct-
ing brilliant and sophisticated causal models and theories that often
have little correspondence to social reality. My model-building process
takes its point of origin in a focus on the challenges to papal authority

that are being posed by the lay movement in the Church, and on various responses of the papacy to these threats. I see these lay-papal conflicts as expressions not only of internal organizational struggle, but also of other conflicts, such as the class and national-ethnic conflicts which inevitably appear inside, and in the environment of, an organization as vast and diversified as the Catholic Church.

Is the interest in the laity on the part of the Vatican and the episcopate (through Catholic Action, Christian Democracy, and certain organizations for the lay apostolate) directed toward mobilizing the laity in the defense of the interests of Church authorities, or toward the sharing of power and increasing of grass-roots participation in the decision-making processes of the Church? It is my hypothesis that the first alternative fits the evidence rather more than the second.

This problem has various aspects. Are the coercive and manipulative means of control used by Church authorities to keep the laity in line constant and necessary aspects of Church organization, or did they come about mostly because Church leaders are habituated to and fascinated by the use of political and economic power? Has there been a move away from physical to psychic coercion, and from coercive to normative means of control? Is the present insistence on dialogue and participation an effort to recover ground lost by the necessary abandonment of coercive power, or a willed decision to liberalize and debureaucratize the Church in order to meet the democratic aspirations of contemporary men and women, and of the Catholic laity more specifically? These questions will be answered by an examination of the demands put forward along these lines by Catholic lay people who are involved organizationally at the supradiocesan level. We shall see if there are noticeable differences among the demands when we categorize the laity by international geocultural regions and by age. Then we shall see how the papacy has reacted to these demands.

A second, and secondary, aim is to lay the groundwork for an explanation of papal mechanisms of control in the light of the politics and the economics of the Vatican. Most attempts at explanation of papal authority stress religious-theological and personal-psychological factors. While these factors have a certain impact, I think that they are usually overemphasized and that not enough attention, in the analysis of the moving forces in Church policy and in hierarchical organization, is given to the area of political and financial interest. Finally, I examine unresolved dilemmas and tensions that exist in the Church because of the perseverance of antipodal aims at the heart of the present crisis.

2. OUTLINE OF THE STUDY

The book is divided into an introductory chapter, three parts containing two chapters each, and a concluding chapter. The material is presented in a roughly chronological framework. I am particularly interested in looking at the changing patterns of lay pressures for change and of authoritarian papal control, especially in the recent period from Pius IX to Paul VI.

Chapter 1 spells out the plan, the aim, and the general methodology of the study, with emphasis on the reasons why I think a focus on papal control and lay demands is important from a sociohistorical point of view.

Part One concentrates on the past history of the lay-papal relationship. Chapter 2 traces how authority has developed historically in the Catholic Church, from the beginnings of Christianity, and how Church officials have responded, over the centuries, to major challenges to their authority. Chapter 3 looks at the way Church authorities in Rome have related to the organized lay apostolate between 1950 and the end of the second Vatican Council (Vatican II), with special attention to the two World Congresses for the Lay Apostolate held in Rome in 1951 and 1957, and to John XXIII and Vatican II's relationship with the organized Catholic laity.

Part Two focuses on the third World Congress for the Lay Apostolate, held in 1967, two years after the close of Vatican II, at a critical period of Paul VI's pontificate. In chapter 4 we see how Church authorities responded to threats to their control that manifested themselves at the congress. Relying mainly on the techniques of participant observation and documentary analysis, this chapter shows how the Vatican tried to keep a tight control over the lay leaders whom it had invited to participate, how it responded to lay pressures and demands, and what selection and control mechanisms were used.

Chapter 5 builds on information collected through a sample of the national delegates present at the 1967 congress. The survey was made in order to highlight the nature of the pressures and demands for more lay power in the Church and the Vatican's response to them. Some of the opinions and attitudes tapped here constitute an important set of lay demands—the demands of the officially recognized lay leaders active at the supradiocesan level.

Part Three examines the sources and present manifestations of papal control over the Catholic laity. Stressing political and socioeconomic considerations for an understanding of the Vatican-laity relationship since the middle of the nineteenth century, it gives particular attention to the evolution of Paul VI's pontificate after 1967.

Chapter 6 investigates the political and socioeconomic roots of papal authority and control in the Church from the time of Pius IX to the end of John XXIII's pontificate. It pinpoints some of the factors that have influenced developments in the Vatican-laity relationship, and shows how the ideology of reigning popes and increasingly active laymen was closely entwined with the international sociopolitical situation, and with the situation in Italy. Papal power in recent times cannot be understood if we do not look at the historical relationship of the Vatican vis-à-vis contemporary society and the state. Inevitably, much of the focus is on developments in Italy and Rome, the strategic centers of contemporary Catholicism. The shaping of Church policy by Italian politics and by socioeconomic developments in Italy, especially during the last hundred years, is shown to have been an important factor in the growth of papal power since Pius IX.

Chapter 7 focuses on Paul VI's pontificate, and on the reasons for his turn to the right after the close of Vatican II. It stresses the relationship between the papacy and the organized lay associations, and between both of these and Italian politics and society.

Paul VI's conservatism in the years following Vatican II retained some elements of liberalism. The chapter seeks to show how this "progressive conservatism" must be distinguished from the extreme positions of reactionary traditionalists like Archbishop Marcel Lefebvre and his followers, who went so far as to reject papal authority because of Paul VI's refusal to repudiate the decisions of Vatican II.[9]

Henri Fesquet, the religious editor of *Le Monde* and one of the most perceptive of Vatican experts, wrote just after Vatican II a small book whose title was "Has Rome Been Converted?" He answered the question mainly in the affirmative, supporting with evidence from the Council his belief that the Vatican was being won over by progressives. But Fesquet soon reversed this opinion, publishing in 1968, after Paul VI's trip to Bogotá, a book entitled "A Church in a State of Mortal Sin," in which he showed that the Catholic Church had not changed much, after all, since the days of Pius XII, thus agreeing with another leading Vatican expert, perhaps the foremost living authority on the modern papacy, Carlo Falconi, who wrote an entire book in 1968 to describe and explain Paul VI's surprising turnabout a few years after Vatican II.[10] Falconi sees the conservative 1968 declarations and actions of Paul VI as an inevitable consequence of the liberalization made possible by John XXIII and Vatican II.

Chapter 7, like chapter 6, gives some attention to the political roots of the papacy, but goes farther in that it briefly examines the finances of the Vatican and notes some of the links between economic power and political and religious ideology. Is it really true that the financial dealings of the Vatican flow from ideological necessities, or could not a case be made that the relationship between these variables is at least reciprocal? This issue has as yet received little attention from sociologists. As Bryan Wilson points out:

> In Western Christianity . . . property came to be owned by a unified church corporation once the Hildebrandine reforms had established a celibate clergy. Indeed, the Roman church, in spite of disendowment in various countries and periods, is one of the largest corporate property owners in the world, even if one leaves out of account its specifically undeployable wealth in the form of church premises and religioartistic assets. This wealth is controlled by specialized agencies which the hierarchy has empowered, and their functions are not open to lay scrutiny. The power of these agencies and the extent to which economic action is dictated by spiritual or political considerations have never been subjected to sociological analysis. The church is a large shareholder in many, especially Italian, enterprises and operates in the capital markets of the world.''

Finally, chapter 8, the conclusion, summarizes the data from the preceeding chapters, returns in a more analytic and classificatory fashion to the problem of the means of control being used by the papacy as its authority is increasingly challenged by both lay and clerical forces, and gives a glimpse of what the findings of this study might mean for the future of papal control over the laity in the Church, and for the future of sociological research on that topic.

I have limited my investigation in order to focus attention on certain definable and researchable issues. It would be presumptuous to try to analyze an organization as large and as complex as the Catholic Church without limiting drastically the questions of interest. Here I am preoccupied with papal control over lay elites. More precisely, I look at the religious and political ideology and practice of lay leaders at the international and national levels, and at their interaction with high Vatican officials.

The autonomous development of the lay sphere that was gaining ground under John XXIII continued under Paul VI, but it suffered from the climate of suspicion created by his fear of doctrinal and political deviations and by the general crisis of Catholicism. During the third World Congress for the Lay Apostolate, in 1967, it was clear that the pope and his curia were protagonists of a sort of struggle for power in the Church, along with the Catholic bishops from around the world whose representatives were meeting in the first Synod of Bishops, and with the laymen who were present at the lay congress. The first World Congress for the Lay Apostolate, in 1951, cannot be understood if we forget that it was essentially the brain child of Msgr. Giovanni-Battista Montini (the future Paul VI), then Pius XII's under-secretary of state for Ordinary (i.e. internal) Affairs. Similarly the second World Congress, in 1957 near the end of Pius XII's pontificate, cannot be evaluated if we are unaware of the tension that existed during the mid-1950s between the conservative pope and curia, on the one hand, and the weak "left" opposition, on the other, best symbolized by student and worker Catholic Action groups and by Montini, whom Pius exiled to the archbishopric of Milan in 1954.[12] Oriented as they were to different sectors of Italian politics and social classes, Pius XII and Montini were not, of course, entirely autonomous actors. It is for this reason that the data pertaining to the third World Congress for the Lay Apostolate, which was the point of departure of my investigation, have been put in the larger ecclesiastical and political context, and that I have used a sociohistorical perspective to complement the insights on the laity obtained through survey data and interviews. Catholic organizations being what Gianfranco Poggi has called "sponsored organizations," it is inevitable that a study which takes them as its point of departure ends up giving a lot of attention to the hierarchy and especially to the Vatican.[13]

Much attention is given to the papacy because of its central importance in Catholicism. If Richard Neustadt was able to say that Americans are more and more dependent on the temperament of the man who sits in the White House,[14] *a fortiori* can we say that Catholics are very dependent on the temperament of the man who sits on the throne of Saint Peter, since the pope is an absolute ruler, elected for life, who is not accountable to any judiciary or legislative control. In general, institutional factors are very important, but the position and personality of leaders should never be discounted as having no weight.

3. METHODOLOGY AND HISTORY

It is not always easy to obtain access to sizable groups of religious leaders, at the national and international level, with questionnaires or interviews. The third World Congress of the Lay Apostolate, held concurrently with the first Synod of Bishops, also meeting in Rome, afforded a unique opportunity to obtain information about an international elite of lay Catholics. My main instrument of data collection was a questionnaire distributed to a sample of the congress participants.[15] Since that technique was not sufficient to generate the type of information needed, interviews with informants and participant observation were also used. I had studied sociology in Rome from September 1961 to June 1964, and during 1966 had obtained more than a hundred interviews with Catholic lay leaders in France. Further, in 1972, as a journalist for Radio-Canada and with a group of Vatican-watching journalists, I had accompanied Pope Paul during his December trip around the world. These experiences proved very helpful for an understanding of what has been going on in the Church in recent years. For the most part, however, my study is based on analysis of documentary materials obtained from the Permanent Committee for International Congresses of the Lay Apostolate (COPECIAL) and the Council on the Laity, or publicly available in libraries and elsewhere. The following journals and periodicals have been particularly useful: *Acta Apostolicae Sedis* (for papal pronouncements), *Aggiornamenti sociali*, *La Civiltà Cattolica*, *Concilium*, *La Documentation Catholique*, *Etudes*, *L'Espresso*, *Informations Catholiques Internationales*, *La Lettre*, *The National Catholic Reporter*, *L'Osservatore Romano*, *Social Compass*, *Testimonianze*, and *The Laity Today*.

It is my hope that this study yields some information on the continuing conflict in the Catholic Church between the forces of domination and control and the pressures and demands for change and autonomy. It makes use of eyewitness accounts and participant observation, the analysis of empirical data, and examination of some of the historical factors of influence, particularly those active during the past hundred years. To help in this latter examination, an effort is made to place the papacy, particularly the popes of the twentieth century, in sociological and political focus and to treat the emerging lay elite in the same manner.

Because the present crisis is not merely religious, but part of a general cultural-institutional breakdown of traditional forms that became world-wide during the 1960s, it is important to use a structural approach and to look at that breakdown in the context of social history, giving due importance to economic, political, and ideological factors.

The Roman Catholic Church is a structure that has existed over most of the history of western civilization. In fact, to say that it has been instrumental in giving birth to western civilization would not be an exaggeration. The organizational image that still most often comes to mind when reference is made to the Church is that of a pyramidal or monarchical structure. On the top is the pope, the Supreme Pontiff, with his chief assistants and advisers, the cardinals, who also hold the top positions in the Roman Curia. Below the cardinals come the various types of bishops and monsignors: the archbishops and metropolitans, the resident bishops, the vicars and prefects apostolic, abbots and prelates and apostolic administrators. Below these august figures are pastors, priests, brothers, and nuns. Finally, at the bottom, in another world practically, is the great mass of the faithful, the laity. The development of this stratified and basically two-tiered conception of the Church, shaped during many centuries of history, was challenged at Vatican II, and other, more collegial, models were considered in its place. One such model is that of an organism, a body, the mystical Body of Christ. Another is that of a new Israel, the pilgrim people, the people of God. A third is that of an open community where those in positions of authority consider themselves to be the servants, rather than the masters, of the whole community. This third model seems to be the original form that predominated in the early Christian church.[16]

I use the structural-institutional model, since it seems the one that most closely approximates the present reality, and distinguish five major categories in the structure of the Church: the papacy, the Roman Curia, the bishops (i.e. the episcopate), the priests, and the laymen. By the word "Vatican" I mean the first two. (Theoretically, "Vatican" refers to the pope's state, while "Holy See" refers to the ecclesiastical institution; in practice the distinction has little value for the researcher, since it is used mostly by Church officials to cover the political nature of many of the papacy's activities.) By "hierarchy" (Church officials or Church authorities), I mean the first three categories; by "clergy," the first four; and by "Church," usually all five. Some cardinals work in the Roman Curia only, some run a diocese, and some have the responsibility of a diocese and are also officers of the curia.

The study views the Church primarily (but not only) as a bureaucratic organization. We shall see whether Weber's characterization of the Church as a monocratic (as opposed to a collegial) variety of bureaucracy—that is, as the pure type of bureaucratic organization—is still adequate today.[17] We shall see whether the bureaucratization is diminishing, and if so, whether it is limited by traditional and patrimonial elements rather than by democratic and collegial types of restraints.

A Neo-Marxian approach, sensitive to Weber's preoccupation with bureaucratization and intent on viewing the Catholic Church as an ideological apparatus of social legitimation, brings a further contribution to our understanding of that organization. Bureaucracies are not only instruments that control their members; they are also structures in which power is concentrated in the hands of higher officials who are usually members of the ruling elites and classes, and who use their power over people and resources to help maintain and reproduce (rarely to challenge) the various social systems in which they operate. Consequently, bureaucracies often become the locus of internal struggles between officials and members which reproduce wider social struggles between social groups and social classes. I want to see whether this kind of approach can be applied to the Church. Instead of looking at the function that religion or Catholicism as a whole plays in the social structure, I look at various groups or actors inside Catholicism, their different positions and interests, their interaction, and especially their conflicts, over time, in varied situations and social structures. Sociology has made us increasingly aware that religious bureaucracies are very much determined in their origin, development, and decline by the other social institutions that form their social context. Most contemporary sociologists would agree that religious organizations help reproduce the socioeconomic structure, even if generally the economic base has a determinant effect on religious organizations.[18]

The reproduction and legitimation functions of religion are not necessarily conservative functions. Religion is often an opiate, but it can also be, sometimes, a stimulator of social upheaval, as Marx, Engels, and Kautsky have acknowledged.[19] Religion can sacralize or legitimate the social order, but can sometimes desacralize or work to change it. In their book on the Protestant Episcopalian church in the United States, Charles Y. Glock, Benjamin R. Ringer, and Earl R. Babbie write: "In some countries, the church has been the center of established political control—in others the seat of revolution."[20] Interestingly enough, in the Catholic Church both functions are operative, but with varying strength, depending on the actors and the situations, and also on time and place. The two roles have always been available to those who wished to fill them, and the dialectic between the two groups of actors has been as important to the drama of the Church as the religious ritual. As we shall see in the following chapters, the conservative and comforting functions have been mostly monopolized by the Vatican, and the lay movement has chiefly, but not exclusively, appeared as one of the challengers of that conservatism.

Marx, Engels, Kautsky, and Weber have written about the internal conflicts inside various religious traditions and they have inspired much of the later work sensitive to this preoccupation.[21] A structural-institutional approach of the Marxian-Weberian type, in opposition to the structural-functional approach, not only makes us look at an organization as the locus of conflicts of power (both internal and external), but also forces us to analyze it historically and dialectically.

My survey of participants in the third World Congress for the Lay Apostolate would have little meaning if I did not place the congress in its historical context with the necessary social and political background. Thus, I attempt not only to consider the Catholic Church as a concrete social structure, but also look at it in its historical setting. That is why I move from a discussion of the history of the Vatican in relation to lay developments to an analysis of the lay congresses of recent years. Then I examine the relationships of the Vatican to European, and particularly Italian, politics over the past hundred years or so. I conclude with an analysis of the situation under Paul VI.

Among contemporary sociologists there is an increasing awareness of the importance of the historical dimension of social institutions, and of the fact that valid theory can be generated from the study of historical materials. Madeleine Grawitz notes in her textbook on social science research (a textbook which has come to be considered the major one in the French language):

> It is certain that sociology, because of its recent development in terms of limited, concrete, and contemporary research, has too often kept its distance from both history and theory. Its own progress and the need to reach the level of explanation are bringing it back today toward both.[22]

In the present study, historical materials are used extensively to put the data in perspective. An effort is made to discuss the issues in a larger sociohistorical context, as Dennis Wrong suggests sociologists should more often do: "The most fruitful questions for sociology are always questions referring to the realities of a particular historical situation."[23]

Irving M. Zeitlin, in his lucid critique of contemporary sociological theory, insists on the same idea:

> The study of the changes a social system undergoes requires, among other things, a study of its history. . . . The social scientist who studies a social structure without studying its history will never truly understand any given state of that structure or the forces operating to change it.[24]

Zeitlin goes on to show that Marx, Weber, and even Durkheim all stressed the causal role of history.[25]

My object in using historical materials is not, obviously, to uncover long-forgotten facts about the leadership of the Catholic Church, or to make a contribution to Church history. It is, rather, to get a socio-logical perspective for an understanding of the social and political background of the present situation in key sectors of Catholicism. What is attempted here is a radical and critical reconstruction of his-torical process in order to reveal the relations between certain forces of control and domination and certain forces of protest and democratiza-tion operating in the religious sphere.

Franz X. Kaufmann, a leading specialist of the sociological study of the Catholic Church as an organization, points to the fact that research on the Church is "turning more and more toward the complex prob-lems of ecclesiastical organization."[26] Kaufmann points, however, to the limits of a pure sociology-of-organizations approach. Such an approach should be complemented with an orientation toward the study of the social constitution of the Church and the points of view of a sociology of knowledge, because of the intimate amalgamation of problems of organization and of meaning ("signification"), the problems of organization and ideology.

Like the Bolshevik party, the Vatican is, above all, an organizational weapon in the hands of the papacy and other top ecclesiastical officials. Religious ideology has increasingly become subordinated to organiza-tional imperatives.[27] Among these internal and external organizational imperatives, organizational control of lay elites seems to have become a major preoccupation and necessity for Church authorities, and conse-quently it should be a major focus of interest for the sociologist of religion.

In his book on modern organizations Etzioni mentions that orga-nizational control is seriously affected by the environment in which an organization operates, and that the environmental conditions that affect the normative power of organizations are quite difficult to see. He notes that organizational competition and the nature of the organi-zation are important determinants of the effect of environment on the organization. He ends his study of organizational controls with the following paragraph:

> We know little about the effect of organizational environment on control even in Western societies. The study of this relationship in other cultures, especially in less developed and nondemocratic soci-eties, remains one of the major tasks of social scientists. Similarly, we

know much more about control of low-ranking participants than of high-ranking ones, and clearly the control of the higher ranks is at least as important. Finally, we need to know more about the dynamics of control. How do changes in leadership affect changes in the level of alienation? What kinds of leadership emerge as alienation changes? Does reduction in scope always support normative control? What are the limits of effective socialization as a means of minimizing control and maximizing commitment, of increasing by the same effort both organizational effectiveness and satisfaction of the participants?[28]

Although I do not presume to be able to answer all these sociological questions in this book, I shall at least lay some preliminary groundwork that may help in answering some of them. I shall do this by attempting to build a classificatory model of means of control that is somewhat more refined and developed than Etzioni's very popular and useful one, a model that will be constructed after an analysis of concrete historical and empirical data scrutinized in the light of the Marxian-Weberian theoretical tradition.

PART ONE

The Historical Background

II

The Papacy and the
Origins of the Lay Movement

From its inception, the Catholic Church has moved gradually from grass-roots democracy and collegial authority to a vast concentration of power and authority in the hands of the clergy and hierarchy, and especially in the hands of the pope and his curia. This development has been accompanied by the alliance of these ecclesiastical leaders with the dominant classes and elites in civil and political society. The present chapter describes this evolution from the beginnings to 1951, when the Vatican held the first World Congress for the Lay Apostolate, an event which marked the beginning of a new stage: the emergence of an international lay Catholic movement, and the efforts of the Vatican to control it.

1. EARLY CHRISTIANITY UNDER
THE ROMAN EMPIRE: "LAÏKOS"

Joachim Wach has pointed out that most religions have developed "constitutions" which sanction and legalize a clergy-laity kind of distinction within the membership.[1] In most religions, this de facto distinction has been based on differing background characteristics, such as age, sex, intelligence, lineage, and status, and also on religious qualifications, such as personal charisma, religious virtue, useful knowledge, magical achievement, or special service. As differentiations appeared, they were perpetuated in a rigid clergy-laity distinction through various means. One of these was the routinization of personal charisma or its replacement by the charisma of office—through descent or co-optation, through the monopolization of economic, political, and intellectual resources, through careful transmission of religious information, through the elaboration and systematization of beliefs, through formalization of cultural and ethical practices, and through insistence upon the idea that clerical-lay distinctions partake of the sacred-secular dichotomy.[2]

In ancient Judaism, as Max Weber has shown, the priests, linked with the ruling classes, were somewhat less important and influential than the prophets, who had closer ties with the lay masses. It was only after the Exile that the "genuine 'spirit' of the prophecy . . . vanished because the priestly police power in the Jewish congregation gained control over ecstatic prophecy in the same manner as did [later] the bishopric and presbyterian authorities over pneumatic prophecy in the early Christian congregations."[3] These prophets, often the vocal defenders of the exploited and oppressed against the ruling and dominant classes, have been described as "revolutionary leaders."[4] They were also usually laymen, although there were exceptions, like the prophet Jeremiah, a priest who strongly attacked his own priestly caste.

In ancient Judaism this struggle between the priests allied with the ruling classes (both internal and external) and the lay prophets allied with the masses was a constant reality. When Christianity first emerged, it was largely a lay protest against the scribes and Pharisees and other upholders of priestly power. Jesus and his apostles were not from the priestly tribe.

A glance at the etymology of the words *laity* and *clergy* aids understanding of these socioreligious categories within the Catholic Church. In the Greek of the Septuagint Old Testament, *laos* usually means the "people of God" as a whole, in opposition to the *ethnè*, the pagan nations, the Gentiles.[5] This meaning was carried over by the Judeo-Christians to refer to the "new" Israel, the Christian church in general.[6] The New Testament view of authority in the church was based on functionality and service rather than on legality, dignity, and power. The leaders were those who had certain charismatic gifts and who were chosen by the apostles or by the community to render certain religious services to their religious brothers and sisters.[7] They were called overseers (bishops) and elders (priests). The *laos* was not a

body separate from these leaders and dominated by them. Although in
the Greek language the word *laos* referred to the mass of the people, as
distinguished from their rulers and leaders, this usage does not occur
in the Bible except in a few places in the Septuagint translation.[8] The
more comprehensive meaning, just described, is the one generally
found in both the Old and the New Testament. The laity-clergy dichotomy as we know it today is never mentioned in early Christian
documents, because it did not exist as such. The earliest functional
classifications we know of in the Christian communities around the
Mediterranean are those of apostles, disciples, prophets, overseers,
elders, and deacons, never those of priests (or clerics) and laymen.

The early Christian gatherings were local churches, presided over by
a number of elders. Then the elders, along with the rest of the membership, elected an overseer. At first this overseer, or bishop (epis-
copos), was only "primus inter pares," but his authority grew, influenced in good part by pagan and Jewish conceptions of priesthood, and
especially by the fact that he controlled the funds of the local church.[9]

The first use of *laïkos* in the sense of "the masses" appears in a letter
written to the Corinthians by Clement of Rome around A.D. 96. The
letter is a strong Paulinian defense of Corinthian bishops who had been
dismissed by a rival party. It expresses loyalty to the empire and has a
certain tone of Roman arrogance (the obedience of Roman legion-
naires is cited as an example to be followed, in the church organization, at a time when Roman emperors were persecuting Christians).
The doctrines of apostolic succession and irremovability of the clergy
are among those affirmed by Clement. He makes use of *laïkos* to mean
the rank-and-file members of the church, as opposed to the clerical and
episcopal leaders.

With the increasing Romanization of the Western church during
the second century, this definition of *laos* and its derivative *laïkos* rapidly prevailed, especially among the Gentile Christians. From the third
century onward, the definition of *laos* as people distinct from church
authorities becomes the only accepted one. This evolution is interesting especially in the light of the parallel, but different, case of the
work *kleros*.

2. THE RISE OF PRIESTS AND BISHOPS

"The term 'kleros' means 'lot' or 'portion' in Greek. Originally, it
meant the whole body of the 'people of God,' but it was applied in the
Christian community to those primarily or exclusively entrusted with

teaching, administering the cult, and caring for social needs.''[10] Thus *laos* and *kleros*, two words referring to the same reality, the "people of God," came to designate two discrete parts of it, as control of the community passed to the bishops and their clerical bureaucracy, while the prophetic voices that had spoken for the masses were gradually muffled. Soon these officials came to consider themselves as primates, rulers over the church community and its "lay" members.

Many historians have noted this transformation inside the early Christian churches. Kenneth Scott Latourette writes:

> As early as the beginning of the second century a distinct cleavage had begun to appear between clergy and laity, and this in spite of the fact that in the first century every Christian was held to be a priest unto God. By the end of the second century the clergy had clearly become a separate "order," that designation having probably been derived from the designation given to Roman magistrates in a tightly stratified society.[11]

A little further on, Latourette is even more explicit:

> As we have suggested, increasingly the Church centered about the clergy led by the bishops and especially around the bishops. As early as the beginning of the second century a differentiation between clergy and laity began to be seen, and as time passed a priesthood developed which was regarded as the Christian counterpart of that of the ancient Jews. The development of the clergy and of ranks in the clergy may in part have been influenced by the example of the kind of officialdom which characterized the Roman Empire, especially during the later years of the period which we have been describing.[12]

Ernst Troeltsch, in a chapter on the foundations of the early church, part of his classic study, *The Social Teachings of the Christian Churches*, describes this development:

> The rise of the clergy as a body of men entrusted with the leadership and government of the Church meant that, owing to the need of the organization itself, the clergy as a class were always striving to perfect their own organization; the old charismatic gifts and free offering of service were logically transformed into a hierarchical sacerdotal system, which placed the bishop and the clergy in a special category by themselves, which was contrasted with the rest of the community, called the laity.[13]

From the third century onward, the practice of popular elections and grass-roots participation was gradually eliminated. Furthermore, the charismatic and spiritual leaders of the community were displaced by upper-class men who were important because of their power in the financial-material affairs of the church. Episcopal and clerical power was extended into the domains of preaching, selection of officials, and ownership of property. As Karl Kautsky writes:

> The teachers were deprived of their freedom and subordinated to the bishop. Soon nobody dared to speak in the community assembly, the church, without previous permission from the bishop; that is, nobody outside of the community bureaucracy directed by the bishop, the clergy, which set itself more and more apart from the mass of the fellows, the laity.[14]

Kautsky goes on to show how the increase in the power of bishops and priests finally suppressed all traces of democracy and facilitated the acceptance of Christianity as the religion of the ruling class of the empire:

> The community soon lost the last remnant of its original democracy, the right to choose its officials. As the bishop and his men gained independence and greater power in the community, it became easier for him to get the community to choose men acceptable to him. He became the man who in fact filled the offices. In choosing the bishop himself the power of the clergy in the community always insured the election of their own candidates. It finally reached the point where the clergy alone chose the bishop, and the mass of comrades in the community had only the right to confirm or reject the choice; but this too turned into an increasingly empty formality. The community finally sank to the level of an applauding mob to whom the clergy presented the bishop that had been chosen for them, so that they could shout hurrah for him.
>
> This constituted the final annihilation of the democratic organization of the community, and put the final seal on the clergy's absolutism; the clergy had been transformed from a humble "servant of God's servants" into their absolute master.
>
> It goes without saying that the property of the community now became in fact the property of their administrators, though not their personal property, but that of the bureaucracy as a corporation. The church property no longer was the common property of the comrades, but the property of the clergy.
>
> This transformation was mightily supported and hastened by the official recognition of Christianity at the beginning of the fourth century. On the other hand, this recognition of the Catholic Church by the emperors was but a consequence of the fact that the bureaucracy and episcopal absolutism had already absolute power.

> So long as the church was a democratic organization, it was com-
> pletely opposed to the essence of the imperial despotism in the
> Roman Empire; but the episcopal bureaucracy, absolutely ruling and
> exploiting the people, was quite useful for imperial despotism. It
> could not be ignored; the emperor had to come to terms with it,
> because otherwise it threatened to grow too strong for him.[15]

At first, Christianity had been an expression of the political and
ideological resistance of oppressed people and lower classes against the
domination of the Roman ruling class, a resistance which eventually
spread to the center of the Roman Empire itself, and even to the
houses of some of the patricians. As Greek and Roman models of
authority and organization replaced the more democratic Jewish forms
of community, bishops with their growing entourage came to define
their positions of authority as a divine right to rule rather than as
opportunities for service. Local, grass-roots democracy was supplanted
by central coordination by the most influential of the bishops.

It is not surprising, in the light of the internal development of this
powerful "episcopal bureaucracy," that Christianity was accepted not
only by rich and powerful Roman converts, but by the Emperor
Constantine himself, who proclaimed it the official religion of the Empire in 313. Kautsky's contention that religious and political elites
were of the same social class, and that they found it in their interest to
use a popular religious movement to buttress their privileged position,
was summarized by Troeltsch in a 1913 article:

> According to this view, purely economic conditions are the cause
> of class stratification, and each class is reflected in a metaphysic and a
> religion that protects its existence and interests. Christianity is then
> the utopian, otherworldly reflection of the unorganized, wretched,
> and helpless proletariat of late antiquity. This purely religious and
> therefore powerless organization of the proletariat, which was out of
> step with the social evolution of the time, was soon subjugated by
> the ruling classes. Through certain changes in its dogma and ethic, it
> was made to serve the interests of property and power. The original
> proletarian character of the Christian movement has been able to
> break through only occasionally.[16]

From the stage when the laity chose the bishops and priests, the
Catholic Church evolved. Although the laity had a say in many aspects
of Church life during some parts of this evolution the stage was
reached where Church officials came to take upon themselves all the
important aspects of decision making. In the Greek Orthodox Church

there remain today some vestiges of earlier times when the laity had some control over church affairs, even if effective power has passed to the hands of the bishops there also.[17]

The alliance of Church and Empire, and the threat of heresies, helped stabilize and reinforce the power and prestige of bishops (and to a lesser degree of priests) and contributed to the reinforcement of the pre-Christian dualism between clergy and laity. Rank-and-file laymen became secondary members of the Church, mere recipients of spiritual goods from the bishops and "their" clergy. Even the deaconate, instituted by the apostles to free their action from material preoccupations, was transformed into a subordinate and transitory function leading to the priesthood.

Troeltsch describes this further development of concentration and stabilization of power in an elite and the concomitant elimination of part-time workingmen from the honorary episcopal and presbyteral post:

> Only gradually did the intellectual and well-to-do people press into the ministry, like Cyprian, for instance, and it was only after the church had received the legal right to hold property, and after the imperial privileges of the post-Constantine period, that the bishops became a ruling class.[18]

The communitarian aspects of the Church were gradually superseded by the creation of an authoritarian, hierarchical system. The de facto authority of this wealthy spiritual caste was given biblical and liturgical legitimation through a reinterpretation of certain texts of the New Testament and the creation of a special ceremony for the consecration of bishops.

In this regard, Antonio Gramsci notes that the effect of the alliance of the hierarchy with the emperor was not only to give certain corporatist advantages to the bishops and to neutralize the influence of the rank-and-file, but to consecrate Christianity as the official ideology of the empire and turn the Church into an ideological legitimation apparatus of the state. From then on, the Church structure seriously started to imitate the structure of the empire, for example in regard to the transfer of some aspects of the cult of the emperor to the person of the pope.[19] This is essentially what the German sociologist Max Horkheimer affirms, in an essay entitled "Thoughts on Religion," in his *Critical Theory*: "Christianity lost its function of expressing the ideal, to the extent that it became the bedfellow of the state."[20]

In his study of the organization of the early Christian churches, Edwin Hatch notes that at the beginning of the fourth century, when

Christianity was still the religion of a persecuted sect, "the government of the Churches was in the main a democracy," but "at the end of the century, the primitive type had almost disappeared: the clergy were a separate and governing class."[21] This momentous transformation, according to Hatch, came about because, by becoming the religion of the state, Christianity saw its officials gain various privileges, such as exemption from public burdens and from ordinary courts, which created a clerical caste that lorded it over the rest of the people. By allowing the churches to hold property, and by bequeathing vast fortunes to them, Constantine also turned the clergy away from the necessity to work for a living:

> The effect of the recognition of Christianity by the State was thus not only to create a class civilly distinct from the rest of the community, but also to give that class social independence. In other words, the Christian clergy, in addition to their original prestige as office-bearers, had the privileges of a favored class, and the power of a moneyed class.[22]

One more development, however, was necessary in order to turn the Church in an image of the state: the further centralization of power in the hands of one man, the Pontifex Maximus, the Supreme Pontiff, the bishop of Rome.

3. THE BISHOP OF ROME BECOMES THE POPE

Inside the hierarchy, because of his close connections with the governance of the Roman Empire, the bishop of Rome became the most influential of the Christian bishops.[23] The bishops of the major cities of the empire—Alexandria, Antioch, Constantinople, and Rome—had come, thanks mostly to the centralizing impulse given by Constantine's convocation of the Council of Nicaea (325), to be known as patriarchs, and the bishop of Rome to be considered the father of the patriarchs. So as the "pater patriarcharum," he naturally took the name of *papa* (pope). Between the second and sixth centuries the increase in the power of the Roman patriarch, now pope, reached new heights in the pontificates of Leo the Great (440–461), savior of Rome from Attila the Hun, and Gregory the Great (590–604).[24] Gregory, who was in his time the real ruler of Rome, firmly established the supremacy of the pope within the Church.

In 752, in an effort to free Rome from the rule of the weak Byzantine emperor, Pope Stephen II enlisted the aid of Pepin the Short, king of the Franks. It was Pepin's son, Charlemagne, who confirmed the pope in his temporal rule over Rome and its surrounding territories; in return, the pope consecrated Charlemagne and crowned him Holy Roman Emperor. This church-state liaison was not an unmixed blessing for the Church's independence nor did it long persist in the original form of the benevolent protection of the pope on the part of the Holy Roman Empire. Like Constantine and his successors, the barbarian rulers took it upon themselves to usurp the hierarchy's power, even in purely ecclesiastical affairs. They constantly intervened in the business of the Church, convening councils and naming their protégés to lucrative ecclesiastical positions. Bishops and abbots became princes of the Church. As their worldly power grew, the spiritual influence of these men was eroded by their secular loyalties and interests. Church affairs became a variant of state affairs. Neglected and exploited by their religious leaders, the lay masses—and the lower clergy as well—remained superstitious, ignorant, and powerless.

In a way, things had come full circle. By taking away power from the rank-and-file laymen, the clergy and bishops, including the pope, had only succeeded in giving the control over the Church back to a single group of laymen, the temporal rulers. In a recent history of the church, the volume dealing with the period from 888 to 957 carries the significant title: "The Church in the Power of the Laity," alluding to the encroachment of these powerful laymen in the selection of bishops and abbots.[25]

Under the control of the Roman nobility during the tenth century and the first half of the eleventh, the papacy was filled mostly by unscrupulous and incompetent men. The feudal system had a stranglehold on the Church, manifested partly in simony and other abuses, which provided justification for the reformist movement of the eleventh century. Intense revivalist movements swept across Europe then and awakened the religious and political conscience of peasants and townspeople alike. Monks were active as leaders of these movements.

Monasteries, founded by lay protesters against the establishment of the Church on a clerical basis and against accommodation to the empire, had remained small but constant centers of opposition to the symbiosis between Church and State well into the medieval period. Actual resistance to feudalization was difficult, since the hierarchy was easily able to co-opt promising young men from the lower classes by means of a stratagem Karl Marx has described:

> The circumstance that the Catholic Church in the Middle Ages formed its hierarchy with the best brains from among the people, without regard to estate, birth or wealth, was one of the principal means of consolidating priestly rule and the subordination of the laity. The more a ruling class is able to assimilate the most prominent men of the dominated class the more stable and dangerous its rule.[26]

In other words, potential reformers could be assimilated into the Church authority structure, a situation which often led them to abandon radicalism and prophetism for careerism.

Nevertheless, with the backing of their reformist lay followers, the monks did succeed, through the Cluniac reforms, in depriving feudal princes and their ecclesiastical protégés of many of their Churchly privileges. A key reform was the papal decree of 1059, which placed the election of the pope in the hands of the college of cardinals and led to the election of the monk Hildebrand as Pope Gregory VII in 1073.

Gregory VII reorganized the Church, using the hierarchical system of the Roman Empire as a model and setting the stage for his successors' victory over secular authority. In weakening the power of the bishops, however, his reforms reinforced the papal power against all lower, nonpapal authority within the Church community. According to Max Weber:

> In the Catholic Church, first the feudal and then all independent local intermediary powers were eliminated. This was begun by Gregory VII and continued through the Council of Trent, the Vatican Council, and it was completed by the edicts of Pius X. The transformation of these local powers into pure functionaries of the central authority was connected with the constant increase in the factual significance of the formally quite dependent Kapläne [auxiliary churchmen supervising lay organizations], a process which above all was based on the political party organization of Catholicism. Hence this process meant an advance of bureaucracy and at the same time of "passive" democratization as it were, that is, the leveling of the governed.[27]

Therefore, one consequence of the liberation of the Church from the encroaching secular princes was the formation of a legalistic concept of authority and hierarchy, resulting in greater power for the pope, especially in the internal affairs of the Church. Furthermore, Gregorian reforms of priestly life, such as mandatory clerical celibacy, and Gratian's influential *Due Sunt genera Christianorum* ("There are two kinds of Christians") crystallized the separation between clergy and laity.

4. CONTRADICTIONS INSIDE THE CHURCH

During the Middle Ages, the clerical class that governed the Catholic Church became the dominant part of the ideological apparatus of the feudal system. The clergy also played an important economic and social function. Bishops were feudal lords with vast estates, and clerics were omnipresent in the arts, the social services, and even in the administration of justice. An internal tension existed in the Church between the functions of legitimation of the feudal order, carried on mostly by the Church hierarchy, and of defense of the oppressed, fulfilled by the lower clergy, the lay protesters, and the new religious orders. Some of these orders, like the Franciscans, were originally lay movements, but were co-opted and to a great extent transformed by the papacy.

Inside the Church hierarchy, the most visible contradiction (just as today) was between papal authority and episcopal—more precisely, conciliar—authority. The battle was gradually won by the papacy, largely because of its success in co-opting the grass-roots protesters. Franz Neumann refers to this in a discussion on caesaristic and totalitarian dictatorship:

> It might be noted, however, that elements of caesarism also arose in the Roman Catholic Church out of the struggle between papal sovereignty and the conciliar position. The mendicant orders, representing the democratic element, were enlisted in the papal cause against the aristocratic element, whose program was conciliar.[28]

This democratic protest movement itself was, like the upper levels of hierarchical authority, divided in two major orientations. Both Engels and Gramsci distinguish between two types of protest movements during the Middle Ages: the urban-bourgeois movement and the more radical popular-protest movement. The rising bourgeoisie wanted to be freed from the tutelage of the ecclesiastical feudal apparatus, in the socioeconomic, political, and cultural arenas. Ecclesiastical laws against moneylending for interest were resented by the new class of urban businessmen, and canon law and Latin, for example, were challenged by lay jurists and intellectuals. In spite of appearances, the major conflict was not between the pope and the upper clergy, but between religious and secular aristocrats on the one hand and the rising communes on the other. The masses of poor peasants still did not count for much in society. The popular protest movement in which they participated was mainly the struggle of the "Third Estate" against the other two, but it was also partly a pacifist revolt of the exploited masses against the conservative nobles and the hierarchy. Gramsci shows that when the crisis was very serious, Church authorities used physical force (i.e. the secular arm, the Inquisition) to maintain their position. When the split was less severe, they used a tactic which later became the favorite control mechanism of Church authorities. That tactic consisted in the elimination or co-optation of the leaders of a movement, and the integration, after that, of what was left of it into the official organizational structure of the Church through the creation of religious orders. If the salvage operation was not successful, then exclusion and condemnation and sheer force were used as a last resort. Coercion was sometimes necessary, since organizational and normative methods of control were not always sufficient. In most cases, as happens in the modern state, the mere fact that officials could resort to violence, if they needed to, was sufficient to assure a substantial amount of conformity. The occasional use of force served as a mighty deterrent, and generally complemented quite effectively the preferred normative and organizational forms of control. Yet in spite of all this, the lay protesters kept up their challenges to ecclesiastical authority.

The fate of these vigorous lay protest movements, which were partly responsible for forcing ecclesiastical reforms in the late Middle Ages, has been described by Gramsci:

> The heretical movements of the middle ages, as simultaneous reactions to the political interference of the Church and to the scholastic philosophy of which it was an expression, on the basis of social conflicts determined by the rise of the communes, were a breach between the masses and the intellectuals inside the Church, which was healed by the rise of the popular religious movements absorbed by the Church in the formation of the mendicant orders and in a new religious unity.[29]

This "new religious unity" was expressed by papal integration of such "popular" orders as the Franciscans, opponents of episcopal authoritarianism and clericalism, into the Church structure.

As a countermeasure aimed at keeping their lay roots, the Franciscans established within their organizational framework a "Third

Order," a classification open to laity willing to live according to a simplified version of Franciscan rules. Other orders, notably the Dominicans, did likewise, and religious affairs remained popular with rank-and-file laity. The Dominicans, preaching and teaching in urban centers, contributed to a grass-roots revival of lay religiosity and the development of university scholarship. The Third Orders, however, and the lay brothers and nuns, were closely held in check by priests and by Church authorities.

Church officials, while willing to take advantage of the revival of religious interest to strengthen their own position, viewed this grass-roots ferment with mistrust and soon effected the subordination of the new orders to the central Church and the elimination of most vestiges of the ancient autonomy of the laity:

> Above all, that independent lay Christianity was restricted, and the outlet which it still possessed in the ancient canonical election of bishops was closed; especially the right of examination which had been granted to the laity as a defence against simonist priests was withdrawn, and retained only by the Pope and the legates. As the influence of Princes and the nobles had been withdrawn from the Church, so now the influence of the people was withdrawn. The sacraments again became entirely independent of the moral character of the priests. Laymen were also excluded from any share in the administration of Church property. The priesthood was clearly distinguished from the laity in dress, liturgical language, and way of life. The priests alone were now entitled to preach, and all cooperation of laymen in public services was forbidden. Theology (technically and scholastically) set itself in opposition to all popular literature, and law became a highbrow affair of the jurists.
>
> The financial system which was now necessary for the newly centralized ecclesiastical system emphasized and strengthened the ecclesiastical taxes, and consumed the property of the poor, exactly as the previous seigniorial Church had done. The hated tithe, which could not be delivered to the simonist priests, was now demanded in full by the new Gregorian Church.[30]

The new orientations given to the Church by Gregory VII lasted for nearly two centuries. The subsequent period of decline of papal authority from the end of the thirteenth century, which culminated in the battle between three popes for the Roman seat, was accompanied by violent challenges from grass-roots movements. Protecting its authority with European political alliances, the papacy emerged, by the end of the fifteenth century, as a stronger central organization with little orientation toward reform movements. From that time until the present century, papal authority over a submissive laity has been little challenged:

> Humanism and the Renaissance, secular politics and the complete victory of the Curia, made an end of it [the sect movement], and since then in Italy and in Southern Europe the ecclesiastical institution has had nothing more to fear from a sectarian Christianity. This is one of the reasons why no movement on the lines of the German Reformation was ever possible in Southern Europe.[31]

5. CENTRALIZATION AND COUNTER-REFORMATION

From Clement IV (1265–1268) on, the popes centralized much of the power of Church nominations in the hands of themselves and their curia. Papal taxation increased with this new effort at centralization, because curial and legation expenses had increased, especially while the pope was living in Avignon away from his Italian territories. The popes were also financing numerous wars and diplomatic intrigues. These financial and political operations contributed greatly to the decline in popularity of the papacy. During the Renaissance, larger numbers of educated laity had a renewed interest in lay participation in Church affairs, but this was by no means an extensive, grass-roots involvement. Efforts at reform of the Church from within by Erasmus and some of his disciples, such as Sir Thomas More, were cut short by the Protestant Reformation. Because of Protestantism and a growing secularization of political and social life, the Church occupied itself somewhat less with political affairs, becoming more and more preoccupied with internal problems.

Lutheranism and Calvinism were religious revolutions of the rising bourgeoisie of Western European countries against feudal Catholicism. They were also, as Gramsci notes, a manifestation of national-popular opposition to the elitist and reactionary cosmopolitanism of the over-Italianized Roman Church—in contrast to the Renaissance, which had been an ambiguous cultural movement of intellectuals and aristocrats cut off from the masses of people and easily co-optable by Church leaders.[32]

The Counter-Reformation succeeded, as had the eleventh-century reform movements, in only further centralizing and clericalizing the Catholic Church's organizational structure. Jacob Burckhardt, in his classic study of the Renaissance, says about the papacy:

The institution that developed during the latter years of Clement VII, and under Paul III and Paul IV, and their successors, in the face of the defection of half Europe, was a new, regenerated hierarchy, which avoided all the great and dangerous scandals of former times, particularly nepotism, with its attempts at territorial aggrandizement, and which, in alliance with the Catholic princes, and impelled by a newborn spiritual force, found its chief work in the recovery of what had been lost. It only existed and is only intelligible in opposition to the seceders. In this sense it can be said with perfect truth that the moral salvation of the Papacy is due to its mortal enemies. And now its political position, too, though certainly under the tutelage of Spain, became impregnable.[33]

The Council of Trent responded to lay demands for liberation from too burdensome a clerical tutelage with an even more stratified conception of the Church of Rome. The Counter-Reformation view of ordinary laymen as subjects rather than as participants accentuated the growing breach between the clerical culture of Catholicism and the new secular society of Europe. Although some ardent counter-reformers, such as the Jesuits, who founded their first lay sodality in 1567, were aware of the possibilities of mobilizing the bourgeois laity in the service of the Church, Catholicism continued to be the dominant ideology of feudalism and of monarchical regimes, and Church authorities continued to prefer alliances with the upper classes to cooperation with the rising Third Estate.

The breach between Church authorities and lay masses was such that once again coercion was needed to maintain control. This time, however, psychic rather than physical coercion was used, because it was no longer possible to resort to brute force. Legalism, formalism, obedience, discipline, and the suppression of all remnants of internal democracy became the major preoccupation of Church authorities. Unable to succeed in this task by themselves, they were increasingly inclined to rely on the help of the absolutist regimes, and in turn to become an ideological legitimation apparatus of the state. The Counter-Reformation, like all restorations, appears to have been a desperate effort to reestablish a vanishing order, an effort which inevitably strengthened the forces of change which it sought to block.

Certain nationalistic Catholic movements—Gallicanism in France, Josephism in the Austrian Empire—attempted to ally reformist ideas with national political power as Protestant reformers were doing, but Spanish domination of the papacy from 1559 to 1713 reinforced a conservatism which forced loyal laymen into a conformist attitude.

During the seventeenth and eighteenth centuries, the waning of Spanish and Portuguese power and the increase in national fervor in various European countries undermined some accommodations that the papacy had made with temporal powers. But as kings and lords felt their power slipping away, they found it useful to collaborate with Church authorities who were happy to reciprocate. The alliances of throne and altar during the final decades of the Ancien Régime (and even afterward under Napoleon and the Restoration regimes) probably account for much of the anticlericalism and laicism in the liberal-democratic and Socialist movements of the nineteenth century, not only in France but in most of Europe.

As the papacy found its power continuing to decline in the temporal sphere despite numerous accommodations with secular rulers, it turned to an aggrandizement of its jurisdiction inside the Church, at the expense of bishops, priests, and laymen.

6. REVOLUTION, NATIONALISM AND THE PAPACY

The period during and immediately following the French Revolution was a difficult one for the papacy. Catholics, especially in France, were split on the question of religious reform and political revolution. In certain areas, many laymen and quite a few priests, especially the lower clergy, not only sided with the revolutionary movement but were active in its launching, in spite of the determined opposition of Pius VI (1775–1799) and of nearly all the French bishops. In 1799, when Pius VI died in southern France, anticlericalism was so widespread that it seemed like the end of Catholicism in France, even the end of the papacy. But Pius VI was to have a shrewd successor, Pius VII (1800–1823).

With Bonaparte, Pius VII negotiated a concordat in 1801 which healed the crisis occasioned a few years earlier by the revolutionary "Civil Constitution of the Clergy," a concordat which proved as lethal to the French bishops' conservative Gallicanism as it was advantageous to the papacy and to Bonaparte. Dissolving the entire French hierarchy, Pius VII then consulted Bonaparte in the naming of sixty new bishops. He also initiated a papal policy of concordats and treaties with monarchs, a policy perpetuated by his successors which culminated in the Lateran Agreements between Mussolini and Pius XI in 1929. Napoleon's restitution of the papal states gave the papacy a geographical base which, ironically, was sanctioned by the Congress of Vienna (1815). This put the pope in an awkward political position vis-à-vis temporal rulers. It contributed to maintaining his role as a political rather than as a purely religious leader.

The treaty signing between Church and State that marked so much of early nineteenth-century European politics has been an outward sign of a last effort by declining despots to save their power through recognition of mutual interests. Church authorities acknowledged their common cause with the temporal princes, but their accords were unable to curb a growing radicalism and nationalism among their subjects.

Some of these temporal princes were able to use rising bourgeois nationalism to their advantage, but the popes, Pius VII and Gregory XVI (1831–1846) especially, when they were not jousting with the monarchs, turned their attention to reinforcing their grip over what they could really control: the Roman Curia, the bishops and the priests, and the emerging laity. Internally, papal dominance grew, and the clerical role vis-à-vis the laity was expressed in one of Gregory XVI's bulls:

> Nobody can be ignorant of the fact that the church is a nonegalitarian community, in which God has ordained one group to govern, and another to obey. The latter are the laymen, the former the clergy.[34]

In France, conservative royalist and ultramontane (i.e. pro-Rome) lay leaders like Joseph de Maistre, Louis de Bonald, and Chateaubriand accepted this dependence on traditional authority in all spheres of life. Meanwhile, under the leadership of Félicité Robert de Lamennais, some ultramontanes started attacking the monarchy and tried to convert the papacy to the cause of liberty and revolution. These efforts were fruitless. The liberal but ultramontane ideas of Lamennais's circle of Catholics, expressed in his journal *L'Avenir*, were opposed by all that was conservative in European Catholicism at the time, loyalist Gallican bishops, conservative Austrians, anti-Mazzini and anti-Risorgimento forces in Italy, and by the pope himself, the reactionary Gregory XVI.

The election of the young and liberal Giovanni Maria Mastai-Ferretti, Pius IX (1846–1878), seemed at first to vindicate the Lamennais position, thanks to the new pope's early flirtation with reformism and liberalism. From this beginning, his pontificate rapidly turned into one of the most reactionary in the history of the Church, on both religious and political grounds. Pius IX fought liberalism and opposed the crusaders for the reunification of Italy, especially those radical republicans like Garibaldi who wanted to make Rome the new nation's capital. His famous *non expedit* of 1868, which prohibited Italian Catholics from participating in electoral politics, only succeeded in putting the papacy at a disadvantage. Italy was gradually united despite the opposition and condemnations of Pius IX.

Just before Rome was taken over by the Italian forces, in 1870, the first Vatican Council promulgated the dogma of papal infallibility, a development which further increased the internal power of the pope and his central bureaucracy at a time when the temporal power of the Church had reached a low point. The papal infallibility doctrine dealt a blow to the illusions of those Catholic liberals who still hoped that Pius IX would reconcile the Church with democracy and other modern ideas and ideals.

7. THE LAY AWAKENING

It was during the pontificate of Pius IX, however, that the Catholic laity began to awaken.[35] The failure of monarchical restoration movements in the nineteenth century, the gradual extension of popular suffrage, and the increasing laicization of political life gave rank-and-file laymen in many countries an importance which they had not enjoyed previously, when the close relations between higher authorities of Church and state had rendered unnecessary the use of the laity as an instrument of clerical influence. Now the laity's higher level of education and their increasing political power in the secular sphere forced the hierarchy to take them into account, especially since they now exercised considerably greater freedom of expression and action outside the Church. In France, the layman Montalembert suggested that French Catholics should, like Belgian and Irish Catholics, organize themselves into associations of laymen and affect public opinion rather than rely on arrangements between Church and government authorities. While the archbishop of Rouen disagreed, saying that it was not the mission of laymen to take care of the affairs of the Church, other bishops were willing to accept the idea of lay participation. Among these was Msgr. Parisis, bishop of Langres, who wrote a pamphlet, "The Role That Laymen Must Play Today in Questions Pertaining to the Freedom of the Church."[36] This particular episcopal intervention constituted a major breakthrough. Even if it did not accept the laymen's direct mission in the Church government, it recognized their role in the action of the Church and the increasing dependence of Church authorities on the laity in the democratic state. Laymen of a more conservative cast, such as Louis

Veuillot, also called for greater lay Catholic involvement in politics and even in Church affairs, but under strict supervision and control of the clergy and hierarchy.

The revolutions of 1848, because of the spirit of democracy and liberation which they aroused in Europe, were another turning point for Catholic laymen. Not only did Church authorities need their support, but laymen, on their own, began demanding a greater and more active role in the Church. The nature of their involvement had been altered irrevocably, and never again would they be entirely submissive to the clergy. When the pope failed to provide leadership for the emerging laity, some members of the hierarchy and clergy allied themselves with the new forces of progress. Indeed, in many countries the combined leadership of some prominent clergymen mobilized the enlightened social consciousness of the laity. Among these progressive clergymen were Henri Lacordaire, who revived the Dominicans; Dom Prosper Guéranger, who revived the Benedictines; Msgr. Félix Dupanloup, who was the leader of liberal Catholicism after 1849; and Bishop Wilhelm Emanuel von Ketteler, who was one of the founders of Christian socialism; they inspired the socially progressive Catholics in the French- and German-speaking worlds.

Another such progressive priest was the Italian philosopher Antonio Rosmini, who had hoped that Pius IX would become a progressive religious and political leader. Rosmini tried, unsuccessfully, to get the pope to accept the reunification of Italy. He also wrote a strong critique, "The Five Wounds of the Church" (1848), which suggested that two of the major problems of the Church were the separation of the people from the clergy in the public cult, and the nomination of bishops by secular powers. In his opinion, bishops should be chosen by the laity, and both together should select priests; thereby the split between the laity and Church officials would be eliminated, and the Church would be made more independent of secular authorities. Rosmini's book was put on the Index of Prohibited Books in 1849, although by 1854, one year before his death, his works were finally judged to be free from censure by the Congregation of the Index.

The awakening of the Catholic laity was manifested in the Lay Congress of Mainz, organized in 1848 by bishops and laymen. At this meeting a multinational group of Catholic laymen and clerics, whose opinions differed vastly from those of the pope, discussed the burning social issues that concerned them, and established an association devoted to solving "the great problem of the day, the social problem."

Some liberal Catholics continued their efforts to influence Pius IX to reverse his conservative positions, but most bishops and clergy sided with the self-willed "prisoner of the Vatican," and with those in the Roman Curia who could manipulate the papal office. The gulf between the Church and modern liberal society widened.

The third quarter of the nineteenth century was filled with the struggles of liberal and social Catholics against traditionalist and monarchist Church leaders. Efforts to create Catholic political parties were opposed by the pope, who feared that such parties would involve laymen in helping governments in their attempts to dominate the Church, as Gallicanism had nearly succeeded in doing. But that does not seem to have been their aim. The lay movements of the late nineteenth and early twentieth century sought an alliance between pope and laity that would be more attuned to liberal causes than was the conservative Church bureaucracy. Their aspirations, generally not encouraged by the papacy, were expressed at lay congresses, organized on the model of the 1848 meeting at Mainz. Some of the ideas developed at these congresses made their way into the teachings of Pope Leo XIII (1878–1903), and the meetings themselves served as organizational bases from which Catholic Action (i.e. that part of the lay apostolate which is both organized and under the jurisdiction of the hierarchy) and even Catholic parties, such as the German Center Party, developed. As early as 1863, for example, a congress of Catholic scholars was organized in Munich, without the permission of the hierarchy, by Joseph Ignaz von Döllinger, a Bavarian theologian. The congress published a call for freedom of intellectual inquiry in science, in philosophy, and, up to a certain point, in religion. That same year, a similar congress was held in Malines, Belgium, but here the emphasis was on religious tolerance and political freedom. In October 1864 another such congress was held in Malines. The famous distinction between thesis and hypothesis was liberally used by those present at this congress. A Catholic state was considered to be ideal in theory (the thesis), but separation of Church and state was considered to be acceptable in practice (the hypothesis). This was an effort by liberal lay Catholics to reconcile the Church with the emerging liberal-democratic system.

These three congresses were followed in 1864 by the antiliberal encyclical, *Quanta Cura*, and the papal condemnation of Döllinger and Montalembert, the German and French leaders of progressive lay Catholicism. The encyclical had been drawn up by Cardinal Antonelli, Pius IX's reactionary secretary of state and leader of the integralist faction in the Roman Curia.

Despite the condemnations, progressive Catholics organized another lay congress at Malines in 1867. The same year, a lay movement of a different orientation was founded in Italy, the "Società della Gioventu Cattolica," the first real organization of what later came to be known as Catholic Action. Like the Jesuit lay sodalities founded in the sixteenth century, the Società was largely composed of aristocrats and wealthy members of the bourgeoisie, but its aim was social rather than religious and spiritual. Intended as an answer to the anticlericalism of the post-Risorgimento Italian government, it was not a political party but a force operating indirectly in the political sphere.

Pius IX immediately approved the Società, seeing in it a useful instrument for the promotion of papal goals, especially the restoration of lost papal territories, and for fostering the survival of the traditional Church by strengthening its defenses against liberalism and modernity. Joseph La Palombara considers these political papal aims as being the main reasons for the development of Catholic Action:

> Catholic Action represents a new form of the Church's intervention in the political life of the country after the Church lost the temporal power it exercised prior to Italy's reunification.[37]

Pius XII admitted as much in his speech to the first World Congress for the Lay Apostolate, in 1951, when he described the Catholic lay movements of the nineteenth century as efforts to recapture the intimacy of the "beneficent" relations which existed between Church and State before the French Revolution.[38]

Despite these origins and the generally conservative cast of its membership, the Società della Gioventu Cattolica was an important step in the formation of an active lay movement. It was the president of that association who suggested that lay Catholics in Italy should meet once a year in a congress in order to solidify the community life of Catholics and their social influence in an increasingly secular world. Thus Catholic Action came to be identified with the "Opera dei Congressi e dei Comitati" (Apostolate of Congresses and Committees), a federation of many Italian Catholic organizations active at the parish level.

The first annual meeting of the Opera dei Congressi, at Venice in 1874, had as its theme the necessity of Christian education. The declaration issued by that first congress called upon Catholics to involve themselves in concerted and unified action to give the Church maximum strength and efficiency, since the liberals' separation of church and state had deprived the Church of all the backing it drew from its alliances with secular powers:

As a consequence, an unfettered revolution threatens the Church, limiting her freedom and her public action; and with the Church in these straits it falls to the Catholics to make up for the government's failure to defend the Church.[39]

In 1875 a permanent national liaison committee was established to insure stability and continuity for the organization. Under clerical supervision, local parish committees of at least five members were organized. It was these parish-level groups, called Catholic Action, that constituted the strength of the Opera dei Congressi, permitting it to function at both national and local levels. The diocesan and regional coordination came much later.[40]

The congresses followed closely the Vatican's line on temporal affairs, namely, noninvolvement in electoral politics and involvement in social issues such as education. Doctrinal influence, not the winning of parliamentary seats, was the objective of the congresses. In 1881, for example, Leo XIII asked the delegates to:

> . . . regroup Italian Catholics in a common and unified action for the defense of the rights of the Holy See, and the religious and social interests of Italian Catholics, in conformity with the desires of the pope and under the direction of the episcopate and the clergy.[41]

In the last quarter of the century, the activities of Catholic Action consisted mainly of an involvement in social and spiritual affairs under the pope's guidance. Speaking of that period, Poggi writes:

> The term "catholic action" as it was used in these years (without capital letters) refers, therefore, to a vast number of associated groups connected by the Opera's parish and diocesan committees, and loosely brought together at the top by their participation in the annual congresses.[42]

By the turn of the century, the Opera dei Congressi, increasingly centralized and powerful in Italian political and religious life, became the arena for warring factions of the Catholic left, right, and center.[43]

In France, similar conflicts between divergent ideological groups became more and more frequent at about the same time. The conservative and authoritarian orientation that prevailed during the nineteenth century was increasingly challenged by the Catholic liberals, especially by the Christian Democrats and the "social" Catholics.

An effort was made by the aristocratic lay leader Albert de Mun (founder of "L'Oeuvre des Cercles," a paternalistic association aiming at occupying the workers' leisure hours) to create a Catholic party on the model of the parties existing in Germany, Austria, and Belgium, but the various overlapping divisions among French Catholics (monarchists and republicans, conservatives and liberals, Gallicans and ultramontanes), and the consequent opposition of Leo XIII in 1885, killed this project before it could get off the ground. Leo XIII, who wanted to break the alliance of French Catholics with the monarchy, and to unite them with the moderate republicans, did not want another Catholic party like the German Center Party.

In Italy, Catholic Action's opposition to the liberals caused them to flirt with the growing mass social consciousness. But when socialism came to seem more dangerous to the Church than the liberal government, Catholic Action conservatives and allied bishops put pressure on the Vatican to relax its policy of non-cooperation with the liberals. Thus, by the end of the century, the movement that had been intended to fight liberalism became—first in local politics, then in national elections—a moderate, proclerical support for liberalism against more radical forces.

Leo XIII, less intransigent than his predecessors toward modernity, democracy, and scholarship, reversed many of their conservative positions on social, political, and theological issues. Several European lay congresses were held during his pontificate—for example, those held between 1888 and 1900 under the inspiration of Msgr. Maurice d'Hulst.

The idea of lay congresses even spread to America, but the Baltimore Lay Congress of 1889 was so strictly under hierarchical control that floor discussion of papers was not permitted, despite their having been screened in advance by an episcopal commission.[44]

8. PIUS X AND BENEDICT XV

In 1903 the death of Leo XIII and the election of Pius X (1903–1914) severely checked the movement in European Catholicism toward liberalism in both religious and nonreligious spheres. The new pope, taking the name of Pius to signify his attachment to the ideas of the conservative popes who had preceded Leo XIII, initiated a reign of intellectual terror. His attitude toward the lay movement is represented by his 1907 encyclical *Pascendi Gregis*, in which he said: "Note here, Venerable Brethren, the appearance already of that most pernicious doctrine which would make the laity a factor of progress in the church." Pius X thus returned to the tactics of psychic (or hierocratic) coercion that had been the hallmark of Pius IX's reign.

Replacing Leo's progressive secretary of state, Cardinal Rampolla del Tindaro, with the archconservative Cardinal Rafaele Merry del Val, Pius X encouraged the development of "integralism," an extreme right-wing reaction against what he called the "modernist heresy." Progressive Catholics were reprimanded for not accepting the divinely ordained distinctions of social classes. "Sodalitium Pianum," the secret inquisitorial society founded and directed by Msgr. Umberto Benigni (later Mussolini's informer), operated freely as a Vatican-sponsored doctrinal and political spying agency. Antimodernist purges took their toll among laity and clergy. This reactionary period of the early part of the twentieth century was to have lasting effects on the development of contemporary Catholicism.

Foreign influence, mainly German, was blamed for the progressive ideas that had infected French and Italian Catholicism. Pius X's condemnations of political activism among Catholics were really made only against progressive political movements and people. He censured "Le Sillon," the progressive French lay movement founded by Marc Sangnier, but tolerated Charles Maurras's extreme right-wing "Action Française." He waited six years before meeting the general of the Jesuits, whom he suspected of being favorable to modernism.

Catholic Action in France was boxed in ideologically between Sangnier's Sillon and Maurras's Action Française. Its most important organ was the Action Catholique de la Jeunesse Française (ACJF), which had been founded in 1886 by the politically conservative but socially involved layman Albert de Mun. The ACJF, from the beginning, had leaned toward the progressive orientation called "social Catholicism," but it refused to take a partisan stand in favor of Christian Democracy. There were congresses of French Christian Democrats in 1896, 1897, and 1898, but the ACJF refused to become involved in those party meetings, in spite of its growing sympathy for that political option. Pius X's reversal of Leo XIII's stand on the necessity for French Catholics to rally to the republic, and his condemnation of Sangnier on May 26, 1910, dealt a severe blow to the progressive wing of French lay Catholicism as it existed in Le Sillon, in Christian Democracy, and in the ACJF. In spite of these difficulties, the progressive French Catholics continued to develop various organizations to promote their ideas and their ideals: institutes, social secretariates, periodicals focusing on social problems, the yearly "semaines sociales," Catholic professional associations, and Catholic trade unions (which merged into a national confederation in 1919). The organizations formed during this period laid the ground for the later creation of a short-lived Catholic party (the "Mouvement Républicain Populaire") and the flowering of specialized Catholic Action for workers and students.

One of the Italian victims of the Vatican ultraconservatives was Don Romolo Murri, who was trying to found a progressive Italian Christian Democratic party, independent of the control of Church authorities. He had been encouraged by Leo XIII into making his movement dependent on the Opera dei Congressi and accepting an ecclesiastical assistant for it, a move which had served to increase the group's legitimacy among Catholics. But Pius X, soon after his election as pope, dissolved the Opera dei Congressi and replaced it with a federation of unions controlled by the bishops of Italy. To replace the Opera dei Congressi Pius X created the Electoral Union, the Popular Union, and the Socioeconomic Union (made up of economic, labor, and welfare organizations).[45]

In 1904 Pius X condemned Murri's efforts, at a congress in Bologna, to organize an autonomous Christian Democratic party. Seeking to escape Vatican strictures, Murri's group then changed its name to the National Democratic League, dropping the appellation "Christian," and declared itself a nonconfessional association with members inspired by Christian ideals. Nevertheless Pius X made a public condemnation of the League in July 1906, suspended Murri *a divinis* in 1907, and excommunicated him two years later after he got himself elected as a deputy of the left.

There was, even within the Church, a certain opposition to Pius X and his conservative allies. Progressives who had withstood the purges obtained at least a breathing space during the next pontificate, that of Benedict XV (1914–1922). Dissatisfaction with Pius X's reactionary pontificate was so general that even the usually conservative college of cardinals was anxious to find a successor as much like Leo XIII and unlike Pius X as possible. When Pius died, the college of cardinals chose as pope a newly named cardinal, Giacomo Della Chiesa, who had been a protégé of Leo XIII's progressive secretary of state, Cardinal Rampolla. The conclave ended after three days, when Della Chiesa finally gathered the 38 votes he needed to defeat the curia's candidate, Cardinal J. Serafini, who finished with 18 of the 58 votes. Pius X and Merry del Val had forced Della Chiesa to leave an important position in the Secretariate of State to become archbishop of Bologna, and had denied him the cardinalate until after Rampolla's death, a form of ostracism which only increased his "papability" in the change-over after Pius X's death. As Benedict XV, he quickly acted to reverse the reactionary trend within the Vatican.

Forty-eight hours after his election, the new pope replaced Merry del Val with Cardinal Ferrata as head of the Secretariate of State and when Ferrata died, three months later, named Cardinal Gasparri, another Rampolla protégé, to that post. He suppressed the reactionary Sodalitium Pianum and took to task the antimodernist heresy hunters. During his eight-year pontificate, he generally took liberal positions on questions of change within the Church in response to the changing outside world. His short and progressive pontificate can be compared to the more recent one of John XXIII, sandwiched as it was between a reactionary and a conservative pontificate. Had he lived longer, he might today be acclaimed like Leo XIII and John XXIII, the two other progressive popes of these last hundred years.

Benedict's papacy was extremely crucial to the evolution of the lay movement. As archbishop of the diocese of Bologna he had been in contact with the Popular Union of Count Giuseppe Dalla Torre and Marquesa Patrizzi; as pope he supported this association of lay Catholics and made it a key element in his reorganization of Catholic Action. He fostered a differentiation between the sociopolitical and the moral-religious spheres because he wanted Catholics to be autonomously involved in politics without confusing political action with religious obligations.

In a letter to a friend in 1875, long before his election as pope, Benedict XV had written:

> Certainly one of the many needs of our times is to bring into being a true lay apostolate: I don't need to write to you at length about this, for you will remember all we used to say about it at the university.[46]

He seems to have wanted above all the development of a lay apostolate in religious, social, and moral spheres rather than an authoritarian curbing of Catholic conservatism. However, his policy of giving more autonomy to lay Catholics in the political and economic arenas favored the growth of progressive and independent organizations which themselves inhibited the conservatives' power.[47]

The development under Benedict XV of popular-based organizations and of the Popular Party, a relatively progressive Catholic political party, was strongly checked by the rise of fascism in Italy. It was stopped completely after the election of Pius XI as pope in 1922. But these Italian organizations created during Benedict XV's pontificate gave birth to the lay Catholic movement that emerged in Italy after World War II. Shaped by Italian politics, the Italian lay Catholic movement nevertheless had numerous links throughout Europe with other, more progressive lay groups, links which helped sustain it during the two quite conservative Pius papacies which followed.

Although Benedict XV did not openly indicate preferences in the political arena, he approved the independent organization of Catholic labor confederations, cooperatives, and mutual aid and insurance societies; and when these new groups took over the functions of the old Socioeconomic Union and the Electoral Union, he suppressed the latter, thus indicating once more the gulf between his policies and those of his reactionary predecessor.

He also allowed the independent development of the Popular Party, the heir to Romolo Murri's Christian Democratic party which Leo XIII had encouraged and Pius X had suppressed. Luigi Sturzo, a former aide of Murri, resigned in 1919 from his position as head of Italian Catholic Action to found the new party, with the tacit approval of Benedict XV. Older Catholic organizations remained under Church authority and became a new kind of Catholic Action that was limited to religious and educational goals.

Leadership in both the political and the religious organizations passed from proclerical moderates to the more liberal men who had been active in the Christian Democratic party and the Electoral Union. These included Sturzo, Giovanni Gronchi, and Giorgio Montini (the father of the future Paul VI), as well as other laymen who were moderately progressive on social issues and quite independent vis-à-vis the pope and the Italian hierarchy.

9. PIUS XI, CATHOLIC ACTION, AND FASCISM

The conclave of 1922 was a lively one. Pitted against each other in the race for the papal seat during most of the conclave were the moderate Cardinal Pietro Gasparri and the archconservative Cardinal La Fontaine. Early voting had clearly eliminated the progressive Cardinal Pietro Maffi and the reactionary Cardinal Rafaele Merry del Val. Once again, the protagonists of the Leo XIII–Rampolla line were in conflict with the inheritors of the conservative Pius IX–Pius X legacy, but this time the progressives stood no chances of winning. Benedict XV had named too few cardinals during his short term as pope. They could only hope to avoid the worst. Anticipating that he could not win a sufficient number of votes to be elected, Cardinal Gasparri swung the votes of the moderates and progressives who backed him to a dark horse, Cardinal Achille Ratti, the new archbishop of Milan. Cardinal Gaetano De Lai, leader of the other faction, then approached Ratti and assured him of the votes of the conservatives if he would agree to get rid of Gasparri as secretary of state. For this clear attempt to fix the election, De Lai and Merry del Val were both excommunicated during that conclave (a technical excommunication lifted immediately after the conclave). Ratti, who was elected, retained Gasparri as secretary of state until 1930, when he replaced him with the nuncio to Germany, the brilliant Msgr. Eugenio Pacelli, the future Pius XII. The apparent victory for the moderates turned out to be a victory for the conservatives, because Pius XI (1922–1939) rapidly revealed himself to be quite a conservative pope.

Both Pius XI and Cardinal Gasparri wanted, above all, to resolve the "Roman Question," the uneasy relationship between the Vatican and the Italian state which Pius IX had bequeathed to his successors. As cardinal of the diocese of Milan, Achille Ratti had hailed Benito Mussolini, the leader (*duce*) of the Fascist Party, as a "man sent by Providence," and had blessed the Fascist banners in his cathedral on November 4, 1921. As Pius XI, he was obviously impressed with the policies of the new government, especially with the concessions that Mussolini was obviously ready to make to Catholicism. Pius XI and his secretary of state agreed to dissolve the Popular Party and to transform Catholic Action into a strong "nonpolitical" alternative to that party. In order to get a favorable settlement of the Roman Question from Mussolini, Pius XI made it clear that Catholic Action was not to pursue courses contrary to those of fascism.

An authoritarian man, fearful of socialism and communism, Pius XI was inclined to think that Vatican interests would be better protected by a strong conservative regime than by a party of liberal Catholics operating in the democratic arena. He also feared that a Catholic party might be forced, under pressure from its centrist but anticlerical allies, to block political concessions to the Vatican on the question of the lost papal territories. Not liking, or feeling that he did not need, the Popular Party, he contributed to its demise in order to help the Fascists consolidate their power, and he legitimized his gesture by saying that what really interested him was a religious rather than a political type of involvement for lay Catholics.

The labor organizations suffered the same fate as the Popular Party, and the control of all Catholic Action organizations became centralized in the hands of the Vatican. In 1923, Pius XI restructured Italian

Catholic Action more or less as it is today. Catholic Action comprised the Federation of Catholic Men, the Union of Catholic Women, the youth organizations (separate for males and females), and the Italian Federation of Catholic University Students (FUCI, with male and female branches). The Central Committee (Giunta Centrale) was composed of a general president named by the pope, the presidents of the six branches who were elected by lay leaders at the local level, and two other members, named by the pope. All officers at all levels were laymen, except for the chaplains, who were clerics named by the episcopate. It was these clerics who proposed the names of lay leaders for nomination by the Church hierarchy at the local level. In sum, there was a certain degree of lay autonomy, in spite of some Vatican and clerical control.

Under Pius XI, Catholic Action was supposed to be purely religious and educational, but it actually supported the collaboration of Catholics with the official Fascist organizations, at least during the 1920s, before the Lateran Agreements.[48] Thus, in Italy, Church and State reached a mutually profitable détente. Pius XI, under the influence of conservatives like Pacelli, preferred diplomacy and concordats to Catholic parties as a solution to the Church's need for a link with the modern world. Catholic parties were difficult to control, unpredictable, and too much influenced by liberal and radical ideas. A clerically controlled Catholic Action, working at the level of young people's and adult's socialization, was far more malleable. Adroitly defining the reorganized Catholic Action as an organization for the "participation of the laity in the apostolate of the hierarchy," Pius XI gave a new impetus to Catholic Action as a conservative, tractable group that the Vatican could support.

Even so, Mussolini, who had been in power since 1922, was to find that Catholic Action, as the sole major Italian organization outside his control, was not compatible with his notions of governing. He even came to see it as a threat to his rule. The Fascists accused the ex-Popolari (members of the suppressed Popular Party) of having moved into Catholic Action, especially in the FUCI, and of using certain Catholic Action groups as an organizational base on which to build an opposition to the regime.

Meetings of the FUCI, because Fascist youth groups had made violent attacks on them, often had to be held secretly, sometimes in the Roman catacombs. The other branches of Catholic Action, those that were based on age and sex and were much more easily controlled by the clergy, were less antagonistic to fascism. But Catholic Action as a whole gradually became the Church's first line of defense against fascism in Italy.

The conflict between the Fascist youth groups and the Italian youth branch of Catholic Action over recruitment of members came to a head in 1931. Mussolini dissolved the youth and university branches of Catholic Action. Pius XI, by now quite vigilant toward fascism's encroachment on the Vatican's prerogatives, retaliated with the encyclical *Non abbiamo bisogno*. Although it was a scathing denunciation of the regime's attacks on Catholic Action and Catholic education, the encyclical led to an agreement, on September 2, 1931, betwen the Vatican and the government. The agreement put Catholic Action under greater control of the bishops and further restricted it to purely religious ends, but it also permitted Catholic Action to continue existing, recruiting, and organizing.

After this compromise with Mussolini, the FUCI continued to function discreetly as a rallying point for some young anti-Fascist Catholics who were to become the leaders of the Italian Christian Democratic Party after the war. Although he was promoted to a quieter position in the Secretariate of State, FUCI's chaplain Msgr. Montini (later Paul VI) kept in touch with these young men during the 1930s and 40s. In 1939 the Fascist journal *Regime Facista* accused Alcide De Gasperi (later prime minister), Msgr. Montini, Count Guiseppe Dalla Torre, and Guido Gonella (the last two were editors of the Vatican paper *L'Osservatore Romano*) of preparing an eventual rebirth of Sturzo's Popular Party. Gonella was also a leader of Movimento Laureati, the university-graduate branch of Catholic Action, which became a leadership recruitment ground for the Christian Democratic Party after World War II; later on, he led a conservative faction of the Christian Democrats. Aldo Moro, slated to become another top Christian Democrat (he was secretary of the party and then prime minister of the country between 1963 and 1968, and again between 1974 and 1976, and was killed by the Red Brigades in 1978), was Gonella's colleague in the high echelons of the Movimento Laureati. The personal and ideological ties formed under fascism by these young anti-regime intellectuals became important in post-World War II Italian politics. After the war, Catholic Action and the Christian Democratic Party, instead of being rather distinct paths for social involvement by lay Catholics (as in the case of Catholic Action and the Popular Party after World War I), functioned together closely. Even the more conservative branches of Catholic Action, like Luigi Gedda's Youth Catholic Action, became a sort of pressure group inside the

Christian Democratic Party and a springboard which Gedda used to create the "Comitati Civici," a network of "Civic Committees" which backed the Christian Democrats at election time.

Italian Catholic lay leaders since World War II, within both Catholic Action and the Christian Democratic Party, have been conspicuously dependent on the Vatican and the Italian episcopate and clergy. They have, to this day, failed to regain the autonomy and freedom enjoyed during the reign of Benedict XV, when the lay movement had a mass base relatively independent of Church authorities.

The hierarchical mandate in the lay movement, a legacy from the Fascist era, is in good part responsible for the subsequent state of dependence. Both Pius XI and Pius XII insisted strongly on the importance of the mandate, although their positions on the topic of sociopolitical involvement were ambiguous and quite dependent on the existing political context. With papacy and hierarchy securely in charge, the Catholic lay movement could be used as a means to support the conservative positions of the papacy in the sociopolitical realm, and progressive laymen could be discouraged from active participation in sociopolitical activities.

When the lay movement had progressive proclivities, in the early 1920s, Pius XI stressed the principle of noninvolvement in political affairs in an effort to help fascism and block socialism. But when noninvolvement in political affairs by Catholic Action after World War II could have favored the left, Pius XII reversed that policy and encouraged "temporal" involvement, since it was now necessary, in order to block the left, that Catholic Action operate as a conservative pressure group. Temporal involvement was encouraged only when it was in accordance with the conservative orientation of the papacy: meanwhile, obedience to the hierarchy and the Vatican remained the cornerstones of Catholic Action.

Antonio Gramsci has discussed the consequences of Catholic Action's dependence on the Vatican:

> The weakness of every national C.A. organization lies in the fact that its action is continuously limited and interfered with by the demands of the international and national policy of the Holy See. To the extent that each national C.A. organization grows and becomes more massive, it tends to take shape as a real political party, whose directions arise from the internal demands of the organization itself. But this development can never become organic because of the Holy See's intervention.[49]

10. ITALIAN CATHOLIC ACTION
UNDER PIUS XII

Catholic Action continued to be a battleground for conservative and liberal lay forces under Pius XII (1939–1958), who made a fresh effort to attach the lay organization firmly to conservative hierarchical control. Forty-eight hours after his election, declaring that Catholic Action was an episcopally guided collaboration between laity and bishops, Pius XII changed the statutes of Italian Catholic Action to put members of the clergy in positions as directors. Although not pressured by external politics as was Pius XI in 1931, Pius XII nevertheless turned the lay organization into a clerical preserve.

There were open protests. Dissatisfied lay leaders, participating in Catholic Action pilgrimages, attended papal audiences to cheer the dead Pius XI rather than the new pope, to the consternation of the Vatican.[50] At about the same time, in 1939, Pius XII lifted the papal condemnation of Charles Maurras's right-wing Action Française, showing clearly where his sympathies lay—at a time when such a sign of papal favor was very important for the forces of fascism in Europe.

A commission of cardinals representing the Italian bishops was named by Pius XII to direct Catholic Action, and to select the lay presidents of all six branches, as well as the ecclesiastical assistants. A prelate was named as director at the national level. For all practical purposes, it was now a clerical organization tightly controlled by the hierarchy, rather than a lay organization. Not until 1946 did laymen regain a little of the power they had held prior to Pius XII's election. Even that did not really serve to liberalize or radicalize Catholic Action, because the most progressive elements were moving out, into the Christian Democratic Party and the parties of the left, and Catholic Action was burdened with many members known to have been supporters of the Fascist regime.

Although Pius XII's 1939 transformation of Catholic Action did not give Fascist leaders any direct control, in many ways it helped the government. Catholic Action was now virtually controlled by the bishops, who, in Italy, were even more favorably disposed toward fascism than was the Vatican. Consequently, Catholic Action gradually became more conservative.

When Italy joined the war, the clerical and lay leaders of Catholic Action (for example, President Luigi Gedda of Youth Catholic Action), encouraged Catholics to enroll in the army. In an audience with Catholic Actionists on September 4, 1940, Pius XII exhorted the men to give their lives, if necessary, for their country, and praised the government for giving religious education to Italy.

Catholic Action generally stayed out of the Resistance; Gedda, in 1943, even formally advised Catholic Actionists not to participate in it. Some young Catholics founded a Catholic left party, but it was squelched by Msgr. Montini in an *Osservatore Romano* note of January 2–3, 1945, a theological condemnation which was reaffirmed on May 6 of the same year. All through the war, Msgr. Montini of the Vatican Secretariate of State and others in the Vatican, including Pius XII, pushed for the political unity of Catholics inside a single Catholic party, the Christian Democrats. Liberalism replaced conservatism as the major orientation of the Vatican. All efforts were put into strengthening the Catholic party and in maintaining as much unity as possible among Catholics. Even the minor center and right-wing parties sympathetic to Catholicism were not encouraged, so as not to disperse the resources of the Church. The Italian Communists and Socialists were so strong near the end of World War II that the conservatives in the Vatican went along with Montini's ideas, minimizing conflicts with some of the more progressive Christian Democratic leaders in order to avoid a victory of the left at the polls.

In April 1945, Montini sent a public letter in the pope's name to Msgr. Gremigni, national director of Catholic Action, encouraging 850 Catholic Action leaders then meeting in Rome to become active in social affairs and public life. And Pius XII, in his address, warned these same leaders against adhering to "theories and social systems which the Church has repudiated or against which the faithful have been warned."

The new line was to press Catholic Actionists into involvement in social and political issues, in the Christian Democratic Party, and against the Socialists and the Communists, who were lumped together under the term "social-communists." Vatican persuasion expressed itself in various ways. In August 1945, for example, the Consistorial Congregation (now called the Congregation of Bishops) sent a document to all Italian bishops on the question of the right to vote. This circular was a *non expedit* in reverse, exhorting bishops to preach that Catholics had a strict obligation to vote. The document gave the bishops detailed instructions on how to influence the faithful in their electoral behavior:

> Catholics can give their votes only to the candidates or lists of candidates that are sure to uphold and defend the observance of the laws of

God and the rights of religion and of the Church, both in private and in public life. The closer the programme and practical activity of a candidate or of a list of candidates comes in justifying and backing this certainty, the greater will be the peace of mind that Catholics can have in feeling free to vote for them.[51]

In 1946, some minor changes inside Italian Catholic Action gave back to laymen a certain measure of autonomy which had been removed in 1939. Some laymen suddenly became important figures in the Italian Church. Vittorino Veronese, secretary-general of the FUCI in 1939, had been called to Rome in 1943 by Montini and, through his influence, been made secretary-general of Italian Catholic Action in 1944. He became general president in 1946. The real power, however, lay with the more conservative Luigi Gedda, president of the men's section, who had succeeded in placing one of his followers in his own former position as president of the youth section by intervening directly with the pope to stop the nomination of a progressive friend of Veronese, Giuseppe Lazzati. Gedda was a shrewd and somewhat ruthless politician, intent on stopping the Christian Democratic Party's collaboration with Socialists and Communists.

After the war, Gedda tried to centralize Catholic Action, giving more power to the Vatican and the Central Committee, and to involve it in politics in order to defend his and Pius XII's conservative ideals. Although not yet second in command in Italian Catholic Action, after Veronese, Gedda gradually became the more powerful of the two, because he had the backing and support of Pius XII.

Italian Catholic Action's first major forays into politics were organized along the lines of a mass mobilization of Catholics to stop a political takeover of Italy by the Socialists and Communists. This mobilization was suggested in an important article by Jesuit Father Ricardo Lombardi in *La Civiltà Cattolica*. At the September 7, 1947, rally in St. Peter's Square, which the *Osservatore Romano* of September 8–9 called "the most impressive filial homage that religious history has ever recorded," Pius XII encouraged Catholic Action to become more involved in civic affairs. In March 1948, in a speech to the pastors of the city of Rome, he reiterated the 1945 instructions to Italian bishops:

It is a strict obligation for those who have the right to do so, men and women, to participate in elections. He who abstains from voting by laziness or by lack of interest commits what is essentially a grave sin, a mortal sin . . . The voice of conscience imposes on every sincere

Catholic the duty to vote for the candidates or the lists of candidates who offer really sufficient guarantees for the protection of the rights of God and of souls, for the real good of individuals, families and society, according to the laws of God and the Christian moral doctrine.[52]

But rallies and exhortations were not enough. As the 1948 elections approached, there was panic in the Vatican because of the grass-roots support for the Communist Party, especially in southern Italy. Gedda suggested a solution: the creation of civic committees in all of Italy could give Catholics the organizational base needed to fight for the Christian Democrats in the elections and apply pressure so that it would remain a right-of-center party. Based on Father Lombardi's ideas about grass-roots mobilization of all Catholic forces, these "Comitati Civici" were simply local groups of the leaders of all Catholic associations existing in their area. To circumvent the 1929 Concordat's ban on political activities by Catholic Action, the Civic Committees held no formal links with that movement, although in practice most of its organizers and members were active in Catholic Action also. Priests, specifically prohibited from entering politics by the concordat, were even more active mobilizers than were the laymen. Through the Civic Committees, an all-out effort, aided by Vatican, United States government, and private-enterprise funds, was made to get votes for the Christian Democrats. The threat of the enormous popularity of the Italian Communist Party was menacing enough to the Vatican to cause it to make a complete about-face on Catholic Action's orientation toward political involvement.

Thanks to the activity of the civic committees, the 1948 elections were an overwhelming victory for the Christian Democrats. By so decisively stopping the "forces of socialism" at the polls, the Christian Democrats were able to form a government without the support of the other political parties.

Now the progressive wing of the Italian Catholic lay movement was forced, by the success of Gedda and his Civic Committees, to grant these committees permanent legitimacy. In July 1948, the General Assembly of Catholic Action at Siena gave Gedda an important victory by voting to keep the Civic Committees alive. Veronese himself, as general president of Italian Catholic Action, had to make the announcement of the decision, though it must have seemed an unhappy one to him. The pope's message to the Assembly—sent through Msgr. Montini—indicated approval of the Civic Committees by congratulating Catholic Action on the "continued renewal of its methods of work which made it discover and utilize the most opportune and efficacious means of action."

But the left-wing laymen were not ready to give up control of Catholic Action to Gedda. Giuseppe Lazzati, whose nomination as president of Youth Catholic Action had been previously blocked by Gedda's intercession with the pope, and who was now a newly elected Christian Democratic member of parliament, wrote an article attacking Catholic Action's politicization. Appearing in November 1948 in *Cronache Sociali*, the periodical of left-leaning Christian Democrats, the article quoted the liberal French Thomist philosopher Jacques Maritain to support the argument that Catholic Action should stay out of politics.

Gedda retaliated with an attack on "certain transalpine philosophies" and on those Catholics who dared to "dispute and judge the right of the Church to use particular competences and methods appropriate to its goals," and with a defense of Catholic Action's intervention in politics:

> Fascism imposed on Catholic Action twenty years of difficulties and wanted to keep it in the sacristy. These politicians [the liberal Christian Democratic critics of Catholic Action] would like us to return to that state. . . . If through Catholic Action it is the Civic Committees that they are trying to hit, then we would say that not only is it ingratitude, but also stupidity. Italian Catholics are avant-garde Catholics; we must not attack the cement which unites them and destroy the dam which has stopped the tides of disorder.[53]

Around the same time, in the name of the necessary unity of Catholics, Gedda and Pius XII were also active in an operation to form a Catholic trade-union confederation in order to break the unity of the labor movement.

Veronese and, more discreetly, Msgr. Montini, backed by the Movimento Laureati, by the FUCI, and by minorities in the other divisions of Catholic Action, leaned somewhat toward Lazatti's position, whereas Pius XII was more sympathetic to Gedda, who controlled both the adult and the youth sections of Catholic Action. In 1949, Pius XII, who had publicly affirmed that the June 1948 victory for the Christian Democrats had been due to the merciful intervention of divine providence, named Gedda general vice-president of Italian Catholic Action. Veronese was thus slowly becoming nothing more than an honorary president, since Gedda now controlled the General

Committee and had the favor of the pope. This was a hard blow for the progressive wing of the Catholic lay movement in Italy, both in Catholic Action and in the Christian Democratic Party. However, when two further Gedda operations ("Plan S," for the reinforcing of Catholic trade-unionism at the expense of the Socialist and Communist workers' movement, and the "Crusade of the Great Return," for the recuperation of fallen-away Catholics) floundered badly, in 1949 and 1950, the Veronese faction in Catholic Action once again became more critical of the Civic Committees. But Pius XII, directly in May 1950 and through the Vatican-controlled *Osservatore Romano* and *La Civiltà Cattolica* in 1951, reiterated his support for Gedda and his committees. The 1951 administrative elections in Italy hurt the Christian Democrats badly, but Gedda continued to push for his committees and to use them as a right-wing pressure group against his liberal adversaries in the Christian Democratic Party and as a springboard for his control over Catholic Action in Italy.

Carlo Falconi sees this opposition in Catholic Action as an opposition between purist idealists (Veronese) and practical spirits (Gedda).[54] It was that, in part, but there is little doubt that the conflict was much more a conflict between two different political positions, one liberal and one conservative. In the 1920s, wanting to block the involvement of lay Catholics in progressive political action and thereby aid Mussolini's rise to power, Pius XI had proposed an apolitical Catholic Action. With the Fascist party now dead, Gedda and his conservative mentors in the Vatican carried their war against socialism into the Christian Democratic Party, attempting to eradicate any leftist tendencies that might develop. To help in this, Pius XII did not hesitate to reverse his predecessor's line on the question of Catholic Action's political neutrality. Now that the danger of a leftist alternative was present once again, and that a Fascist or a conservative restoration was out of the question, the Vatican opted for a centrist alternative, banking on the Christian Democrats. Every effort was made, however, to turn that option into a center-right rather than a center-left coalition whenever the fragile centrist base was too small and allies were needed elsewhere on the political spectrum to keep the Christian Democrats afloat. Thus the opposition between humanization and evangelization —or more precisely the opposition between civic (i.e. political) involvement and religious apostolate—was not the central issue it was often made out to be, in Catholic Action and in the Church generally. At about the same time, in France, Catholic Action and priest-workers were fighting for greater freedom to get involved in political and social issues, but, strangely enough, they were told by the Vatican that Catholic Actionists and priests should not become politically active. The reason for the discrepancy in the reactions of the Vatican to the French and Italian situations is simple: in Italy, political involvement meant supporting the center and the right, a position which was agreeable to the Vatican, whereas in France, political involvement of priests and laymen would have meant a leftist involvement, an option which was unacceptable to the Vatican. The numerous crises of Catholic Action in France have always been a result of the tension between progressive laity and clergy involved with nonclerical Communist and Socialist parties, and conservative churchmen who felt they had to censure whatever political organizations they could not lead.

When the Belgian priest Joseph Cardijn founded the Young Catholic Workers (JOC) in the mid-1920s, Pius XI did not protest. On the contrary, he congratulated him for trying to win back the working class which the Catholic Church had lost during the preceeding century. A branch of specialized Catholic Action like the JOC, progressive but noninvolved politically, and firmly controlled by Church authorities (as was the case with the FUCI in Italy), was deemed acceptable, since political noninvolvement and hierarchical control were sufficient compensations for the group's progressive proclivities.

In Italy, where Church authorities under Pius XII wanted Catholic Action to be politically conservative, the more liberal Catholic Actionists brought up Pius XI's old ''no politics'' argument to try to prevent the use of lay organizations for conservative political aims. Sensing that it was impossible to switch Italian Catholic Action to a progressive political view, they sought to minimize the damage by trying to stop all political involvement of Catholic Action and by stressing the religious apostolate. This group would likely have pressed for political involvement, if the involvement had had a chance of being liberal rather than conservative. Since that appeared impossible, the liberal laymen in Catholic Action stressed the idea that Catholic Action should be a lay apostolate aimed at transforming men and society through nonpolitical means, rather than a centralized, clerically controlled bulwark against the left.

Because a centrist alternative to the Socialist and Communist left could only succeed in maintaining itself in power in Italy if it expanded its base by moving either to the right or to the left in a significant manner, the split among Catholics increasingly manifested itself between those who were left-leaning and those who were inclined to favor a coalition with the Monarchists, the Liberals and the neo-Fascists. Pius XII favored this last option. He became increasingly conservative after the 1948 elections, excommunicating those who voted Communist and putting more and more pressure on the Christian Democrats for an opening to the right.

In the religious arena, the pope became more conservative. His 1950 encyclical *Humani Generis*, directed against some of the progressive theologians who were to become the periti (experts) of Vatican II, has been compared to Pius X's antimodernist *Pascendi*. Further, the dogma of the bodily assumption of Mary into heaven (1950), the destitution of Archbishop Charbonneau of Montreal because of his working-class sympathies in an important strike, the attempted canonization of Pius IX, and the actual canonization of Pius X were accumulating indications of a turn toward the right. The tightening of control over Catholic Action, then, was just one more manifestation of Pius XII's conservatism.

11. TOWARD THE FIRST WORLD CONGRESS FOR THE LAY APOSTOLATE

Even the Vatican's 1949 decision to accept the suggestion of Veronese and Montini to hold a world congress for the lay apostolate at Rome in 1951 was intended as a way to strengthen the conservative position. There were effective advantages for both the liberals and the conservatives in the Church for holding such a congress. The Vatican conservatives hoped to extend their control over the various international organizations that were prone to develop activities and ideas outside the sphere of influence of the hierarchy. On the other hand, liberals like Veronese and Montini were hoping that the congress would break the monopoly of conservative and clericalist Italian Catholic Action over the lay movement.

The papacy wanted to use Catholic Action and indirectly the Christian Democratic Party as its secular arm to control not only Rome and a few small territories (as had been the case before the loss of the pontifical states), but the whole of Italy. The first World Congress for the Lay Apostolate, held in Rome in October 1951, gave Pius XII the occasion he needed to reaffirm strongly his idea that the lay apostolate should intervene in the political-social sphere, but should be "subordinated to the ecclesiastical hierarchy."[55] A woman journalist, whose husband was head of the delegation of the International Federation of Catholic Men in October 1967, wrote about that congress:

> The holding of the first Congress for the Lay Apostolate (1951) was due chiefly to the support given by the Holy See, precisely by the

then Substitute of the Secretariate of State, Msgr. Giovanni Battista Montini, now Pope Paul VI. At that time some feared and others hoped that the growing lay movements would be taken up in the arms of Mother Church and coordinated along the lines of the old "Catholic Action" which was nothing but the extended arm of the hierarchy.[56]

This quotation describes fairly well the problem of the lay Catholic movement, in Italy and elsewhere, in relation to the hierarchy and to the Vatican, not only in the late 1940s and in the fifties, but even into the late sixties and early seventies.

In substance, then, there were two tendencies in the Italian lay movement, and these two tendencies had affinities with various orientations in other countries. On the one side were traditional Catholic Action organizations, differentiated according to age and to sex, conservative and sponsored by the hierarchy, still integralist and clericalist in orientation but with a new anti-Communist slant that had developed after the war. On the other side was the politically liberal and somewhat socially aware Christian Democratic orientation, supported by Catholic university graduates, intellectuals, and the newly re-created workers' groups. The people representing this latter tendency were not rabid anti-Communists, and they were rapidly becoming more radical, as was the case also with Catholic Action workers' groups in France and elsewhere. But, by and large, these liberals were really just sophisticated conservatives, or, more precisely, progressive conservatives and moderate centrists.

Pius XII and Luigi Gedda, among others, were the sponsors of the first orientation described above, whereas people like Msgr. Montini and Vittorino Veronese were among the leaders of the second, more ambivalent one.

In this chapter we have seen how the Christian church grew from a relatively communitarian lower-class Jewish sect into a highly organized Gentile church with close ties to the rulers of the Roman Empire. It developed an increasingly centralized hierarchical structure which supported and at times even dominated the existing political structures. As the Roman Empire in the West faded from the scene, the pope became a sort of religious counterpart image of the former emperor. The papacy from the time of Constantine, through the period of the rise and fall of feudalism, to the time of the emergence of the modern nation-state, acquired considerable authority in society and in the Church, relegating the lower clergy and the laity to secondary positions. When the Protestant Reformation and the French Revolution swept away many of the traditional, mainly coercive, means of control of Church officials over its grass-roots constituency, the papacy regained prominence by making alliances and concordats with political rulers. And as the laity started to build a strong movement that threatened to gain some independence vis-à-vis papal authority, the Vatican used co-optation and condemnations as means of control. The laity, particularly Italian Catholic Action, became an instrument of the conservative policies of the Vatican. Lay Catholic organizations came to be viewed by the Vatican as a "reserve clergy," as extensions of clerical and hierarchical influence in secular society, to be used in the political arena whenever it was advantageous. It was in this latter context that both liberal and conservative churchmen agreed to hold the first World Congress for the Lay Apostolate in 1951.

III

Centralizing the Lay Movement: The First Two World Congresses for the Lay Apostolate and Vatican II

In the hundred years beginning with the mid-1850s the influence of the laity in the Catholic Church expanded as never before. Centralization of this broadening and powerful movement culminated with the two World Congresses for the Lay Apostolate held in Rome during the 1950s. These meetings provided an international forum for the assembled lay representatives, but they also made it easy for the Vatican to control and co-opt the laity's international leadership.

The consolidation of the Catholic International Organizations (CIOs), an influential federation of international groups, and the establishment of the Permanent Committee for the International Congresses for the Lay Apostolate represented papal efforts to orient the development of the lay movement. Nevertheless, they served also as important instruments for the expression of moderate lay opinion, itself the end product of a century of lay activity.

1. THE FIRST WORLD CONGRESS FOR THE LAY APOSTOLATE

The convocation, in October 1951, of the first World Congress of the Lay Apostolate brought together Roman Catholic laity from seventy-four countries. It was the first truly international assemblage of representatives of lay Catholic organizations. The officially stated goal of the congress was to unite all the laymen involved in various types of apostolate and to set up guidelines for their work.[1]

Beyond the official statements, it is important to see the congress in the context of the Italian struggle between the two distinct orientations toward lay involvement in religious and political affairs described in the previous chapter.

Vittorino Veronese, who had become president-general of Italian Catholic Action, with the backing of the influential Msgr. Montini and the approval of the Vatican, took the initiative to convene this congress. Le Cour Grand-Maison, one of the presidents of the congress, in his closing speech to the delegates thanked Veronese for having been the "inspirator, organizer, and animator of this meeting."[2] Montini had persuaded the pope that such a meeting would be to the Vatican's benefit, and Pius XII and his conservative officials in the curia supported the idea of reviving the tradition of lay congresses, because they believed they could use these international gatherings to extend their own authority in the growing world-wide Catholic organizations and to pursue the goal of bringing Italians back under the influence of the Church, as the 1950 Holy Year had tried to do.

Even the leader of the lay opposition to the Montini-Veronese group, Luigi Gedda, acknowledged that the "principal merit for this congress" belonged to Veronese.[3] Gedda, then vice-president of Italian Catholic Action, attended as head of the Italian delegation and played an active part, but with very different goals from those of Montini and Veronese, who had put the international meeting in motion primarily to broaden the perspectives of Italian Catholic Action, and thus to weaken the conservative trend in the Italian lay movement.

Veronese hinted at this when he said, in his speech to the congress, that he hoped the congress would result in "a deeper and more general reciprocal knowledge of the various aspects of apostolic experience in different countries."[4] In an interview given to Desmond O'Grady in 1968, he also said:

> As president of Italian Catholic Action in 1951, I took the initiative to convoke the first world laity congress. The main value of the congress was that for the first time it brought together those engaged in the lay apostolate. Previously the structure had been vertical— students throughout the world were linked, as were Catholic women's organizations, and so on—but this was the first attempt at a horizontal grouping of the laity, united as laity.[5]

One of Veronese's major objectives in 1950 was to open up the conservative Vatican to the liberal perspectives of the Christian Democratic leaders of the new Italy. Count Guiseppe Dalla Torre, editor of the Vatican daily *L'Osservatore Romano* under various popes, recalls in his memoirs that Veronese, in 1950, had created an elite Catholic group of intellectuals, the "Circolo di Roma," with the idea of bringing together Vatican officials and important political and diplomatic lay figures for lectures and discussions.[6] Count Dalla Torre had good contacts both in the Vatican and in the Christian Democratic Party, and it was for this reason that Veronese chose him to be the Circolo president, insisting that he stay on in that office for as long as possible. Dalla Torre recalls in his memoirs an unforgettable meeting to which Veronese had invited as speaker the Christian Democratic chancellor of West Germany, Konrad Adenauer. These recollections give a good indication of the liberal strategy Veronese was using in the early fifties to counteract the more conservative tendencies in the Vatican and in Catholic Action.

As president of the organizing committee for the World Congress for the Lay Apostolate, Veronese was able to influence the direction of the congress and the choice of topics for discussion. His aim of encouraging Italian Catholic Action to align itself with world trends, rather than for international organizations to model themselves after the Italian lay movement, was suggested in his speech to a preparatory conference just before Christmas 1950: "We must be capable of putting universal reality before selfish interests and nationalism." At that time, he also stated his hope that the congress would "really open the soul to universal conceptions."[7]

At this planning meeting of a hundred experts, from fifteen international organizations in twenty-two countries, the topics for the October meeting were chosen: (1) today's world, (2) doctrine, (3) formation (i.e. training), (4) social involvement, (5) international responsibilities. The last two topics were the most important for the liberal lay figures in the congress. In his important speech at the congress itself, Veronese, who had been chosen by the Vatican to be secretary-general of the congress, expressed his hope that this international meeting would give Catholics a broader knowledge of various apostolic experiences in different countries and a clear perception of the duty to be active in international organizations. He suggested that other such congresses be held regularly at both international and national levels.

In a low-key and diplomatic way, Veronese and his friends underplayed certain themes, such as the subordination of the laity to the hierarchy, and stressed certain others, such as collaboration *with* the hierarchy. Similarly, they talked of the variable forms of the lay apostolate rather than of Catholic Action itself, which represented a narrower perspective and had greater undertones of hierarchical control and conservative involvement in politics. The pope's address to the congress strongly emphasized the subordination of Catholic Action to the hierarchy, whereas the speech by Maria Vendrik, a delegate from the Netherlands who was to become a member of the Council on the Laity in 1967, suggested that rules and insistence on subordination be toned down in favor of love:

> We do not question the necessity of the subordination of laymen to the hierarchy, but we wonder if the fact of insisting on this subordination does not create an obstacle to the full exercise of lay responsibility. We think that subordination could perhaps be efficiently guaranteed by spiritual means, that charity and love of the Church will do more than juridical rules. We ask lay information be oriented above all to the growth of love for the Church, the Mystical Body of Christ.[8]

At the World Congress of 1951, a new group of lay leaders emerged from among the officers of the international lay organizations. The most conspicuous participants, those on the organizing committee or in other prominent positions, were usually officers of already strong organizations, especially Catholic Action, or were upper-class notables in their own countries. Professor Ramón Sugranyes de Franch, secretary-general of Pax Romana–International Movement of Catholic Intellectuals (MIIC), gave a major address, quoting Msgr. Montini in asserting the importance of international activity for the Catholic lay movement. De Franch emerged as a key figure at the congress and, like some others active there (Mieczyslaw de Habicht, Rosemary Goldie, Maria Fievez, Maria Vendrik, Martin Work, Prince Karl zu Löwenstein, Jean Larnaud), became in 1967 one of the members of the newly created Council on the Laity.

Some twelve hundred people were present at the 1951 congress. They came as representatives of thirty-eight Catholic International Organizations of lay Catholics from seventy-four nations, and seventeen ethnic groups-in-exile (these were chiefly anti-Communist refugees from East European nations).[9] Experts and guests were also counted in the total.

A distinction was made at the first congress (and also at the second and third), between international and national delegates. The national delegates (Catholics from each country were allowed a maximum of

twenty) were primarily Catholic Action leaders and their selection was
heavily controlled by the Church hierarchy in the various countries.
At this meeting the more autonomous and internationally minded
laymen active in the CIOs (each CIO was allowed a maximum of ten
delegates) were conscious, some for the first time, of the heavy hand of
the Vatican. This fundamental distinction between international and
national delegates mirrored, up to a certain point, the difference
between the more autonomous and internationally minded laymen
active in the CIOs and the hierarchically controlled Catholic Action
leaders from the various countries represented. On the other hand,
because of the congress a new life was infused into the CIOs. The
Conference of Catholic International Organizations was created to
replace the Conference of Presidents of the CIOs, a permanent secretariate was set up in Geneva, and statutes were drawn up with the
approval of the Vatican.

A full-page photograph of Pius XII begins the first of the two
volumes of the congress's proceedings, published by the Vatican. The
pope's prayer and major speech, in various languages, occupy fifty of
the opening pages of the 400-page volume.[10] The remainder and the
second volume are devoted to the business of the congress, consisting
of selected speeches by laymen and (predominantly) clerics, and reports
on workshops devoted to twenty separate topics: mass media, intellectuals, charities, family, catechism, childhood, youth, health, school,
work, professions, civics, sports and leisure, missions, parishes, international life, minorities, women, art, and unity.

Italian lay leaders figured prominently in the proceedings—more so
than in the subsequent congresses—but the prevailing influence at the
first World Congress was the combined authority of the Vatican and
the national ecclesiastical hierarchies. This is evident from the two-
volume proceedings, which consist mainly of statements by members
of the clergy and a few carefully selected laymen.

Many non-Italian lay leaders were surprised at the close Vatican control of this international meeting. John M. Todd, an English layman
present as a delegate, has described the screening of the ''conclusions''
printed as the congress's official statement:

> On the second day of the Congress messages reached various dele-
> gates, including a member from the English Delegation, asking them
> to come to a meeting which was to be the inaugural meeting of the
> Commission of Conclusions, of which they were to be the members.
> The commission was a working party whose task was to draw up a
> document to be submitted to the President of the Congress as suit-
> able for publication as the conclusions of the Congress, also to draft a

second brief document for the Holy Father. The chairman of this commission was a layman, the secretary and assistant secretary were priests. At the first meeting, a draft of proposed conclusions drawn up by Msgr. Pietro Pavan, a member of the commission, was put before the commission. During the subsequent four days, groups of members of the commission were asked to fill out the various sections of this document; nearly all this work was given to ecclesiastical members of the commission. It was made clear that this was to be the document which was to go out to the world as embodying the conclusions of the deliberations at the Congress, that substantial additions by way of practical suggestions arising out of the work of the Congress would not be accepted, and even that small additional phrases attempting to make matters more precise would be censored and possibly removed or weakened in their phraseology. These facts became clear as suggestions were made, and as sentences which the commission had accepted were found to be missing from the document when it returned from the typists. The second document, for the Holy Father, was intended to be less general, and it was stated that it would be confidential and would not be printed. This was duly drawn up, but the same process as before took place. Sentences which the commission had accepted had disappeared when the document returned from the typists' office, and subjects brought up by members of the commission were banned. (The subjects are amongst those referred to in this article.) The commission was thus prevented from saying what it wished to the Holy Father.[11]

Backstage operations of the type described by Todd, engaged in by carefully selected ecclesiastical assistants, are not uncommon control mechanisms in lay Catholic organizations. That they were deemed necessary at this congress, where the Resolutions Committee consisted of participants who had already been thoroughly screened, gives a measure of the precautions which the Vatican was taking to assure that no discordant voice would be heard that could embarrass the pope and the hierarchy.

Individual workshop recommendations played a minor part in the workings of the first World Congress, and the published conclusions were a discreetly balanced selection of conservative and liberal views. Both groups spoke of the need to increase worldly involvement, although in different terms. The conservatives talked of saving souls, while the liberals affirmed the primacy of the spiritual sphere over partisan political action and stressed the need for social action on the international level. All described the Church as the Mystical Body of Christ, but the liberals tended to talk also of the Church as the people of God, rather than in juridical-hierarchical or organismic terms, as was the case with the conservatives. Contrarily to the liberals, the conservatives put great emphasis on the sufferings of refugees from behind the Iron Curtain, and on their own great love and respect for the person of the pope. Although the congress opened with an address by Msgr. Joseph Cardijn, a progressive prelate and the founder of the Jeunesse Ouvrière Catholique, it was the pope's sermon which was the high point of the whole meeting.

This congress, more than the two that followed, can be seen as a mirror of the internal rivalry in Italian Catholic Action. The outcome of this liberal-conservative contest was not evident until after the congress was concluded and the international delegates had gone home, although the sequel might have been predicted from the pope's statements.

Pius XII's speech, delivered midway in the congress, was an unmistakable reply to any who looked to him for arbitration of the contest. His statement on the importance of participating in affairs of state, which could be interpreted as reflecting the Vatican attitude on Italian politics, seemed to be a clear vindication of Gedda's conservative position. In addition, Pius XII clearly delineated his opinion of lay activity within the Church. To fill the gap left by shrinking numbers of priests, he encouraged lay collaboration in Church affairs, but he strongly emphasized the subordination of these lay participants to the ecclesiastical hierarchy.

The liberals paid tribute to the pope, but they balanced their homage with references to the importance of the whole Church and of its constituent parts, the hierarchy, the clergy, and the laity. Not so the conservatives. Gedda, for example, got somewhat carried away and said: "Our meeting with the Vicar of Christ in a few minutes will lift our enthusiasm to a supreme intensity."[12]

In spite of the pope's speech, and other similar addresses (perhaps even because of them, since now it was possible to see clearly where the Vatican stood), the congress brought out in the open some of the new perspectives Veronese and Montini had encouraged and it laid the groundwork for the birth of a moderate lay opposition to the Roman Curia on an international level.

Most recommendations favored a better training and an increasingly active participation of Catholics in various sectors of activity, especially at the international level. Some proposed resolutions were submitted by individual or national delegations and published as such in the proceedings, but they were not acted upon. Voting on motions was just not a very important activity at the first World Congress for the Lay Apostolate. Only three resolutions were put to the vote and passed: one encouraging the laity to work toward "the union of all Christians in the unity of the Church"; a second calling for the internationalization of Jerusalem and of the Holy Places to guarantee their security, and for aid to the refugees of the Arab-Israeli war; and a third appealing to all Catholic people that they give better assistance to refugees.[13]

Any victory that the liberals might have claimed in having held such a congress was short-lived. On January 23, 1952, *L'Osservatore Romano* published an announcement of the creation of the Permanent Committee for International Congresses for the Lay Apostolate, a group formed for the purpose of coordinating Catholic lay congresses at the international level. It was this organization (COPECIAL) that was to manage the two future international meetings, and numerous regional meetings besides. Veronese, given the job of secretary of the new paper organization, was actually being kicked upstairs. Following the Italian spring elections, Gedda replaced Veronese as president of Italian Catholic Action, and it was reported that Veronese learned of his "resignation" from that position only after it was announced in *L'Osservatore Romano*. Two years later, Msgr. Montini was relieved of his powerful position as undersecretary of state and sent to Milan as archbishop, by a similar "removal through promotion." These changes, made directly by Pius XII, were primarily results of divergent views on Italian politics. Since outright demotion is only used in cases where the victim is considered to be untrustworthy and unreliable (for example in the case of a radicalized archbishop like Msgr. Joseph Charbonneau of Montreal), the person removed through promotion often retains a high degree of loyalty to the organization.

2. POWER STRUGGLES IN ITALIAN CATHOLICISM, 1951–1957

Veronese, barred from the leading role in Italian Catholic Action, took up his new duties as secretary of COPECIAL with great industry. At the level at which he worked, new ideas were being disseminated about the mission of the laity, but the financial dependence of COPECIAL on the Secretariate of State did not leave Veronese much freedom.

With seminal funds from the pope, the Pius XII Foundation was created in 1953 "to support and promote Catholic international works of the lay apostolate." Funds were solicited world-wide, and the

Secretariate of State appointed a five-member board to administer the foundation, whose funds went mostly to the Conference of the CIOs and COPECIAL. As long as Msgr. Montini was influential in the Vatican, Veronese's position was tolerable, but when Montini was transferred to Milan, Veronese was left quite isolated.

Opposition to Montini within the curia came to a head in 1953 when Msgr. Domenico Tardini, the pope's other chief aide within the Secretariate of State, refused to accept the cardinalate, in order, it has been said, that Montini should be forced to refuse as well. The play worked perfectly, and at the consistory of 1953, Pius XII announced that both men had declined the cardinalate. Montini was thus blocked from the chance to become secretary of state, a position which would have greatly helped him become the successor to Pius XII. During the illness of Pius XII in early 1954, to the great consternation of the conservatives in the curia, Montini, because of his official position in the Secretariate of State, took on increasing responsibilities in the government of the Church. A future cardinal who was then working in the secretariate, Msgr. Angelo Dell'Acqua, went so far as to say: "At that time, I would say, Monsignor Montini was running the Church."[14] There is little doubt that Montini's authority was being challenged by the growing power of a group of conservatives that Carlo Falconi has called the "Vatican Pentagon."[15] Comprising this group of five influential and reactionary men were Cardinals Alfredo Ottaviani, Giuseppe Pizzardo, Nicolo Canali, Adeodato Piazza, and Clemente Micara. On November 3, 1954, while Pius was convalescing, Msgr. Montini was named archbishop of Milan, an appointment that immediately removed him from the Roman scene. Pius XII did not even consecrate him, although he did make a short radio speech for the ceremony.

Many have assumed that Montini was exiled from Rome because of his previous disagreements with the pope and with conservative curialists on sociopolitical issues and on the question of priest-workers. Other observers attributed the removal to his criticisms of nepotism and irregularities in Church finances. This view was partly substantiated by charges, published just before Pius's death in 1958, that Enrico Galeazzi, an architect who aided Pius XII with Church finances during the entire pontificate, had—along with the pope's nephews Don Carlo and Don Guilio Pacelli—made personal gain from Pontifical Aid Organization dealings. Xavier Rynne has suggested, as yet another source of disagreement between Montini and Pius XII's curia, that the curia objected to Montini's pressure for Vatican cooperation with nondenominational international organizations, such as UNESCO, that were working for peace and social justice.[16]

After 1954, with Montini out of the Vatican and Pius XII increasingly ill, the conservatives in the curia strengthened their influence. The powerful old cardinals, supported by lesser and younger clerics, consolidated their power through a kind of interlocking directorate within the central Church bureaucracy. They were thus able to increase considerably their influence over bishops, priests, and lay people. Falconi, among others, has well documented these facts.[17]

Meanwhile, power struggles in Catholic Action, both in Italy and in France, had given the liberals a small degree of leverage, but the conservatives succeeded in retaining control of these sponsored lay groups. In Italy, Carlo Carretto, Gedda's successor as president of Young Men's Catholic Action (GIAC), had begun to oppose Gedda but was forced to resign in 1952. A second young reformer, Mario Rossi, was forced out of the same presidency in 1954. The reformers had been trying to "shift the emphasis from age divisions to category divisions in the GIAC"[18] as had been done in France and Belgium, where groups of workers and students had formed separate Catholic Action organizations that spearheaded the demands for change that traditional Catholic Action refused to endorse. This effort to move away from Vatican control toward a more radical intellectual and political position was simply overwhelmed by Gedda's superior organizational power. After Rossi's "resignation," the FUCI (5,488 members) and the Movimento Laureati (12,643 members) were easily brought into line. Numerically, they could not counterbalance the four branches of general Catholic Action, controlled by Gedda, which numbered, at least on paper, more than 2.5 million members (284,455 men; 597,394 women; 556,752 young men; 1,215,977 young women). But they continued to oppose Gedda quietly and prudently, by insisting on internal educational work rather than on external political action, and by not participating in Gedda's conservative initiatives on the political and religious fronts.

In Italy, on the lay scene, except for the rapidly solved crises of Catholic Action, very little was happening during the mid-fifties. The slow rediscovery of the mission of the laity nevertheless gradually eroded the traditional views about Church organization. There was a proliferation of initiatives in the area of teaching theology to the laity. These courses were, as Falconi has shown,[20] simply watered-down versions of what was being taught to future priests in seminaries, and they did not have a very profound impact, except perhaps to inform the laity about the lack of adaptation of the clerical culture of the theologians.

More significant for the development of the lay movement was the publication, in 1953, of Yves Congar's study for a theology of the laity, even if the climate was not quite ready then for a general accept-ance of his ideas.[21] It was only after the election of Pope John XXIII that Congar became a sort of semiofficial theologian of the laity. In 1963, after the first session of Vatican II, he suggested that in the next sessions lay experts be allowed to speak on problems of the modern world, and his suggestion was accepted; but during the fifties he was considered to be much too radical.

3. THE SECOND WORLD CONGRESS FOR THE LAY APOSTOLATE

Given the conditions in the Vatican after 1954, it is not surprising that the second World Congress for the Lay Apostolate in 1957 looked very much like a replay of the first. One difference was that the Italian laity played a much less important role than in 1951, when Italian had been an official language and the secretaries of the workshops and the organizers of the congress itself were Italians. In 1967 the role of the Italians would be even more discreet than in 1957. At all of the three congresses there was an almost complete absence of the Italian radical lay movements and personalities; those present were establishment types, docile creatures of the hierarchy, with just a few exceptions.

In 1957 the Vatican and Gedda controlled the congress much more tightly than in 1951, even though the liberal intellectuals of Pax Romana were also quite influential. In cooperation with the interna-tional JOC, these liberals, operating mostly through COPECIAL, succeeded in giving to the congress a certain progressive tone. Veronese was still secretary-general, and Rosemary Goldie, a relatively progressive woman who had previously worked for Pax Romana in Australia and at Geneva, was effectively in charge of the secretariate.

There were more people in attendance in 1957 than in 1951. There were approximately two thousand participants, and they came from more than eighty countries. The delegates were very similar in social and ideological background to those who had come in 1951. In fact, many of the 1951 delegates returned in 1957.

After 1951, COPECIAL had published the proceedings of the first World Congress and various other materials about the lay movement, and had organized numerous preparatory meetings not only in Europe but also in the Third World. In April 1953, COPECIAL brought together a group of international experts on the laity at Gazzada, in Italy, to study the recently published proceedings and to discuss possible themes for the 1957 world congress. A second meeting, at Castelgondolfo in October 1954, finally decided that "Basic Formation for the Lay Apostolate" would be a major theme. Two further meetings were held, at Gazzada again in March 1956 and at Paris in 1957, to make the final preparations for the congress. COPECIAL also helped to organize an African preparatory meeting at Kisubi, Uganda, in December 1953 and an Asian one at Manila in December 1955.

The second World Congress for the Lay Apostolate opened on October 5, 1957. In his address, again the high point of the meetings, Pius XII reiterated his condemnation of the emancipation of the laity and his opposition to an autonomous international federation of lay groups. Throughout the congress there was the same special attention to the "victims and martyrs of the Church of Silence,"[22] in the best tradition of the Cold War.

In addition to the pope's opening talk, the assembled delegates heard a first-session speech by Cardinal Giuseppe Pizzardo, a hard-line curialist, and addresses by such conservative Jesuits as Cardinal Ottavianni's adviser Sebastien Tromp, professor at the Gregorian University, and Pius XII's adviser, Ricardo Lombardi, the founder of the conservative Movement for a Better World (who nevertheless became, under Pope John XXIII, a somewhat more progressive cleric: as a matter of fact, the curia banned his explosive book on Church reforms from Catholic bookstores in Rome when it appeared just prior to the 1962 opening of Vatican II). The closing address was made by the reactionary archbishop of Genoa, Cardinal Giuseppe Siri, whom curia reactionaries were hoping would be the next pope. But an equal number of liberal prelates and clerics were on the list of congress speechmakers: Archbishop Montini, Msgr. Gerard Philips of Belgium, the Chilean bishop Manuel Larrain, and liberal priests such as Louis-Joseph Lebret, O.P. (who has written about and worked for the development of the Third World and whose thought was important to Paul VI's social encyclical *Populorum Progressio* published on March 26, 1967) and George Delcuve, S.J., the founder of the religiously avant-garde catechetics institute "Lumen Vitae" in Belgium.

Most speeches by clerics manifested the same cult of the personality of Pius XII and of hierarchical authority that had been so common at the 1951 congress. Even the liberal clerics could not avoid sounding somewhat conservative, especially since the themes of the congress did not lend themselves to very critical perspectives.

On the lay side, there were major speeches by such famous Catholics as Francis Sheed, Alfredo López, Maria Vendrik, Romeo Maione, Prince Karl zu Löwenstein, Thomas Kierstens, Aldo Moro, Jean-Pierre Dubois-Dumée, Joaquín Ruiz-Giménez, Joseph Folliet, John C.H. Wu, Auguste Vanistendael, Antoine Laurence, and Vittorino Veronese, many of whom had been key figures in the first World Congress and would continue to play active roles in the official international lay movement.

While the theme of the training of lay apostles, as had been decided in Castelgondolfo in 1954, remained as one of the three main themes of the 1957 congress, it was given somewhat less prominence than the other two, the doctrine of the place of the laity in the Church, and the situation of the contemporary world as faced by lay apostles.

The question of Catholic Action was even more to the fore than in 1951, expecially in the speeches of the conservatives. Pius XII stressed the importance of Catholic Action, although he widened the meaning of the term to include other forms of organized and mandated lay apostolate. Cardinal Suenens made himself the advocate of that position, in his efforts to broaden the concept of Catholic Action to take in the Legion of Mary, a lay organization which he was actively promoting. These discussions had the effect of legitimizing the existence of lay organizations outside officially mandated Catholic Action. They also spurred COPECIAL to start, in 1958, an inventory of existing lay Catholic organizations at the national and international levels. This panorama of the lay scene, which was presented to the Council Fathers at Vatican II in 1963,[23] illustrated the wide variety of forms of lay Catholic organizations, and showed that the lay apostolate was a much broader affair than Catholic Action.

The sole non-Catholic observer at the congress, a German Protestant who attended as a journalist, remarked in a speech given ten years later at the third World Congress that the contest between Catholic Action and nonmandated lay organizations was an issue that was important to the participants of the second congress. Dr. Hans-Ruedi Weber wrote:

> Ten years ago, the Congress began with a Latin Mass and an address by your Holy Father, Pope Pius XII. This address was the starting

point for heated discussions throughout the Congress about the relationship between the hierarchy and the laity, between Catholic Action with a capital C and Catholic action with a small c. Such an inner Catholic organizational discussion tended to overshadow the excellent things said at the same Congress, for instance about the mission of the Church in the modern world and about lay spirituality.[24]

In 1957, as in 1951, the participation of the mass of delegates was minimal, in comparison to that of members of the clergy and of a few influential lay personalities. The majority seemed to have been spectators rather than participating delegates. Weber described the level of participation in the following manner, in a 1968 article: "The lay participants in the Congress at Rome were very, very obedient and submissive children."[25]

The speeches were practically the only activity. The absence of discussion, recommendations, and grass-roots participation, in contrast with what happened at the 1967 congress, was noted by the Canadian lay leader Romeo Maione, in an interview given me on October 25, 1968. In 1957 there was a "meeting of sore seats," he said, and in 1967 a "meeting of sore throats."

In 1957, as in 1951, the latent conflict expressed itself in the speeches. The conservatives emphasized the dependence of lay organizations upon the hierarchy, and insisted on the importance of anticommunism and of the Christianization of the temporal order, specifically through the use of the mass media. Stressing spiritual formation for the laity, they invoked Mary, rather than Christ, in their prayers and in the conclusion of their speeches. In addition, they raised objections to such liberal terminology as "lay theology" and "emancipation of the laity."

On the liberal side, the JOC, which had just finished its international meeting in Rome, was influential, chiefly through its president, Romeo Maione, who had been assigned by COPECIAL to work on the preparation of the congress. In the liberal view, collaboration between laity and clergy took precedence over lay subordination to the hierarchy, and one speaker, a Cuban delegate named José Lasaga, said laymen should be witnesses and not apologists. The Church itself was described by some liberal speakers as God's people on the march, and the lay apostolate was depicted as a variegated movement with communal rather than hierarchical characteristics. Evangelization and biblical and spiritual formation took precedence, in the liberal speeches, over political action, but there was nevertheless much talk of Third World poverty and of the need for international awareness and work for social justice. Some mentioned the necessity of a world government and others called for more scientific knowledge of the contemporary world. Msgr. Larrain of Chile even spoke of the "priesthood" of the laity and of the layman's prophetic role.

Because of the climate existing in the Vatican in 1957 (Pius XII's fin-de-règne can in many ways be compared with Pius IX's and Pius X's reactionary pontificates), the liberals were on the defensive at the second World Congress, but in their speeches they nevertheless succeeded in putting up some token resistance to the prevailing conservative mood. Veronese, for example, praised diversity, comparing the lay apostolate to an orchestra where each has a different part to play. He also quoted his good friend Msgr. Montini, then in relative disgrace, in his speech to the delegates. Montini, on the other hand, departed from his written text to quote Jacques Maritain, at a time when Maritain was still considered a dangerous radical by the conservative members of the Roman Curia. Montini's presence at the congress was his first official appearance in Rome since his Milanese "exile" in 1954. A 1956 attack on Maritain by the Jesuit Antonio Messineo in *Civiltà Cattolica* had been widely interpreted as a broadside at Montini and his liberal associates. As a result, their mention of Maritain and the general progressive tone of their speeches at the 1957 meeting could be viewed as courageous efforts to block complete conservative control of the lay movement.

The liberals were able to do little except hold the line, but it is doubtful whether they would have been able to continue doing even that for long after the congress, had it not been for the death of Pius XII in 1958. Immediately after the congress, the COPECIAL staff published the proceedings in three volumes and, along with other progressives, waited patiently for better days. Veronese, named director-general of UNESCO with the backing of the Christian Democratic government of Italy, left his position at COPECIAL.

In December 1958 an unexpected change came to the Vatican on the heels of the death of Pius XII. Conservative cardinals, unable to elect Siri to the papacy, and anxious to avoid a liberal like Montini, turned to an older candidate. They could not have known that the election of John XXIII would bring about a more radical transformation of the Church than had occurred at any time in recent centuries.

4. ACCESSION OF JOHN XXIII

The election was lengthy and difficult because neither conservatives nor progressives could obtain the two-thirds majority necessary to elect their candidate. The stalemate was described in the Italian press as being between the Pacellians (followers of the late Pius XII) and the Montinians. It was reported that some conservatives had approached the seventy-seven-year-old Cardinal Angelo Giuseppe Roncalli, patriarch of Venice, to offer him their votes in return for a promise not to make Montini his secretary of state, and that the deal had been refused.

Although known for his progressive stands, Roncalli was also recognized as a simple, pious man with few enemies. The mode of his emergence during the contested election is alluded to in his diary:

> As the voting in the Conclave wavered to and fro, I rejoiced when I saw the chances of my being elected diminishing and the likelihood of others, in my opinion most worthy and venerable persons, being chosen.[26]

Eleven turns of balloting took place during the three days of the conclave, a sign that it was not an easy election but rather a compromise one, as Pope John himself acknowledged:

> When on 28 October, 1958, the Cardinals of the Holy Roman Church chose me to assume the supreme responsibility of ruling the universal flock of Jesus Christ, at seventy-seven years of age, everyone was convinced that I would be a provisional and transitional Pope.[27]

The well-known story of John XXIII and of the second Vatican Council would not warrant a lengthy discussion here, but it is worthwhile to review briefly a few points important to an understanding of the third World Congress for the Lay Apostolate and its aftermath, and to a general understanding of the question of papal control of the laity in the Catholic Church.

It is quite understandable that the more progressive cardinals would have voted for Roncalli. The French cardinals, who knew him well because of his ten years in Paris as nuncio, were in his favor, and since they represented a sort of opposition to Pius XII's pontifical style, they succeeded in persuading some non-Italians to vote for him (it must be remembered that Pius XII had left a college of cardinals with a majority of non-Italians). Because of Roncalli's "low profile" and old age, however, the conservative cardinals (mostly Italians of the curia) may have believed that the papacy would make a more conservative man of him, as it had of others before him. Even if he did try to initiate changes, they may have reasoned, at his age he would have little time and energy to outmaneuver the curia and carry his reforms through. Also, the fact that he had always wisely stayed clear of curia intrigues meant that he had no strong enemies (and no powerful friends either) there, a clear advantage at a time when a compromise pope was needed.

The particular flavor of his papacy, so strikingly different from that of the aristocratic churchmen who both preceded him and followed him, is generally attributed to his peasant background, but the man had other qualities. Pope John's diplomatic abilities, developed during a thirty-five-year-long career in the service of the Vatican in countries as varied as Bulgaria, Turkey, and France, were certainly outstanding. In addition, as a historian with wide knowledge of the Church's past, the new pope was able to choose from a range of historical models in his effort to free the papacy from its Vatican "prison" and start a program of Church reform.

Calling quickly for a general council to reassess the Church, he mobilized the most powerful weapon at his disposal against the curia: the bishops, accompanied by the bishops' theological advisers, often influential men in their own right. He also made use of that other decisive force in any ideological struggle: the power of public opinion, both inside and outside the Church. Within the council, Catholic laymen and priests who hoped for a victory of the progressive forces in the struggle could only be spectators in the hierarchical contest that Pope John was determined to carry through. But outside the walls of St. Peter's, the pressure and support from journalists, writers, and lay groups proved to be decisive elements in what has been called Pope John's revolution.

Montini's fortunes took a sharp turn for the better because of Pope John's accession. Within the month, the new pope had created twenty-three new cardinals. Montini was first on the list, but he was closely followed by Tardini, who was named secretary of state. Although John had not accepted the deal proposed by the conservative anti-Montini curialists, he was evidently disposed to compromise on this point.

It was soon obvious, however, that the new pope was already grooming Montini to become his successor. Pope John announced in January 1959 the calling of an ecumenical council (Vatican II) to update the Church. Montini greeted the news of the council with enthusiasm and was soon at work on its Central Commission and on other commissions in preparation for it. Later, during the 1962 session of Vatican II, it was said that the pope advised Montini to steer clear of active participation in the debates in order to avoid making enemies. In fact, Montini spoke only twice during the 1962 session, and did so in a very circumspect manner. He was invited by Pope John to stay in the papal apartments during that session.

Tardini and other conservative curialists expressed only reluctant approval for this projected reevaluation of the Church, a grandiose plan that could hold little worth for those who wished to maintain the status quo. From the time of the announcement of Vatican II, Pope John's relations with Tardini and his conservative associates were distinctly cool. Here is how Carlo Falconi describes the revolutionary character of Pope John's announcement of Vatican II:

> At a distance of eight years from what the conservative wing of the Senate of Cardinals described as the *coup d'état* of 25 January 1959, the revolutionary character of that event is apparent to all. With it, in fact, Pope John put an end to his predecessors' authoritarian monologue and gave the word to the whole Church, bishops, priests, and laymen included; he dealt a blow at Roman centralization and at the privileges of the Curia, opening the way to recognition of the pluralism and federalism of the national and continental Churches, he reconsecrated the primacy of the Church's spiritual mission, subordinating to its pastoral ends the legalism of its lawyers and the temporalism of its diplomatists; he gave an impulse to the progressive secularization of the ecclesiastical community by extending greater responsibilities to laymen; and, finally, he brought the Catholic Church in a certain sense into the vanguard of ecumenism, thrusting it towards an embrace not only with other Christian communities but even with other faiths.[28]

Using the old argument of nonintervention in politics—the position so often invoked by anti-Fascist liberals in Italy since early in the twentieth century—Pope John declared that charity and prophecy, in his papacy, would take precedence over politics and diplomacy. And indeed, many found in his pontificate a brief resurgence of the prophecy and charisma that had characterized the early Christian church. John's announcement of nonintervention in politics was made for the hierarchy and clergy only and he also indicated that he was not, for the Italian Catholic laity, opposed to the "opening to the left" that the Christian Democratic Party was trying to implement. John XXIII did not oppose the involvement of Catholics in the secular arena; what he rejected was conservative clerical impingement in socioeconomic and political matters.

5. POPE JOHN AND COPECIAL

Within the official Catholic lay movement, the new pope had a more direct effect. Late in 1958 he relieved Gedda of the presidency of Catholic Action. Gedda was allowed to keep control of the Civic Committees, but they were temporarily deactivated. Catholic Action became much less important than during the two preceding pontificates, whereas COPECIAL suddenly became much more than the paper organization it had been until then. Those liberal members of the Catholic lay elite who had been active in COPECIAL and who had planned and taken part in the two lay congresses at Rome were to feel their efforts rewarded during the new pontificate. Toward the end of May 1959 the COPECIAL staff established contact with some thirty lay officers of national and international organizations and with certain theologians. This group was asked to make an evaluation of the two congresses and of COPECIAL itself, which had been in existence seven years. Discussion of a third lay congress was also under way. On August 6, 1959, *L'Osservatore Romano* announced the pope's restructuring of COPECIAL, a reorganization which included the naming of a board of directors partly composed of prominent laymen. This step, which consisted of putting important lay leaders into a bureaucratic structure that had always been wholly clerical, was something definitely new in the Catholic Church.

The board of directors for COPECIAL was initially composed of Professor Silvio Golzio, president of the Italian Movimento Laureati; Prince Karl zu Löwenstein, president of the Central Committee of German Catholics; Claude Ryan, national secretary of Canadian Catholic Action; Juan Vásquez, president of the International Federation of Catholic Youth; Jean-Pierre Dubois-Dumée, of the International Catholic Press Union; and Ramón Sugranyes de Franch, president of Pax Romana-International Movement of Catholic Intellectuals. The August 6, 1959, issue of the *Osservatore Romano* reported:

> According to the new dispositions of the Holy See, the orientation of the work is entrusted to the Board of Directors, while the Roman Secretariate will continue to fulfill an executive role. Miss Rosemary Goldie is appointed executive secretary to the Committee. The Committee will continue to be assisted by the Ecclesiastical Commission, presided over by Cardinal Pizzardo.[29]

On October 24–26 the first meeting of the board was held in Rome. It was decided that the directors would meet twice a year, and that at least one of the two annual meetings would always be held in Rome, in order to facilitate contacts with Church authorities and with the Ecclesiastical Commission of COPECIAL. In 1960 there were various additions to the board, and to the Ecclesiastical Commission. That same year Pope John approved the board's plan for a third congress to be held after Vatican II, and COPECIAL published the first issue of a bulletin, *Lay Apostolate*, to appear three times a year in English, French, and Spanish.

In November 1961 and February 1962, meetings were convened in Rome by the Ecclesiastical Commission and by the board of directors to discuss the theme of "unity" in preparation of the third World Congress. The European Congresses for the Lay Apostolate in 1960 and 1966, especially the latter, were important landmarks in the preparation of the congress. There were also some meetings in Rome in July 1964 and March 1966 to set down the program and the themes of the third World Congress. In 1966 and early 1967, top members of the secretariate of COPECIAL went to various countries for consultations about the congress, and an organizing committee met frequently in order to prepare in detail the functioning of the congress.

COPECIAL also made an inventory of existing Catholic organizations active in the lay apostolate at the national and international levels. In 1963 the results were published in an 83-page booklet.[30] It lists the organizations in each country and then divides them into four groups, depending on the kind of organized lay apostolate that existed in the country:

1. Countries that have a unitary national Catholic Action (e.g. Italy)
2. Countries that have a general or specialized Catholic Action (e.g. France)
3. Countries that have a federative Catholic Action (e.g. the Philippines)
4. Countries where the term Catholic Action is employed in a generic sense only, or not at all (e.g. the U.S.A. and England)

Part of the booklet deals with the lay apostolate at the international level and divides the Catholic organizations operating at the international level into four categories:

1. Members of the Conference of the CIOs
2. Associates of the Conference of the CIOs
3. Organizations which collaborate with the Conference of the CIOs
4. Other Catholic international bodies

This labeling is quite revealing, in the sense that it shows how dependent COPECIAL still was on the framework that Italian Catholic Action had imposed on the organized laity, but it also points to a possible breaking-up of that framework by the introduction of other types of lay organizations in the officially accepted organized lay apostolate. Although lay apostolate organizations were classified according to their degree of closeness to unitary Catholic Action or to the Conference of the CIO, the organizations farther away from these two prototypes were given an aura of legitimacy by their inclusion in the lists.

A copy of the booklet was given to all the bishops attending Vatican II, and copies were also widely distributed among a larger public composed of clergy and laity. Its impact was far-reaching: it served to manifest the new dynamism of COPECIAL and of the organized lay apostolate generally, and it greatly contributed to raising consciousness in the Church during Vatican II on the question of the thrust of the lay movement.

6. LAY PRESENCE AT VATICAN II

Most of the bishops and other churchmen who convened in Rome on October 11, 1962, for the opening ceremonies of Vatican II were not exactly revolutionaries, but, as was the case generally, now that the complacent fifties were over, they were in the mood for change. The lay auditors, invited to observe and in some small measure to participate, were not particularly progressive either, most of them being liberals of the Montini-Veronese orientation, but they also were caught up in the general atmosphere of fascination with reform. Lay presence at the Church council was, itself, a departure from tradition. Twenty lay delegates, chosen by Vittorino Veronese, at the Secretariate of State's request, were present at the opening session. The delegation, with Pope John's approval, had been composed of representatives of COPECIAL, of the Conference of the Catholic International Organizations, and of other national and international organizations. The pope had also invited Jean Guitton—a French Catholic intellectual and close friend of Archbishop Montini who had experienced difficulties with the Holy Office and the *Osservatore Romano* in the early fifties —to be a lay observer at the first session.

These laymen were no more than observers, but at least they were present. After the death of Pope John in June 1963, the new pope, Paul VI, named ten more lay auditors for the second session. This enlarged lay delegation sent a dutifully grateful message to the participants in the second session of the Council:

> Conscious of the historical event which has taken place as a result of the decision of the Holy Father to invite qualified lay auditors to take part as observers in the Council sessions, these auditors consider it a

duty to express to the Council the emotion, joy and profound gratitude of the laity whom they have the honor to represent and to fulfill this responsibility by attentively following the work of the Council and its decisions, and redoubling their prayers for its success.[31]

Henri Fesquet (in *Le Monde*), Xavier Rynne, and quite a few other commentators ridiculed this message, pointing to its colorless clerical tone and content as unworthy of an adult laity. It is not surprising, however, that these particular laymen would have produced such an innocuous and pompous declaration, since nearly all of them had been carefully selected from among the moderate leaders of the lay movement. At the third session, in the fall of 1964, fifteen more lay auditors were named, seven of whom were women. And at the fourth and last session in 1965, there were other additions, so that finally the number of lay auditors totaled forty-two (29 men and 13 women), and the lay guests totaled nine (7 men and 2 women). Most of these representatives of the laity were chosen because they were officers of important, officially recognized Catholic organizations.

These passive observers were not, of course, the only laymen who were taking an interest in Vatican II. Carefully and copiously reported in the world press, Vatican II was being listened to and looked at by Catholics (and non-Catholics) the world over. Nevertheless, if one were to make a list of Church-approved Catholic lay elite at the beginning of Pope Paul's pontificate, the names of those present at the council might serve. They were not a group that would spearhead a challenge to papal power, as one can readily see from the following complete list of the auditors and guests, with some of their organizational links (as reported in the French Catholic daily *La Croix*):

Auditors

SILVIO GOLZIO (Italy), president of the board of directors of COPECIAL

JEAN GUITTON, of the French Academy

M. DE HABICHT, permanent secretary of COPECIAL

EMILE INGLESSIS (Greece), director of the general secretariate of the International Federation of Catholic Men

JEAN LARNAUD (France), secretary-general of the International Center of Liaison with UNESCO

RAIMONDO MANZINI (Italy), editor of *L'Osservatore Romano* and president of the International Catholic Press Union

JAMES NORRIS (U.S.A.), president of the International Catholic Commission on Migrations

HENRI ROLLET (France), president of the International Federation of Catholic Men

RAMÓN SUGRANYES de Franch (Spain), president of Pax Romana—MIIC, president of the Conference of the CIOs, and member of the board of directors of COPECIAL

AUGUSTE VANISTANDAEL (Belgium), general secretary of the International Federation of Christian Trade Unions

JUAN VÁSQUEZ (Spain), president of the International Catholic Youth Federation and member of the board of directors of COPECIAL

VITTORINO VERONESE (Italy), former director-general of UNESCO, president of the first two World Congresses for the Lay Apostolate, and former secretary-general of COPECIAL

FRANCESCO VITO (Italy), rector of the Catholic University of the Sacred Heart of Milan and vice-president of the International Federation of Catholic Universities

EUSÈBE ADJAKPLEY (Togo), regional secretary for Africa of the International Catholic Youth Federation

JOHN CHEN (Hong Kong), president of the diocesan Council for the Lay Apostolate

PAUL FLEIG, president of the World Union of Catholic Teachers

LUIGI GEDDA (Italy), president of the World Federation of Catholic Physicians, former president of Italian Youth Catholic Action, and former president of Italian Catholic Action

JOSÉ MARIA HERNÁNDEZ, president of Philippine Catholic Action

PATRICK KEEGAN (Great Britain), president of the World Movement of Christian Workers, and member of the board of directors of COPECIAL

BARTOLO PÉREZ, president of International Young Catholic Workers (JOC)

STEPHEN ROMAN (Canada), layman of the Byzantine rite

STEFAN SWIEZAWSKI, Catholic University of Lublin (Poland)

LEON DE ROSEN (France), president of the International Christian Union of Business Executives

K. C. CHACKO (India)

RAOUL DELGRANGE (Belgium), former president of the Bureau Catholique International de l'Enfance

FRANK DUFF (Ireland), founder and president of the Legion of Mary

BARON WALTER VON LOE (Germany), former president of the International Bureau of Movements of Adult Rural Catholics

MARTIN H. WORK, executive director of the National Council of

Catholic Men (U.S.A.) and member of the board of directors of COPECIAL

PILAR BELLOSILLO (Spain), president of the World Union of Catholic Women's Organizations

ROSEMARY GOLDIE (Australia), executive secretary of COPECIAL

IDA GRILLO, Women's Union of Italian Catholic Action

MRS. JOSEPH MCCARTHY, National Council of Catholic Women (U.S.A.)

ALDA MIRELLI, president of the Missionaries of the Kingship of Christ, and of the Italian Women's Center

MARIE-LOUISE MONNET (France), president of the International Movement for the Apostolate of Independent Social Milieus (MIAMSI)

MARQUISE AMALIA DI MONTEZEMOLO (Italy), president of the Apostolate for Spiritual Assistance to the Armed Forces

ANNE-MARIE ROELOFFZEN, general secretary of the World Federation of Catholic Young Women and Girls

GERTRUD EHRLE (Germany), member of the Bureau of the World Union of Catholic Women's Organizations

MARGARITA MOYANO LLERENA (Argentina), president of the World Federation of Catholic Young Women and Girls

GLADYS PARENTELLI (Uruguay), vice-president of the International Movement of Catholic Agricultural and Rural Youth (MIJARC)

H. SKODA (Czechoslovakia)

MR. AND MRS. JOSÉ ALVÁREZ ICAZA, founders of the Christian Family Movement in Mexico

Guests

L. C. BAAS (Netherlands), president of the National Center of Catholic Action

JOSEPH FOLLIET, vice-president of the "Semaines sociales de France"

JEAN LINDEMANS (Belgium), secretary-general of the Catholic International Education Office

JEAN DE MIERRY, former vice-president of French General Catholic Action

M. DU ROSTU, vice-president of the World Union of Catholic Women's Organizations

JOAQUIN RUIZ-GIMÉNEZ CORTÉS (Spain), professor in the Faculty of Law of the University of Madrid, and former ambassador to the Holy See

ANDRÉ RUSZKOWSKI, professor at the Pontifical University of Peru

and secretary for external affairs of the International Catholic
Film Office

THADDÉE SZMITKOWSKI, secretary-general of the CIO Information
Center at the U.N.

MARIA H. C. VENDRIK (Netherlands), former president of the World
Federation of Catholic Young Women and Girls, and member of
the National Committee of Catholic Action in Holland.

This long list of names and organizational affiliations gives us some
indication of the type of laymen who had become prominent in the
affairs of the Catholic Church during the pontificate of Pope John and
the early years of Pope Paul's pontificate.

Pope John's reforms in the lay sphere did not go very deep. Since he
was very busy with the curia and the bishops, the protagonists of
Vatican II, he was reluctant to get involved also in major struggles in
the lay Catholic movement. What he did was to accept as lay representatives at the council those lay leaders of Catholic organizations
who had been present and active in the lay apostolate since the first
World Congress for the Lay Apostolate, rather than just Catholic
Action people. In the lay sphere, he let those laymen who had been the
loyal opposition to Pius XII's conservative orientation take a greater
role than the one they had been able to play during the fifties. Essentially, this meant that the Veronese-Montini orientation became dominant over the Gedda–Roman Curia line.

Most of these laymen remained active in lay affairs after Vatican II,
and we find many of them in important positions at the third World
Congress and in the Council on the Laity. The official leadership level
of the lay sphere is one area where there was a direct transition from a
Pacellian to a Montinian orientation, without the charismatic Ron-
callian transition period. At the grass-roots level, we have a very different picture. The ferment brought about by the transformations in
contemporary society and by Vatican II has continued unabated
through the 1970s. There, John's charisma had much stronger effects
than at the elite level among the laity.

7. DEBATE ON LAY PARTICIPATION
AT VATICAN II

The democratic and socialist revolutions of the past century had not
left the mass of Catholic laymen unaffected. Those laymen, no longer
the obedient servants of paternal prelates, had been pressing for more
recognition and greater participation in Church affairs. During the

1950s their demands had grown more urgent and had become disturbing to some members of the hierarchy. Although the numerous crises
in French and Italian Youth Catholic Action were considered to be
deplorable episodes by conservative Italian curialists, many bishops
insisted that it had become necessary to redefine the status of laymen in
the Church, whatever the risks might be.

Thus, during the third session of Vatican II, a lengthy debate on the
lay apostolate led to the formulation of the Schema on the Apostolate
of the Laity. Cardinal Fernando Cento, president of the Commission
on the Lay Apostolate, indicated the novelty of such a move: "This is
the first time in the history of the Church that the theme of the apostolate of the laity has been taken up in the deliberations of a council."[33]

Many bishops, aware of their isolation from worldly affairs, saw the
laity as a channel by which they could regain entry into "the world."
As mediators between rank-and-file Catholics (and non-Catholics) and
the hierarchy, the members of the lay movement might act for the
bishop, as his eyes and ears. They might even speak for the bishop, on
certain occasions. Msgr. Larrain of Chile expressed this view to the
Council Fathers:

> Laymen must constitute the bridge that will serve to present the
> problems of the world to the Church, and the Gospel to the world.
> To fulfill this important mediation function, organizations must be
> flexible, and Christians must be aware of the signs of the times and
> active in the world.[34]

Similar contributions were made by Cardinal Fernando Cento of the
Roman Curia, Msgr. Leven of the United States, Msgr. Caillot of
France, Msgr. Ruotolo of Italy, Msgr. Donze of Tulle in France, and
Msgr. Heenan, archibishop of Westminster.[35]

Although many prelates protested that it was not for purely utilitarian reasons, such as the current crisis of clerical manpower, that
they were pushing for a greater role for laymen, it was clear that the
Commission on the Lay Apostolate had not been established only because the intrinsic dignity and importance of the laity had just been
discovered. The need for new collaborators, more attuned to the
modern world than were priests, nuns, and brothers, worked with the
pressures coming from laymen themselves for a greater say in Church
affairs to create the new orientation.

Theologically, this new role was legitimized by the use of the biblical notions of "the people of God," and "the priesthood of the faithful." Some reactionary prelates, among them Cardinals Ruffini of
Palermo, Bacci of the curia, and Siri of Genoa, had manifested their

aversion to these expressions during the second session of Vatican II. Many others had warned against the danger of granting so much freedom to the laity that the hierarchy's prerogatives and freedom of action would be curtailed. Bishop Hengsbach of Essen, Germany, had countered these objections during that same second session, saying there was greater danger in not recognizing the laity's responsibility, since the hierarchy needed the laity's help to fulfill its own responsibility. Had not the Holy Spirit, he added, descended on Apostles and laity alike at the first Pentecost in Jerusalem?[36]

During the third session of Vatican II, in 1964, five days of debate preceded the drafting of the Schema on the Apostolate of the Laity. Many prelates were disappointed with the final wording of the schema and publicly stated their objections. Significant portions of the text had been cut out and moved to other documents, to be discussed and voted on later during the council. The most interesting theological parts had been transferred to the Schema on the Church, discussion of lay activity was moved to the Schema on the Church in the Modern World, and consideration of roles in missionary activity was moved to the Schema on Missionary Activity.

These alterations left a truncated text which was, according to Bishop Alexander Carter of Sault-Ste-Marie, Canada, "conceived in the sin of clericalism." Carter also protested that the laity had been consulted too late to be able to make significant changes in the schema. Cardinal Joseph Ritter of St. Louis used similar harsh words, faulting the text for its clericalism, its legalism, and its favoritism toward Catholic Action.

Another critic, Bishop Eugene D'Souza of Bhopal, India, objected to the use of a quotation from Saint Ignatius of Antioch, "Let nothing be done without the bishop." Calling the quotation "clerical totalitarianism," he said:

> Laymen must be treated as brothers by the clergy and the latter must no longer attempt to usurp responsibilities which properly belong to the former. Why could they [laymen] not represent the Church in international organizations, why could there not be laymen in the Roman Congregations, and why could not laymen serve in the diplomatic service of the Holy See?[37]

In a major speech to the Council on October 9, Cardinal Suenens of Malines-Brussels objected to the expression "Catholic Action," asking, as he had done at the second World Congress for the Lay Apostolate in 1957, that Catholic Action be broadened to include other types of apostolic action. On October 12, Archbishop John C. Heenan of Westminster reiterated the Anglo-Saxon prelates' view that the expression "Catholic Action" was not adapted to certain countries, and that there should be the freedom to use the term "lay apostolate" instead. He also called for a secretariate of the laity to be staffed by laymen who had taken a lead in the lay apostolate in their own countries.

The debate was concluded with a speech by Patrick Keegan, a lay auditor, a speech so conciliatory that Xavier Rynne sarcastically remarked that "his speech appeared to have been clericalized."[38] There was also a promise by Bishop Hengsbach that the Commission for the Lay Apostolate would revise and improve the text and resubmit it at a later date. It was, in fact, voted on a year later, at the fourth session of Vatican II, on November 10, 1965. Only two votes were recorded against it, but it was generally considered to be a drab and clerical text, in which few revisions had been made since the third session. A recommendation that a special secretariate for service and promotion of the lay apostolate be constituted in Rome was one of the few contributions to the development of lay power, but even this was ambiguous since a Roman secretariate could very easily lead to greater Vatican control over the laity at the supradiocesan level. The text, however, was more open in its definition of legitimate lay organizations, admitting others besides Catholic Action, but insisting on the importance of links with the hierarchy.

There was little consultation of laymen between the third and fourth sessions. The lay auditors and guests who had viewed the often interesting debate over the lay apostolate schema were offered no opportunity to participate. It is highly probable that, had they been consulted, they would not have contributed much anyway, considering who they were and what they said when they spoke on other occasions.

In response to Pope Paul's encyclical on Church dialogue, issued at the beginning of the third session, an internationally representative group of 182 laymen presented the council and the pope with a plea in favor of freedom in the area of birth control. But the new pope had already reserved the verdict on birth control to himself, appointing early in 1964 a special "Commission for the Study of Problems Relating to Population, Family, and Birth." Already, Paul VI was showing signs of his reluctance to change the conservative positions enunciated by Pius XI (and reaffirmed by Pius XII) at a time when the Fascist cult of the prolific mother was at the height of its popularity in Italy.

The lay petition, thus, had little influence, but it was evidence that not all laymen were represented by the docile group of 42 auditors and nine guests, whose presence at Vatican II was hardly noticeable among the 2,300 prelates. It must be conceded, however, that their docility was partly due to the nature of the control exercised by the Vatican over lay participation. Since the Vatican gives the laity statuses that are tentative and limited in time (and dependent for their perpetuation on the "good conduct" of the incumbent), laymen who keep waiting to be in a secure position to speak out never get to that position because the Vatican does not permit such an occurrence to come about. Those who nevertheless do speak out lose their legitimacy, since they are immediately removed from office or, if that is impossible, their organization is isolated and stripped of all official standing.

The third session of the council, like the second, ended in frustration for both the progressive majority and the conservative minority. The former had been forced to postpone the vote on religious liberty and to make compromises with the conservatives on collegiality and ecumenism. The latter realized that they were fighting a losing battle, and that all they could do to minimize the damages was to maneuver for delays and minor revisions. There was criticism of Pope Paul from all sides, for his indecision and his minor concessions to the conservatives which satisfied neither the conciliar right nor the conciliar left.

In fact, Pope Paul was turning out to be the real "transition pope" that the more conservative electors of John XXIII had hoped for, a compromiser and a temporizer, an old man more interested in preserving than in transforming. Paul VI was essentially a product of Italy's upper classes, an intellectual and a politician who, by the time of his accession to the papacy, had spent most of his life enmeshed in curial and Italian politics. As Msgr. Montini, he had, during the forties and fifties, worked with progressive lay and clerical forces to reinforce his and his associates' position against Roman Curia reactionairies. As archbishop of Milan, he had been considered one of Italy's most progressive prelates. At the beginning of his pontificate, Paul VI continued to fight entrenched conservatism, using the laity and the bishops against the curia and many Italian cardinals. In doing so, he was following the example of Gregory VII, who, in the eleventh century, had reinforced the position of the papacy against the seignorial church with the aid of laymen.[39] But after minor initial reforms in the curia and the college of cardinals, Pope Paul found himself in the position of opposing the demands for further reforms that were coming from the laity, lower clergy, and bishops.

Like many liberals, and like many Italian Christian Democrats, the progressive Msgr. Montini, once elected to power, took a much less progressive position. At a certain point in his development, his progressive inclinations hardened and he was to henceforth be the opponent of those pressing for change, even if some traditionalists still saw him as a leftist.

Thus the Catholic Church found itself in a situation similar to the one of the early fifties, with a conservative pope backed by an even more conservative curia. The gap was growing between the Vatican and its liberal and radical critics among laity, priests, and bishops. The pope, who functioned as an isolated enlightened despot, had few contacts with the Catholic masses and the changes that confronted them. Although the spirit of Pope John continued to pervade the sessions of Vatican II, the new direction under Pope Paul served somewhat to constrict the boundaries and curtail the excitement of the historic council.

New ground was broken, however, with the sections pertaining to the laity in the council's text *Lumen Gentium*, on the Church, which had separate chapters devoted to "the people of God" (i.e. to the Church as a whole, hierarchy, clergy, and laity) and to the laity. In the first draft of *Lumen Gentium*, a single chapter on both of these topics preceded a chapter on the hierarchy. After much discussion, during the second session of the council, on collegiality and the priesthood of all the faithful, the chapter on "the people of God" was separated from that on the laity and placed before the chapter on the hierarchy, which was followed by the chapter on the laity.

In the chapter on the laity, the traditional distinction between clerical and lay status is reaffirmed, but laymen are described as having an autonomous role to play as apostles in the world. Within the Church, laymen remain dependent on the hierarchy, and the absolute authority of the pope is reaffirmed in unequivocal terms: "The fullness of the power of the Roman Pontiff is not to be jeopardized."[40] There is, however, a certain breakthrough for laymen when it is said that their importance, dignity, responsibility, freedom, and initiative are to be promoted by the "sacred pastors." Laymen are no longer depicted as mere collaborators and it is there that a comparison with the traditional view shows striking change.

The apparent tension between *Lumen Gentium*, which stresses the baptismal mandate to the apostolate and which seems to encourage a prophetic and autonomous type of action, and the *Decree on the Lay*

Apostolate, which emphasizes the hierarchical mandate for an organized apostolate under the jurisdiction of bishops, did not escape the attention of commentators, so it is not surprising if many lay leaders have been playing down the *Decree* and giving more attention to *Lumen Gentium*, while Vatican conservatives do just the opposite.

In addition, the famous *Pastoral Constitution on the Church in the Modern World* and the *Declaration on Religious Liberty* were other council documents which had major implications for the development of the Catholic laity. For example, the council participants, by accepting the principle of "responsible parenthood" in the pastoral constitution, while leaving the decision about birth control methods to the pope, planted the seeds of future challenge to the conservative stand that Pope Paul was to take. A French Communist sociologist, Antoine Casanova, in an analysis of the question of the laity at Vatican II, has stressed the radical implications of the council's ideas concerning laymen:

> The change in the order of presentation of chapters, the triumph of a biblical style over a juridical style, and the promotion of the expressions "people of God" and "common priesthood" activated, at the level of theology itself, an irrefutable implantation of popular and democratic values. Equal in religious dignity, direct beneficiaries of Christ's mediation (which surpasses Mary's and the hierarchy's mediation without eliminating them), these people can be considered as responsible beings and as the makers of their own history at the level of salvation—a divine salvation with human dimensions that cannot be realized except in a collective way, that passes through the transformation and the animation of a social world—where workers have a specific role inasmuch as they are the image of the god who came to live "as a slave." Even the definition of authority is more humble; the text avoids presenting the hierarchy as being above the Church. The hierarchy is shown as being among the people of God and at their service.[41]

The assessment of these documents has been lengthy, because there were ramifications of Vatican II that went beyond the documents even though they were based on them. Pope Paul had opened the fourth and last session with the announcement of the convening of the Synod of Bishops requested by the council. By this time, it was evident that a synod would be a more congenial meeting for Pope Paul than the planned lay congress was likely to be, since bishops are much more dependent on the Vatican than laymen. Both meetings, which were to bring Church and lay leaders of emerging nations to Rome, would produce new directions for the laity, but a congress of laymen would be much more difficult for the Vatican to control than a synod of bishops.

The Post-Council Commission, at its meetings in early 1966, made the proposition that a laity council be founded. At first, the Vatican did not want to create both the Council on the Laity and the Justice and Peace Commission, but because of strong criticism from progressive priests and laymen, it was finally decided to have both under the same president, Cardinal Maurice Roy of Quebec.

On July 7, 1966, the Vatican named a provisional committee to prepare the new lay institutions called for by Vatican II. It was made up of three clerical and four lay members, the latter including Vittorino Veronese and Rosemary Goldie. The Conference of Catholic International Organizations manifested its displeasure at not having been consulted at that important stage. The provisional committee suggested that the secretary and one of two vice-presidents be members of the laity. The Vatican finally decided to have members of the clergy as president, vice-president, and secretary of the Council on the Laity, and members of the laity as vice-secretaries only. Twelve lay persons were named as members of the Council on the Laity. They were asked to sign a pledge of secrecy (one of the Vatican's favorite control devices), but they all refused. In a press conference on January 13, 1967, three days after Paul VI's *motu proprio* letter which created the Council on the Laity, Veronese stressed that the number of lay members of the Council on the Laity would be extended beyond twelve, and that representatives of the nonorganized and individual apostolates could be included in the future. A few months later, after their first plenary session, the Council on the Laity expressed satisfaction with the wide scope of freedom given to them by the pope. At that meeting they received explanations about the relationship of the Council on the Laity to the hierarchy and the Roman Curia. As might be expected, their margin of autonomy was quite thin.

8. DIRECTIONS: HIERARCHY AND LAITY

The return of prophecy and charisma to the Church, in the person of Pope John, represented a process of "continuity in change" rather than a truly transformed religious hierarchy. Vatican II, the naming of many new non-Italian cardinals, and the publication of *Mater et Magistra* and *Pacem in Terris* seemed, to many observers, to be new departures, but were, according to one analyst, "necessary reformulations of

norms and beliefs in the Church . . . made possible without basic alter-
ation of this ultimate criterion of legitimation and authenticity.''[42]
Many of the new conservatives in the Vatican after 1968 were men
who had been liberals in the fifties; the new progressives were clearly
more radical than these liberals had ever been. Since the issues had
changed, the moderate reformist views of the liberals of the fifties now
appeared to be quite conservative. One of the most important effects
of Vatican II for lay Catholics was the demythologizing of Church
authority through the news coverage of Vatican II. On television and
in newspapers, they heard the bishops and members of the Roman
Curia labeled as progressives, moderates, conservatives, and reactionaries, and they saw these same august prelates engaged in down-to-
earth partisan polemics and politicking. It made them aware of the
human and secular aspects of their Church and it may have embold-
ened some of them when their turn came to participate in Church
affairs during the lay congress in 1967.

Public reports of the discussions and votes of Vatican II revealed
rather accurately the secular and religious ''politics'' of the participating Catholic hierarchy. According to Antoine Casanova, a definite
majority of the 2,300 prelates were liberals (around 1,900), a good
number were conservatives (around 300), and a small group were radicals (not more than 100).[43] Quite a few well-publicized incidents
during each of the four sessions of Vatican II made it clear to everyone
that the hierarchy was not a unanimous chorus of heavenly voices.

This discovery made restrictions on lay expression of opinion all but
obsolete. If politicking was permissible for clerics, it should *a fortiori* be
acceptable for the lay members of the Church. In this sense, the controversies of Vatican II anticipated and paved the way for the third
World Congress for the Lay Apostolate, which was to be a far livelier
spectacle than the two earlier lay congresses. Thanks to Vatican II, to
its liberating climate of ideological struggle and the relatively progressive documents it produced, positions which were barely legitimate in
1951 and 1957 were so generally accepted in 1967 that they received
only token opposition at the lay congress, as we shall see in the following two chapters.

PART TWO

*The Third World Congress
for the Lay Apostolate*

IV

The Unfolding of the Congress

The third World Congress for the Lay Apostolate, in October 1967, constitutes a good observation point for looking at papacy-laity relations during Paul VI's pontificate, since it came nearly five years after his election and two years after the opportunity to develop his personal orientation toward the lay movement and its demands. In the ten years since the preceding congress, the Catholic Church had endured numerous changes, some of them more apparent than real. John XXIII and Vatican II had come and gone, and at the international level momentous socioeconomic and political changes had taken place. This congress might reveal whether John's pontificate and Council had really made an impact on the exercise of papal authority toward the laity, and on the laity's desire to press for changes in religious and ecclesiastical matters. Now that he was in the top position of power, and not one of the leaders of the informal opposition anymore, what would Montini's attitude and practice be toward the increasingly critical stands of the Catholic laity? Would he take Pius XII's autocratic approach, would he encourage decentralized participation and disarming frankness as John XXIII had done, or would he develop some new approach? Scrutiny of the 1967 congress will help to answer these questions and to illustrate the types of mechanisms of control prevalent in the operating procedures of the Vatican. A congress is an ideal situation in which to observe the functioning of an organization, because in a short period of time and without the habitual screens that veil its operations, the organization reveals much of its policies, strategies, tactics, and goals. In the case of a secretive organization like the Vatican, it offers one of the rare chances for observation with a certain degree of visibility.

October is usually one of the busiest months of the year at the Vatican because it is then that many international Church meetings are held. October 1967 was particularly hectic: the first international Synod of Bishops and nearly a dozen other international meetings of Catholics were taking place in Rome. The most important of these numerous meetings was the third World Congress for the Lay Apostolate, scheduled for October 11 through 18 at the Palazzo Pio, a few blocks from St. Peter's Square. Compared with the Synod of Bishops, which met over a period of thirty days, the third World Congress for the Lay Apostolate had a tight schedule: seven days of closely packed meetings and workshops on the general theme "God's People on Man's Journey." The first portion of the congress (October 11–14) was devoted to a series of eight workshops studying "Man Today," and the second (October 15–18) to a similar series on "The Laity in the Renewal of the Church." Each workshop was subdivided into language groups. This twofold division of the activities of the congress (i.e. "Man Today" and "The Church") was closely linked to two of the major documents produced by Vatican II: *Gaudium et Spes*, which spoke of Christian involvement in today's world, and *Lumen Gentium*, the dogmatic constitution on the Church, which characterized the Church as being the people of God. The transition between the two series of workshops was to be a key address by the pope and a lecture on "God's Call" by Yves Congar, a progressive French Dominican theologian and author of an important book on the laity during the fifties.[1]

1. THE ORGANIZERS AND THE PARTICIPANTS

Because the organizers of and the participants in the third World Congress for the Lay Apostolate were an easily definable assemblage of the international Catholic lay elite, they suited one of the goals of the present study: to describe and explain the relationship between the Vatican and lay Catholic leaders at national and international levels. Although many have remarked, as shall be seen later, that these people were not truly representative of the Catholic laity, they nevertheless constituted a close approximation to an international lay Catholic elite, although one would have to append the modifier "Vatican-approved."

The organizers were largely the members and consultors of the Council on the Laity, founded by Paul VI in early 1967, and the officers of various Catholic International Organizations. Many of them had been auditors at Vatican II, or had been members of COPECIAL. The other participants, mostly officers of national Catholic organizations and of CIOs, were called "national delegates" and "international delegates" respectively. A few representatives of nonofficial, nonsponsored, nonstructured groups were invited as experts or as auditors, rather than as official delegates. Thus, officially, the congress was a fairly representative meeting of officers and leaders of those lay Catholic organizations controlled by the Church hierarchy. They were what one might call the Vatican-endorsed international lay Catholic establishment.

Participation in the 1967 congress was open to national delegations, limited to thirty persons per country (of these, up to six could be clerics), and to international delegations, of a maximum of five members from organizations affiliated with the Conference of the CIOs and of three from Catholic organizations not affiliated with the Conference of the CIOs. The leaders of these delegations formed an assembly of heads of delegations that was to meet at least three times during the congress to vote on resolutions prepared by the Resolutions Committee. Finally some experts, observer-consultants (i.e. non-Catholics), auditors, and the press were also present at the congress.

The Organizing Committee, created by COPECIAL, appointed the president of the congress (Vittorino Veronese), four co-presidents, and the twenty members of the Steering Committee. Eleven members of the Steering Committee were members of COPECIAL's board of directors, and it was in the committee that the effective power resided. The Steering Committee was assisted by the Ecclesiastical Commission, comprised of priests and bishops appointed by the Vatican, and by a congress secretariate whose secretary-general was Rosemary Goldie, executive secretary of COPECIAL. Looking at this organizational structure and realizing that both COPECIAL and the Steering Committee were, in effect, named by the Vatican, one can see how difficult it would be for any "subversive" ideas to find a forum in this congress.

Most of the documents had been printed before the opening of the congress. These included a list of participants, indicating their affiliation and nationality, the major speeches and working papers to be presented, and a set of rules to govern the actions of the participants. Little was left to chance or improvisation.[2] According to these regulations, the Steering Committee was to meet daily at noon, during the congress, to analyze the proceedings and make decisions necessary for the "orderly conduct of sessions and other functions." It nominated the members of the Resolutions' Committee and chose the presidents and secretaries of all the eighty groups of the workshops.

The only aspect of the congress which had any semblance of democracy was the assembly of heads of delegations, which came about, as a sort of afterthought, because of pressures exerted by some delegations during the preliminary organizing stages. There did not seem to be much danger that anything explosive would come out of that assembly either, especially since the president and vice-presidents of the assembly were nominated by the Steering Committee. All in all, it was a pretty tight ship, and the Steering Committee seemed to have everything well under control when it convened in Rome a few days before the congress was to open.

Concerning national delegations, it was required that four-fifths of the maximum of thirty members should be lay persons. For most countries, the delegations consisted of one representative of each of the most important officially recognized lay organizations. National episcopal conferences, through their subordinate agencies, were often instrumental in the selection of the national delegates. In many delegations, Catholic Action or similar "mandated" or "sponsored" groups (the National Council of Catholic Men and the National Council of Catholic Women, in the case of the United States) dominated. A few delegations were so lopsidedly conservative that there were protests. Youth and worker movements from Spain, for example, sent their own "unofficial" delegation because they considered that the bishops' list of delegates did not represent them. There was a similar protest from the Irish laity.

The COPECIAL Organizing Committee, under contradictory pressures from conservatives in the Roman Curia and from liberal Church elements, slightly counterbalanced the selection bias by inviting some well-known progressives (e.g. Dorothy Day of the *Catholic Worker*, Tom Cornell of the Catholic Peace Fellowship) as experts. In national caucus meetings, the experts sometimes voted along with the regular delegates and nobody objected.

Although the organizers made extraordinary efforts to get funds for travel expenses for representatives from poorer countries, the laymen in the most advantageous position to participate were the more well-to-do and those who happened to live closer to Rome. The United States and Malta, for example, sent full delegations of thirty members, while many Asian and African countries had a small number of delegates, some of whom were people already studying or working in Europe. Third World countries were thus able to have some delegates without overly burdening the budget allowed for travel grants.

René Didier, visiting professor of social welfare at the University of Montreal and president of the International Catholic Union of Social Services, in a report on the congress in the Montreal daily newspaper *Le Devoir*, had this to say about the selection bias in certain national delegations:

> Undoubtedly, the weight of the hierarchy in certain regions of the world is still quite heavy. Let us add to that problem two other difficulties, distance and lack of funds, which falsified the real situations. This is what pushed certain delegates from Latin America, Africa and Asia to say, sometimes with vehemence and passion, that this congress was, once again, that of the Whites, the Rich, the Westerners and the Europeans. In all justice, we must underline the great effort at solidarity which expressed itself, notably by the granting of travel funds to the poorer delegates; but a much more important effort would have been necessary to permit a participation that would have been more in tune with reality.[3]

Institutional identification and the availability of travel expenses were key determinants of an individual's or an organization's presence at the congress. Several commentators, including James O'Gara, a liberal Catholic journalist from the United States, have mentioned the importance of these two factors.[4] The selection procedure for national and international delegations brought to the congress representatives from organizations that were already differentiated along age, sex, occupational, national, and even class lines. Hence, the delegates could not be a completely homogeneous group. On the other hand, there was a smaller ideological and political difference of views than one might have expected of such a large world-wide assembly. O'Gara had this impression of the delegates' attitudes:

> It is not easy to generalize about a gathering of 2,500 people, but some national delegations were clearly more progressive than others,

and inside every national delegation I had any contact with there was a wide variation in attitudes. Some delegates were traditional, old-line Catholic Action types interested in reforming but at the same time wanting to preserve traditional structures, men and women with whom most bishops would be quite comfortable. Others— probably the minority as far as I could tell—were quite unconcerned with the hierarchical mandates or even approval; they want drastic reform in the Church and they want it fast. This conservative-liberal division, I should emphasize, is not along lay-clerical lines. There are a number of priests here, as chaplains, observers and one thing or another, and the differences among them are at least as marked as those among the lay delegates. Indeed, very often the "radical" priest seems more of a rebel than his lay counterpart, if only because he usually knows more theology to be radical about.[5]

Bob Walsh, secretary of the English Laity Commission and a member of one of the most progressive national delegations, was pleasantly surprised by the orientation of the delegates:

Walsh said he felt that perhaps the point that came through most at the congress was how "progressive" the delegates were. Remembering that in many cases the delegates were appointed by their bishops, he said that "It was remarkable not only how well they had learned the lesson of Vatican II but how willing they were to build on it.[6]

The Norwegian sociologist of religion, Edvard Vogt, was similarly impressed by the congress and even referred to it as "the Laity's October Revolution."[7] In a more reserved vein, the Jesuit Giuseppe De Rosa, in a 1967 article in the Vatican-controlled publication *Civiltà Cattolica*, said of the congress, "It is certainly one of the most meaningful events in this post-conciliar period."[8]

The empirical survey presented in the next chapter confirms and clarifies these general impressions. The Vatican had anticipated the restive mood of the laity, and, consequently, had taken numerous precautions to insure that everything would run smoothly and without risky last-minute improvisations. The Vatican seems to have judged that a maximum of preparation and control, tempered with some appearance of autonomy and freedom, would avoid dissatisfaction and recriminations. Thus the members of the Ecclesiastical Commission named by the Vatican were not chosen among the conservative curialists. Such liberal clerics as the African bishop Jean Zoa, the Panamanian bishop Mark G. McGrath, the Italian Jesuit Roberto Tucci, and the Italian ghost-writer of Pope John's *Pacem in Terris*, Msgr. Pietro

Pavan, were among those selected for that commission. This ecclesiastical commission, named specifically for the congress, greatly overlapped the Ecclesiastical Commission of COPECIAL. Cardinal Maurice Roy, known in Quebec as a moderate liberal, was president of both of these commissions, as well as president of the Council on the Laity.

One outcome of the congress that the Vatican wanted to avoid was the creation, or the demand for the creation, of a permanent international organization of the laity composed of people chosen by some partly democratic procedure. Thus, in anticipation of the congress, in January 1967, the Consilium de Laicis, or Council on the Laity, was created as a part of the Roman Curia. The Vatican chose the fifteen members of the council and its seven lay advisers from among lay Catholics who had been prominent during the preceding fifteen years in COPECIAL, in Catholic Action, and in various international Catholic organizations. Seven bishops and a superior-general of a religious order were named as ecclesiastical advisers.

Many leaders of Catholic organizations were offended by this undemocratic, centralizing act, and their resentment may have contributed to an iconoclastic mood among some of the congress participants. The very creation of the Council on the Laity was a blow at the autonomy of the Geneva-based Conference of Catholic International Organizations. At the time of the creation of the Council on the Laity, the Vatican grant to the Conference of CIOs was suspended without notice and its permanent secretary was persuaded to come to Rome as one of the council's two vice-secretaries.

The Latin name "Consilium de Laicis" was itself an indication of the desire to show that the council was an agency *on the subject* of the laity, a council *on* rather than *of* the laity. The Vatican did not want to call it "Consilium Laicorum" (Council of the Laity) for fear that this could have been interpreted as meaning that the council belonged to the laity. In fact, the documents of COPECIAL first translated "Consilium de Laicis" as "Council on the Laity." Later the less paternalistic and more ambiguous translation "Laity Council" was hit upon and frequently used also.

2. THE PREPARATIONS AND THE OPENING DAY

The third World Congress for the Lay Apostolate was preceded by numerous preparatory meetings, most of them under the auspices of COPECIAL, the organization created by Pius XII the year after the first congress. By May 1959, less than two years after the second congress and just a few months after Pope John's announcement of Vatican II, COPECIAL organized a planning session at Montallegro, in Rapallo, Italy. Thirty experts, most of them lay leaders active in COPECIAL, attended this three-day meeting to lay the groundwork for the 1967 congress.

In 1961, as we saw in the preceding chapter, John XXIII reorganized the Executive Committee of COPECIAL, enlarging its membership and giving it greater importance. Following this, various other organizing meetings were held to hammer out the general lines of the future congress, and on July 23, 1965, Cardinal Amletto Cicognani, the Vatican secretary of state, announced that the third congress would be held in October 1967.

In September 1965, the board of directors of COPECIAL, gathered for its semiannual meeting, decided upon a plan for the preparation of the congress on a world-wide basis. In March 1966, at the Domus Mariae in Rome, the program of the congress was defined and elaborated by a group of fifty international experts, most of whom were laymen linked closely with COPECIAL, with Vatican II, with the CIOs, and with Catholic Action in various, mostly European, countries. Five groups were formed to help the board of directors of COPECIAL, and an organizing committee of seven lay persons was constituted. These seven lay persons, by their strategic positions in various lay organizations, and by their participation in numerous lay endeavors sponsored by the Vatican in previous years, were what one might call the upper echelon of the lay power elite in the Catholic Church. They were Professor Sugranyes de Franch, chairman, former secretary-general, and former president of Pax Romana; Professor Vittorio Bachelet, general president of Italian Catholic Action; Prince Karl zu Löwenstein, president of the Central Committee of German Catholics; Patrick Keegan, former president of the JOC and of the World Movement of Christian Workers; Maria Vendrik, member of the Communication Center for the Church and the World (Netherlands); Mieczyslaw de Habicht, former general secretary of the Conference of the CIOs; Vittorino Veronese, former president of the Italian Catholic Action (1946–52), former secretary of COPECIAL (1952–1958), former director general of UNESCO (1958–61), and president of the Banco di Roma. All were members of the board of directors of COPECIAL, and all later became members of consultors of the Council on the Laity, except for Veronese, who was appointed to two other new branches of the Roman Curia, the Pontifical Commission for Justice and Peace and the Papal Commission for Social Communications Media.

COPECIAL also organized, for May 1966, a meeting of 120 delegates from eighteen European countries to make further plans for the congress. That same year, similar meetings were held in Latin America and North America, and itinerant consultations were made, by Marie-Ange Besson and Rosemary Goldie of the COPECIAL Secretariate, in Africa, Asia, and Oceania during 1966 and 1967.

In addition, COPECIAL had launched a vast international inquiry on the topic of "lay participation in the renewal of the Church since Vatican II," sending an open-ended questionnaire to national organizations involved in the coordination of the lay apostolate and to international Catholic organizations. In some countries, the questionnaire was simplified and adapted to local conditions, then published in Catholic periodicals, and individuals and groups sent in their answers to the periodicals. Although not very systematic, the inquiry gave the congress organizers some means of assessing the mood of lay Catholics from sixty-five countries and thirteen international organizations. It was an instrument intended to help COPECIAL find out what the laity's expectations were. It avoided controversial issues and focused on problems such as the diffusion and application of Vatican II documents, especially in the liturgical and apostolic spheres. What mainly seemed to emerge in the responses to the inquiry, as presented in a 48-page pamphlet distributed to the congress participants, was the confusion and traditionalism of some sectors of the Church. Probably because of the type of groups surveyed (the same essentially that would send delegates to the congress), very few radical demands were presented. It appeared from the pamphlet that the laity would be quite satisfied to succeed in getting the moderate reforms of Vatican II actuated.

On the basis of this inquiry, which was analyzed in the summer of 1967, the organizers of the congress had no reason to fear an October Revolution. Although they were aware by then that their elimination of nonorganized and nonmandated sectors of the laity from participation would be a major criticism of the congress, the inquiry probably contributed to the sense of security which led to a certain relaxation of controls. They did not realize that the format of their questionnaire, the type of questions asked, and the manner of collecting responses created biases that made it impossible for them really to tap the mood of the restive laity at the grass roots, or at the level of the articulate elites that would be present. Their surprise and dismay at the orientation taken by the congress would have been less had they not been led thus to expect a tranquil assemblage.

On the two days immediately preceding the congress, separate and restricted meetings were held in Rome for the Asian, African, and Latin American delegates. These continental meetings were held to "facilitate contact and collaboration between delegates and experts from these regions" (according to an instruction sheet sent to the participants by the COPECIAL Secretariate and to "aim at giving an introduction to the congress and try to explain its philosophy" (according to the minutes of the Steering Committee of the congress). At the meetings for Asians and Latin Americans, delegates expressed their desire that particular emphasis be given to certain issues, such as lay independence, world justice, and cooperation with non-Christians. The Asians specifically asked that ecumenism, already an important part of the program of the congress because of the developments which had occurred in that area (e.g. Cardinal Bea's Secretariate for Unity and other initiatives of John XXIII) since the 1957 congress should henceforth be extended to include non-Christian religions as well as other Christian denominations.

The congress opened with a plenary session. Among those present were Aldo Moro, president of the Council of Ministers of Italy (who had been chairman at the 1951 and 1957 congresses), and approximately thirty bishops, archbishops, and cardinals. Vittorino Veronese welcomed the participants as president of the congress, an honor bestowed upon him because of the central role he had played at the two previous congresses and in COPECIAL, and also because of his long-standing friendship and collaboration with Pope Paul. (In 1946, Montini, as head of the section of Ordinary Affairs in the Secretariate of State under Pius XII, had succeeded in having Veronese named as general-president of Italian Catholic Action and Moro as president of the Italian Federation of Catholic University Students. In 1939, Veronese had been chosen as general secretary of FUCI, which Montini had earlier served as chaplain.) Desmond O'Grady, in a feature article on Veronese in 1968, called him "the prominent Catholic layman par excellence."[9] Veronese was considered to be the person responsible for the organization of the 1951 and 1957 World Congresses for the Lay Apostolate, in his capacities as general-president of Italian Catholic Action (1946–1952) and secretary-general of COPECIAL (1952–1958). As leaders of the progressive wing in the

Vatican, in Catholic Action, and in the Christian Democratic Party, these three men, Montini, Veronese, and Moro, had remained close friends as they emerged as important religious, cultural, and political figures in postwar Italy.

The "introductory lecture" at the congress was given by Dr. Thom G. K. Kierstens of the Netherlands, secretary-general of the International Christian Union of Business Executives. Kiersten, a progressive, described what he considered to be some of the major problems of man today, and what a Christian's contribution to their solution might be. He called for a "democratization of theology," an updating of Christian ethics, and a reorientation of the Church toward service to the world so that the Church might more adequately cope with problems of war and peace, of the thirst for freedom and unity, of the equality of women, of Third World poverty, of radical injustice, of alienation, especially among the young in the increasingly affluent countries, and of rising expectations and increasing turbulence in developing countries. The major prerequisites for this reorientation, according to this Dutch businessman and intellectual, would be a greater autonomy of speech and action for the laity, better lay-clergy relations and communications, and organizations that would function with democratic procedures and be open to change. The potential conflict between the newly formed Council on the Laity, as a branch of the Roman Curia, and the more democratically run Conference of the CIOs was alluded to by Kierstens when he said, referring to democratic procedures:

> In this regard, we might draw attention to the experience of the Conference of International Catholic Organizations, whose activities threaten to be overshadowed somewhat by the new institutions now created. Let us not forget that this Conference, however imperfectly it might have worked, was and still is the only example of free initiative on the part of the lay or committed Christians, on the international plane, [and] that it is a democratic institution which, with the necessary transformation and finance, could still do tremendous work for the Church. There is a Dutch saying that one does not throw away old shoes before one is sure that the new ones fit perfectly.[10]

The tension between the Council on the Laity and the CIOs, which Kierstens referred to, originated in the tension between the Vatican-based COPECIAL and the more independent Conference of the CIOs during the fifties. The relationship between the CIOs on the one hand and COPECIAL and its successor, the Council on the Laity, on the other is a very complex one which I shall try to elucidate farther along in this study. Suffice it to add at this point that many delegates to the congress, especially among those representing CIOs, expressed their dismay at the way the Council on the Laity had been formed. The Steering Committee of the congress, which greatly overlapped with the Council on the Laity, tried at various times during the congress to explain the role and functioning of the Council on the Laity, but this did not stop the criticism.

3. THE ISSUES OF FREEDOM AND AUTONOMY

Throughout the third World Congress for the Lay Apostolate, some participants and journalists expressed their opinion that the Steering Committee was trying to "steer" a tight course between the democratic pressures of some lay participants and the autocratic pressures of their hierarchical overseers in the Roman Curia. The opening day provided a good example of this intention, and subsequent statements and responses that occurred within the official agenda indicated how difficult the voyage had proved to be.

Kierstens, undoubtedly influenced by the ferment in the Church in the Netherlands, opened with a speech which was blunt and frank. Its insistence on freedom and autonomy set the tone for the discussions and exchanges that were to follow. Kierstens hit exactly on some of the issues that progressive participants wanted to raise and that the Vatican would have rather bypassed.

These same issues were to be, during the ensuing week, those which brought out the latent tension between the somewhat democratic-minded heads of delegations and the more prudent Vatican appointees. The tension would be apparent not only in the meetings of the heads of delegations, but in the workshops of delegates, and in the official speeches as well. A good statement of this tension, and of the way the moderate lay leaders hoped to resolve it, was expressed in the closing speech of the congress, delivered by Joaquín Ruiz-Giménez, one of the most influential members of the Steering Committee and of the Council on the Laity:

> It is not a question of opposing the hierarchy with a sort of "laymen's union," and still less of carrying on something like a huge "class struggle" in the Church, the members of the Hierarchy having the power and the laity being more or less out to win it. . . .
> It is not a question either of refusing obedience, but of giving it its

most profound and original meanings, so that it reflects the awareness by the layman of this joint responsibility with the Hierarchy in
the dynamism of God's people.

The realization of this "vital community," at the same time hierarchical and democratic—in the deepest and purest sense of both
terms—requires between pastors and people a reciprocal dialogue
which is increasingly authentic and confident, and participation of
the people at the preparatory stage in decisions which have to be
taken by authority.[11]

Like Veronese, Ruiz-Giménez had been long a friend of Paul VI.
He was a former secretary-general of the Confederation of Catholic
Students of Spain, an observer at Vatican II, and a left-leaning Christian
Democrat. *Le Monde* described him on July 30, 1966, as the unchal-
lenged leader of the left wing of the Christian Democrats in Spain. He
had been president of Pax Romana, ambassador of Spain to the Holy
See, and minister of education in Franco's government; in 1963 he was
expelled from Franco's Phalange for his liberal ideas. The Pax Romana
connection was very important for his career as a lay leader of Montinian tendencies, as it has been for many other influential lay members
of COPECIAL and the Council on the Laity. Rosemary Goldie, who
replaced Veronese as executive secretary of COPECIAL and later became associate secretary of the Council on the Laity, also came to her
position as the highest-ranking woman in the Roman Curia via the
Pax Romana organization. This extract from Ruiz-Giménez's closing
speech illustrates well his long-term relationship with the pope:

It is only right that we speak of our gratitude, sparingly so that it
does not appear flattery, but with sincere feeling, for the essential role
played in all this [i.e. in the congress] by the one who was Monsignor
Giovanni-Battista Montini, and who today sits in the chair of St.
Peter.

I keep as one of the most vivid souvenirs of my life the homily I
heard one morning in this city of Rome, during a Mass celebrated in
the intimacy of a group of university students of Catholic Action. I
have never forgotten those words of Msgr. Montini on the sense of
the Church and the role of the layman, commenting on a text from
St. Paul; some years later, they took root deeply in my mind and
with even greater promise in the address that Msgr. Montini, then
Archbishop of Milan, made to the Second World Congress for the
Lay Apostolate in 1957; they blossomed again, enriched, in Cardinal
Montini's speeches to the Second Vatican Council, to crystallize

today in the messages of the Vicar of Christ. Indeed, before, with, and since Pius XII and John XXIII, Paul VI has contributed providentially to the dynamism and vital presence of God's people in the world.[12]

The key issues of freedom and autonomy were raised at the first meeting of the assembly of heads of delegations. It has been decided by the organizers of the congress, in consultation with Vatican officials, that some form of contact would be established with the Synod of Bishops. But the assembly of heads of delegations rejected the bland message of greetings to the synod fathers prepared by the Steering Committee and already distributed to journalists. The assembly requested a delay to consult the delegations so as to be able to draft a stronger text. Thus a certain element of democratization was initially introduced in the congress itself by this "representative" assembly. By asserting itself in such a forceful manner, it indicated that it would use the power it had (given it by the regulations of the congress) to examine and to revise or adopt all texts emanating from the congress instead of functioning as a docile rubber stamp for the Steering Committee. The new message for the bishops called for the creation in the Church of representative structures in which the laity would be chosen by elections rather than by clerical co-optation.[13]

This new message to the Synod of Bishops was discussed in a frank and uninhibited way and finally approved in principle by the assembly of heads of delegations on Saturday, October 15 (subject to further amendments). It was voted on the following evening, and was presented to the bishops by a small delegation, headed by a woman, on October 17, the last day of the congress. At the same first meeting of the assembly of heads of delegations, the head of the Dutch delegation proposed a motion calling for publication, in the proceedings of the congress, of the texts of all resolutions proposed to the assembly (by five delegations, as the rule stipulated), even if not adopted by the assembly and the plenary session of all delegates. The assembly adopted the Dutch resolution, which insured the expression of minority views.

Then the assembly elected the Canadian Romeo Maione as its president, an act that brought greater democracy into the assembly proceedings and further extended its very limited autonomy. Maione's role as president was to be especially crucial in the rough going toward the end of the congress. Although the congress had been planned to insure that every detail would remain under the control of the Steering Committee and the Ecclesiastical Commission, already a certain element of the impromptu had introduced itself. What had been planned as a triumphal pageant began to look a little like a town hall meeting.

The orientation of the assembly of heads of delegations was greatly influenced by Maione, a progressive Italo-Canadian who had been president of the international Young Catholic Workers (JOC). Maione had spent two years as an organizer for the second congress, having been commissioned for that job by some of the organizers of the 1957 congress, the liberal friends of Msgr. Montini (Maione jokingly but affectionately referred to them as the "Pax Romana Mafia" in an interview I had with him on October 25, 1968) who were then in conflict with conservative leaders of Italian Catholic Action. These same organizers ran the 1967 congress, according to Maione, and arranged to have him elected president of the assembly of heads of delegations. Maione proved to be more interested in being responsive to grass-roots preoccupations with social justice and democratization than in remaining loyal to his Christian Democratic intellectual friends and to the former Msgr. Montini. He saw to it that nothing stopped the resolution-making process of the assembly, even when this meant extending meetings far into the night. Maione has, since the 1967 congress, resigned from his job as director of the Canadian Bishops' Development and Peace Organization to return to work in the labor movement in Montreal, and then at the Canadian International Development Agency in Ottawa.

The second day of the congress, Thursday, October 12, opened with a plenary session consisting of a panel discussion by experts on the theme "Man Today" and of "personal witnessing" by participants from various countries and sectors of Catholic activity. By their focus on specific life situations, these addresses created, as intended, a psychological climate suitable for the group study meetings which followed.

The speakers included the British economist Lady Jackson (Barbara Ward), the Italian Jesuit Roberto Tucci, the American astronaut James A. McDivitt (many delegates were upset by the propaganda aspect of his presence and by the showing of two United States Information Agency movies on war that were sympathetic to the U.S.A.), and Stanley Hebert, a black American, who attacked racism.

4. THE BIRTH-CONTROL CONTROVERSY

In the afternoon of October 12 the first series of workshops—on man today—began with small-group discussion on each of eight themes:

spiritual attitudes, the family, cooperation between men and women, tensions between generations, social communication, social and economic development, peace and world community, and migration. Each theme was discussed in five language groups. Each group was guided by a discussion leader and a secretary appointed by the Organizing Committee, which had also prepared an outline of problems to be discussed. Despite these careful arrangements, discussions were often quite lively and controversy erupted in some groups. As usually happens in such gatherings, some workshops were more popular than others. Those on the family and on social and economic development had the highest numbers of participants. About four hundred attended the workshop on the family. Many delegates saw in this workshop an ideal forum to make known their position on birth control. Since, at the time of the congress, Pope Paul had not yet taken his tough final stand on birth control, they hoped to influence his forthcoming decision by passing a strong resolution on the subject. The discussion on birth control had not been anticipated in the agenda for the family workshop, but all five language groups took it up spontaneously.

Table 1 indicates the different wordings of the "birth control" or "responsible parenthood" motions in each of the five language groups, plus the breakdown of the final voting on this issue in each group. Because the formulations were not identical, as can be seen from the key extracts reported in the table, the group figures can only be approximately compared. Nevertheless, since these figures indicate the general ideas of the delegates, they are important in shedding light on what became the major post-congress public issue: birth control and, more specifically, the delegates' positions on the birth-control question. It is on this issue that the lay demands for change were expressed most forcefully and that the authoritarian and manipulative character of the papacy and the Roman Curia manifested itself most clearly during and after the congress.

The fifth group, which had two hundred participants, was subdivided into two English-language subgroups and one French-language subgroup. The proceedings do not give the voting figures for one of the English subgroups and for the French subgroup, but they do report that a pro–birth-control motion was passed by the French subgroup. The wording of the motion of this subgroup was similar to that of the English subgroup reported in table 1, because the discussion in both subgroups originated from a proposed motion prepared beforehand by the caucus of a progressive CIO. My recollection as an observer in the French subgroup is that the motion was passed with an

TABLE 1 *Acceptance of Birth Control in the Workshop on the Family*

Groups	Group 1 English-Spanish	Group 2 English-German	Group 3 French-German	Group 4 French-Spanish	English subgroup of Group 5 English-French
Formulation	"Paternity must be responsible"	"Parents should be free to choose methods of contraception"	"It should be left to their conscience . . . to decide the question of method"	"The group asked the Magisterium to listen to the opinion of Christian laymen"	"Responsible procreation . . . essential condition for the harmonious development of family life"
For	32	15	30	Circa 57[a]	50
Against	4	11	0	. . .	0
Abstain	1	2	2	. . .	0
Absent	13	12	3	. . .	0
Total	50	40	35	57	50

SOURCE: *Man Today: Proceedings* 2:103–115.

[a] "This resolution was approved almost unanimously by the 57 participants" (*Man Today*, p. 112).

overwhelming majority. The motion from the English-speaking sub-group asked for a "clear declaration on responsible parenthood in line with the Council teaching and putting the accent on the dignity of man," but recognized also that "problems concerning the principles of conjugal ethics are subject to the authority of the Magisterium" (i.e. the teaching function of the Church).

In spite of the missing data, the table indicates that a clear majority of the participants in the family workshop were in favor of leaving the choice of birth-control methods to the conscience of individual Catholics. The survey data presented in Chapter V confirm this inclination for the national delegates, who were generally more conservative than the international ones.

When Cardinal Maurice Roy, after the congress, attempted to interpret a portion of a resolution on development (discussed later in this chapter) favoring "responsible parenthood" as an endorsement of the magisterium's primacy over conscience on the birth-control question, there was little in the published statements or resolutions of the lay delegates to support him.[14]

The family workshop as a whole failed to submit a resolution to the assembly of heads of delegations, as it might have done. Its difficulties were noted in the official workshop report, which clearly does not support Cardinal Roy's contention:

> It must be recognized, when one considers the total of 400 participants in groups and sub-groups of Workshop No. 2, that a majority emerged which considered that, if husband and wife must be responsible for the decision as to the number of their children, it is also for them to decide in conscience on the choice of methods to be used, in an attitude of respect and love, and in the light of the great perspectives of God's design. However, lack of time did not allow the regrouping of the different motions put forward and the submission of a resolution to the Workshop participants for their reflection and vote.
>
> Those in charge of the Workshop were all the more inclined not to present a motion on this point when they learned that rather parallel resolutions coming for other Workshops, would be submitted to the vote of the Heads of Delegations.[15]

Another draft resolution on family planning was submitted to the Resolutions Committee by five national delegations, but it could not be voted on for lack of time. This text, which was published in the proceedings of the congress, stated:

As laymen, we are convinced that responsible family planning is necessary to guarantee the integrity of matrimonial love and of the family institution in a world where the total population is growing at such an accelerated rhythm. In the line of this unambiguously moral and Christian perspective, we are of the opinion that the choice of the means to prevent a new conception should be left to the conscience of the married couple, with due considerations for medical, psychological, economic and sociological insights.[16]

These documents all seem to show that many lay delegates wanted the Vatican's position changed, not because they wanted a relaxation of a high moral standard but because they considered the existing rules to be outdated and even immoral. This seems to indicate that the fight of these laymen for democratization of the Church was not an attempt at the seizure of power by an elite group but simply a move to oblige Church authorities to be more attuned to modern and changing ideals and values of a moderate liberal nature.

5. HIERARCHICAL CONTROL MECHANISMS

On the morning of Friday, October 14, delegates arriving for the continuing workshop sessions found, stacked on tables and benches in hallways and workshop rooms, hundreds of copies of a one-page statement, hitherto secret, made three days earlier by Cardinal Maurice Roy of Quebec, president of the Ecclesiastical Commission of the congress. The document had a bombshell effect on the delegates. Printed with the Latin original on one side and a translation in English, French, Dutch, German, or Spanish on the reverse, it was apparently an official summary of a talk Cardinal Roy gave on October 11 to a meeting of bishops who were attending the congress in various capacities. Cardinal Roy began by asking the bishops to refrain from intervening too frequently in the workshops, in order that they should not disturb the laity's freedom of expression. Here is the first part of his text:

SUMMARY OF THE REMARKS OF H.E. CARDINAL MAURICE ROY,
PRESIDENT OF THE ECCLESIASTICAL COMMISSION OF THE
THIRD WORLD CONGRESS OF THE LAY APOSTOLATE,
11TH OCTOBER 1967 AT HOTEL COLUMBUS

With great joy the Ecclesiastical Commission of the Congress invited to the fraternal banquet the Most Excellent Bishops taking part in the Congress.

H.E. the Cardinal President of the Commission said how happy he was to see so many bishops present. Nevertheless the Congress did not want to provide the Bishops with a special place in the Congress hall, and particularly for the good reason that they would thus be able to remain with their own delegations. Indeed, one of the points of this congress would then be this kind of contact between pastors and lay faithful.

For the time being there will be only this one meeting of the Bishops with the Ecclesiastical Commission: we hope nevertheless that it may be possible during the second part of the Congress to have another such meeting.

The Bishops will participate in various workshops that are moreover an essential part of the Congress. His Excellency the Cardinal therefore sincerely and confidentially communicated to Their Excellencies the Bishops how they should take part in the workshops: it is quite certain that the presence of the Bishops is a very good thing, but it should not change the essential character of these discussions, the object of which is direct and concrete dialogue between laymen.

The course of the workshops will not be easy: there is already a linguistic difficulty (they will be in two languages); those who participate in the discussions do not know each other well; the Steering committee is new and perhaps not well prepared. . . . If however, certain Bishops intervene too frequently in the discussions, these latter will in a way be disturbed because the laymen will not dare to speak with full freedom; there would then be discussions of theology or by theologians. . . .

But in the second part of his message, Cardinal Roy assured the bishops that laity would not go "uncorrected," and explained the congress mechanisms that would insure that the Vatican would have the last word:

It does not seem impossible that in the discussions of the laymen some unorthodox points might be made. . . . In a congress that a Bishop would have in his own diocese, he would himself have the office of correcting. Here, however, the situation is different. The Holy See has appointed a certain Ecclesiastical Commission to watch over the doctrine of the Congress. This Commission will have its permanent seat at the Palazzo Pio, where it will always be possible for the Ecclesiastical Commission to help the direction of the Congress in drafting the conclusions. On the other hand, each workshop has an Ecclesiastical Assistant whose task will be to see to it that the discussions are doctrinally correct. The Bishops can always, even after the sessions, make known the points to be corrected. Finally the Bishops will have frequent occasions to see these laymen attending the Congress from their own countries, and even be able to hint at the amendments they consider necessary.

The Bishops are asked to pass on this message to the priests and religious taking part in the workshops.

Most delegates were shocked by what they considered to be not only paternalistic clericalism but downright manipulation on the part of the hierarchy. The heads of delegations, who had naïvely passed the Dutch motion to get minority positions published, now realized that even majority positions, voted by the assembly, might not be made accessible to the public in their original form, if found to be doctrinally incorrect by the Ecclesiastical Commission. The official regulations of the congress had discreetly stipulated that the Steering Committee would be assisted by an ecclesiastical commission, but not that the commission had been appointed by the Vatican to watch over the doctrine of the congress even to the point of helping draft the conclusions and making corrections to points made by laymen "even after the sessions." Few had realized that the assistance to the Steering Committee actually meant control and censorship of democratically-made decisions. As a matter of fact, the regulations had not mentioned the Ecclesiastical Commission at all in the stipulations for texts to be adopted by the congress:

> These texts—statements, resolutions, motions, etc.—will be proposed in written form by the Steering Committee, by at least five delegations or by the workshops. They shall be examined and put to the vote in the assembly of heads of delegations. Texts adopted by a majority of two-thirds of the assembly shall be presented for adoption in plenary session and published as emanating from the Congress.[17]

Thus, what was to be presented to the world as the result of democratic processes and grass-roots lay deliberation would, in fact, be the resolutions of a congress whose statements could not only be influenced by episcopal "hints," but also altered by clerical "corrections." The Dutch delegates were especially upset, and their leaders talked openly of leaving the congress and returning home in protest. Participants speculated not so much on the document's authenticity (it seemed authentic enough, with the Latin original on one side of the sheet and the translation in one of the five major languages of the congress on the other) as on the source of the leak. One of the members of the Steering Committee, Joseph Amichia, presiding over the Saturday plenary session, remarked: "The Committee can only admire the efficiency of the clandestine means used to diffuse this secret text to the whole Congress."[18]

At noon, the Steering Committee discussed the issue and invited Cardinal Roy to address the next day's plenary session in order to reassure the delegates. His reply to the incident, reproduced in a press release the same day, did not deny his authorship of the text, but tried to give the impression that in his talk to the bishops he had actually said something different from what appeared in the text. The printed Latin text was perhaps intended only for internal Vatican circulation, but no one denied that it was an authentic reproduction of a text emanating from the cardinal's office. Since Cardinal Roy could not flatly deny his authorship, he could only intimate that he had not really read the text as prepared and say that he had been misinterpreted. His press release was a masterpiece of curial diplomacy. Glossing over the second section on the role of the Ecclesiastical Commission (in the press release he did this by feigning to summarize that second part), he stated that his intention was not to put emphasis on the "doctrinally correct" character of the congress but on its development as "truly a lay congress." The English press release of his Saturday reply can be compared with the English translation of his speech to the bishops, quoted above:

> ATTENTION: THIS LAST PART OF THE PRESS RELEASE IS AN EMBARGO
> UNTIL 4 P.M. TODAY, SATURDAY 14TH OCTOBER
>
> At the beginning of this afternoon's Plenary session on the first series of the workshops, Cardinal Maurice Roy, President of the Ecclesiastic Commission of the Congress, spoke to the delegates a few words of explanations to clarify a misunderstanding which arose after his speech to the Bishops, on Wednesday evening. Here are the words of the Cardinal:
>
> "Three days ago, speaking to a group of about thirty Bishops, on the occasion of a reception, I said to them:
>
> "If you wish to attend one or other of the workshops, you will be most welcome; but do see to it that your presence does not change the essential character of these meetings, the purpose of which is to assure a frank, realistic dialogue among the laity.
>
> "If the Bishops and priests speak too often the workshop may well become a discussion among theologians, for theologians are capable of speaking at considerable length. . . . Let us leave to the laity—and they are numerous—time to express themselves.
>
> "It may undoubtedly happen, in the heat of the discussion, that one or other of the laity may speak in a manner that to us may seem inexact from the point of view of the Church's Doctrine. This might also happen in a meeting of priests. In his own diocese a bishop might feel obliged to make a correction, for it is his mission to teach. But

here the situation is different. If a lay person errs, there will surely be another lay person to express a more exact opinion. In addition, in each workshop, there is an ecclesiastical assistant who can help in replying to more difficult theological questions.

"In a word, I asked the bishops and priests to leave all initiative to the laity and to assure that the congress retain its character—that of a discussion among lay persons.

"I deeply regret that some persons misunderstood my thought and have attributed to me, far too generously, intentions which were not mine at all. My only desire then as now is that the bishops and priests have confidence in you and that your congress be truly a lay congress."

The COPECIAL bulletin *Lay Apostolate* which came out after the congress repeated the press release's version of that famous speech. It also cut off before the more incriminating section but went further by omitting the last two summarizing paragraphs of the press release.[19]

Cardinal Roy's document and his talk to the bishops angered many delegates and may thus have pushed them to take a small measure of extra freedom. In any case, they were thereafter on guard against the possibility of undemocratic moves by the organizers or by the Vatican. It is probable that the incident contributed greatly to the frankness and lack of inhibition which characterized discussion during the remaining days of the congress.

At the plenary session on Saturday afternoon, the workshop secretaries gave their first summing-up of workshop discussions. Reports on birth-control issues brought warm audience response. When the speaker for the family workshop groups announced that the majority of discussants had declared themselves in favor of freedom for married people to choose the means of birth control that they considered best for themselves, the congress participants applauded loudly.

6. PAPAL CONTROLS AND COMPLAINTS

On Sunday, the scheduled events were Paul VI's mass and sermon in the morning, Father Yves Congar's plenary session lecture in the afternoon, and the third meeting of the assembly of heads of delegations in the evening.

The pope's sermon was not the center of attraction of the congress as Pius XII's speeches in 1951 and 1957 had been. A *New York Times* reporter noted the difference:

One participant found this change [between the 1957 and the 1967 congresses] most striking in the attitudes of laymen towards addresses by two pontiffs:

"When Pope Pius addressed us in 1957," he recalled, "it was the major event of the congress. Hours were spent in discussion and exegesis of every phase. This year, Pope Paul's speech passed almost unnoticed. Insofar as it was discussed at all, in private groups, it was to point out how far behind the congress it was."

There was even discussion in one large group of mixed nationality, of sending a deputation to the Pontiff to express disappointment with his admonitory tone. The project was abandoned out of concern for the Pope's current ill health.[20]

In his address, Paul VI stressed the importance of social involvement in pressing issues,[21] but attacked secularization and laicization, instructed laymen not to infringe on the authority of the hierarchy, and warned them that they should not "act without the Hierarchy, or against it, in the field of the Father of the family."[22] According to the *National Catholic Reporter*, "Several delegates . . . criticized the sermon. A Belgian editor, Jan Grootaers of the Belgian periodical *Die Maand*, said the Pope's sermon was 'far behind the congress.'"[23] The *New York Times* reported that this papal "warning appeared to be aimed at discouraging moves within the lay congress directed toward the establishment of a permanent lay organization."[24]

If the summoning of the three World Congresses for the Lay Apostolate and the creation of COPECIAL and the Council on the Laity were intended to bring the lay movement under more direct control of the hierarchy and especially of the Vatican, then it is understandable that Paul VI would stress the question of obedience. But it is also understandable that many of the lay leaders present at the 1967 congress were not prepared to be docile.

Newsweek's religion reporter Kenneth Woodward noticed the lack of docility: "Predictably, the Pope's statements drew negative reactions from most laymen. 'The Holy Father,' said one, 'missed a moment of history. He could have used this opportunity to indicate new ways to make the voice of the laity heard.'"[25] The Rome weekly *L'Espresso*, one of the best-informed sources on Vatican affairs, judged that Pope Paul was taking a halfway position between those curia prelates opposed to lay participation in Church affairs, and the lay participants who wanted a share of the decision-making. In line with this interpretation, it is even possible, as some participants speculated, that Cardinal Roy's controversial speech to the bishops on October 11 was just as much aimed at pacifying these conservative curialists as at curtailing the delegates' forays into the realm of ecclesiastical decision-making.

Some laymen were careful to distinguish, in congress discussions, between "decision-taking" acts, which they conceded should remain the prerogative of the bishops, and "decision-making," a process in which laymen should be permitted to participate. But despite this shrewd distinction, which recalls the difference between monarchical rule and parliamentary government in the English system of constitutional monarchy, the pope's message and Cardinal Roy's ill-fated attempt at control made it clear that the pope and the bishops were not enthusiastic about allowing the laity to share even minimally in Church power. They had no intentions of peaceably dwindling into the role of figureheads like the English royalty and House of Lords. Unable to solve the difficult problem of collegiality between themselves, the pope and the bishops were not eager to release any of their often crucial decision-making power to laymen. It was only many centuries after the granting of the "Magna Carta" that democracy with its similar distinction between "governing" and "ruling" dealt the death blow to monarchical regimes that had survived democratic revolutions. And the Roman Curia was even less inclined than the pope and the bishops to recognize this new force of the laity which was so difficult to control. Vatican radio and *L'Osservatore Romano*, for example, did some selective reporting of the congress, omitting most references to such problems as birth control and the redefinition of authority, and stressing instead the triumphalistic and gigantic aspects of the event. As usual, these Vatican media served as the front line of defense for the beleaguered central authority of the Church. Lay interference with clerical prerogatives was perhaps a matter best not mentioned, lest it further accentuate the crisis of confidence which was starting to develop in the post–Vatican II period of the pontificate of Paul VI. Like the *New York Times*, the *Osservatore Romano* can be said to publish "all the news that's fit to print," except that in the Vatican newspaper's case, the word "fit" applies only to news that coincides with the conservative views of the Roman Curia. As Cardinal Montini had said in 1961, the *Osservatore* reports what it thinks should have happened, rather than what has really happened.

Contrary to Pope Paul's call for a religious reconsecration of the secularized temporal order, Congar's speech, delivered by a fellow Dominican because of Congar's illness, stressed the importance of recognizing the autonomy of the temporal order, and the need not only for "welcoming events and seeing in them a call from God" but also the need to "challenge some of their aspects and to use in their regard what we may call the critical function of faith."[26] Congar not only encouraged lay involvement in politics, but also held it to be desirable that Christians should

> group themselves to mediate, not only in a Christian way but as Christians, on the principle of free association started from below, without a mandate of the hierarchy, whether on the purely religious level or on the temporal level, in general conformity to the rules of Catholic faith and discipline.[27]

In contrast to Paul VI's statement that the Church expected "substantial aid for the functioning of her institutions" from "a generous laity, faithful to its leaders and well organized,"[28] Congar spoke of the necessity that the Church have "information from the bottom, and structures for information and dialogue," and of the necessity for "cooperation of all the people of God, clergy and laity, pastors and faithful."[29] At the time his speech was written, Pope Paul's favorite theologian could not have known of the strict paternalism that would be expressed in the morning papal address. But to someone not aware that the text had been prepared and printed before Paul VI's address became public, it could seem indeed that Congar was offering a silent criticism of the latter, by not even mentioning lay obedience and deference to pope and hierarchy, which Paul VI considered to be the cornerstone of the lay apostolate.

The Sunday evening assembly of heads of delegations clearly set itself in opposition to the pope's hard line on lay subservience. It had already, the night before, approved in principle the text of a new memorandum to the Synod of Bishops in replacement of the official one prepared in advance by the Steering Committee. The final text adopted on Sunday night included a call to the bishops to accept a wider definition of the collegial sharing of authority in the Church. The memorandum stressed that many laymen wanted active participation in the elaboration of Church orientations and effective association with the responsibilities inherent in the Church's mission.

A key passage in this memorandum specified some of the "indispensable conditions" for lay participation, particularly that "Representative structures should be established at the different levels of the organization of the Church" and that "The laity will be elected to these structures."[30] This memorandum was one more indication that, in the orientation of Catholic international lay leaders, something fundamental had changed since the time of Pius XII. The era of the layman who is satisfied to pray and pay had definitely come to an end. Indeed, if these carefully screened laymen now wanted representative structures and elections, what would a more representative group have demanded?

7. THE LAY DEMANDS: FROM WOMEN'S LIBERATION TO DEMOCRATIZATION OF THE CHURCH

The demands and complaints of the lay delegates were not limited to questions of democratic participation in Church affairs. Other substantial issues were raised which were just as disturbing for the pope and his curia.

On Monday, October 16, the second series of eight workshops began, but the interest of the participants in this series was not so great as in the first. Now it was the resolution-making process that held their attention. A session for auditors entitled "The Laity in the Renewal of the Church," the theme of the second workshop series, and a symposium, "The Year of the Faith," were held in the main auditorium of Palazzo Pio that day, but these were prearranged affairs with speeches and without any audience participation.

Elsewhere, throughout the day, individuals and groups lobbied for strong motions against racism and against the war in Vietnam. The Polish philosopher Georges Kalinowski circulated an open letter urging Catholics in the United States to pressure their government to stop its military activities, especially the bombings, in Vietnam. *L'Avvenire d'Italia*, the liberal Catholic daily published in Bologna, reneged on a promise to Kalinowski to publish the letter, but it later appeared in the *National Catholic Reporter* and several European Catholic periodicals.[31]

The assembly of heads of delegations did not have time to vote on most of the resolutions that were presented to it. Thus the resolution against the Vietnam war was not voted on because of lack of time and not because of a failure to get the required sponsorship of five delegations, as Archbishop McGucken of San Francisco later alleged in a report on the congress to the National Conference of the Catholic Bishops in Washington, D.C.[32]

On Tuesday, the 17th, the main event was the fourth meeting of the assembly of heads of delegations. There were 24 draft resolutions before this assembly. At the first part of the meeting, during the afternoon, a resolution on the handicapped was adopted unanimously. Another, on the role of women in the Church, presented by St. Joan's

International Alliance (a Catholic women's group which was lobbying for the ordination of women, among other things) was adopted with some amendments. The amended resolution, instead of expressing the "desire that women be granted by the Church full rights and responsibilities as Christians, both as regards to laity and the priesthood," as the original motion had proposed, stated more mildly:

> The World Congress for the Lay Apostolate wishes to express its desire that women be granted by the Church full rights and responsibilities, and a serious doctrinal study be pursued on the place of women within the sacramental order and within the Church.[33]

A third resolution was passed condemning all forms of racial discrimination and urging all men and institutions to eradicate racism. The meeting adjourned for the ecumenical service at 6 P.M., but reconvened afterward for a session, the stormiest of the congress, which lasted from 9 P.M. until 2:15 A.M. This session began quite peacefully, with the quasi-unanimous acceptance of a resolution on the fight against oppression, which read as follows:

> The Third World Congress for the Lay Apostolate, meeting in Rome, basing itself on the Gospel, and on Christian tradition as expressed by Vatican II concerning the right of each man and of human groups to have and develop freely their own personality in a given society:
>
> noting that everywhere in today's world persons and groups are suffering oppression—in the political and economic sphere, as well as in the religious, social and cultural sphere;
>
> urgently calls to mind the Christian's duty to side with those who are oppressed, regardless of their race, ethnics, religion, ideology and social class;
>
> requests those Christians who through their geographic location are closest to the oppressed, to come to the assistance of their brothers; to participate actively in their efforts to achieve freedom from oppression; and to take part in any action that seems tò bring about their emancipation;
>
> requests those Christians who cannot directly influence the situation to give witness to their solidarity with those being oppressed, by giving them moral and material support, and by using their influence —whether through the U.N., or through governments, or through appropriate international bodies, whether non-governmental, Christian or non-Christian.[34]

This strong stand was followed by a unanimous resolution on peace and the world community, which spoke of the need for peace, justice, brotherhood, disarmament, unity, development, and respect for human rights.

The next resolution to be discussed and voted on was a long statement on development. One section of this resolution raised the question of birth control, and it was in the discussion of this section that the contest over the birth-control issue occurred.

When it became obvious that the resolution on the family, as well as numerous other resolutions, would never even be presented to the assembly of heads of delegations for lack of time, those wanting a strong stand on birth control put all their energy into the passage of the development resolution which contained the following clause on demographic expansion:

> In view of the agonizing problem of *demographic expansion*, they [the participants in the congress] recall:
> (1) the duties of states to have a policy that is realistic and respectful of man, in particular of responsible freedom of the couple, but that such a policy should not be an excuse for a delay in development, nor a substitute for efforts to realize it, and free from any geopolitical intervention of the great powers
> (2) the social duty of husband and wife towards responsible parenthood
> (3) the duty of Christians to participate in the efforts towards education
> (4) the very strong feeling among Christian lay people that there is need for a clear stand by the *teaching authorities of the Church* which would focus on fundamental moral and spiritual values, while leaving the choice of scientific and technical means for achieving responsible parenthood to parents acting in accordance with their Christian faith and on the basis of medical and scientific consultation.[35]

There was some opposition, especially from a few delegates from certain Middle East and Latin American countries. Shouting arguments ensued, and some catcalls and much applause were heard during the heated debate on this clause. A Lebanese representative branded the resolution a heresy and stormed out of the meeting. The text was approved shortly after midnight, with 67 in favor, 21 against, and 10 abstentions. The vote was barely sufficient to give the development resolution the two-thirds majority it needed to become an official position of the congress.

Two additional resolutions were passed in the early morning hours of this final session of the heads of delegations, but neither provoked a controversial vote. One, on "Social Communication Media and the

Press," protesting limitations to freedom of the press, passed unanimously. The last resolution, "Follow-up of the Congress," was a statement that had been approved in substance in the Sunday memorandum to the bishops, but was important for the aftermath of the congress. It stressed the need for more participation of laymen in decision making at all levels in the Church and asked for a more democratic approach to the selection of laymen for membership in an enlarged Council on the Laity. It passed with only one unfavorable vote. The resolution diplomatically thanked the pope for the creation of the Council on the Laity and then proposed:

> That this Congress respectfully request the Holy Father to enlarge the composition of the Council on the Laity in accordance with democratic processes so that it may become truly representative of the multiple cultures, organizations and forms of the Lay Apostolate in all parts of the world, taking into account a just geographical representation;
>
> that the enlarged Council on the Laity accelerate the democratic establishment of structures on the Laity at all levels across the world.[36]

This eighth and last resolution voted by the assembly of heads of delegations was published not only in volume 2 but also in volume 3 of the proceedings, where a special note from the COPECIAL secretariate was added. This note illustrates very well the difficult position of the lay curialists of the Council on the Laity, torn between the demands of the laity and the pressures from the conservatives in the Vatican:

> The "democratic" processes referred to here and elsewhere in this volume, especially in the reports of Workshops Nos. 4, 5 and 6, concern mainly the method of selecting lay people to work in the new pastoral structures which are being set up in the Church after the Council. As far as possible, it is hoped that these lay people will be elected by those they are to "represent."
>
> The concept of "democracy" invoked here will be better understood in the light of certain distinctions drawn by Vittorino Veronese in an address given to the Italian Bishops' Conference on February 19, 1968: "It is one thing to speak of democracy in the Church as a juridical system analogous to that of civil institutions—parliamentary and governmental—and another thing to speak of a democratic sense, that is, an open, loyal and direct manner in relations between the various members of God's People, Hierarchy, clergy and laity, based on the reciprocal responsibility consequent on the essential diversity of ministries and the corresponding charisms. Democracy as a struc-

ture and rule of law is not applicable to the Church, any more than aristocracy, oligarchy or anarchy are applicable to it . . ." When laymen, at the World Congress or in a particular country, ask to share, not in the responsibility of making decisions, which is reserved exclusively for the Hierarchy, but in the elaboration of decisions and the plans for carrying them into effect, they are not claiming an unjustified right, but wanting to fulfill a duty . . . to be available for consultation and for participation in pastoral care, that is, pastoral charity.[37]

A letter from Cardinal Maurice Roy to the assembly of heads of delegations expressed the interest of the Council on the Laity, over which he presided, in the discussions of the congress, especially in the congress's suggestions for the development of the Council on the Laity and for its future collaboration with various associations for the lay apostolate. The letter made no reference at all to the numerous suggestions made during the congress concerning democratization. This appeared to some participants to be a subtle (and unwarranted) pressure on the heads of delegations not to insist on this issue in the final draft of the resolution.

At the plenary session that met to summarize the second series of workshop discussions, democratization was once more a central question. At the plenary meeting, on Wednesday, the 18th, Workshop No. 5, on renewal of Church communities, recommended

> that everywhere co-responsible Councils be established at national, diocesan and parish levels: that each Council be truly representative of all the laity (men, women, and youth, coming from various movements, as well as non-organized Christians); that the lay members be freely elected by the laity. . . .[38]

Workshop No. 6, which was concerned with the "aggiornamento" of lay organizations, also made the following recommendation in its general report: "The organizations should be democratic in their structure and procedure."[39] In addition, one of the groups of Workshop No. 6 had voted the following resolutions on the structure of the Council on the Laity and on the necessity of a permanent Church synod:

> Resolved that the organizational structure of the Council on the Laity established by his Holiness, Pope Paul VI, be changed so as to create a body truly representative of the laity, and at least two thirds of its members be freely elected by the laity. . . .
>
> It is our desire that a Synod of the Church be created as soon as possible and that this be the body to help the Holy Father in the

government of the Church, and that it consist of representatives of the Hierarchy, priests, religious and laymen.[40]

When we consider the far-reaching implications that such changes would bring about in the organizational structure of the Catholic Church, it is not surprising that the COPECIAL secretariate repeatedly found it necessary to relativize the scope of the workshop conclusions:

> Is it necessary to stress again, as we did in presenting the previous volumes, that the reports from the Workshops, which we publish here as we received them, are not meant to be "a doctrinal treasure to be kept intact," but at the most "a provisional synthesis, subject to all kinds of amendments and corrections"?[41]

The issue of the democratization of the Church and the problem of birth control were the considerations that turned the congress into a significant event. According to James O'Gara:

> Every time any speaker urged reform in either area [democratization in the Church and birth control], the applause was immediate and thunderous. On these two points at least, majority sentiment clearly seemed to fall on the side of change.[42]

In his book on the Church, the progressive biblical scholar John K. McKenzie wrote:

> In October 1967, the world synod of lay delegates convened at Rome at the invitation of the Pope surprised the world and frightened the Pope by calling for an early declaration relaxing the rigid teaching of the Roman Church on contraception. This was an instance of how lay councils can be vehicles of a lay consensus, and it happened a remarkably short time after the Second Vatican Council.[43]

All clerical reactions, however, were not as unreservedly sympathetic as that of Jesuit McKenzie.

8. HIERARCHICAL AND PAPAL REACTIONS AND THE UNRESOLVED CRISIS

At the concelebrated mass which preceded the plenary session of Wednesday, October 18, Cardinal Valerian Gracias, archbishop of Bombay, indicated in a subtle manner that, at least in his opinion, the delegates had gone a little too far. After noting the growing role of the laity in the affairs of the Church which the congress had manifested, he said: "That was the purpose of all these deliberations in which you have participated—expressing yourself freely and wisely, and at times unwisely—fully convinced that our faith is not static but has to be dynamic."[44]

Cardinal Roy was noticeably displeased by the congress's stand favorable to birth control. In yet another more or less shrewd curialist move, he tried to minimize the damage which his earlier guidelines to bishops had, unsuccessfully, tried to prevent. Here is the text of a note which he had the COPECIAL staff print at the end of the section on birth control of the resolution on development, in the proceedings of the congress as well as in the COPECIAL bulletin:

> In *L'Osservatore Romano* of October 20th, 1967, H.E. Cardinal Roy, president of the Ecclesiastical Commission of the Congress, pointed out, with regard to point II D of Resolution IV, on Development, in relation to "responsible parenthood," that the text is a factual statement of the feeling expressed by Christian lay people, who look with confidence to the Church's teaching authority.
>
> As regards in particular the words, "leaving the choice of scientific and technical means . . . to parents acting in accordance with their Christian faith," these are obviously to be interpreted in the sense clearly indicated by the Second Vatican Council, in Nos. 50/B and 51/C of the Constitution Gaudium et Spes, i.e. "Christian faith enlightened by the Church's magisterium."[45]

It is not so obvious that the lay delegates at the congress meant "Christian faith" in this issue to be "Christian faith enlightened by the Church's magisterium." It is more likely that they meant "Christian faith enlightened by conscience." Conscience was the word used in the birth-control resolution that, for lack of time, did not get to the vote; this resolution did not manifest any special confidence in the magisterium of the Church. The resolution asked "that the choice of the means to prevent a new conception be left to the conscience of the married couple with due consideration of medical, psychological, economic, and sociological insights."[46] The omission of "theological insights" from this list, and especially the omission of any reference to the magisterium of the Church, would lead one to conclude that in the case of conflict between the dictates of the magisterium and an individual conscience, the voice of conscience was meant to prevail. This is confirmed by the fact that the resolution on development, which was actually approved, expressly asked the magisterium to "focus on fundamental moral and spiritual values" and to leave the choice of technical means to parents.

After the congress, the Dutch and American delegations protested publicly against Cardinal Roy's interpretation. They said the meeting had indeed called for a change in the Church's stand on birth control.[47] The data from our survey, presented in the next chapter, also clearly contradict Cardinal Roy's interpretation. The lay leaders were not in agreement with the position hitherto set forth by the Vatican, and were politely but firmly requesting that this traditional position be liberalized.

At the closing session, Vittorino Veronese read a short telegram sent to him as first president of the congress by Cardinal Amletto Cicognani in the name of the pope. The telegram, by focusing on the pope's satisfaction, not with the congress and its conclusions, but with the filial telegram sent by the laity and with the "happy development of lay apostolate attested by the large number of participants," seemed to indicate that the pope was not pleased with the congress. This was confirmed when, on December 23, in his address to the college of cardinals, Paul VI hinted at what it was that had not pleased him about the congress:

> Among the events of the last six months which concern the Church's internal life and activity, The Third World Congress for the Lay Apostolate—held in Rome from 11 to 18 October last—has an outstanding place, for the subjects dealt with, for the number and quality of its participants and for its future consequences and its repercussion throughout the world.
>
> Many things were said at this meeting, and much has been written about it, and very well written, even if everything cannot be given unreserved approval and agreement. . . .
>
> We should like all these sons and daughters . . . to keep engraven in their hearts one impression: the Pope's love for them, the trust he places in them, and the invitation he addresses to them to work always in loyal harmony with the Church's magisterium and with the Hierarchy, whose only desire is to see them carrying out the tasks assigned to them by the recent Council.[48]

In February 1968 the members of the Vatican-appointed Council on the Laity met and, evidently influenced by the congress resolutions and by the memorandum to the Synod of Bishops, recommended to Paul VI that he expand the Council on the Laity membership to give better representation to various social and geographical sectors of the laity. They did not, however, make any mention of democratic processes in the selection of these new members. They knew Paul VI was firmly opposed.

In a general audience, Pope Paul replied by speaking strongly of the importance of the organized lay apostolate, in particular of Catholic Action. He then launched an attack on lay movements that lack close relations with the hierarchy and that speak out too critically of the Church. This public speech had been preceded and was followed by the blossoming of numerous Catholic protest groups throughout the world.[49]

These bitter remarks, coupled with the pope's June 1968 encyclical on birth control, substantiated what many observers had noted since the end of Vatican II: that the Roman leadership of the Catholic Church had really not changed very much. Now it had stopped its ears to the plain speaking of the lay movement. But in the laity, change was irresistibly under way. The third World Congress for the Lay Apostolate showed that even lay leaders largely selected by Church authorities and under pressure by pope and curia were ready to make, in 1967, strong demands for increased responsibility and participation in Church affairs.

Squeezed between the intransigeance of his curia and the increasing disintegration of mass support for his views, unable to cope with the new situation with perspectives different from the limited ones developed as a liberal intellectual influenced by the Neo-Scholastic clericalism of Jacques Maritain, Charles Journet, and Jean Guitton, Pope Paul evidently decided to give in to some of the curia's demands. When he and his entourage realized that the changes brought about by Pope John's opening of windows were not going to stop after Vatican II, they reverted to time-tested control techniques, many of the same ones used against Montini and his friends by the Roman Curia and Pius XII in the fifties.

The unsuccessful efforts to keep the lid on the lay congress of 1967 and to minimize its effects afterward were the first of a series of events which were to transform the pontificate of Paul VI from a continuation of Pope John's into something like a restoration of Pius XII's. Henri Fesquet, religious editor of *Le Monde*, wrote after the congress:

> The government of the Church will undoubtedly take some time to consider in their true light the positive elements of this congress. Certain members of the Roman Curia will surely be tempted, according to their old tactic, to completely ignore and deprecate it.[50]

What Fesquet and others did not seem to understand, at least immediately after the congress, was that not only a few members of the curia were disturbed by the rebelliousness of the congress, but the pope himself and even liberal elements of the hierarchy, such as Cardinal Roy. It might take much longer than Fesquet anticipated for the government of the Church to see that 1967 meeting in a more positive light. So far, no fourth World Congress for the Lay Apostolate has been proposed.

Another lay congress may have to give way to a revised form of international meeting, a synod where "safe" laity and priests will be admitted to participate with the bishops. Something of this sort might have been initiated when, during October 1967, a group of the lay delegates to the congress were invited and did attend one of the meetings of the concurrent Synod of Bishops.

But even a joint laity-bishop meeting seems remote in view of the bishops' expressed displeasure with the 1967 congress's demands for representative and democratic lay structures. It must be kept in mind that the bishops, too, admonished the laity, reminding them that "it is up to the Hierarchy—as the conciliar decree *Apostolicam Actuositatem* tells us—to promote the apostolate of the laity, provide it with spiritual principles and support, direct the exercise of this apostolate to the common good of the Church, and attend to the preservation of doctrine and order."[51]

The conservatism manifested by the hierarchy and by the first Synod of Bishops contrasts with the defiant mood of the lay delegates to the Third World Congress for the Lay Apostolate:

> The real caution of the bishops of the Synod was shown by the contrast with the nearly 3,000 Catholic laymen who attended the concurrent World Congress on the Lay Apostolate. Original predictions that they were a tame group of "official laymen" who would not challenge the status quo were rudely shattered from the beginning. Their main preoccupations were self-determination, democracy in the Church and a social and ecumenical Christianity. (There were as many non-Catholics on their program as there were Catholics.) They caused the most stir with a resolution asking that the decision on birth control be left to individual parents, but their requests for an elected body to represent them in Rome is potentially as subversive. It is worth noting that their resolution on birth control published but not adopted for lack of time, goes farther than the action of the bishops.
>
> All this was a bit much for Roman ways and the pope took the occasion of a mass to warn them against neglecting guidance of the

hierarchy. The effect of the warning was largely to cause annoyance among its hearers. The mood of the laity seemed to be that it will accept leadership but not mere attempts to force them into obedience.[52]

The rigidity of the pope and of the hierarchy did not augur well for the future of the democratic participation of laymen in the decision-making processes in the Church during the remainder of the pontificate of Paul VI. It remains to be seen whether John Paul II will reverse Paul VI's policies in this area.

The hope expressed by Dr. Hans-Ruedi Weber, journalist and ecumenicist, however, still seems far from becoming reality. The only non-Catholic present at the 1957 World Congress for the Lay Apostolate, Dr. Weber was one of nearly a hundred Protestant and Orthodox observer-consultants in 1967. He said:

> Has the time for *Catholic lay* Congresses not passed? Must we in the future not have congresses of the whole people of God, composed of Catholics, orthodox and Protestants, the laity and what you call the ministerial priesthood?[53]

It is impossible to predict whether such a type of congress will ever come to pass. But it is possible to understand what happened at the 1967 congress and before, and why. If it is true that this third World Congress for the Lay Apostolate "revealed the power of lay contestation in the Church," and that this lay contestation "represents in its own way an aspect of dialogue between the laity and the hierarchy,"[54] then one of the best ways to understand this "dialogue" (or more precisely this lay challenge to papal and to hierarchical authority and control), is to take a good look at who these laymen were and what they thought and wanted. To these concerns the following chapter will be devoted.

V

The Lay National Delegates: A Sociological Survey

The preceding chapter has told in some detail how the delegates to the third World Congress for the Lay Apostolate advanced certain demands for change and reform in the Catholic Church. These demands, which were addressed to the Vatican and to the hierarchy, were concerned in particular with the problems of democratization of ecclesiastical structures and modification of various official moral and religious norms considered to be in conflict with current practices and values. That chapter also described how Vatican authorities and congress organizers reacted to these lay pressures. The present chapter pursues the analysis of that congress, with the help of empirical materials obtained in a survey of the lay national delegates. Here, then, I characterize the participants to the congress in some measure, and try to assess up to what point they were willing to accept the authority of the pope and other Church officials.

From the preceding chapter, one will have obtained a general idea of the opinions of the lay delegates on various subjects. One will have obtained also some notion of the social, political, and religious characteristics of the lay leaders who were chosen as delegates to the congress, but all this was quite impressionistic, based on participant observation by journalists and other people present, including myself.

Here the delegates are considered in a somewhat more systematic manner. After a brief description of the methodology used in my questionnaire survey, and of the major social, political, and religious characteristics of the lay national delegates, I examine the opinions of these people on Church authority. Then a brief report of these same characteristics and opinions is presented, separating the delegates by the geographic-cultural regions they represented, and by age.

1. METHODOLOGY

The participants, both lay and clerical, in the third World Congress for the Lay Apostolate were divided into five general categories by the organizers of the event. The *international delegates* were all representatives of international organizations, most of which were affiliated with the Conference of Catholic International Organizations, and they tended to voice the official positions of their associations. The *experts*, *observers*, and *auditors* were not really full-fledged participants in the congress. All those grouped in these four categories constituted barely a half of the participants. It was the delegates of the fifth category, the *national delegates*, who constituted the other half of the participants. These people did not come as representatives of specific organizations as such (although most of them were prominent activists in lay organizations in their country), but as representatives of the lay apostolate of their countries as a whole. It was fairly easy to see where the officers of JOC–International, Pax Romana, St. Joan's International Alliance, or the progressive sociologists from FERES (Fédération Internationale des Instituts de Recherches Socio-Religieuses) would stand on various questions, because these international organizations have a history of official involvement in all sorts of issues; but it was nearly impossible to know what kind of people had been selected as national delegates simply by looking at their organizational affiliations. For these reasons, I decided to limit my study to the national delegates. Consequently, a questionnaire was drawn up and administered to them in order to discover who they were and what were their major orientations toward ecclesiastical authorities and toward various aspects of the ongoing discussion concerning Church reforms and social change.[1]

Since the four official languages were English, French, Spanish, and German, the final version of the questionnaire was constructed simultaneously in French and English, and then translated into Spanish and German by sociologists whose native languages these were. It was distributed to a random sample of 25 percent of the lay national delegates present at the third World Congress for the Lay Apostolate. The national delegates totaled around 1,400. After excluding bishops, priests, and nuns, there were about 1,200 lay national delegates.

The sampling method used was that which Leslie Kish calls "systematic selection," a variant of stratified random sampling.[2] The sample was drawn from the official list of national delegates, on which the names had been grouped by continent and by country. I chose every fourth lay person on the list, beginning with the name corresponding to a randomly chosen number between one and four. This gave me a sample which was representative of the lay national delegates, and at the same time it gave me a sample in which countries and continents were represented in a manner proportional to the number of national lay delegates that they had at the congress.

Delegations were too small to make possible an analysis by country, but I was able to regroup the various countries in a certain number of geocultural categories permitting me to make international regional comparisons. The sample contained 293 names. I distributed the questionnaire to 290 of these individuals, either directly or with the help of the heads of delegations. A total of 212 usable questionnaires was collected in boxes placed in the lobby of Palazzo Pio, or by mail afterward. This constitutes a return rate of 73 percent, a percentage generally considered quite high for a questionnaire distributed at a congress or convention.

2. SOCIAL AND POLITICAL BACKGROUND AND ORIENTATIONS OF THE LAY NATIONAL DELEGATES

A sociopolitical and religious profile of the sample will give us a good idea of the kinds of persons selected to come to the congress as lay national delegates. There were 103 countries sending national delegations to the congress, but many of these delegations had only a few lay members. The 212 persons who answered the questionnaire came from 76 of these countries. Grouping of these 76 countries in six major geocultural categories gives the following distribution of delegates: Africans, 11 percent; Latin Americans, 19 percent; Asians, 11 percent; English-speaking (outside Africa and Asia), 18 percent; Western Europeans (British Isles excluded), 26 percent; and Eastern and Southern Europeans, 15 percent. By race 76 percent were white, 10 percent were black, 8 percent were Oriental, and 6 percent were of mixed racial background. Only 3 percent of the lay national delegates studied were manual workers; 9 percent were sales or clerical workers, while 22 percent were managers or proprietors, and the majority (51 percent) were in the professions. Most were of urban origin: only 21 percent had lived on a farm or in a village of fewer than 2,500 inhabitants during their childhood.

Most ranked well above average in education, and a little above average in income. Only 26 percent earned less than $3,000 (U.S.) a year; 28 percent earned between $3,000 and $6,000; 19 percent, $6,000 to $9,000; 9 percent $9,000 to $12,000; and 14 percent more than $12,000. By 1967 international standards, this is not very low. In answer to a question asking how they would describe their personal wealth in comparison with the population of their respective countries, 23 percent said "rich," 62 percent said "about average," and only 15 percent said "below average." Only 23 percent did not finish the twelfth grade in school, whereas 42 percent had between thirteen and sixteen years of schooling, and as many as 34 percent had gone to school for more than sixteen years. Along with these, other indications of a high level of education were the fact that 56 percent said they considered themselves to be intellectuals, and that 50 percent said they read more than ten books a year.

There were more men than women at the congress. In the sample 59 percent were males, as opposed to 41 percent females. In age distribution, 35 percent were under thirty-five years of age, 25 percent were over fifty, and the rest, 39 percent, were between thirty-five and fifty. Finally, 56 percent were married, 40 percent were single, and 4 percent were widowers. There were no divorcees, and only one person was separated from his spouse.

In order to determine political orientation, the delegates were asked how they would vote if they were living in Italy. The Italian political spectrum is a very wide one, extending from the far right to the far left and comprising most possible intermediate options. It was hoped that by this technique, I could compare delegates from countries with very different political systems. Unfortunately, but not surprisingly, exactly half of the delegates in the sample said they did not know enough about Italian politics to reply. As for the other half, 4 percent left the question blank; 4 percent said Communist or Socialist; 6 percent, Social Democrat; 34 percent, Christian Democrat; and 1 percent, Liberal or Republican; none said Monarchist or neo-Fascist. This is quite a high proportion of people leaning toward a Christian Democratic option. Chapters 2–4 on the historical and political and economic backgrounds of the international lay movement help us understand the reason for the high percentage of Christian Democratic sympathizers. The selection process obviously operated here. Since the Christian Democratic Party in Italy can include political options ranging from extreme right to moderate left, the large proportion of delegates choosing that alternative does not yield much information about the respondents' leanings on socioeconomic and secular political issues, but it does indicate what kind of Catholics were selected. Other questions helped make the political picture a little clearer.

Asked how they would characterize themselves on a general political spectrum, the majority of the sample considered themselves to be centrists and moderates. Percentages were as follows: 2 percent said they were very conservative; 22 percent, moderately conservative; 33 percent, moderately liberal; 15 percent, highly liberal; and another 15 percent, left or radical. Since it is always hard to pinpoint concretely what these categories refer to, especially when self-evaluation is used by an international group of people, a few specific political questions were asked. Replies to these questions showed a three-way (conservative–liberal–radical) split among the delegates, a split where the liberal center nevertheless covered most of the political terrain. This was visible also in the answers to a question as to whom they would like to see elected as president of the United States in 1968: 58 percent indicated Robert F. Kennedy, and only 7 percent indicated Richard Nixon. Martin Luther King and other left candidates received a total of 9 percent; President Lyndon B. Johnson, 4 percent; Governor Nelson Rockefeller, 2 percent; and Governors Ronald Reagan and George Romney each, 0.5 percent. Another indication of the respondent's moderate liberal political opinions came from answers to a question on the American intervention in Vietnam: 11 percent favored escalating the war and increasing the war effort; 61 percent a stop to the bombing followed by negotiations; 9 percent, gradual withdrawal of American troops; and 12 percent, an immediate and unconditional withdrawal. This liberal tendency was further revealed in replies to other political questions: 26 percent favored (72 percent opposed)[3] suppression by the Church of all military chaplaincies, to indicate opposition to war; 74 percent favored (23 percent opposed) immediate admittance of Red China into the United Nations; 69 percent favored (30 percent opposed) the development of the United Nations into a world government; and 84 percent said they would (13 percent said they would not) like to see individual countries give up some power so that the United Nations could do a better job.

Communism did not seem to represent as serious a threat to this sample of Catholic lay people as one might have imagined. Sixty-two percent indicated it would be all right for a Catholic to cooperate with a Communist in a common political action (37 percent said it would not). As many as 75 percent of the respondents agreed (23 percent disagreed) with the statement that it is possible to be a good Catholic and a Socialist at the same time. Asked if they concurred with the statement that there was no room in the Church for people who believe in communism, 32 percent said yes and 66 percent said no. Furthermore, 18 percent would (81 percent would not) like to see books written by Communists excluded from public libraries. Finally, in response to questions about Cuba, 43 percent of the delegates agreed to a statement that actions of the United States toward Cuba were comparable to those of a colonial power trying to suppress movements of national liberation within its colonies, and 4 percent favored an American invasion of Cuba, while 93 percent opposed it.

On racial issues, 21 percent said they believed (77 percent said they did not believe) that white people in the United States have a right to live in an all-white neighborhood if they want to, and that blacks should respect that right. And only 11 percent were opposed to the taking of public stands by the Church in favor of racial integration. Acceptance of immigration quotas can be viewed as an index of a conservative racial bias. Yet 67 percent of the delegates indicated that they agreed that immigration quotas are immoral and that anyone should be able to immigrate freely into another country (31 percent disagreed).

Opposition to taxes on the rich to be redistributed in social benefits to the poor is generally considered to be another good index of conservatism. When asked if their country should have higher taxes for richer people to provide low-rent public housing to low-income families, only 7 percent definitely disagreed, another 11 percent disagreed somewhat, 34 percent agreed somewhat, and 45 percent agreed definitely.

Another issue which generally gives a good clue to a person's or group's political orientation is the question of capital punishment. Conservatives are usually more favorable to the death penalty. In our sample, 53 percent definitely agreed that "capital punishment (i.e. the death penalty) should be abolished," 18 percent agreed somewhat, 15 percent disagreed somewhat, and 13 percent disagreed definitely. The relatively high proportion of people who do not have a strong opinion on this, and especially on many of the other issues just examined, in spite of the fact that these are issues on which people generally have strong and definite opinions, again points to the fact that the lay national delegates tended to be people of moderate opinions, liberals and centrists rather than determined leftists or rightists.

One last general question should be mentioned. The delegate sample was asked to agree or disagree with the idea that the way to make needed changes in society was through gradual evolution and not by radical reform. As expected, the great majority agreed (definitely, 35 percent; somewhat, 38 percent), but 18 percent disagreed somewhat and 8 percent disagreed definitely. These responses further point to the tentative conclusion that the national delegates were mostly political middle-of-the-roaders, leaning toward liberalism more than toward conservatism or radicalism, even if there were also small hard-core groups at each end of the political spectrum.

3. RELIGIOUS INVOLVEMENT OF THE DELEGATES

Not surprisingly, most of the national lay delegates questioned were highly involved in Catholic organizational life. Of the sample, 67 percent were already interested and active in organized lay apostolate programs during their adolescence and early adult years. At the time of the survey, 66 percent were working or had worked, at least in a part-time capacity, for some Catholic organization.

Fifty-three percent indicated they attended at least two weekly meetings of Catholic groups, exclusive of mass, whereas only 28 percent said they attended that many nonreligious meetings each week. Some 70 percent said that half or more of the organizations in which they were active were Catholic, and 77 percent said that half or more of the time they spent in the close company of people outside their family (for work, leisure, business, meetings, etc.) was spent with fellow Catholics. The two best friends of 86 percent of these delegates were Catholics like themselves, and 49 percent said that half or more of the periodicals and newspapers they read were Catholic. Thirty-six percent had a relative who was a priest, 88 percent said they were on very good terms with members of the clergy, and 11 percent said they themselves were former seminarians or novices.

Since the sample was composed of national delegates to the congress, it was to be expected that their interests and concerns in religious affairs would be centered on organizations at the national level. Only 9 percent did not report involvement in national organizations;

these reported organizational connections at the local (i.e. parochial and diocesan) level (2 percent), the international level (5 percent), or a combination of local and international levels (2 percent). Of the 91 percent reporting some national-level organizational activity, the majority (52 percent of the whole sample) mentioned all three organizational levels (local, national, and international), 12 percent of the whole sample mentioned local and national levels, 19 percent national and international levels, and the rest the national level only.

The picture presented by the national lay delegates is, therefore, one of intense participation in religious organizations, particularly at the national level, as well as great involvement with other Catholics in their personal lives.

As far as their ritual participation is concerned, only 6 percent did not go to mass every Sunday, and 61 percent went at least twice a week. And if the obligation to go to Sunday mass were to be suppressed (37 percent were in favor of such a change in Church laws) 85 percent would still continue to go to weekly mass. Seventy-eight percent received communion every week, 80 percent went to confession at least every two to three months (they reported a slight tendency to go less often since Vatican II), 59 percent recited grace at least once a day and 85 percent prayed in private at least once a week. Nevertheless, 59 percent said that a person who does not go to church can still be a good Christian. Only 4 percent participated "often" in unofficial house masses where the liturgy is not celebrated according to canonical rules. Six percent had done so quite a few times, 8 percent a couple of times, and 4 percent once. Of the 76 percent who reported never having participated in such liturgies, some (33 percent) said they would like to if they had a chance, and the others (43 percent) were opposed to doing it.

It is interesting to note that as many as 19 percent of the survey sample had at least one non-Catholic parent, that 14 percent did not receive Catholic baptism as infants and were converted and baptized during their youth or adult life, and that 24 percent never attended Catholic schools. In answer to a question about the financing of parochial schools, 23 percent did not want these institutions to be supported by public taxes. Moreover, 17 percent thought that, in their own countries, the Catholic Church should not try to maintain Catholic schools at any level. Only 21 percent gave 10 percent or more of their income to the Church, although 42 percent thought that this should be required as an obligation of all Catholics.

Another dimension measured was religious knowledge. We asked four questions in an effort to assess the delegate sample's biblical knowledge. Fewer than half (48 percent) of the national delegates knew that the Book of Acts is not an eyewitness account of Jesus' ministry. On the other hand, 69 percent were able to write down the names of at least seven of the authors of the Gospels and Epistles, and 68 percent were able to pick out of the names of the three Old Testament prophets from a list of six names that also included Paul, Deuteronomy, and Leviticus. Finally, 38 percent succeeded in giving the names and the authors of four important social encyclicals written by popes during the last hundred years. Such knowledge of religious facts is well above average for Catholic laymen, but it is still less than what one might expect from laymen who are so highly involved in various religious activities.

One of the most important aspects of a person's religious life is that person's faith: the beliefs and opinions about sacred entities and affirmations. While many of the questions, as noted above, sought to tap the opinions of the delegates on various nonreligious topics, they were also asked certain questions about traditional Christian beliefs. Many of the questions were the same ones that Glock and Stark used in their San Francisco Bay Area survey and subsequent national survey.[4] When asked if they really knew that God exists and had no doubts about it, 77 percent said yes, a smaller percentage than the 81 percent that Glock and Stark obtained in 1963 for Bay Area Catholics[5] and the 85 percent they obtained a year later nationally.[6] On a question about the divinity of Jesus, 79 percent of the national delegates sample agreed with the statement that "Jesus is the Divine Son of God and I have no doubts about it," whereas in Glock and Stark's Bay Area sample 86 percent agreed.[7] Thus it appears that there were fewer believers at the Rome Congress for the Lay Apostolate than among the rank-and-file Bay Area laymen. This was not quite the case, however, because those who indicated that they fundamentally believed in the existence of God and the divinity of Jesus but sometimes experienced doubts were more numerous among the lay national delegates' group (15 percent for God and 14 percent for Jesus) than in Glock and Stark's Bay Area sample (13 percent for God and 8 percent for Jesus). Thus, if we add the firm believers to the occasional doubters, the total number of believers in both surveys is approximately the same (94 percent for belief in the divinity of Jesus for both samples, and 92 percent for lay delegates and 93 percent for Bay Area Catholics for belief in God).

For a large proportion of lay national delegates, questions of belief, as opposed to other aspects of religious behavior, were not considered to be the central core of their Christian involvement. As many as 88 percent agreed with a statement that the best mark of a person's religiousness was the degree of that person's concern for others, and 38 percent agreed with a stronger statement that what a man believes about God doesn't matter a great deal as long as he leads a life of concern for others. This doesn't mean, however, that concern for others was the only other aspect of religiousness which they considered to be essential: 60 percent indicated they thought God to be as concerned with submission to authority as with the way one treats his fellow man.

4. OPINIONS OF THE DELEGATES ON CHURCH AUTHORITY AND POWER

When asked to respond to questions about their opinions on Church authority, the lay national delegates to the Rome congress displayed markedly less unanimity than they had shown on questions of faith. The lay national delegates' responses to this group of questions suggested that their firm institutional, ritual, and ideological links with the Church (described in the preceding section) did not necessarily lead them to adhere to the traditional currents of Catholic thought on the issues of Church authority. Questions on these issues showed the lay national delegates to be liberals rather than conservatives or radicals, but showed also that they had a definite leaning toward change rather than toward stability. On this point the lay national delegates manifested a critical stance which it would have been difficult to predict from the nature of the selection process that brought them to Rome for the congress, and from their answers to some of the questions analyzed in the preceding section.

When asked if they agreed with a statement that permanence and stability, rather than change, must be aimed at in the work of the Church, only 32 percent agreed, while 65 percent disagreed. Nearly all of them (96 percent) agreed that "criticism is necessary in the Church." And many were indeed ready to make criticisms: for example, 74 percent agreed (and 24 percent disagreed) that "the Catholic Church relies too often, in its everyday operations, on authoritarian and secret procedures." While 51 percent agreed that "the use of censorship (like imprimaturs) is an acceptable way for the Church to fulfill its teaching mission," 47 percent registered a lack of agreement with that statement. More than half agreed that the use of honorific titles such as Excellency, Holiness, and Eminence should be abolished (36 percent disagreed), and only 38 percent said that the reform of the Roman Curia was proceeding at a satisfactory pace (58 percent disagreed). As many as 20 percent of the lay national delegates felt that "the Church as an institution is corrupt and should be radically transformed," while 79 percent did not think so. This was not much lower than the percentage (23 percent) who felt that the Catholic Church was not playing an important role in the world on questions involving international social justice, world peace, and the development of peoples (77 percent thought it was an unimportant role). When asked who their favorite theologian was, 25 percent spontaneously mentioned progressive theologians Yves Congar or Karl Rahner, men who had been in trouble with the Roman Curia in the fifties; most other names mentioned were also well-known progressives, and very few mentioned conservative figures. When asked to indicate their favorite pope, from Pius IX to Paul VI, 61 percent marked John XXIII. Most of the others indicated a preference for Paul VI (17 percent), or for Pius XII (12 percent); none chose Pius XI or Benedict XV, 1 percent chose Pius IX, 2 percent chose Saint Pius X, and 1 percent chose Leo XIII.

The Netherlands, France, and Germany, in that order, were the three countries where the Catholic Church was most often considered to be in an ideal situation (by 19 percent, 15 percent, and 12 percent of the delegates, respectively). The fact that these three countries, where Catholicism is generally considered to be most progressive, and the challenge to Vatican authority greatest, were chosen over all others seems to indicate, like the preceding questions about theologians and popes, that the national delegates tended to lean toward a reformist rather than an integralist position on the issue of Church authority. This was confirmed by the fact that the delegates' favorite Catholic periodical was the progressive French fortnightly published by Catholic laymen, *Informations Catholiques Internationales*.

Concerning Vatican II, only 2 percent had negative feelings toward it, 1 percent because it was too revolutionary and the other 1 percent because it was not revolutionary enough. Another 1 percent had positive feelings toward Vatican II because it did not make changes that were too revolutionary. But the immense majority (97 percent) were positive toward Vatican II for reasons related to change and progress: 42 percent indicated that the council was "a great renewal" and 55 percent that it was "a step in the right direction."

Concerning another of Pope John's major goals besides Vatican II, the reform of canon law, 2 percent said canon law should remain as it is, 4 percent said it should be eliminated completely rather than re-formed, and 3 percent did not answer the question. The others (91 percent) felt it should be reformed, 40 percent saying it should be adapted and updated, and 51 percent agreeing that it should be revamped and simplified, with room left for future innovations.

Only 37 percent agreed that "the strengthening and consolidation of members' loyalties to the Church is much more important than adapting and opening the Church to the modern world" (60 percent disagreed). On the other hand, 71 percent agreed that "Catholics should obey all the prescriptions and rules of the Church" (28 percent disagreed). These two questions again show the somewhat ambivalent nature of the group of lay national delegates. They seemed to be attached to the Church, but were definitely inclined to press for changes and reforms in the ways in which authority is exercised. They wanted acceptable leaders whom they could obey.

Two questions in the survey permitted one to get a rather clear picture of the lay national delegates' opinion on the controversial issue of birth control: 61 percent agreed (and 35 percent disagreed) with a statement saying that birth-control pills should be considered by Church authorities as an acceptable way of regulating the size of a family, and approximately the same number (62 percent) were positive toward the statement that good sex education in high school should include knowledge of methods of birth control. These responses on birth control seem to undercut the interpretation given by Cardinal Maurice Roy in *L'Osservatore Romano* of November 20, 1967, concerning the state of mind of the delegates, as discussed in chapter 4. A majority seemed to desire a change in the traditional birth-control position of Church officials although this majority was not overwhelming.

In general, then, the delegates' attitudes toward Church authority show that the delegates were neither reactionaries nor revolutionaries; they accepted the necessity of obedience, but wanted officials to be less rigid. They tended to fall on the liberal rather than the conservative side of the religious spectrum.

There were other indications that pressure for change among this group of lay leaders was moderately high. In an area where Church officials were often criticized, such as questions of their power and their wealth, the moderately liberal and slightly critical perspective of the lay national delegates was also evident. Forty-three percent of them agreed (and 55 percent disagreed) with a statement that the Catholic Church in their own countries spent too much money on building schools and churches, and not enough on helping the poor. And 47 percent agreed (50 percent disagreed) that religious institutions should not get tax exemptions for financial investments (as is the case in some countries). Finally, 34 percent agreed (and 59 percent disagreed) with a statement affirming that "the Catholic Church is allied to financial powers," and 64 percent would (35 percent would not) have the Vatican publish periodical reports on its finances (investments, expenses, income, etc.).

On the question of political power, 40 percent would (and 59 percent would not) have the Church divest itself of the remnants of its temporal political power (i.e. the Vatican State, nunciatures, etc.). Concerning the separation of church and state, 85 percent indicated that church and state should be separate and independent as institutions (12 percent disagreed). Furthermore, 52 percent responded negatively to a statement on the usefulness of Christian trade unions and Christian political parties for the Church's mission (45 percent responded positively). A similar number, 54 percent, considered that sufficient reasons were lacking for the Church to maintain separate Catholic institutions in nonreligious spheres such as education, trade-unionism, social services, and party politics (43 percent disagreed).

This does not mean, however, that the delegates believed that Christians should not be preoccupied with social and political issues. When asked if churches should stick to religion and not concern themselves with social, economic, and political issues, only 16 percent agreed and 85 percent disagreed. The wording of the question may have elevated that last percentage. Still, it is evidently not involvement in worldly affairs by Christians or even by the Church as such which was faulted; it was separate Catholic organizations with a narrow denominational focus that the majority of the sample would not subscribe to. This was confirmed by the similar responses to a question which asked if respondents agreed or not with a statement that the Church should keep out of political matters, not expressing its views on day-to-day social and political activities.

Thus, it is evidently important, in determining the respondents' attitudes, to specify the kind of political involvement they might approve or disapprove. It seems that the delegates rejected conservative denominational interference in temporal matters rather than ethical involvement by Christians in social and political affairs. If as many as 76 percent (versus 23 percent) disagreed with Camillo Torres, the Colombian guerrilla priest, that "every Christian who is not a revolutionary is in a state of mortal sin," it is perhaps as much because they disagreed with the concept of "mortal sin" as because they were opposed to revolutionary political involvement! This is further indicated by the 90 percent (versus 9 percent) who asserted that Catholic organizations should be active in peace movements. And to ward off any impression that most of the national delegates favored some new form of clericalism, albeit of a liberal or radical type, suffice it to mention that 62 percent (versus 32 percent) considered that the movement toward secularization of modern society should be encouraged rather than opposed by Christians, and 81 percent that the Catholic Church should do much more than at present to encourage and promote scientific research (17 percent disagreed).

5. OPINIONS ABOUT EPISCOPAL AND PRIESTLY AUTHORITY

Since the mid-sixties, episcopal power and the status of the priesthood have been among the most frequently discussed issues within the Catholic Church. Collegiality was the most troublesome issue of Vatican II; and the Synod of Bishops, which has met five times between 1967 and 1977, has considered, but not solved, the delicate problem of the relationships between the pope, the Roman Curia, the bishops, the priests, and the remainder of the Church community.

Responses to the questionnaire seemed to indicate that the lay national delegates had fairly definite attitudes toward future collegial relationships among Church authorities. Presented with a statement that the international Synod of Bishops should have decision-making rather than mere advisory power toward pope and Curia, 73 percent of the lay national delegate sample indicated assent, and 26 percent dissent. Nearly half (46 percent) agreed (and 52 percent disagreed) that the pope should be elected not by the college of cardinals, but by the Synod of Bishops or by some other unspecified method. Indicating approval of even greater decentralization, 77 percent of the respondents agreed that local people at the diocesan level (rank-and-file clergy and laity) should be given a more extensive role in the nomination of bishops. Only 22 percent disagreed with this idea.

In addition to questions about episcopal and priestly roles, the questionnaire listed a series of five attributes that might be expected of bishops and pastors (see table 2). Respondents were asked to indicate if they considered the attributes important or not, both for bishops and for pastors.

TABLE 2   *Percentage of Lay National Delegates (N = 212)*
Who Cited Certain Listed Attributes as Being Important
for Religious Leaders

Attribute	Important for bishop (Percent)	Important for pastor (Percent)
Teacher of Christian principles and doctrine by word and example . . .	96	96
Sacramental-spiritual role	94	94
Informal friend and servant of the community	70	83
Participant and leader in social issues	65	58
Administrator and manager	61	47

Listing the tabulated responses in rank order showed the same priority among the five attributes given for both bishops and pastors. But for two attributes—"informal friend and servant of the community" and "administrator and manager"—the percentage of respondents indicating assent was quite different for the two categories of spiritual leaders.

The responses indicated a higher expectation for a pastor than for a bishop to be an "informal friend and servant of the community," although 70 percent would expect the bishop to have that attribute also. On the other hand, a somewhat greater expectation was placed on bishops than on pastors to be good administrators and managers, and to be participants and leaders in social issues. Concerning the pastors' role as "informal friend and servant of the community," which 83 percent of the respondents selected as important, 73 percent (versus 27 percent) indicated in their response to another question that they thought priests in their own countries should have a good working relationship with people of all classes and races. Fifty-seven percent, however, signified also that clergy and hierarchy were not giving good examples of Christian poverty (43 percent disagreed).

Some dissatisfaction with the clergy (or with those responsible for the situation of the clergy) may have been expressed by the response to another question: 95 percent (versus 4 percent) of the lay national delegates favored a statement that major seminaries be substantially transformed so that future priests would be better prepared. In addition, 50 percent agreed (and 48 percent disagreed) that minor seminaries for the training of future priests should be phased out of existence. If the lay national delegates had been satisfied with their clergy, they would have had little reason to be so harsh vis-à-vis their seminary training.

Much publicity has been given to the fact that many priests feel that they have been overlooked in the recent rediscovery of episcopal collegiality and in the opening of vistas to the laity. There is no doubt that there is now a full-fledged crisis of the clergy in the Catholic Church. Priests are working in secular jobs, organizing, protesting, resigning, and marrying in incredible numbers. Some questions asked in the survey of lay national delegates go to the heart of the controversies over these developments, which are often referred to as symptoms of the crisis of authority in the Church.

Only 4 percent thought the cassock was acceptable garb in public for a priest; 33 percent preferred a dark suit and Roman collar, and 35 percent a suit with a small distinctive insigne, while 27 percent thought he should wear anything he likes, even without any distinctive identification. On the question of housing, only 41 percent insisted on separate clerical quarters, such as rectories and monasteries, for priests; the others (56 percent) did not insist on such a restriction. Only 30 percent were opposed to giving diocesan priests freedom to marry. The 65 percent who were not opposed to priestly marriage divided along the following lines: 20 percent favored it only for priests who had actually left the priesthood, and 5 percent indicated they would not oppose priests' marrying as long as it was done before ordination; 29 percent indicated they didn't care whether priests married before or after ordination; and 11 percent indicated they would not be opposed to marriage after ordination. On the issue of priests' organizing, 56 percent opposed (and 42 percent favored) the idea of priests' forming unions in order better to resolve their problems with diocesan curias.

These opinions and attitudes about priests and bishops again point to the fact that the lay national delegates were mostly moderate liberals, critical of Church authorities but not radically opposed to them, intent on transforming the Church but also quite attached to it.

6. OPINIONS ON LAY POWER AND PARTICIPATION

Since lay power and participation were the fundamental issues at the third World Congress for the Lay Apostolate, the lay national delegates' opinions on these issues will now be examined.

The questionnaire included diverse questions on the topic, and the answers gave a rather clear idea of where the national delegates stood. My previous research in France and the United States had indicated some key issues under discussion by Catholic laity. Eight of these lay problems were presented and the survey respondents were asked to rate the seriousness of these in their own countries. The results are shown in table 3.

It can be seen from the table that most respondents thought laymen's unwillingness to participate to be a serious problem (81 percent). The size and impersonality of parishes were held responsible for lack of participation by 72 percent of the sample, but domination of

TABLE 3   *Seriousness of Various Problems of the Laity in Respondent's Country (in percentages)*

Problem	Serious	Not serious	No answer
(a) Inaccessibility of the bishop and his co-workers to ordinary laymen	57	39	4
(b) Too much pressure on the members for financial contributions	35	62	3
(c) Parishes are too large and impersonal, thus reducing possibility for communal fellowship and spontaneous relationships	72	25	3
(d) Lay activities are too often dominated by the pastor or other members of the clergy	66	32	2
(e) Lay initiative, even if undertaken in the spirit of the Council, is not rewarded or recognized	59	36	5
(f) The parochial schools require too much time and resources in relation to the total life of the Church	44	52	4
(g) Too few laymen take on responsibilities and commitments that are offered, thus indicating that much of the problem of a participating laity is due to the attitudes of the laymen themselves	81	14	5
(h) Lay groups and organizations are too competitive and divided to get anything important under way	45	36	16

lay activities by the clergy (66 percent), the absence of rewards for lay initiative (59 percent), and the inaccessibility of the bishop and his coworkers to ordinary laymen (57 percent) were also marked as problems of considerable seriousness. It may well be that the unwillingness of laymen to participate, indicated as the major problem facing the laity, was largely a result of the other problems listed above. Pressures on lay members for financial contributions was considered to be a serious problem by only 35 percent of the lay national delegates.

Ivan Vallier and Rocco Caporale, in their cross-national study of lay Catholic leaders, looked into the question of the demands of the laity: "The chief demands," they write, "are not for relief from traditional moral prescriptions but for a series of new opportunities to participate in the functioning of the Church."[8] To test this statement, the lay national delegates were asked if they were more interested in participating in the functioning of the Church than in being relieved of traditional moral prescriptions.[9] Eighty-eight percent said they were, and only 7 percent did not favor this statement. This shows clearly that greater participation in the decision-making processes was indeed desired by most lay national delegates, and that change in traditional moral norms was secondary in their minds. Eighty percent marked that many decisions in the Church should be taken through broad participation at the grass-roots level rather than by people at higher echelons of authority. Fifty-two percent indicated that lay participation was moving ahead rapidly enough in their country, and only 31 percent reported that laymen already had enough autonomy of action and speech in Catholic organizations. A similar small number, 30 percent of the sample, signified agreement with a statement that it was better for lay Catholic organizations to be mandated and juridically controlled by the hierarchy. Disagreement with these two statements was indicated by 68 percent of the lay national delegates. Conversely, 87 percent said that laymen should be collegially co-responsible, with priests and hierarchy, for the Church.

Rating the importance of types of lay participation in decision-making, 45 percent selected policy making and goal setting as the most important Church activities for laymen today. Another 24 percent put the emphasis on liturgy or public worship, 12 percent selected control and administration of parochial and diocesan resources and funds, 9 percent chose the selection of Church leaders as the most important lay activity, and only 2 percent said laymen should not participate in Church decision-making.

On a more limited issue, 73 percent of the lay national delegates agreed that priests' homilies at mass should sometimes be replaced by a dialogue between priest and congregation or by homilies delivered by qualified laymen. On the question of a preferred model for the lay apostolate, 66 percent chose militant groups working in close collaboration with the hierarchy, 11 percent preferred militant groups working independently of the hierarchy, 13 percent preferred individual laymen independent of the hierarchy who would stress exemplary personal lives, and only 7 percent opted for individual laymen who were obedient and respectful toward the hierarchy and who would also stress exemplary personal lives. The answers to this question, when viewed in the light of other opinions and attitudes which were critical of hierarchical control, point to the possibility that hierarchical control is generally disliked because of its interference with social action. It seems then that it is not authority per se and organization per se that are rejected but authority and organization that impede a militant lay involvement in programs for social justice.

Respondents who, in other sections of the questionnaire, said that the hierarchy was impeding lay involvement may have here been expressing the same notion more clearly. Any block to militant lay groups might be opposed by these respondents, as we can see by the answers to another question, where 66 percent agreed that highly organized groups were much better for the apostolate than loosely defined groups or individuals working on their own.

One of the major characteristics of traditional Catholic Action associations, nevertheless, was rejected: the division by sex and by social class. As many as 83 percent thought that Catholic associations should not be separate for men and women, and 74 percent did not favor separation by social class either. Thus a larger percentage of the sample rejected the organizational principle based on sex that the other principle founded on what Poggi calls "milieu-based specializations" or "milieu organizations."[10]

These lay national delegates were willing to accept some clerical authority as long as it was not a dominating or manipulative control. When asked what was the best position for a priest to take in parochial organizations on matters outside faith and morals, only 2 percent said that he should take a position of complete control. Another 8 percent selected "power of final decision only," 65 percent indicated "advice and direction only," and 24 percent chose having the priest share an equal vote with his parishoners. As many as 90 percent would see laymen consulted by the pope, bishops, and priests before statements should be made about Catholic positions on temporal issues.

Questioned about the usefulness of boards of laymen to assist priests in their duties, 59 percent of the sample favored having such boards, with members partly elected and partly appointed. Another 37 percent favored boards wholly elected by parishioners. Only 3 percent said the boards should be appointed by priests, and a mere 1 percent said there should not be any such board at all.

From these responses, it seems that objections to clerical and hierarchical power are based on feelings that the leadership can be authoritarian, ill informed, or too conservative. The replies of the lay national delegate sample clearly indicated a wish to exercise influence, of varying kinds and degrees, in Church activities.

The lay national delegates, in summary, were not radicals in social and political issues, but rather people with centrist or moderate liberal ideas. Nevertheless, on the religious level, they were quite traditional as far as practices were concerned, and quite reformist as to their beliefs, opinions, and attitudes on selected religious issues. There is no doubt that in a matter like birth control they considered the traditional position of Church authorities to be ill founded and in need of change. Finally, in the area of lay participation in Church decision-making, they generally wanted a greater share of power and responsibility. They definitely were not a group of power-hungry, anti-authority types intent on making a revolution in the Church. They were critical of, but not fundamentally opposed to ecclesiastical authority. They might be willing to rock Peter's boat in order to be heard, but they certainly were not interested in trying to seize the rudder and even less in trying to sink the boat.[11]

7. GEOCULTURAL DIFFERENCES IN SOCIAL BACKGROUND AND IN SOCIAL AND POLITICAL ORIENTATION

Comparisons of ideology between various categories of delegates inside our sample, using background characteristics as independent variables, are not very illuminating. When the organizers of the congress and the national ecclesiastical hierarchies chose the lay national delegates, they evidently had in mind an ideal of an involved but moderately liberal layman. They selected delegates who represented a broad range of background characteristics (age, sex, social class, profession), but who had little ideological variety. In other words, merely by looking at the selection process, one could anticipate that the lay national delegates would be quite different on background (independent) variables but rather similar on dependent variables (i.e. on attitudes and opinions). For this reason, I shall select for examination only the two independent variables, namely, nationality and age, which have a certain usefulness for my purpose of description and comparison.

One of the main sources of differentiation in the delegates to the third World Congress for the Lay Apostolate was regional and cultural variation. To study this differentiation, the national delegates in the study were divided into six large geocultural categories: Africans, Latin Americans, Asians, Western Europeans (minus the Anglo-Saxons), Southern and Eastern Europeans, and delegates from Anglo-Saxon countries of Europe, North America, and Oceania.[12]

This division allows a comparison of delegates from the Third World (Africa, Asia, Latin America) with those from more industrialized countries. Southern and Eastern European countries were grouped, because many Eastern European delegates were refugees living in southern Europe who had lived in eastern Europe at a time when the two areas were economically, politically, culturally, and religiously quite alike. There were not enough delegates from eastern Europe to warrant a separate category, and regrouping them with Southern Europeans seemed to be the most appropriate thing to do.

Before going on with this differential description, it is important to note that the culture of a region does not constitute a single causal variable, but is rather a conglomerate of life experiences, values, and norms acquired in the socialization process in a given geographical area.

A general overview of the main differences between the various geocultural groups is summarized in table 4.

As the table indicates, the Latin Americans and the Western Europeans had the fewest delegates over fifty years of age. The Anglo-Saxons had the oldest delegation, with 36 percent over fifty. Women were underrepresented in the Southern and Eastern European, African, and Asian delegations. Only the Anglo-Saxon delegation had a majority of delegates who were women.

The Europeans, especially the Southern and Eastern group, had the highest level of schooling, followed by the Asians. Of the Asian national delegates, 61 percent had attended school more than sixteen years, putting them ahead of the Anglo-Saxons (54 percent). The Africans were the lowest in this category, with only 17 percent who had attended school more than sixteen years.

Broad differences between geocultural groupings were indicated in responses to a question on the variable "wealth." In answer to the

TABLE 4 *Social-Background Characteristics of Lay National Delegations, by Geocultural Categories*

Characteristic	Africans	Latin Americans	Asians	Anglo-Saxons	Western Europeans	Southern and Eastern Europeans	Total	N
Percent of people over 50 years of age	25%	14%	33%	36%	18%	32%	25%	(53)
Percent of women	21%	45%	38%	54%	44%	32%	41%	(86)
Percent with 16 or more years of schooling	17%	55%	61%	54%	66%	77%	58%	(122)
Percent of those who said they were wealthy or very wealthy	8%	45%	8%	31%	20%	13%	23%	(49)
Total	(24)	(40)	(24)	(38)	(55)	(31)	. . .	(212)

question: "Compared with the people in your country, what would you say your economic situation is?" the following replies could be checked: very wealthy, wealthy, average, below average but not poor, and poor. Only 8 percent of both the African and the Asian delegates said they were wealthy or very wealthy. Furthermore, 46 percent of the Africans and 29 percent of the Asians said they were "below average" on this variable. But there was a surprising difference between these two Third World groups and the other one, Latin America. Among the Latin Americans, 45 percent responded "wealthy or very wealthy," and only 8 percent "below average." The proportion of Latin Americans who selected "below average" was slightly higher than the proportion of Southern and Eastern Europeans (13 percent) selecting this option, and about the same as the Anglo-Saxons (8 percent) and Western Europeans (6 percent).

The selection of the "below average" option by such small percentages of the lay national delegates may have been partly caused by a system under which many delegates paid their own way, an arrangement which tended to favor the well-to-do. Since most Africans and Asian lay leaders could not afford the expense of tickets from their countries to Rome and back, delegates were often selected from among people already living in Europe or working full time for the Church, whose fare was, in most cases, paid for by Church authorities. A system of travel grants was set up, however, to permit poorer delegates from African and Asian countries to come to the congress. That the Asians and Africans had, besides paying their own way, these options for getting to the congress probably explains why most of the African and Asian delegates indicated they were not wealthy; the grant system, which favored them, permitted a fair number of poorer delegates to attend. Furthermore, the selection of many African and Asian delegates among young people studying or working in Europe also contributed to make these delegations less wealthy than the others, which were often made up of people who could pay their own way.

Instead of considering each question separately, as in the preceding sections, I shall use indices to compare delegates from various geocultural regions on certain political and social orientations. All of these indices were constructed with at least three questions each and validated with at least two other similar questions. For example, for a racism index, the possible answers to three questions indicating a racist attitude were spread out along a four-step Likert scale (definitely agree, agree somewhat, disagree somewhat, definitely disagree), and a score varying from 0 to 3 was given for each answer. A person could, consequently, obtain a total score ranging from 0 to 9. After the index was validated by a test of its capacity to predict racism with the use of two other similar questions, I regrouped the ten categories of the index into three categories, each containing about the same number of cases. By this method three categories of delegates were obtained, and they were labeled nonracist, slightly racist, and most racist.

The percentage of nonracists for each geocultural category is indicated in table 5.

Looking only at percentages of nonracists in each geocultural category, we find that the least racist are the Latin Americans, and the most racist are the Asians. One might not have anticipated that Asians would rank high on a racism scale. But the fact that the scale contained items specifically aimed at uncovering anti-black feelings, and the added fact that Asians were also the most conservative national delegates, may possibly explain this finding.

On a scale of political conservatism, the Asians also scored highest, as table 6 indicates.

The African countries' aggregate, on the conservative-radical index, produced the second highest percentage of "radicals," the lowest—much lower than that of the others—percentage of "conservatives," and the highest percentage of "moderates," making them the least conservative of the six groups.

Two anticommunism scales were built, one for political anticommunism, one for religious anticommunism. Religious anticommunism will be considered in a later section of this chapter. Political anticommunism scales are reported in table 7, along with data on scales for nationalism and civil liberties.

TABLE 5   *Percentage of Nonracists, by Geocultural Categories*

Category	Percent	Total N
Africans	54%	(24)
Latin Americans	60%	(40)
Asians	21%	(24)
Anglo-Saxons	49%	(38)
Western Europeans	44%	(55)
Eastern and Southern Europeans	39%	(31)
All	45%	(212)
	(N = 97)	

TABLE 6   *Political Conservatism, by Geocultural Categories*

Category	Radicals	Moderates	Conservatives	Total	N
Africans	35%	56%	9%	100%	(23)
Latin Americans	31%	48%	21%	100%	(39)
Asians	13%	44%	43%	100%	(23)
Anglo-Saxons	34%	29%	37%	100%	(38)
Western Europeans	23%	43%	34%	100%	(53)
Eastern and Southern Europeans	40%	33%	27%	100%	(30)
Average for total	29%	42%	29%	100%	(206)

On the question of political anticommunism, all geocultural groups were quite similar except the Asians, who only had 13 percent ranking low on anticommunism. The nationalism index was made up of two questions on attitudes toward the United Nations and one question on freedom of immigration. The Southern and Eastern Europeans were the least nationalist, whereas the Africans scored highest on nationalism. On the index of civil libertarianism, the Africans and Asians were the least favorable (the questions asked pertained to freedom of expression and conscientious objection), and the Anglo-Saxons and the Latin Americans were the most favorable.

In summary, the differences between the six geocultural groups on various social background characteristics and sociopolitical orientations were not very pronounced. The Africans were poorer and had fewer years of formal schooling than the others. Their delegations had fewer women, fewer conservatives, fewer anti-Communists, but also more nationalists and fewer of those favoring civil liberties than had the other geocultural groups. The Latin Americans scored themselves as richer, and as highly favorable to civil liberties and racial integration. The Asian delegations contained relatively high proportions of people under fifty years of age and of men. These Asians also had proportionally stronger tendencies toward racism, political anticommunism, and conservatism, and they were not very favorable to civil liberties. The Anglo-Saxon delegations had the highest proportion of women delegates. These delegations indicated the highest percentage of support for civil liberties, but were second-lowest on the nationalism scale. The Eastern and Southern Europeans had the highest educational level, and were the most internationalist of all the geocultural aggregates. On almost all these scales, the Western Europeans took a middle position.

These data on the social background and sociopolitical orientations of the national delegates lead to the conclusion that there were, finally, few differences between the geocultural groups, and even between the Third World delegates and the others in these respects. In spite of the small differences uncovered for some variables, especially in social background, there were no very fundamental cleavages on political and social opinions and attitudes, except perhaps in the case of the Asians, who were more conservative than the others. This relative homogeneity may have been due to the particular efforts made by the organizers of the congress, and by local Church leaders, to select delegates representing a certain range of social conditions and a somewhat narrow range of moderate political and social options, as mentioned above.

8. DIFFERENCES IN THE RELIGIOUS INVOLVEMENT AND BELIEFS OF DELEGATES

A consideration of the religious involvement of the delegates from the six geocultural regions shows that the differences among them were not very considerable. The Europeans were more prone to read Catholic newspapers and other periodicals, with 50 percent affirming that half of the periodicals they read were Catholic. The others indicated that their reading included a somewhat smaller proportion of Catholic newspapers and periodicals, probably because fewer of these are published outside Europe.

The Africans were nearly all former students of Catholic schools, and it was among Western Europeans that the smallest percentage (67 percent) of Catholic school alumni was recorded. The Latin Americans had the highest proportion of delegates affirming that the majority of the organizations to which they belonged were Catholic. The Anglo-Saxons were not so likely as the others to be members of Catholic organizations only. Compared with the other geocultural groupings, the Africans reported the lowest number giving a high proportion of their income to the Church. The Anglo-Saxons reported giving proportionately more of their income to the Church than the other five groupings.

An index of sacramental participation was constructed, similar to one developed by Greeley and Rossi in their study of Catholic schools in the United States.[13] This index used three questions, pertaining respectively to frequency of participation in communion, mass, and confession. The Asians were the most active Catholics, as far as sacramental participation was concerned, and the Eastern and Southern Europeans the least so.

An index of biblical knowledge used the two questions about the New Testament and one about Old Testament prophets. On this index, the Europeans and Latin Americans obtained the highest scores, and the Asians the lowest.

None of the above differences in religious involvement would seem to be very important or systematic. In the area of beliefs, however, a surprising divergence between the geocultural groups was found. The Asians, Africans, and Latin Americans, in that order, turned out to be more orthodox (on Glock and Stark's index of orthodoxy) than the Eastern and Southern Europeans and the Anglo-Saxons. But the least orthodox (or fundamentalist, since in my opinion Glock and Stark's orthodoxy index is really a measure of fundamentalism rather than of orthodoxy) were the Western Europeans, as table 8 indicates.

The Asians were not only the most conservative and anti-Communist, as I have already shown, but they were also the most orthodox of the six groups, with the Africans and Latin Americans close behind.

Additional indices measured various aspects of the religious beliefs and opinions of the national delegates to the 1967 Rome congress. I followed the same procedure as for the indices relating to social and political attitudes, described above. Tests were made to evaluate the validity and sensitivity of each of the indices. In most instances, face validity was decisive, but in all cases the predictive power of the index was ascertained. Each Likert-type question had four possible answers (definitely disagreed, disagreed somewhat, agreed somewhat, and definitely agreed), and a score ranging from 0 to 3 was assigned to each answer. This meant that final total scores could range from 0 to 9 for an index constructed with three questions. The index was then validated in the following manner: scores on the index were correlated with scores obtained from answers to other questions that measured the same type of orientation.

Without going into the details of index construction for the various measures of religious ideology, I present in table 9 the differences between the geocultural groups on religious problems under current discussion. Only percentages of those who scored high on these opinion and attitude questions are listed, so as to facilitate the reading of this rather far-ranging data.

TABLE 7 *Political Opinions and Attitudes, by Geocultural categories*

Opinions and attitudes	Africans	Latin Americans	Asians	Anglo-Saxons	Western Europeans	Southern and Eastern Europeans	Total	N
Percent low on political anticommunism	39%	30%	13%	33%	37%	35%	32%	(68)
Percent low on nationalism	29%	48%	50%	35%	46%	68%	48%	(102)
Percent pro civil liberties	17%	55%	21%	56%	48%	42%	44%	(92)
Total	(24)	(40)	(24)	(39)	(55)	(31)	—	(213)

TABLE 8 *Orthodoxy Index, by Geocultural Categories*

Orthodoxy	Asians	Africans	Latin Americans	Anglo-Saxons	Southern and Eastern Europeans	Western Europeans	Total	N
High	61%	58%	55%	45%	45%	16%	45%	(88)
Low	13%	13%	18%	24%	35%	51%	29%	(61)

TABLE 9 *Percentage Scoring High on Various Indices of Religious Ideology, by Geocultural Categories*

Index	Africans	Latin Americans	Asians	Anglo-Saxons	Western Europeans	Southern and Eastern Europeans	Total	N
Clericalism	25%	25%	30%	31%	21%	19%	25%	(53)
Religious anticommunism	39%	40%	45%	28%	44%	48%	41%	(86)
Religious radicalism	25%	38%	25%	51%	55%	52%	44%	(91)
Alienation toward the Vatican bureaucracy	79%	65%	62%	56%	41%	57%	57%	(121)
Ecumenism	13%	20%	29%	23%	22%	19%	21%	(45)
Pro-lay participation	50%	46%	50%	48%	65%	39%	51%	(109)
Pro-lay power	30%	40%	29%	38%	33%	42%	36%	(76)
Pro-"church of the poor"	38%	45%	13%	49%	37%	39%	38%	(81)
Pro-collegiality	46%	50%	42%	46%	45%	42%	43%	(91)
Pro-episcopalism	8%	21%	25%	31%	43%	23%	27%	(58)
Acceptance of birth control pill	46%	57%	67%	57%	81%	62%	63%	(91)
Acceptance of marriage of priests	62%	76%	50%	61%	79%	71%	69%	(141)

My clericalism index indicates a small difference among the six groups. A fourth of the Africans and Latins were clericalist; the percentage was higher for Asians and Anglo-Saxons, and lower for the Europeans. As mentioned above, two anticommunism indices were constructed, one for religious and one for political anticommunism. The index of religious anticommunism was built with questions on dialogue and cooperation with Communists, and on the possibility for a Communist to be a member of the Catholic Church. Religious anti-communism was relatively high for all groups except the Anglo-Saxons, who scored quite low.

One of the rare occasions when a difference was discovered between the Third World countries, on the one hand, and the Europeans and Anglo-Saxons, on the other, was in the case of the religious radicalism index. This was a rather generic index, constructed with questions on Vatican II, canon law, and stability in the Church. The Europeans and Anglo-Saxons showed themselves more favorable to religious change than the Third World delegates.

The Africans were the least alienated from the Vatican bureaucracy, with Latin Americans and Asians close behind, when scored on an index of alienation toward the Vatican bureaucracy. On an ecumenism index, the Asians scored highest and the Africans scored lowest, with all the other groups very close to one another. I recall that during the special meeting for Asians just before the congress, they asked that the concept of ecumenism be broadened in order to include non-Christians.

On the index of sympathy for lay participation in decision making in the Church (in opposition to mere liturgical participation), the Eastern and Southern Europeans showed themselves to be the most moderate, and the Western Europeans the most aggressive. On the other hand, strangely enough, the Eastern and Southern Europeans scored highest on the pro-lay power index; in other words, it seems that what these delegates wanted was real power rather than simple participation.

The Anglo-Saxons and the Latin Americans indicated the greatest desire to see the Church become a church of the poor. On this index, very few Asians scored high. This is somewhat ironic, in the light of the indication by many Anglo-Saxons and Latin Americans, and by few Asians, that they were personally wealthy.

Our pro-collegiality index measured a positive attitude toward a communitarian, grass-roots kind of Church authority, against acceptance of a centralized, bureaucratized, and hierarchical authority. The index of pro-episcopalism is slightly different, in the sense that it measures the degree of sympathy for the power of bishops and bishops' synods, in opposition to the power of the pope and the Roman Curia. There is practically no difference between the six groups on the question of collegiality, except in the case of the Latin Americans, who were more numerous than the others in the category scoring high, but the differences are considerable on the pro-episcopalism index. As many as 43 percent of the Western Europeans scored high on this index, whereas only 8 percent of the Africans were at the same end of the scale. The others fell more or less halfway between these two geocultural groups.

Two other issues showed slight differences between some of the six groups. On the question of acceptance of the birth-control pill, the West Europeans were the group most favorable toward contraception by that method. The West Europeans were also the most likely to accept married clergy, although Latin Americans and Eastern and Southern Europeans were not far behind on this question. The Asians were the group that was less favorable to a change in the celibacy rule; only 50 percent of them score high on this issue, a further indication that they were the most religiously conservative of the geocultural groups.

This description of geocultural differences can be concluded with a few generalizations. Overall, the Afro-Asian delegates showed themselves to be the most conservative in their religious opinions and the most traditionalist in their religious beliefs. On the other hand, the Western Europeans showed some distinctive differences from other groups. They emerged as nontraditionalist believers and as holders of relatively progressive religious opinions and attitudes.

The religious conservatism of the Afro-Asian delegate sample can probably be explained, in good part, by the selection method for delegates to the congress.[14] Travel grants inevitably went to laymen who had shown themselves to be faithful and trustworthy leaders in established religious organizations in their countries. Hierarchy and clergy seem to be firmly in control of organized laity in these two geocultural regions. The lay Catholic organizations of most African and Asian nations rarely show the independence and progressive orientation evident in many equivalent organizations of Western Europe or, to a lesser degree, in those of the Anglo-Saxon world. It is a fairly well-known fact that national and local religious officials in Western Europe are generally progressive and relatively independent of Rome. When conflict arises with the Vatican, a united national front of bishops, priests, and laymen has often opposed the Vatican. The situation is somewhat different in Anglo-Saxon countries, where most of the national hierarchies have shown themselves ready to stand with Rome against the laity and most of the clergy. In Africa and Asia, hierarchy, clergy, and organized laity are rarely in conflict among themselves or with the Vatican; they tend to have a common, moderately conservative orientation, due perhaps to the fact that they are often a minority identified with Western powers, though this situation has been changing rapidly in recent years.

It is impossible to push these kinds of generalizations further, because there are numerous national and diocesan variations, and because there are also wide differences inside these groupings, among laity, clergy, and hierarchy. These remarks, however, should suffice to illustrate my point that the lay national delegates from various geocultural areas represented a certain diversity of orientations as far as their attitudes toward Church authorities were concerned.

9. THE CORRELATES OF RELIGIOUS IDEOLOGY

The relationship between the religious ideology of the lay national delegates and some other variables, such as age, religious behavior, and political ideology, will be explored in this section.

In the religious ideology of the lay national delegates, I found no important or systematic differences as far as most background characteristics (such as social class, occupation, income, self-perceived economic status, education, and sex) were concerned. Examination of the delegates by age and placement on the orthodoxy index, on the other hand, showed the older ones to be more orthodox on religious issues. Table 10 illustrates this quite clearly.

TABLE 10   *Orthodoxy, by Age*

Degree	Under 30 years	35–46 years	50 years and over	Total
Not very orthodox	36%	30%	19%	(29)
Rather orthodox	33%	29%	25%	(29)
Very orthodox	31%	41%	56%	(42)
Total	100%	100%	100%	(100)
N	(73)	(83)	(52)	(208)

Just by examining the percentages, one readily sees that a correlation between age and orthodoxy exists: the older a delegate, the more orthodox he is.[15] The correlation in the table can be expressed statistically in a summary fashion through various measures of association. Since I have two ordinal variables here, the measure called Goodman and Kruskal's gamma (γ) is an excellent choice.[16] Gamma varies in size from 0 to 1. It can also be negative, when we have an inverse correlation. This measure of statistical association expresses both the size and the direction of a correlation between two ordinal variables. The gamma for the correlation that we see in table 10 between old age and orthodoxy is .25. This means that there is indeed a correlation, that it is moderately high, and that it is positive. It is this gamma score that is entered below in the upper-left square of table 11. This statistical technique facilitates analysis by synthesizing much information in a small amount of space. Indeed each gamma score in table 11 summarizes an entire table of percentages similar to table 10. Such a table permits rapid visualization of the correlation between numerous pairs of ordinal variables, without necessitating an examination of a percentage table for each pair.[17]

Here are a few other interesting indications that can be culled from an examination of my correlation matrix. Not only is there a positive correlation between age and a conservative religious ideology, as expressed through orthodoxy, religious rigidity, and religious anticommunism, but there is a negative correlation as well between age and most progressive positions that a Catholic could take on the question of Church authority. The younger members of my sample showed themselves more ready than the older sample members to oppose highly visible Christian institutions and the Vatican bureaucracy, and were more open to ecumenism, lay participation and lay power, Churchly poverty and collegiality, birth control, and a married clergy.

If one correlates certain aspects of religious behavior, such as frequency of participation in sacraments, ritualism, and biblical ignorance, with the elements of religious ideology just considered, the relationships are similar to those observed between old age and religious ideology—that is, positive and high. Sacramentally and ritually active and biblically ignorant laymen are more inclined to be religiously orthodox, rigid, and anti-Communist, favorable to clericalism, Christian institutions, and the Vatican bureaucracy, and closed to religious change, ecumenism, lay participation and power, Churchly poverty and social involvement, collegiality, episcopalism, birth control, and a married clergy.

TABLE 11 *Indices of Religious Ideology, by Age and by Indices of Religious Behavior and Political Attitudes (Gammas)*

	Old Age	Sacra-mentalism	Ritualism	Biblical ignorance	Political anti-communism	Political radicalism
Orthodoxy	.25	.39	.13	.16	.28	-.20
Religious rigidity	.22	.15	.13	.08	.47	-.13
Clericalism	.06	.19	.07	.15	.29	-.30
Religious anticommunism	.24	.08	-.05	.12	.55	-.36
Openness to religious change	-.02	-.09	.03	-.24	-.50	.35
Opposition to Christian institutions	-.22	.12	.02	-.06	-.44	.44
Alienation toward the Vatican bureaucracy	-.14	-.19	-.13	-.12	-.41	.40
Ecumenism	-.22	-.19	-.23	-.02	-.43	.32
Openness to lay participation in Church affairs	-.18	-.16	.02	.00	-.20	.00
Openness to lay power	-.19	-.10	-.05	-.09	-.44	.25
Desire for a "church of the poor"	-.31	-.15	.08	.04	-.19	.21
Collegiality	-.22	-.01	-.06	.13	-.44	.40
Episcopalism	-.02	-.12	-.05	.21	-.42	.23
Desire for social involvement of the Church	-.03	.07	-.25	-.06	.00	.09
Acceptance of the birth control pill	-.18	-.26	-.02	.05	-.31	.22
Acceptance of a married clergy	-.27	-.20	-.20	.03	-.39	.33

We can conclude, then, that three groups—the older lay delegates, those more active on the cultual level, and those less knowledgeable about the Bible—are also those who are less demanding vis-à-vis Church authorities and who more readily accept the controls imposed on them by these officials.

If the analysis is pursued a little further, one can consider the relationship between each of two aspects of the political ideology of the lay national delegates (political anticommunism and political radicalism) and the elements of religious ideology just examined. Scoring high on anticommunism at the political level tends to correlate with orthodoxy, rigidity, and anticommunism at the religious level, as well as with a favorable inclination toward clericalism, separate Christian institutions, and the Vatican bureaucracy, and disinclination toward religious change, ecumenism, lay participation and power, Churchly poverty and social involvement, collegiality and episcopalism, birth control, and a married clergy. Similarly, those who are recorded as politically radical tended to exhibit the opposite inclinations. The only issue for which there was no correlation between political radicalism and an aspect of opposition to Church authorities is on the index that measured the desire for lay participation in Church affairs ($\gamma = .00$). This could be due to the fact that many of the lay national delegates didn't expect much from lay participation anyway, because they think that lay participation, as it is currently granted by Church authorities, is often nothing more than a form of manipulation and co-optation.

10. SOME EXPLANATIONS OF THE CONCLUSIONS ABOUT THE LAY NATIONAL DELEGATES: VATICAN CONTROL OF LAY GROUPS

The survey analyzed in this chapter can be summarized in the following manner: The lay national delegates to the third World Congress for the Lay Apostolate constitute an elite, both from a socioeconomic point of view and from the point of view of their involvement in the religious life of the Catholic Church. They are wealthier and better educated than the average Catholic layman and they are much involved in religious activities of all kinds. Politically, they have a tendency to be moderately liberal. Their religious ideology is not conservative. They are rather liberal on religious issues and moderately critical of Church authority.

The most important differences among the delegates in these areas of religious and political ideology stemmed from the differences in age and the fact that they came from different geocultural regions. Older delegates were less critical of Church authority and they were also more conservative politically and religiously. The Asians were very conservative along both lines, whereas the Africans were conservative on religious questions but not in politics. Finally, I found a high correlation between dogmatic, ritual, and organizational involvement at the religious level, on the one hand, and religious and political conservatism, on the other.

The image of the delegates that emerges from the data helps us better understand the nature of the selection process which brought them to Rome in the first place, and the apparently quite radical nature of the stances that the delegates took during the congress. The organizers obviously wanted "safe" delegates: delegates who would not challenge or embarrass Church authorities; but they also had to maintain a certain degree of credibility. They could not invite only subservient and conservative people. They needed to foster the impression that the laymen invited to the congress were autonomous and independent. They did not, however, want to invite people who would present too radical a challenge to the existing ecclesiastical order. This led to the selection of delegates who were generally neither very conservative nor very radical, of people who were actively involved in the official organizational life of the Church. Being invited to the congress was like a symbolic reward for services rendered to the Church over the years. Quite a few of these laymen, however, had become freer and more critical vis-à-vis Church authorities during the pontificate of John XXIII and during Vatican II and its aftermath. Although still members of organizations controlled by Rome or by national hierarchies, they were intent on making heard what Francis X. Murphy and Gary MacEoin have called "a new sound in Rome."[18]

Gianfranco Poggi has shown that ecclesiastical officials in the Catholic Church are faced with a dilemma: either the Church adapts to a secularized and pluralistic world, or it becomes completely isolated and is threatened with slow extinction. The appeal to the layman through the creation and development of lay organizations like Catholic Action and Catholic political parties was an effort to avoid being trapped in that dilemma. Church officials thus tried to use laymen to maintain their links with the modern world. The laity became a bridge with the world for the hierarchy. Since direct control of lay groups by these officials both stifled the development of the organizations and caused numerous conflicts, indirect control, manipulation, and co-optation became favorite operating procedures. But we know that co-optation is not a one-way street, as Philip Selznick has demonstrated.[19] The parent organization cannot easily co-opt without being itself subverted: individuals or groups cannot be integrated and excluded from all forms of power and participation at the same time.

Wherever Catholic Action has been too strictly under hierarchical control, it has failed to attract large numbers of involved laymen or serve as a link between the modern world and the hierarchy. Since many laymen rejected the tokenism involved in the limited autonomy of Catholic Action groups, the Vatican and the national hierarchies have had to loosen their controls in order for the lay groups to survive and prosper. They have made tremendous efforts to appear open to dialogue, consultation, and participation. The third World Congress for the Lay Apostolate was the most important of a series of efforts by the Vatican to appeal to the laity in an apparently open manner. The fact that it backfired was not due to lack of foresight on the part of Church officials, but to the constraints of the situation. If more conservative and less representative delegates had been chosen for the congress, there would have been less explosive action there, but the whole event would have been scoffed at as a rigidly controlled meeting. On the other hand, if it had been a truly democratic meeting, there would have been less dissatisfaction on the part of the lay activists, but the whole meeting would have blown the lid off St. Peter's basilica. The middle road of pseudo-participation and limited democracy that was chosen was probably the only one that could realistically be taken, once the decision to hold a congress had been irrevocably made.

This solution to the dilemma created many new problems for the central bureaucracy, but these problems are the price the hierarchy has had to pay in order to keep the lay movement in the fold. As control breeds alienation, so freedom engenders independence and disintegration. It is the classic dilemma of authority versus freedom. A central authority structure that is not flexible enough becomes isolated and invites outside challenge to its power. When the Church bureaucrats invited the laity to come to Rome to assume greater participation in Church affairs, the outsiders inevitably became a threat to the stability of the authority structure, no matter how closely lay activists were controlled.

We saw that at the third World Congress for the Lay Apostolate the delegates refused to back the traditional position of Church authorities on internal democracy and on birth control. In addition, the Council on the Laity had previously turned down a hierarchical request that its own deliberations be kept entirely secret. We saw also how the Vatican selected, co-opted, and tried to control the lay leaders at the congress. Also evident was how the delegates reacted to an overly blatant manipulation that could be described as an instance of counterproductive control.

Since in a token granting of autonomy and participation there will always be some elements of the real thing, mechanisms of control by the central power must be subtly instituted. That the Vatican understood this was evident in the discussion in chapter 4 of the devices for keeping the delegates in line and of the various delegates' efforts to challenge these devices. But even manipulation sometimes backfires, and there is often no choice but to revert to authoritarianism or to give a greater degree of freedom. The Church has, in this century, nearly always opted for rigid control when lay organizations have seemed uncooperative. Some Catholic organizations have been subjected to "lay massacres," last-ditch measures in which they are deprived of their leaders or of official recognition. These are not frequent occurrences, since the hierarchy is often able to minimize effective lay participation and maximize clerical control while giving a public impression of the opposite, but they are frequent enough to warrant the conclusion that Church authorities, especially at the Vatican, are unwilling to share their power with rank-and-file members of the Church. Since the 1967 congress, the tendency has been to regress to a slightly more overt form of authoritarianism as far as laity-hierarchy relations are concerned.

In spite of the controls exercised at the third World Congress for the Lay Apostolate and the conservative method of choosing delegates, the laymen who gathered in Rome in October 1967 laid the foundation for a transformation of the norms and structures of the Catholic Church. As a result of the congress and of post-congress conflict between the Vatican and the laity, these same active and well-educated lay leaders—and others also—have become more radical in their religious and political orientation in recent years. The moderate and reasonable delegates who answered the questionnaire just analyzed have asked for greater power in the Church. Their requests have brought a confused response from Church officials, who believe them to be already too powerful but who cannot do without them because they need their support. The trend since 1967 seems to have been a harder line, but it is unlikely that this orientation will endure for very long, because exclusion of laymen from participation in the affairs of the Church is much more dangerous for organizational survival than the risks inherent in a policy of limited and controlled access to positions of decision-making power. Since papal control over the laity is not an end in itself, but rather a means to attain certain goals, some of which are political and economic, rather than purely and uniquely religious, rigid controls could theoretically be abandoned if these goals could be reached through other means. But since it is unlikely that the Vatican will abandon in the near future its preoccupation with economic and political power to revert to its original religious goals, it seems rather inevitable that manipulative means of control will continue to be part of the standard operating policies of the Roman Catholic Church. In the next two chapters, I shall examine this question of how political and economic factors impinge on and influence the actions and operations of the popes and their immediate collaborators.

Although the same time-period already covered in previous chapters will be examined in these two chapters, it will be from a very different perspective. Instead of simply describing the relationship between papacy and laity, I shall try to explain the nature of that relationship, particularly the papal tendency to "lord it over" the laity, by taking into account the down-to-earth political and socioeconomic interests of the Vatican. I shall try to show that papal-lay relations are not only religious but also economic and especially political, the politics of Italy being the most important factor that has influenced papal control over the laity during the past hundred years. In other words, intra-Church policies will be connected to extra-Church realities through the contention that the Vatican controls and uses the laity mainly to further its political and financial interests, and not only to promote religious goals as it officially purports to do. The similarity, then, of the following chapters with what has been examined before is only apparent since the former chapters dealt with internal religious phenomena while the following chapters will add to that a consideration of political and economic underpinnings.[20]

PART THREE

The Sources and Present
Manifestations of Papal Control

VI

The Vatican and Italian Politics

Although my aim until now has not been to make an inventory of the organized lay apostolate, but rather to examine its relations with Church authorities, I have been led, especially in chapters 2 and 3, to give much attention to the Italian situation.[1] But that is not enough. In order to understand the role of the laity in the Catholic Church, and the nature of the controls which the Vatican has used to contain the lay movement, I must go beyond the sphere of ecclesiastical organization and values to examine briefly the political and socioeconomic situation in Italy over the last hundred years. The Vatican's need to control the laity is related to political and economic pressures, not only to religious goals. What I have treated until now mainly as religious and organizational problems can also be examined in the context of politics, and even of economics. As Renaud Dulong has written: "To refuse to look at the Catholic Church in its political dimensions is in itself a political act."[2]

The nature of the present-day relationships between papacy and laity is intimately linked with recent political and socioeconomic developments in Italy, as well as with certain European and international developments such as the growth of nationalist, liberal, Socialist, and Communist movements in modern times.

1. PIUS IX (1846–1878), LEO XIII (1878–1903), AND ITALIAN POLITICS

After revolutionary democrats failed to unit Italy around the middle of the nineteenth century, conservative and aristocratic liberals succeeded in establishing a united and independent constitutional kingdom of Italy in 1870. At the first Vatican Council, that same year, the bishops had declared the pope infallible, but because the Franco-Prussian war made it impossible for France to defend Rome against the threatening Italian troops, the bishops hurriedly left for home. Later that year, Pius IX was rewarded for his continued opposition to Italian unification by the takeover of the papal states. The resistance put up by his international brigade of pontifical Zouaves and Swiss Guards was token; they were no match for the Piedmontese invaders of his territories. His temporal power gone, he retaliated by excommunicating the founders of the unified Italian state. He also advised Catholics not to participate in politics, a strategy subsequent popes were eventually to abandon in their efforts to establish a more realistic position toward the various governments of Italy. Pius IX declared himself "the prisoner of the Vatican" and spent the rest of his life fighting the Italian state, attempting to reestablish the hegemony that the Catholic Church had held during the Middle Ages and that had been gradually eroded by the Reformation, the Enlightenment, and the democratic revolutions. The ill-fated politics of Pius IX can be seen in the context of an effort to return to those golden medieval days of the alliance of throne and altar, when churchmen were often more powerful than kings.

During the last hundred years, the dream of restoring Church dominance in the western world has inspired many pontiffs. After a century of Italian unification, the policies of Paul VI were a product of the search for a way of reestablishing some degree of Catholic hegemony. The strategy had been changed to fit the situation. Instead of a policy of alliances with traditional reactionary powers, Paul VI backed a Christian Democratic Party, a tightly controlled apostolate, and a class-collaborationist form of neocapitalism. Between Pius IX and Paul VI lay a century of religious and political developments, a mixture of diplomacy, intrigue, and struggle, in which the Catholic laity's role became increasingly important, both inside and outside the Church. Catholic Action and more generally the organized lay apostolate had become key elements in the Church's design for becoming, once again, the foremost universal religion, a sort of civil religion not only of the West but of the whole world.

The neo-Guelfist dream of a Catholic Italy united around the papal throne, which the newly elected Pius IX promoted, and which the first Italian Christian Democrats revived in a less clerical fashion at the end of the nineteenth century, still constituted the reality of the Vatican policies. The Christian Democrats were the papacy's new Zouaves, except that the papal realm had been extended to all of Italy rather than being limited only to the ancient papal states that Pius IX tried desperately to keep under his control.

Cardinal Ferrata reported that he was told by Pius IX, shortly before his death, that everything had changed around him, that his system and his policies had served their time, that he was too old to change his orientation, and that it would be the work of his successor to impart a new direction to the papacy. The problem was even more complex for his successor, Leo XIII (1878–1903), because during most of his long pontificate anticlerical republicans with little desire for reconciliation with the Church were in power in both France and Italy. Moreover, Leo XIII did not want to give up the papacy's claims to lost territories and privileges by recognizing the Italian state. Although in the social and political arena he was more progressive than Pius IX (he blocked, for example, the creation of a conservative political party in Italy), there were strict limits beyond which he would not go.

In 1876, two years before Pius IX's death, the moderate monarchists (the liberal right, as they are often called) who had run the government of Italy for sixteen years were replaced in power by followers of Mazzini and Garibaldi who, although strongly anticlerical, had reconciled themselves to the constitutional monarchy. This change of rulers, added to the fact that Leo XIII had been a Roman Curia diplomat under Pius IX, and not a bishop from an Italian diocese where collaboration with the state was a necessity, helps to explain his reluctance to change Pius IX's policy concerning Catholic participation in Italian national elections.

Much of the program of the social Catholics near the end of the nineteenth century represented an effort to move the masses away from communism and liberalism, rather than a genuine desire for their socioeconomic and political emancipation. Because the Church was still at odds with the rising bourgeoisie for having despoiled it of its feudal privileges, it made occasional bids for the sympathy of the workers. Read in this perspective, Leo XIII's corporatist encyclical *Rerum Novarum* (1891) appears as a much more conservative document than it is often pictured to be. Far from being a "Magna Carta" for workers' rights, it was an effort to reconcile workers with the Church by making certain concessions without coming out too strongly against the very strong power of the capitalists. And in this sense it was an anti-socialist manifesto. Thus, during the latter part of his reign, Leo XIII spelled out a social program which effectively reconciled the Church with the ruling bourgeoisies, without overly antagonizing the working class. This program was neither liberal nor socialist, although it was definitely more sympathetic to liberal democracy than to socialism. Leo XIII condemned socialism, as his predecessors had done, and he openly encouraged French Catholics to rally to the republican form of government rather than try to reestablish the monarchy, saying that he considered a return to a monarchical type of government to be an unlikely eventuality in the case of France.

In Italy, the government became very unstable after the 1882 extension of the suffrage. Because of economic problems, violence flared throughout the country. In 1893, in response to a general desire for a strong man who could reestablish law and order, a conservative, Francesco Crispi, was called as prime minister for the second time. He ruled with an iron hand during the last few years of the century.

The Socialist agitation of 1898 brought about government repression not only against workers' associations but also against Catholic organizations, whose intransigency (on the questions of national unity and papal power) supposedly made them objective allies of the left-wing agitators. These difficulties with unpopular government only helped Catholic organizations develop more strongly than before.[3] This revival of Catholic organizational life led to the official founding of Italian Catholic Action in 1898.

Although Leo XIII never entirely abandoned the official Church position set down by his predecessor against Catholic participation in national Italian politics, he weakened the rigidity of Pius IX's *non expedit* when he allowed Catholic participation in local Italian politics. After the replacement of Crispi by the "constitutional" left (i.e. Liberals) in 1900, Catholic intransigeance toward the Italian state was substantially reduced by Church authorities because it was only strengthening the extreme left. Leo XIII gradually oriented the Catholic lay movement toward conciliation with the liberal politicians in power. Since he had asked French Catholics to rally to the republican government, it was difficult for the pope to maintain that Italians should forever continue their boycott of their own national government. After remaining faithful to Pius IX's policy throughout most of his papacy, Leo XIII came, near the end of his life, to accept the necessity of Catholic respect for the established national democratic regime. In the Italian lay Catholic movement at the turn of the century, the main expression of which was the Opera dei Congressi, the emphasis shifted from a conservative defense of papal claims against the Italian state to a gradual social and economic, and sometimes political, mobilization of Catholic masses. In other words, the Opera dei Congressi slowly transformed itself into a relatively progressive Christian Democratic movement with the approval of Leo XIII. This lay movement, because of the political situation in Italy, was moving away from the original defensive Catholic Action orientation into a second state of development, namely, a Christian Democratic Party orientation.

2. PIUS X (1903–1914) AND
BENEDICT XV (1914–1922)

Before becoming pope, the conservative Pius X (1903–1914) had encouraged alliances at the municipal level between Catholics and Liberals against the Socialists. He implemented a similar policy at the national level after he became pope. This reactionary pope, whom Pius XII admired so much that he canonized him, was the reconciliator of the Catholic Church with capitalism and liberalism. By 1903 the Opera dei Congressi was evolving into a mass political organization, a semiautonomous national Catholic Action movement strongly attracted toward a Christian Democratic orientation. Pius X and his curia did not like this new development because they had very little sympathy for Christian Democracy. In the summer of 1904, in order not to lose control over the orientation of the lay movement, Pius X dissolved the Opera dei Congressi, using as his pretext the organization's internal tensions between progressives and conservatives.[4]

Leo XIII had forced the conservative Count Paganuzzi to leave the presidency of the Opera dei Congressi in 1903, thus favoring the members of the more progressive wing of the young Christian Democrats. Pius X, an admirer of Paganuzzi, and a critic of the Christian Democrats' radicalism, replaced both the Opera dei Congressi and Catholic Action with a new kind of Catholic Action consisting of a federation of religious, socioeconomic, and electoral "unions." Thus, Catholic Action became much more encompassing, and through it the Vatican was able to intervene indirectly in Italian politics, defending the social order against the rising tide of socialism. These new Catholic Action unions were used as instruments to transmit instructions to Catholics on how to vote. This was done primarily by the chaplains, and the activity led to further bureaucratization of Catholicism and a concomitant de-democratization of the Church. Max Weber refers to this precise phenomenon as a "passive democratization" and a "leveling of the governed in face of the governing and bureaucratically articulated group, which in turn may occupy a quite autocratic position both in fact and in form."[5]

Under Leo XIII's successor, Pius X, there were various political tendencies inside the Italian lay Catholic movement. There were left-leaning Christian Democrats like Murri and Sturzo, who wanted to create a Catholic party of a moderate left tendency. There were pro-clerical moderates, who were even more willing than the Christian Democrats to follow Pius X's line of support for Prime Minister Giovanni Giolitti's liberal candidates who were ready to make concessions to the Vatican. Finally, there were conservatives, many of them young Catholics, who were sympathetic to the new imperialist nationalism which was to evolve into fascism.

Pius X was concerned about the increasing loss of papal control over the voting behavior of Catholics, and about the potential radicalization of Catholic workers and peasants. He was willing to let Catholics vote to block anticlericals and Socialists, but not to support them. Being an Italian patriot rather than a Roman curialist like his predecessor, the conservative Pius X was the first to admit the possibility of limited lay Catholic participation in national politics, agreeing that Catholics might vote in the 1904 elections. The Socialist Party, which came into being in 1892, was seen as such a threat by this conservative pope that he decided to allow individual Catholics to enter the political arena in order to counter Socialist influence. Firmly opposing and condemning more radical "social Christians" like Murri, who wanted to found a Catholic party, Pius X wanted to develop an antileftist alliance between Catholics and moderate Liberals like Giolitti.

In 1909 the pope went so far as to agree to allow Catholic deputies to hold seats in Parliament. Prime Minister Giolitti was open to the idea of a Catholic alliance. He had succeeded in gaining the support of a group of northern radicals by isolating them from the leftist parties and had managed to stay in power by maintaining a delicate balance between these adherents and his conservative southern supporters. When universal suffrage was established in 1912, Giolitti had to counterbalance the large numbers of new working-class voters who were already favorable to socialism. An alliance with the Catholic Action federation proved to be beneficial to him. A Catholic alliance with the Liberal prime minister was also advantageous to the pope, and both sides were easily able to make small reciprocal concessions. The Giolittians had merely to tone down their anticlericalism. The papacy made itself more open to bourgeois-democratic policies, abandoning the social perspectives initiated under Leo XIII and trading votes for state support of papal authoritarianism inside the Church.

Pius X pushed for a return to the type of lay movement that existed under Pius IX: a conservative Catholic Action oriented toward the defense of Church privileges, this time through participation in elections alongside secular rightists, rather than through abstention. His attitude toward the lay movement, toward both Catholic Action and the Christian Democrats, and his decisions concerning their orientation, thus seems to have been determined by his conservative orientation in political matters. Pius X's position amply illustrates the conservative function filled by the papacy most of the time, and, more generally, the legitimating role played by Catholicism. As long as the threat was felt to come from the Liberals, the Church attacked them, but as soon as the Socialist Party became a serious political force, the Liberals were viewed as allies. Pius X did not hesitate to resort to quite reactionary alliances and actions. The religious witch-hunt against "modernism" that he initiated within the Church, and which even touched the young Angelo Roncalli (the future John XXIII),[6] was not without links to the conservative positions Pius X upheld in the social and economic spheres.

In 1913, thirty-five Catholics were elected to the Italian parliament and, more significantly, as many as 230 of all the elected are said to have previously agreed to uphold the Gentiloni Pact, an agreement whereby they promised not to support anticlerical policies and laws on such questions as divorce, Catholic schools, and religious congregations.[7]

Giolitti nevertheless had overextended himself, creating a government majority too numerous and heterogeneous to maintain. He was forced to pass the reins of government to Antonio Salandra, a more conservative and proclerical leader who also received the backing of the Catholic proclerical moderates. Despite Pius X's success in obtaining proclerical victories in the political arena, internal Church dissatisfaction with the witch hunting during his pontificate probably accounts for the election of a more progressive successor after his death in 1914. In the conclave which had followed the death of Leo XIII, the Austrian cardinals had used an old privilege called the imperial veto to impede the election of Leo XIII's progressive secretary of state, Cardinal Rampolla, as pope. On the first ballot Rampolla received 24 votes and Giuseppe Sarto 5, but on the seventh and last ballot Rampolla had only 10 votes left while Cardinal Sarto had 50. Eleven years later, in 1914, there was no obvious outside political interference during the conclave that elected Pius X's successor, and, as a reaction against the dead pope's conservative policies, it was a protégé of the late Cardinal Rampolla, Cardinal Della Chiesa, who was elected as supreme pontiff. Giacomo Della Chiesa was not a political conservative. This new pope, Benedict XV (1914–1922), was a neutralist during World War I. Italian Catholics had been quite divided on the issue of going to war; proclerical moderates gave a qualified support to the pro-war governments, and the newly formed Central Committee of Catholic Action, which was set up by Benedict XV, objected to the policy of military intervention.

In the very fluid wartime political situation, Benedict XV abolished the electoral *non expedit*, at the request of Luigi Sturzo. He further permitted the founding of a party of Catholics, the Popular Party, by Sturzo and laymen like Giorgio Montini, a former president of the Electoral Union of Italian Catholics. Benedict generally favored autonomy for lay Catholics in the political arena.

Gaetano Salvemini has described how Benedict XV's apparently neutral attitude, in contrast to that of his predecessor Pius X and that of his successor Pius XI, actually helped the Popolari, who could not have founded their party without the pope's tacit approval:

> Benedict XV let spontaneous forces develop in the Catholic movement, without showing any conservative or democratic preferences; with his non-intervention he left the field open for the democratic forces in Italy, saying that the *Partitio Popolare* acted on its own, by virtue of its exclusive responsibility, and not at all by any control by the authorities of the Catholic Church.[8]

In an article written in *L'Ordine Nuovo* in 1919, Gramsci considered the foundation of the Popular Party to be the Italian equivalent of the German Reformation. He saw the new Catholic party as a necessary phase in the process of development of Italy toward socialism, like the Mensheviks in Russia, since that party created solidarity in the countryside where socialism could not penetrate yet, and raised expectations that only socialism would be able to satisfy on the long run.[9]

In 1919, the Popolari elected 101 deputies, to the Socialists' 156. The immediate success of the Popolari came in good part from their appeal to the peasants, which was due largely to a progressive program calling for the breaking up of large estates.

Within the Popular Party, the leaders were more interested in following a centrist line than in defending clerical interests. The clericalists were a power to be reckoned with in that party, although they were counterbalanced by a leftist group preoccupied with social (especially agrarian) reform. At the first congress of the party, in July 1919 at Bologna, Father Agostino Gemelli, a conservative scholar, later to become a Fascist sympathizer, wanted the party to be dependent on the hierarchy and dedicated to the defense of the traditional papal claims; in other words, he wanted it to be a conservative confessional Catholic party. Sturzo opposed him, saying that he wanted to avoid giving the country the false impression that the Popular Party was a front for Catholic Action, rather than an essentially political organization.[10]

This did not please the Catholic conservatives, who were more interested in getting a satisfactory territorial settlement of the Roman Question than in participating with progressive political parties in the solution of the social and political problems of Italy. One of the concessions that conservatives like Gemelli wanted from the Italian state was the public funding of a national Catholic university. As a matter of fact, Mussolini later made that concession and Gemelli was appointed rector of the Catholic University of the Sacred Heart in Milan.

Concurrent with the rise of the Popular Party came the development of Catholic trade-unions. In 1918 a national federation of labor unions replaced Pius X's old Socio-Economic Union, which had stressed employer-worker collaboration of the corporatist type rather than the defense of workers.

The years 1915–1922 saw the gradual disintegration of parliamentary democracy in Italy and a deterioration of socioeconomic conditions. The Popolari, holding to a centrist position, refused to collaborate with the Socialists and, like the proclerical moderates before them, backed the Liberal Giolitti. In spite of their impressive gains at the polls in 1919, the Socialists were unable to gain power electorally without the help of the peasant-based Popular Party, and were unwilling to provoke a revolution to seize power.

Antonio Gramsci explains, in an article on the birth of the Popular Party and in the ninth of his Lyons theses, his idea that the Popolari came about as a result of the Vatican's wish to integrate the Italian peasantry into the framework of the bourgeois state.[11] In his view, however, the Partito Popolare was not solely a party of order created to mediate between ruling and working classes. He describes it as a step in the direction of the left. Although a competitor of the left for the votes of the rural masses, the party helped move these masses, through development of associationism, solidarity, and organization, to a position where reliance on religious myth could be replaced by a need for historical action and political power that only socialism could provide.

On the other hand, Pietro Nenni, the Socialist leader, saw the Popolari as a Vatican-controlled party that "performed a first-rate task of social conservatism" and stopped the Socialists from taking control in 1919.[12] Salvemini, another Socialist, also considered the Popolari to be responsible for preventing the Socialists from taking power.[13]

Giolitti, his power eroding, made a last-ditch effort to hold his centrist coalition together by trying to field a block of candidates, some of whom were Fascists, in the 1921 elections. This time, both Popolari and Socialists refused to play the Giolitti coalition games, and the election results gave Giolitti little to form a government with. Socialists and Popolari were returned in strength, and 45 seats were won by Fascists and conservative Nationalists. Giolitti gave temporary support to another centrist politician, Ivanoe Bonomi. Then Luigi Facta, another centrist, formed a new, uneasy centrist coalition that included the Popolari. Meanwhile the Fascists were becoming more popular and powerful. Coalitions of centrists, Popolari, and Socialists failed to materialize because one of the three groups would inevitably refuse to join the alliance. The Fascists were performing takeovers by force in many parts of the country, and the disunited left and center parties could do little to oppose them. Left-wing Socialists split from the Socialist Party to form the Italian Communist Party, a move which further splintered the anti-Fascist forces. Gramsci himself, between 1923 and 1926, spent much of his time attacking the Socialists instead of trying to develop an alliance with them and the Popolari in order to block the road to fascism.

Thus, Mussolini's rise to power was facilitated by this division of the left-of-center forces. After the king asked him to form a government in 1922, the Fascist leader had little difficulty consolidating his power and eliminating his political opponents. His cabinet obtained a vote of confidence from 306 deputies (including the Popolari), with only 116 votes against. These 116 deputies were the Socialists and Communists.

In a speech on October 3, 1944, Palmiro Togliatti, the leader of the Italian Communist Party, gave an evaluation of these events:

> We remember the experience of the rise to power of fascism in 1920, 1921, and 1922. We remember that in those years one of the

reasons why the reactionary ruling classes were able to grab power and destroy us all, one after the other, was the fact that we could not come to an agreement between the proletarian organizations under the leadership of the Socialist and Communist parties, and the peasant associations under the leadership of the Popular Party.

You might recall that at the congress which we held in Livorno in 1921, when we founded our party, our comrade Terracini, in the political speech which he gave at the congress, accused the leaders of the Socialist party, the reformist and conservative leaders of the Socialist Party, of not having understood the necessity of coming to a political agreement with the Popular Party.[14]

The question of the collaboration between the Communist Party and the Catholic party in Italy is one which has never been resolved. Since these two political formations are the strongest of all the Italian parties, they see themselves as virulent adversaries in the political arena. It was only immediately after World War II that the Catholic party and the Communists were able to form a government together. After that, the Christian Democrats, the political and spiritual heirs of the Popolari, were strong enough to govern by themselves or in alliance with the other parties to the right of the Communists. In recent years, however, because of the increasing difficulties in maintaining the center-left coalition (i.e. Christian Democratic collaboration with the Socialists and Social Democrats) there has been again some talk of a sharing of power between the Communists and the Catholic party. This new alliance, which is coming about little by little, is referred to as the "historical compromise" by the Communists.

3. PIUS XI (1922-1939) AND MUSSOLINI

After the death of Benedict XV and the election of Cardinal Achille Ratti as pope in 1922, the Popular Party of Luigi Sturzo fell into disfavor with the Vatican. The conservative and authoritarian Ratti, who chose the name of Piux XI, was attracted by Mussolini's offer to settle the Roman Question (i.e. the mainly territorial differences between the Vatican and the Italian state stemming from the takeover of the papal states in 1870), on the condition that the Popular Party be kept under control. Some Popolari, especially former proclerical moderates, even went as far as making alliances with the Fascists and participating in Mussolini's cabinet. In addition, 150 Catholic notables signed a manifesto in favor of Mussolini's government just before the 1924 elections. The Vatican, and many Italian cardinals, bishops, and priests, leaned toward the Fascists, creating many difficulties for what was left of the anti-Fascist Popolari (the veterans of Murri's Democratic League and the trade-unionists, essentially).

On October 2, 1922, Pius XI gave Mussolini more direct support by asking the clergy to remain neutral in politics and to not align themselves with the Popolari. He then requested that Luigi Sturzo resign from parliament and disband the Popular Party (June 9, 1923), and finally, the following year, ordered all priests to resign from that party. It was then that Pius XI decided to revivify and give a strong new impetus to Catholic Action, in order to destroy the Popular Party.

Gramsci, in his history of the Italian Communist Party, makes this shrewd observation about the difference between the Popular Party and Catholic Action at that time, a difference which helps us understand why the conservative Pius XI would help suppress the first and favor the second:

> The Italian Popular Party was on the brink of entering into serious conflict with Catholic Action. As a matter of fact, it was increasingly becoming the organization of the lower clergy and the poor peasants, while Catholic Action was in the hands of the aristocracy, the big landowners, and the higher ecclesiastical authorities, who were reactionary and favorable to Fascism.[15]

For Gramsci, Benedict XV's revival of grass-roots Catholic organizations, which culminated in the development of the Popular Party, had brought about an increasingly important role for progressive lay Catholics and a parallel decrease in the hierarchy's control over them: "By the incoercible logic of ideas and events, active Catholics have implicitly become Lutherans."[16] But this new reform could not be of a religious nature; it could only be secular, that is, liberal for the elites and socialist for the masses. Had the Popular Party followed a normal development, according to Gramsci, it would have split, the mass of its poorer members moving into the orbit of a working-class party organization.

Mussolini had little to fear from the badly divided and decimated Popolari, who were already losing many members to antipolitical Catholic Action and even to the Fascists. By changing the electoral laws in 1923, the Fascists and their allies succeeded in getting 65 percent of the vote and two-thirds of the seats in the Chamber of Deputies in the 1924 national elections. The Fascist list obtained 4,500,000 votes, against 645,000 for the Popolari, 448,058 for the

Socialists, 348,540 for the Maximalists, 304,682 for the Communists, and 241,685 for the Liberals. Again the Popolari refused to enter into a common front with the other opposition parties. Alcide De Gasperi, Sturzo's successor as political secretary of the Popolari, tried in July 1924 to propose a coalition between Catholics and moderate Socialists, but his move was opposed by the Vatican. Piux XI preferred the Fascists to a government that would have comprised left-of-center Catholics like De Gasperi in coalition with moderate Socialists. On March 24, 1924, Pius XI had indicated his pleasure at the fact that religion had been reintroduced into the schools and that government subsidies to the clergy had been increased. On December 14, 1925, he would thank the Fascist government for all it did for religion, and, in passing, mention that he had been saddened by an assassination attempt on Mussolini, a clear indication of sympathy for the dictator. On various occasions, Pius even said publicly that Mussolini was a man sent by God.

The *Civiltà Cattolica*, the Vatican-controlled Jesuit periodical, published an article on August 16, 1924, on the "role of Catholics in the present political party struggles in Italy," indirectly attacking De Gasperi because he had called for collaboration between Catholics and moderate Socialists in order to save Italy from fascism. The article defended fascism and opposed any collaboration between the Popolari and the Socialists. Once again, the Vatican's link with the conservative interests of the ruling class and its fear of the left stood manifest and the Catholic Church was made an ally of a repressive regime.

On September 8, Pius XI himself, in a talk to Italian Catholic students, said that collaboration with socialism, as suggested by De Gasperi, would be cooperation in evil. He also attacked the nonconfessionalism of the Popular Party, which "might lead to ignoring even the Catholic confession itself."[17] When some Catholic journalists tried to minimize his opposition to an alliance of the Popolari with the Socialists, the *Osservatore Romano* replied that an anti-Fascist coalition including the Socialists was not acceptable to the pope. Thus Pius XI blocked one of the few moves which might have stopped fascism in Italy.

Mussolini openly established a dictatorship in January 1925, and in November 1926 a government communiqué announced that all anti-Fascist political associations and political parties had been dissolved. De Gasperi was jailed for a few years. Quite a few of the more conservative leaders of the Popolari switched to the Fascists, while some, like Giorgio Montini, simply retired from politics. Montini's son,

Giovanni-Battista (the future Paul VI), newly ordained as a priest, was recruited by Msgr. Giuseppe Pizzardo to work in the Secretariate of State of the Vatican. This was during the time when Cardinal Pietro Gasparri, the secretary of state, and Msgr. Eugenio Pacelli (the future secretary of state of Pius XI, and a future pope himself) were negotiating as many concordats as possible with conservative governments. Msgr. Montini was also made chaplain of the Italian Federation of University Students in 1925, in which office he contributed greatly to making that lay Catholic organization a quiet source of opposition to the Fascist regime.[18]

Pius XI had helped kill the Popular Party in order to please the Fascists and, as noted above, had simultaneously revived Catholic Action as a sort of religious substitute for lay activity. Many of the young laymen who would normally have joined the Popolari came to Catholic Action and started using it as a sort of spiritual bulwark against the totalitarian encroachments of fascism. When Pius realized that the Fascists would not let even Catholic Action alone, and that they were intent on monopolizing the socialization of youth, he decided to defend Catholic Action's right to be active in religious and moral areas. This change of heart vis-à-vis fascism did not stop him from working to get a concordat from Mussolini and from trying to trade off legitimation of the regime against concessions to the Vatican. The pope took full advantage of the fact that conservative and unpopular regimes during the twenties and thirties found it useful to get religious legitimation for themselves. Concordats permitted the papacy to increase its autonomy in the nomination of bishops, but they also often put pressure on lay Catholics so that they would not oppose the conservative regimes that had treated the Church well.

After the Vatican-induced exile of Sturzo and the dissolution of the Popular Party in 1926, negotiations were opened with the government, at the instigation of the pope himself, for the settlement of the Roman Question. The negotiations broke off when a struggle erupted over who would control the boys' and girls' scout movement. When the Vatican relented on that issue, talks were resumed which led in 1929 to the Lateran Agreements, comprising a monetary convention, a treaty, and a concordat.

The financial settlement for the lands confiscated by the Italian state in the nineteenth century amounted to the equivalent of 90 million dollars (in 1929 U.S. funds). This settlement money forms the basis of present-day Vatican wealth. Benedict XV had left the Vatican in a very weak financial posture, but Cardinal Gasparri's and Pius XI's skillful negotiations put the Vatican back on solid economic grounds.

The fact that more than half of this sum was finally paid in government bonds, which Pius XI agreed to keep over a long period, had the inevitable result of tying the Vatican closely to the Fascist regime. It is not too surprising then, that a majority of the Italian hierarchy and clergy, and even the pope, approved and encouraged Mussolini's imperial ventures in Ethiopia and protested against the regime only when some definite interest of the Catholic Church itself was trampled upon.[19]

The Lateran treaty, the second component of the Lateran Agreements, was a momentous event for the Catholic Church. Church authorities in Rome were jubilant. At last the Vatican was being compensated for territorial losses suffered in 1870, and it was finally getting recognized by Italy as a sovereign entity. After more than forty years of uncertainty, the Vatican was now an independent state, with the pope as its temporal ruler, and it was guaranteed its communication with the rest of the world. The treaty also closed the quarrel between the papacy and the Italian state, by giving papal recognition to the kingdom of Italy with Rome as its capital and by making Catholicism the official religion of Italy.

Finally, the concordat concerned religious affairs more specifically. It guaranteed religious education in schools, thus helping the Fascist state structure civil society and maintain its hegemony over the masses, as Gramsci would have put it. The Catholic University of Milan was accredited, and Church laws on marriage were accepted as having legal validity in the civil arena. Priests and members of religious orders were forbidden to be active in politics, and Catholic organizations dependent on Catholic Action were recognized by the government on the condition that they not involve themselves in politics and that they become directly dependent on Church authorities. The concordat thus reinforced the authority structures of the Church in return for assurances that the priests and laymen would not push for social justice and would view fascism with a certain amount of sympathy. In other words, the effect of the quarrels and agreements between the Vatican and fascism concerning Catholic Action was that, in return for the religious legitimation they needed, the Fascist leaders helped the Vatican increase its control over the Italian lay movement. Since Mussolini feared the laity more than the clergy or hierarchy, because the laity could have reorganized a political opposition in the form of a new Catholic party, he demanded that leadership positions in Catholic Action be taken away from the former Popolari leaders, and that the public activities of Catholic Action be drastically curbed.

As anticipated, the Lateran Agreements helped Mussolini sweep the general elections of 1929. Just before the signing, De Gasperi was freed from jail. Unable to find a job in Italy, he went to work as a librarian in the Vatican until the end of the war, when he reemerged to become the unrivaled leader of the Christian Democratic Party.

Dependence on the Church hierarchy and noninvolvement in politics were the two conditions which the Lateran Agreements had put on the existence of Catholic Action associations. However, less than two months after the signing of these agreements, jurisdictional disputes on questions of youth education and Catholic Action erupted. Now that the Populari Party was out of the way, and that he had obtained legitimacy from the Lateran Agreements, Mussolini sought even greater control over lay Catholics.

Relations between the Vatican and Mussolini deteriorated somewhat between 1929 and 1931. The concessions made to Catholic Action had assured the existence of one small island of potential resistance to Fascist control, where Catholic laymen could prepare the eventual rebirth of a Catholic opposition party. This the Fascists resented, fearing that Catholics would relaunch the Popular Party, and they attacked Catholic Action. The pope countered with numerous protests and with a strong anti-Fascist encyclical, *Non abbiamo bisogno* (1931), but relations improved again after the uneasy compromise of September 1931.

Msgr. Montini, who was closely identified with the Popolari and was one of the few staunch anti-Fascist progressives in the curia at the time, lost his part-time job as chaplain of the Italian Federation of Catholic University Students in the fence mending that followed. In compensation, he was given a promotion in the Secretariate of State, becoming one of the closest collaborators of the new secretary of state, Eugenio Pacelli, the future Pius XII, at a time when the Vatican was quite ambivalent about the rise of fascism and much interested in the possibility of developing an alliance of conservative Catholic regimes in southern Europe to counterbalance both Soviet Bolshevism and German Nazism. In 1937, some months after Pius XI's condemnation of both Nazism and communism in *Mit Brennender Sorge* and *Divini Redemptoris*, Montini was again promoted, this time to the key post of substitute secretary for the section of Ordinary Affairs in the Secretariate of State. Throughout all these years he kept in contact with the young Catholic intellectuals he had known in the FUCI. Some of them were to become active in the resistance and several emerged after World War II as leaders of the new Catholic party, the Christian Democrats, and as members of the Italian government. Guido

Gonella, Aldo Moro, Amintore Fanfani, Mario Scelba, Giulio Andreotti, Paolo Emilio Taviani, all so influential in postwar Italy, were close associates of Montini during the war. One of Montini's brothers also became a Christian Democratic politician of some importance.

Montini and his progressive lay friends, however, were a minority in Italian Catholicism during the Fascist era. By and large, the Vatican, the Italian hierarchy and clergy, and many of the official leaders of Catholic Action and other Catholic organizations were on good terms with the Fascist regime. A climate of cooperation and conciliation reigned between church and state. Praise for the Duce was frequent and lavish because of the conservatism of these Catholics and also because of fascism's concessions to the more traditional aspects of Catholicism. All this started to change only when Mussolini began to align himself with the racist doctrines of the Nazis in the mid-thirties, a development which led the pope to reverse his earlier reactionary orientation. When Pius XI finally realized he was being used by Mussolini, who was himself nothing more than a pawn of Hitler, his opposition became irrevocable.

4. THE VATICAN AND THE RISE OF HITLER

The Vatican's policies toward fascist Italy were not something unique, occasioned simply because of the Italian connections. In relations with other reactionary regimes, the same complacent attitude was present. In Germany in the twenties, the Center Party was led to reject the Weimar coalition with Social Democrats and Liberals, and to enter into an alliance with the German Nationalists, at the instigation of papal nuncio Eugenio Pacelli. From 1928 on, the Center Party became a clerical instrument in the hands of the nuncio, who oriented it toward nationalism and dictatorship. The Vatican then decided to let the Center Party be dissolved, in order to negotiate with the Nazi government a concordat which would assure certain privileges to Catholicism, just as the 1929 concordat in Italy had done.

In a semiofficial statement, the Vatican tried to explain its action to dissatisfied Catholics:

> The determination of Chancellor Hitler's Government to eliminate the Catholic Party coincides with the Vatican's desire to disinterest itself from political parties and confine the activities of Catholics to the Catholic Action organization outside any political party.[20]

This coincidence of Vatican and Nazi interests was not purely accidental. The Vatican certainly did not follow that line of political noninvolvement after World War II in Italy when noninvolvement would have favored the left rather than the right. The decision of the Vatican to confine the activities of Catholics to Catholic Action and to approve the suppression of Catholic parties was due to the fact that the Vatican knew it would get more concessions from conservative governments in need of religious legitimation than it would from Catholic parties that had to be careful not to appear too subservient to the Church. Also, those governments' strong anti-Communist and anti-Socialist orientation was an added incentive for the Vatican. Thus it was not because of the desire to stay out of politics, but in order to support right-wing regimes and to combat left-wing alternatives that the Vatican and various members of the hierarchy and clergy suppressed Catholic parties and promoted Catholic Action.

The Vatican's acceptance of the Nazi takeover of Austria, its backing of Franco against the Popular Front government in Spain, and its support of the right-wing armed revolt in Mexico against revolutionary forces seem to have been part of an overall policy. Vatican support of Catholic parties in Germany, France, and Italy after World War II does not invalidate this interpretation, because only the Catholic parties could then block a Socialist-Communist victory.

Hitler's rise to power, thus, was considerably helped by his good relations with the Vatican, and by his own 1933 concordat with the Holy See, which completely destroyed the political power of German Catholics. Pius XI's instructions to Cardinal Faulhaber, archbishop of Vienna, in early March 1933, probably underlay the switch in the German Catholics' position toward Hitler later that month. Cardinal Faulhaber is reported to have said on March 24, after his return from Rome:

> Let us meditate on the words of the Holy Father, who, in a consistory, without mentioning his name, indicated before the whole world in Adolph Hitler the statesman who first, after the Pope himself, has raised his voice against Bolshevism.[21]

Pius XI was indeed fascinated by Hitler, just as he was by Mussolini. In 1933 he told Franz von Papen, who had come to Rome to prepare the concordat for Germany, how pleased he was "that the German government now had at its head a man uncompromisingly opposed to Communism and Russian nihilism in all its forms."[22] Mussolini had suggested to Papen that he quickly conclude the concordat: "The signing of the agreement with the Vatican will establish the credit of your government abroad for the first time.''[22] For the Vatican, legitimation of Hitler's government was evidently a small price to pay in order to get a favorable concordat with Germany.

The Vatican's relations with Germany were directed by Pacelli much more than by Pius XI himself, since Pacelli was the expert in that area. Relations with Hitler's Germany deteriorated somewhat after 1933, because the German dictator did not keep to the agreements he had made in the 1933 concordat concerning education of youth. After the unsuccessful attempt on Hitler's life in November 1939, the Vatican's secretary of state nevertheless sent him the pope's congratulations on escaping this danger.[23] Previous and subsequent Vatican doubts about Hitler's Germany seem to have been due to the failure of the German government to respect the interests of the Catholic Church more than to the European invasions and persecutions launched by the Third Reich. Even the condemnations of certain aspects of Nazism in the 1937 papal encyclical letter *Mit Brennender Sorge* are quite mild when compared with the condemnation of communism in the encyclical *Divini Redemptoris* that appeared eight days later.

The consistent hard line against socialism and communism and the concurrent support of fascism is attributed, by many observers, to the papal secretary of state, Pacelli. He had risen to the position after the resignation of Cardinal Gasparri, whose anti-fascist ideas were straining relations between Mussolini and the Vatican. Pacelli's sympathy for Germany and for authoritarian forms of government became public knowledge during this period. In 1935, former Chancellor Heinrich Brüning was quoted as telling Count Harry Kessler:

> Behind the agreement with Hitler stood not the Pope, but the Vatican bureaucracy and its leader, Pacelli. They visualized an authoritarian state and an authoritarian Church directed by the Vatican bureaucracy, the two to conclude an eternal league with one another. For that reason Catholic parliamentary parties, like the Center in Germany, were inconvenient to Pacelli and his men, and were dropped without regret in various countries. The Pope [Pius XI] did not share these ideas.[24]

During the thirties, at least, Pius XI was not himself truly a Fascist, unlike some Italian prelates. He was a conservative prelate who had made deals with the Fascist government, hoping to solve the Roman Question, protect Catholic interests, and block the rise of socialism. His ambivalent attitude toward the Mussolini regime was expressed both in his occasional efforts to resist government encroachments on the socialization of youth and in his public blessings of concessions obtained from the Fascists.

Pius XI's personal change of attitude toward the two reactionary regimes he had allied himself with may have come about as early as 1936, the year of the formation of the Axis, and possibly even before that. Quarrels arose between fascism and the Vatican, particularly during 1931, 1938, and 1939, but compromises and concessions negotiated relative peace between the two camps during much of this period. When it became clear, in 1938, that Italian fascism would follow the racist and interventionist policies of its German ally, Pius XI made his first strong and unambiguous statement against Nazism. Attitudes throughout the Catholic hierarchy were also confused. Even the pro-Fascist Cardinal Schuster of Milan spoke out against racism and exaggerated nationalism. Pius XI castigated Cardinal Innitzer of Vienna for his support of Hitler, and, later in 1938, addressing a group of Belgian pilgrims, condemned participation of Catholics in anti-Semitic movements and added that Christians were "spiritually Semites." This latter comparison, however, was omitted from *L'Osservatore Romano*'s account of the pope's speech.

Pius XI was preparing a very strong speech against fascism just before his death on February 10, 1939. Pope John XXIII himself made public in 1959, on the twentieth anniversary of the death of Pius XI, the notes of the speech Pius had planned to deliver. In recent years, a controversy has erupted concerning this speech and the mysterious circumstances surrounding Pius XI's death. Posthumous documents of Cardinal Tisserand (the dean of the college of cardinals, who, in a letter to Cardinal Suhard on June 11, 1940, had accused Pius XII of being soft on Nazism) indicate a possibility that Pius XI was assassinated by his physician, Dr. Francesco Petaci, whose daughter was Mussolini's mistress.

More recently, some historians have revealed that Pius XI had secretly commissioned an encyclical against racism and anti-Semitism from Jesuits John Lafarge, Gustav Gundlach, and Gustave Desbuquois in June 1938. The text was finished in September 1938, but apparently the superior general of the Jesuits, Wladimir Ledochowski (a conservative Polish count), held it and tried to block its publication. Gundlach wrote several letters to Lafarge about this, letters which were found in Lafarge's papers after his death in 1963: "On Oct. 16, 1938, Gundlach wrote that Ledochowski seemed bent on 'sabotaging' the encyclical, and on Jan. 28, 1939, he said the Jesuit superior was hindering it."[25] It is not clear whether Ledochowski forwarded the encyclical on racism to Pius XI. In any case, the pope, who had been seriously ill during the fall and winter, was unable to publish it before his death, and possibly did not even have time to read it.[26]

The speech against fascism which Pius XI was hoping to deliver on the tenth anniversary of the Lateran accords between Italy and the Vatican (and which was disinterred in 1959 by John XXIII) had been scheduled to be given as an address to the Italian bishops on February 11, 1939. It went undelivered. When Mussolini learned of Pius XI's death the day before, he is reported to have said: "At last, that stiff-necked man is dead."[27]

Germany's ambassador to the Vatican, writing of Pius XI's growing hostility toward Nazism and fascism, noted several times that Secretary of State Pacelli was exerting a "restraining" influence on the old pope. Pius XI's changes of heart in his last year of life were quickly forgotten after the election of Pacelli as the new pope, on March 10, 1939. Pacelli, who took the name of Pius XII, may not have been as enthusiastic about fascism as the eleventh Pius had been during the first years of his pontificate, but he certainly was not as anti-Fascist as Pius XI had become during the last few years of his life.

5. PIUS XII (1939–1958), THE SILENT POPE

Monsignor Montini was the first person outside the conclave to learn the news of Pacelli's election as pope, by a telephone call from Pacelli himself. Montini's subsequent position from 1939 to 1954 as one of the pope's closest advisers probably explains his passionate defense of Pius XII's silence on the question of the Nazi genocide.

A few days before his election as pope in 1963, Montini wrote that Pius XII feared that speaking out "would have been not only futile but harmful," unleashing "still greater calamities involving innumerable innocent victims, let alone himself."[28] Nevertheless, it is likely that Pius XII's continuing sympathy for the Germans and for conservative and authoritarian types of governments, his fear of communism, and his preference for diplomacy over prophecy also lay behind his silence.[29] Diego von Bergen, the ambassador of the Third Reich to the Vatican, wrote in a 1942 report: "His heart, as I have been assured, is always on the side of the Axis powers."[30]

The justification of Pius XII's opposition on grounds of avoiding martyrdom for himself and other churchmen, or because he feared for the lives of even greater numbers of Jews, can be given some support. On various occasions, he deplored the plight of Hitler's victims and even tried to alleviate their sufferings, but he never did publicly condemn Nazi violence. It may have been that he was, as Rolf Hochhuth has characterized him:

> . . . a fence-sitter, an over-ambitious careerist who, having attained his goal, wasted his time on inconsequential trifles while the tormented world . . . waited in vain for a word of spiritual leadership from him.[31]

Even if one does not agree with this characterization, one must at least admit that Pius XII's fascination with diplomacy and his tendency to consider the political interests of the Church as supreme did not make of him a neutral spectator to the turmoil of the first half of the twentieth century. Although he never went as far as some European bishops in supporting fascism, he certainly never condemned it in the same uncompromising terms he often used for communism. In the early years of his Vatican career, in 1919, he had a traumatic confrontation with a group of German Spartacists who invaded his Berlin nunciature, an experience which may have brought about this acute phobia about communism.

The *Actes et documents du Saint Siège relatifs à la seconde guerre mondiale* indicate the awareness of Pius XII and other high Vatican officials of the extermination of the Jews by Hitler. The documents include an important letter, dated July 8, 1943, from Msgr. Angelo Roncalli, Vatican apostolic delegate to Turkey and Greece, to Msgr. Montini, substitute secretary of state, in which the future John XXIII refers to Nazi pogroms in Poland.[32] This knowledge may have contributed to the extensive efforts in 1943 by Pius XII and by Msgr. Montini to extricate Italy from its alliance with Germany and from the war in general, even if these efforts were also made, evidently, to save Rome from Allied bombing and other reprisals.

Documents released recently in the eighth volume of the *Actes et documents* indicate that Pius XII instructed his nuncios to protest against racial laws and the deportation of Jews, but this seems to have been the farthest that he was willing to go. The nuncios did not protest very strongly or openly. In fact, one of those who is purported to have been the most vehement in his protests was the Fascist-leaning Valerio Valeri, papal nuncio in France, whom De Gaulle considered to be persona non grata after the Liberation!

It is even possible that a strong condemnation of the genocide by the pope himself would have made matters worse.[33] It is difficult, however, to imagine how things could have been worse, and it is possible that this action could have helped. Those who opt for the pessimistic interpretation say there were indications that the pope might have been imprisoned by the Germans. In 1943, after Mussolini's downfall, Hitler, intent on punishing Pius XII because of his role in that affair, prepared a plan to capture the pope and his entourage and to transport them to Germany. Goebbels, Himmler, and General Wolff all later claimed credit for having aborted this plan of the Fuehrer.

An argument frequently invoked by Pius XII and his defenders was the importance of maintaining papal political neutrality. This neutrality supposedly made it impossible for the pope to condemn Hitler and Mussolini openly and strongly. This line of reasoning could hold, were it not for the fact that in the case of socialism and communism Pius XII was not neutral. In fact, he rarely had any scruples about intervening in political affairs when he wanted to condemn the left.

A good example of Pius XII's pseudo-neutrality can be seen in his comment on Hitler's invasion of Poland, when he referred to the invasion in terms that equated the invaders with their victims: "Two civilized people cut swords, shed blood, launch a war of rival interests . . ." Even the veiled allusion to the aggression against a small nation, in Pius XII's Christmas address of 1939, did not refer to Germany's invasion of Poland, but to Russia's intervention in Finland, according to an interpretation given by the Vatican itself to the protesting Germans. As a matter of fact, the allusion was deliberately made ambiguous so that it could be seen to apply to either Poland or Finland, depending on the needs of diplomacy.

When the Berlin correspondent of the *Osservatore Romano*, Dr. Edoardo Senatro, asked Pius XII if he would protest the mass killings of the Jews, the pope is reported to have answered: "Dear friend, do not forget that millions of Catholics serve in the German armies. Shall I bring them into conflicts of conscience?"[34]

A cursory examination of Pius XII's and Montini's stand on the Nazi persecution of the Jews helps to clarify their later stands on other political issues crucial to the development of the lay movement. Paul VI's continued support and defense of Pius XII, in spite of minor differences during their twenty-year association, and his decision to propose Pius XII for canonization as a saint (along with John XXIII) seem to indicate that he did not become a conservative overnight, and that the similarity of his position with that of Pius XII on the questions of Catholic Action and the lay movement was not purely fortuitous, but was probably based on political considerations also.

6. PIUS XII AND POSTWAR ITALIAN POLITICS

After the war, the Vatican's most pressing concern was the internal
political situation in Italy. The only way the Vatican could acquire any
substantial influence in postwar Europe, and avoid losing most of its
privileges in a new Italy, was to become active in politics. The Vatican
had been so compromised by its earlier collaboration with fascism that
it needed to rely on untainted laymen in order to attempt a reinstate-
ment of its political influence in Italy and elsewhere. After World
War I, Sturzo's relatively progressive (and officially nonconfessional)
Popular Party had succeeded in involving Italian Catholics in politics
on a grand scale for the first time. After the downfall of Mussolini, the
Vatican decided to favor its rebirth under the name of the Christian
Democratic Party, and to make it even more dependent on Church
authorities than before.

The two effective powers in Italy at the time, the American-domin-
ated Allied Military Government and the Vatican, easily succeeded in
turning the former Popolari into the strongest Italian political party.
Alcide De Gasperi, the faithful Catholic lay leader who had been secretary and parliamentary chairman of the Popular Party before its
dissolution, and who had been employed as librarian in the Vatican
during the Fascist period, became the leader of the new party. He was
on very good terms with Msgr. Montini, who was often his advocate
with the conservative Pius XII. De Gasperi relied mostly on Vatican
and American aid to control the party and win elections, although he
resented somewhat the efforts of Vatican clerics to control the political
line of the party, preferring to follow, as much as possible, the relatively progressive Sturzo line rather than the conservative directives of
Pius XII and his curia. As for the Americans, they were so worried
about a possible Communist takeover that they did not mind De
Gasperi's liberal ideas.

This is not to say that De Gasperi was a very radical politician. On
autonomy vis-à-vis the Vatican, collaboration with Socialists and
Communists, and like issues he tried to steer a middle course, but
under pressure from the United States government and the Vatican he
eliminated the Socialists and Communists from his coalition government and consolidated the centrist position of his party by making
alliances with other center parties. The United States and the Vatican
also helped the Christian Democrats eliminate three small groups of
Catholic leftists formed at the end of the war: the Left Christian
Democrats (a tendency inside the Christian Democratic Party), the

Christian Social Party (Catholic Socialists), and the Christian Left Party (Catholic Communists). The two last groups were dismantled by the Vatican, with Christian Democratic aid, because they threatened the political unity of Catholics and because they were independent and critical of the Church hierarchy. The pope's secretary of state, in the *Osservatore Romano* of May 6, 1945, invited the Catholics in these two groups to join the Christian Democrats. Most of them appear to have subsequently joined the Communist Party. As for the Left Christian Democrats, they stayed for the most part in the Christian Democratic Party, but not as an organized tendency.

The successful backing of a Catholic party proved to be an astute move on the part of the Vatican. Its success made the Vatican the most powerful pressure group in Italy, a position prepared by the concordat with Mussolini, as P. A. Allum has remarked in one of his penetrating books about Italy:

> . . . the political triumph of Christian Democracy, which had been prepared under Fascism by the protected position secured for Catholic Action in the Concordat, brought the Papacy to the controlling center of state power in Italy.[35]

Some of Mussolini's concessions to the Vatican in the concordat were instrumental in keeping Italy from getting a leftist government after World War II, but it was mostly the massive intervention of Church authorities after the war which assured the victory of the Christian Democrats.

Palmiro Togliatti, in a speech at the Second National Congress of the Communist Party, in April 1945, mentioned that there were difficulties in his party's relations with the Christian Democrats because of

> the influence of a conservative and even reactionary part that attacks us openly, not on political grounds, but in an arena where it is difficult, and even impossible, for us to defend ourselves. Sermons, refusals of absolution and other sacraments, refusal to celebrate a religious marriage, and so on. . . . In this context, the intervention of the ecclesiastical authorities with spiritual measures to create a kind of anti-Communist spiritual terrorism creates a serious situation.[36]

The Communists nevertheless helped the Christian Democrats write the Lateran Agreements of 1929 into the new republican constitution of 1948. They did this in order to attract Catholic votes, but in fact they thus only contributed to strengthening the power of the Vatican and the Christian Democrats. They helped to legitimize further the privileged position given to the Church by the concordat, thus enabling the Vatican to use various spiritual and political means of control to stop rank-and-file Catholics from supporting the Socialist and the Communist parties.

Experience had shown the Vatican that Catholic parties did not always consider themselves directly responsible to Church authorities. Fearing the radicalization of rank-and-file laity in postwar Italy, Pius XII and his conservative curia wanted to exercise control over influential lay leaders. Since the concordat specifically prohibited any involvement of Catholic Action in politics, a position difficult to reverse in the short run, Luigi Gedda's brain-child, the Civic Committees, became the postwar instrument of Vatican political control. Devised as local action associations coordinated by Catholic Action, the Civic Committees proved to be a brilliant innovation for Catholic politicians. They permitted the Vatican to be active in politics without formally appearing to be so.

Postwar Vatican attitudes toward the body politic were based on prewar experiences, but also on an evaluation of what would be deemed acceptable by the laity. When laymen were active in internal, spiritual work, the hierarchy encouraged involvement in conservative political organizations, but when leftist politics seemed to interest the laity, then the call for noninvolvement in politics came out. What was important, then, was submission to the Vatican's conservative policy, rather than the question of involvement or noninvolvement per se. In other words, insofar as Catholic Action did not get involved in leftist politics, the Vatican was favorable to different types of action, depending on the tactical needs of the moment.

During the fifties, some Catholic intellectuals opposed Gedda's type of conservative political involvement, but since they could only counter it with a purely "apostolic" and "spiritual" Catholic Action, they made little headway. It has only been in recent years that significant numbers of Italian lay Catholics have broken from Christian Democracy to involve themselves in leftist political action. This is a far cry from the period of the fifties, when the liberals did not dare go further than to call for more programs of spiritual formation, in order to oppose the conservative political use of Catholic Action by Church authorities.

Thus, after World War II for the duration of Pius XII's pontificate, Catholic Action became, once again, little more than a front for the Church's conservative involvement in Italian politics, although the leaders of the Christian Democratic Party were not always tractable.

On a June 1946 referendum on the form of the Italian state, the Christian Democratic leaders favored republicanism, whereas the Vatican leaned toward a return to the monarchy. After the electorate chose the republic, the Christian Democrats formed, in 1947, a tripartite government with the Socialist and Communist parties. To many Christian Democrat leaders the coalition seemed the best possible way of forming a government, given the difficult political situation in Italy, but De Gasperi, under pressure from the Vatican and the United States, ousted the Socialists and the Communists from the government a few months later. Elections were called for 1948, and numerous reports of clerical involvement in the preelection politics indicated the extent of papal concern.

In the effort to defeat the Socialists and Communists soundly in the upcoming 1948 elections, the pope maneuvered in order to ally the Christian Democrats with right-wing parties. Montini counseled against giving funds to those parties. Finally, funds which came mostly from religious orders and wealthy industrialists in Italy (and from the United States government), were distributed mainly to Christian Democrats, but some money also went to individual right-wing candidates who were on good terms with Church authorities or favorable to the United States, as numerous public disclosures have recently shown.[37]

The elections of April 1948 gave the Christian Democrats an absolute majority of seats in both houses, temporarily disposing of the dilemma of having to choose between left or right alliances. Their overwhelming victory made the centrist Catholic party independent of both Socialists and Communists, and also of neo-Fascists and monarchists. The successful election was due, most observers noted, to the Church's intense campaigning:

> It is generally conceded that only the extraordinary effort of organized Catholicism in 1948—the successful creation of a "Christ or Communism" alternative for the voter—prevented the extreme Left from coming legally to power in the elections of that year.[38]

On July 29, Pius XII accentuated this anti–working-class orientation of his pontificate by calling for a rupture of the unity of the Italian trade-union movement by Catholic workers, in a speech to 60,000 members of the ACLI (Christian Association of Italian Workers). The subsequent creation of a Catholic trade-union movement effectively succeeded in breaking that unity.

The years 1948 to 1953 were a period of economic and political stability for Italy. With his four-party center coalition (which included Liberals, Republicans, and Social Democrats), De Gasperi was at the summit of his power. Despite his debt to organized Catholicism, he compounded his electoral success of 1948 with political success. He thus became powerful enough to avoid Pius XII's most reactionary suggestions and somewhat limit Vatican control over the Christian Democrats. The party itself was a complex mixture of warring factions, but they were held together by the need to continue winning elections and by De Gasperi's conciliatory genius. In 1951 the first local elections gave another victory to the Christian Democrats. The second postwar national elections, in 1953, continued the Christian Democrats in power, albeit with a slightly lower majority than in 1948. The party was well aware that it owed its continued strength to the backing of Italian business and religious interests, and it repaid its supporters with whatever advantages it could.

Joseph La Palombara, in his study of interest groups in Italian politics, thus characterizes the political situation at that time:

> By and large, those who replied to *Tempi Moderni*'s questionnaire [on pressure groups in Italy] consider that the most pernicious influence on Italian politics is exercised by organized business and organized religion.[39]

The 1948 and 1953 victories of the Christian Democrats represented the organic coming together of Roman Catholicism and the Italian bourgeoisie, at the expense of the Italian working class. But, as shown in chapter 3, the key instrument for this victory was the combined power of Luigi Gedda's Civic Committees. Their continued action on various political fronts came, at times, into conflict with the Christian Democrats and with progressives in Catholic Action, but they were so useful electorally to the Christian Democrats that few leaders of these two organizations dared to attack them openly. Gedda was on such good terms with Pius XII and the Roman Curia that he could afford to be on the offensive. On August 7, 1951, just a few weeks before the first World Congress for the Lay Apostolate, Gedda wrote a political attack in the conservative Catholic Action daily *Il Quotidiano* against what he called the "De Gasperi virtuosos." The article is a good indicator of the existence and the intensity of the political split between the two factions of Christian Democrats, the conservatives and the liberals, a split which reflected itself at the religious level in Catholic Action (Gedda and his group versus Veronese and his group) and in the Vatican itself (Pius XII and most of the curia versus Msgr.

Montini and a few like-minded prelates). Many of the religious conflicts we have examined in chapters 2–4 have their origins in these
political conflicts which shook Italy during the pontificate of Pius XII.
The post–World War II struggles in Italian Catholic Action, the tensions at the three World Congresses for the Lay Apostolate, the opposition between Pacellians and Montinians, and later on between followers and detractors of Paul VI, all have their roots in the political
passions and interests of Italy, and specifically of those found inside the
Italian Christian Democratic Party. So much so that in answer to the
question, What is papal power all about? one might very well say: It
has to do mostly with the Italian political situation. Underneath the
religious façade, one finds a lot of very earthly politics.

7. THE "STURZO OPERATION" AND THE END
OF THE DE GASPERI AND PIUS XII ERAS

During the spring of 1952 there was fear among Italian conservatives
of a victory of the "social-comunisti" in the municipal elections in
Rome, where the Socialists and the Communists had presented a
common list of candidates. The Rome municipal elections have always
been very important to the Vatican, mostly because of its considerable
real estate holdings in the capital. An attempt was made by Pius XII
and Gedda to involve De Gasperi's Christian Democrats in an alliance
with the neo-Fascists, the Monarchists, and other right-wing forces.
They put the operation under the patronage of Sturzo (who as an old
priest was more vulnerable to such pressures) in order to get the Christian Democratic Party to agree. Their intention was to tamper with
the official Christian Democratic election list in order to include in it a
number of non–Christian Democratic rightists. They used the conservative Jesuit Ricardo Lombardi to put pressure on De Gasperi. On
April 19, Lombardi told De Gasperi's wife that her husband should
accept the Vatican list, and that if he proceeded with his own electoral
list and the Christian Democrats did poorly, he would be forced to
resign.

On the following evening, Msgr. Montini, who did not agree with
the pope's plan, dined with a friend of the De Gasperis, Emilio
Bonomelli, manager of the papal villa at Castelgondolfo. To
Bonomelli, who was telling him that the Sturzo operation would
break the Christian Democratic Party, Msgr. Montini is reported to
have said:

> It is just what they [i.e. the conservatives in the Vatican] want; they
> have done nothing but repeat for a long time that the party is carry-
> ing us to ruin, and they think that Gedda and his Catholic Action is
> the only efficient force capable of replacing the party and standing up
> to communism.[40]

Bonomelli reported his conversation with Montini to De Gasperi, and
told him he would try to make the pope see the light about the inap-
propriateness of the Sturzo Operation. He convinced Count Enrico
Galeazzi, the man in charge of the Vatican's financial affairs, on this
point, and Galeazzi went to see the pope with the pope's brother,
Prince Francesco Pacelli.

Finally, the rightist candidates became reluctant to give Sturzo some
written assurances that he required of them. Their balkiness may have
stymied the plan as much as any change of opinion the pope might
have had about its validity. At any rate, the *Osservatore Romano*
presented De Gasperi's Christian Democratic candidate list as the
official Catholic list, and Gedda's Civic Committees finally backed the
list.

Luckily for De Gasperi and Montini, the Christian Democrats easily
won the Roman election, and a crisis was averted. The election
victory was also a vindication of the Christian Democrat position,
namely, that they did not need the support of the right to win. In fact,
they might argue that rightist support could be a kiss of death for the
unity of their party, since working-class party members would then
feel freer to back the candidates of left-wing parties.

The Sturzo Operation helps us understand why Montini was subsequently promoted-demoted from the Secretariate of State to the archdiocese of Milan, and why Veronese had similarly been switched from
Catholic Action to COPECIAL. Behind the façade of the religious
apostolate, a political struggle was going on in which Pius XII and his
close friend Gedda were supporting the right inside and outside the
Christian Democratic Party against De Gasperi, Fanfani, and other
supporters of what was then the left faction of the Christian
Democratic Party, known as the "Dorotei line." The key difference
between the two groups was that Pius XII and Gedda wanted a conservative clerical alliance, whereas De Gasperi, Montini, and Veronese
saw conservative clericalism as responsible for a countering anticlerical
radicalism. Their strategy was to co-opt Republicans and some
moderate Socialists into backing the centrist Christian Democratic
Party.

Both groups wanted the defeat of the Socialists and the Communists. To arrive at this end, Pius XII and his followers were willing to favor an alliance of the Christian Democrats with the right. Pius XII preferred Catholic Action to the Christian Democrats, whereas Montini and the other like-minded Christian Democrats put the unity of Catholics in support of the Christian Democrats above all else. Pius XII was unwilling to make concessions to moderate leftists in order to maintain the Vatican's position of strength in Italy. The goals were the same, only the means differed. Pius XII's methods of control were cruder, less sophisticated, whereas Montini, like De Gasperi, understood that the best way to defeat the left was to maintain a center and slightly left-of-center position and to co-opt the moderate Socialists rather than the rightists, whenever coalitions became necessary in order to stay in power.

Conjecturing that they would not forever be able to get as high a percentage of the vote as in the 1948 election, the Christian Democrats made an effort to change the electoral laws, in order to give two-thirds of the seats to the coalition of parties which received fifty percent plus one of the votes. The elections of June 7, 1953, however, effectively destroyed that Christian Democratic effort to rob opposition parties of some of their seats, because the coalition parties failed to get the required percentage of the vote. In the Chamber of Deputies, for example, in comparison with the previous general election, the Christian Democrats and their allies lost some seats, whereas the opposition, left and right, gained some. The law was rescinded the following year. The Christian Democrats were then in the position of having to move closer either to the right or to the left. Since there was little possibility that a repeat of the Sturzo Operation on the national level would be any more successful than the 1952 misadventure, the only way for the Christian Democrats to stay in power was to try, in spite of the Vatican's reluctance, to open up toward the left.

After De Gasperi's death in 1953, the left-leaning faction within the Christian Democratic Party gained control. Fanfani, the leader of the "Democratic Initiative" group, was elected secretary-general of the party in July 1954, opening a whole new era for the Christian Democrats. In spite of papal and curial opposition, closer ties were established with the Socialists, whose leader Nenni had broken from close cooperation with the Communist Party. At the local level, although the Christian Democrats were still greatly dependent on clerical support, Fanfani was able to maneuver his party out of a position of dependence on the Civic Committees of Catholic Action.

In the May 1958 general elections, the right-wing parties lost some seats, while the Christian Democrats and the Socialists gained some ground and the Communists held their own. The Christian Democrats decided to form a new cabinet with center-left tendencies, including a few members of the Social Democratic Party, and obtained the outside backing of the Socialists. The conservatives in the Vatican and in Catholic Action opposed this coalition government, and it was soon defeated in parliament. Antonio Segni, a centrist Christian Democrat, replaced Fanfani as prime minister and continued Fanfani's policy of favoring Vatican-owned companies in the awarding of construction contracts. A forty-day parliamentary crisis, however, led to the resignation of Segni and the formation of a conservative all-Christian Democrat government by Fernando Tambroni in March 1960, since the *Osservatore Romano* (which was still controlled by the conservatives in spite of Pope John's election) had vetoed Fanfani's efforts to include Nenni's Socialists in the government.

8. POPE JOHN XXIII (1958–1963) AND THE "OPENING TO THE LEFT"

Angelo Roncalli's attitude of religious and political openness led to a quite progressive pontificate, even if in many ways it remained marked for a little while by the conservative climate of the Pacelli years. In April 1959 the Holy Office issued a ruling declaring that Catholics should not vote for those who united with Communists and favored their actions. It seems that the Holy Office had not obtained permission from the pope to issue such a warning, because he subsequently made it known that he was henceforth opposed to Church intervention in Italian politics. As patriarch of Venice, he had not opposed the alliance of Christian Democrats with Socialists at the local level, although he had gone along with the Vatican's condemnation of a similar alliance at the national level in 1956.

During Pius XII's pontificate, it was unthinkable for a high-ranking prelate to oppose the official Vatican line on such a fundamental issue. Not even Cardinal Lercaro of Bologna, the most articulate and one of the few progressive men among the Italian cardinals, would have dared to do so. Since both Pius XII and the curia were in substantial agreement to support a conservative orientation, there was not much that could be done by the prelates who did not favor that kind of politics. Under John XXIII, however, because of the deep cleavage between the curia and the pope, both conservatives and progressives at the upper echelons of authority in the Church in Italy felt freer to express their ideas on political issues.

In July 1960, an open revolt of workers and youth in Italy sparked a crisis which led to the fall of the Tambroni government, which existed as a result of the support of the neo-Fascists, Monarchists, and Liberals. Fanfani then returned as prime minister with the backing of the Liberals and the Social Democrats. After the November 1960 municipal elections, the Christian Democrats made a new effort to collaborate with the Nenni Socialists at the local level. Discussion centered on having a real center-left government at the national level. It was around that same time that Pope John indicated his willingness to allow the Christian Democrats to reverse the policy of Pius XII on the question of collaboration with the Socialists.

In 1961 the Vatican prevented all Italian bishops from intervening in the local elections as had been the practice under Pius XII. And when the Nenni Socialists made a coalition agreement with the Christian Democrats in February 1962, one month after the latter's Naples congress which had approved the idea, the Vatican asked all the bishops not to speak out against this completely new turn in Italian politics. Although a center-left alternative had become a necessary one for the Christian Democrats, there was so much opposition to it among conservative Catholics that only Pope John's policy of nonintervention curbed Catholic right-wing activity and made the coalition possible.

Thus, a "nonpolitical" pope showed himself to be a very shrewd politician. By not opposing the opening to the left, he helped the Christian Democrats remain in power, with the cooperation of the Nenni Socialists. He actually saved the Christian Democrats, while helping to move Italy a few notches to the left. But he also contributed to loosening the hold of organized Catholicism on Italian politics. Under Pope John, and partly because of him, many Italian Catholics started feeling easier about voting for parties to the left of the Christian Democrats. The papal acceptance of cooperation with Socialists paved the way for further moves to the left for Italian Catholics.

Before the 1963 general elections, Pope John again asked the bishops to keep silent and refrain from taking a partisan position. The effect of the pope's refusal to permit the intervention of the Italian hierarchy in favor of the Christian Democrats cannot be accurately measured, but they suffered a setback at the hands of the Communists, who got 25.3 percent of the vote, a rise of 2.6 percent from the preceding election.

Fanfani was replaced as prime minister by the moderate Giovanni Leone, and then by the progressive Aldo Moro, a friend of the newly elected pope, Paul VI. Conservatives attributed the Christian Democrats' loss of 1 percent of their vote to Pope John's tolerance toward the left, and described as "stupid blunders" his friendly reception of the Soviet journalist Aleksei Adzhubei (Khrushchev's son-in-law) and the timing of the encyclical *Pacem in Terris*, which coincided with the election campaign.

During his pontificate, John XXIII was the target of numerous attacks from right-wing Catholics who accused him of being a Communist, or a blundering old fool, or both. They recalled that when he was named a cardinal by Pius XII in 1953, he petitioned the pope to have the Socialist president of France award him his red hat, as an old custom permitted, and that when the Italian Socialists held their annual convention in Venice in 1957, not only had he asked them to come and visit him in his episcopal palace, but he had also asked Catholic Venetians to pray for them. For this flirtation with Italian socialism, he had at that time been denounced to the Vatican.[41] The *Osservatore Romano* had even served him a discreet reprimand for that action.

On other questions having to do with politics and the left, Pope John indicated that he was not going to remain tied to Pius XII's conservative stands. Shortly after his election, for example, he summarily dismissed the ambassador of the Polish government-in-exile, thus paving the way for a reconciliation with eastern European Communist regimes. On October 8, 1962, in a meeting with Cardinal Stefan Wyszyński and other Polish bishops, he praised the Poles for their struggle for the defense of their borders against Eastern and Western invaders. In West Germany, the Christian Democratic government of Konrad Adenauer lodged a vehement protest, through its ambassador to the Holy See, but the Vatican's position on the statement remained unchanged.

Conservatives in the Vatican, in Catholic Action, and in the Christian Democratic Party strongly resented John's conciliatory attitude toward Communist regimes and his policy of refusing to get involved on the side of the conservatives in Italian politics. They particularly resented some of the radical implications of his social encyclicals *Mater et Magistra* and *Pacem in Terris*.

Msgr. Pietro Pavan, who is considered to have been the most important figure in the drafting of *Pacem in Terris* (he also revised the early draft of *Mater et Magistra* which a group of Jesuits had drawn up), is reported to have said, in a conversation, that Pope John was convinced that his intervention with Khrushchev on the Cuba crisis had been very important in the turning about of the Soviet ships, and that this had led him to conceive the idea of writing *Pacem in Terris*. If this is the case, it is possible that Pope John considered, after the Cuba crisis, the Soviets to be less of a danger to world peace than the Americans, and that this belief led him to soften the Vatican's position on the center-left operation in Italy and on Communist regimes in eastern Europe. By the time the parliamentary elections of 1963 came along, the green light had been given to the center-left. Both major parties involved, the Christian Democrats and the Nenni Socialists, lost some voters in the process, mostly to the Communists, and this contributed to making the alliance more pressing.

Pope John's progressive political ideas obviously made him very reluctant to encourage the development of Italian Catholic Action, with its concommitant involvement of hierarchy, clergy, and laity, particularly through the Civic Committees, in support of the Christian Democrats. He was more inclined to favor the development of a lay apostolate involved in nondenominational action toward social justice and international peace, letting Christian Democrats act autonomously in the political arena. His position on these matters was very similar to that of Benedict XV, the pope who called him from Bergamo to Rome in 1921, as we have seen in chapter 2.[42]

Pope John even went further than Benedict XV in this desire to free the Church from the hold of conservative politics, since he kept more distance between himself and the Catholic political party than Benedict had done, and positively encouraged lay Catholics to become involved with non-Catholics in the struggle for peace, development and social justice. Pope John's unfinished revolution was an effort to develop a Catholicism which would not be a religious legitimation of socioeconomic and political conservatism, in contrast with the policies of most of his predecessors and their collaborators, who were not only authoritarian religious leaders but also conservative politicians. Their reliance on coercive and manipulative means of control to keep the rank-and-file laity and its leaders under their influence was not a pure dedication to the things of God alone, but a down-to-earth preoccupation with the trappings of political power, territorial imperatives, and financial interests. It matters little that from Pius IX to Pius XII these temporal designs were hidden under the guises of otherworldliness and piety (witness the name Pius, "pious," that they chose for themselves as if the better to veil their common fascination with diplomacy and political power); the fact remains, as is evident in this chapter, that the modern papacy is a political as well as a religious institution. Political considerations often determine the type of orientation and action that is taken, at least as far as the control of the lay movement is concerned. Pope John was perhaps the exception that confirms the rule, though he was also partly a politician, albeit of an ideological tendency different from that of his predecessors. As for Paul VI, whose pontificate was chosen as the major testing ground for this study, it is rather evident, as will be seen in the next chapter, that his use of quite sophisticated means of control over the laity, as well as his return to the more traditional forms of control, was intimately linked with and partly dependent on, his lifelong interest in the exercise of ecclesiastical authority for the legitimation of the neoliberalism of Christian Democracy and for the defense of the privileges of the Vatican in Italian society. In more general terms, we could say that the centralization of authority in the hands of the pope and the increasing use of manipulative types of mechanisms of control by Church officials in Catholicism have come in good part from the influence of the Church's social environment, and more specifically from the Italian political and economic context in which the Vatican operates.

The present chapter has studied that political context, from Pius IX to John XXIII. In the next chapter, the discussion will move on to Paul VI's pontificate. The first three sections will focus attention on religious issues, thus continuing for the latter part of Paul VI's pontificate what chapters 2–5 attempted for previous popes and for the first part of that pope's reign. Section 4 will try to analyze Paul VI's pontificate in its relationship with Italian politics. Finally, section 5 will go beyond both religion and politics to examine the economic underpinnings of the papacy in modern times, especially during Paul VI's reign.

VII

Pope Paul's Pontificate
(1963–1978)

1. A "PROGRESSIVE-CONSERVATIVE" POPE

During the pontificate of John XXIII few people considered Cardinal Montini to be a conservative. In fact, he was then generally thought to be one of the most eager supporters of the pope's innovative policies. His difficulties with Pius XII and the reactionaries in the Roman Curia during the mid-fifties had cast him in the role of a progressive prelate ostracized for his forward-looking views. Even after the death of John XXIII and the election of Montini to the papacy, the public image of him as a potential supporter of *aggiornamento* did not alter drastically. Accustomed to his progressive demeanor, people were slow to realize that he was fundamentally a very moderate man, and that as Paul VI his style of leadership was bound to become increasingly similar to that of Pius XII. It was not until 1968, five years after his election, when he began to take a series of decisions and outline new orientations, that he was revealed in such a light. Nevertheless, a close examination of incidents in Montini's Vatican career shows that his allegiance to progressive Catholicism was never as strong as it appeared at the time of his accession.

Among the chief indicators of Montini as a progressive prelate were his transfer from the Secretariate of State to the archdiocese of Milan and his not being named cardinal by Pius XII. It is true that he had to wait for the death of Pius XII for his cardinal's hat, but he had, after all, been named archbishop of the most important diocese in Italy by Pius, who would not have given him that position if the two had not fundamentally been in agreement on basic issues. Furthermore, Montini's clerical activities in Milan were not exactly what one might call avant-garde. His unrelenting efforts to become archbishop of the workers seem to have been inspired by a strong anti-Communist bias as much as by a desire for social justice. In important matters, Montini was sometimes quite conservative. In June 1960, for example, he sent a secret letter to the Milanese clergy telling them that they had "the duty not to favor the so-called 'opening to the left' at the present time and in the form now envisaged." While not so conservative as Pius XII and the dominant reactionary cardinals in the curia, neither was he a leftist. He was simply a moderate Christian Democrat, a defender of a centrist political line, a "progressive-conservative."

Unlike Pius XII, Paul VI was not a reactionary and authoritarian leader of men. He was rather a sensitive and modest liberal turned more conservative because difficult circumstances pushed him in that direction. He was a "prince of agony, who has been unpoped," in the words of Malachi Martin, a close observer of the Vatican scene.[1] At first he adopted a modern human-relations type of approach to counter challenges to his authority, but little by little he seems to have come to the conclusion that the boss must boss. Fearful of seeing the Church disintegrate, Paul VI showed himself ready to use manipulation in order to maintain his papal control. Not a charismatic and utopian leader like John XXIII, Paul did not believe in prophecy and spontaneity, unless it had a tinge of conservatism, as in the new Pentacostalism.

After John XXIII made him cardinal, an incident occurred which revealed something of Montini's orientation toward his more radical lay Catholic compatriots. In September 1962 the progressive lay Catholic Milanese periodical *Adesso* ceased publication because of pressures from the Holy Office. The periodical was directed by Mario Rossi, who had been forced to resign from his position as leader of Italian Youth Catholic Action by Gedda in the mid-fifties. The Holy Office accused the periodical of being prejudiced against the hierarchy, of upholding unacceptable ideas on lay autonomy, and of being in collusion with the French radical periodicals *Esprit* and *Témoignage Chrétien*. According to a circular sent by the editors to the subscribers, Cardinal Montini had agreed with these curial accusations. In the last issue, the editors wrote: "We do not want to create scandals and we prefer to shut up rather than to edit an *Adesso* which would not be faithful to our convictions. Could it be that, in Italy, they prefer other kinds of laymen, namely obedient executors, rather than men who have minds of their own?"[2]

Montini's siding with the Roman Curia in silencing a voice of the progressive laity was a telling position to have taken just before Vatican II, at a time when Pope John had made it clear that the underhand methods of the curia were not to his liking. This action was a clear indication that Montini did not tolerate the kind of lay intellectual autonomy and emancipation that might bring rank-and-file Italian Catholics out of the tight control of the hierarchy and the Vatican, or out of the fold of Catholic Action and Christian Democracy.

During the first session of Vatican II, in the fall of 1962, less than a year before he became pope, Montini contributed little to the heated debates and struggles inside and outside the council halls. As archbishop of Milan, he sent weekly reports to the Catholics of his diocese, presenting the positions of the various sides in the discussions, seldom indicating his own preferences. Once, in his newsletter, he blamed the members of the curia for not being more open to Pope John's viewpoint, but he did not speak out against the conservative minority at Vatican II, as most progressive bishops and cardinals were doing. It was as if he were taking care not to antagonize the potential supporters of his candidacy as pope among the cardinals.

Throughout Vatican II, both before and after his election to the papacy, Montini steered a noncommittal course, balancing progressive and conservative stands. At the end of the second session, the progressives' dissatisfaction with the meetings was largely due to the new pope's failure to stop the dilatory tactics of the conservative minority. Collegiality, or the sharing of power between the pope and the episcopate, to which he had been sympathetic before his election as pope, now started appearing to him as a potentially dangerous novelty, a possible usurpation of traditional papal prerogatives. Rather than downgrading the college of cardinals and the system of nunciatures and apostolic delegations (the Vatican's foreign service) as some critics had suggested, Pope Paul nearly limited his organizational reforms in these areas to taking away the right to elect the pope from the oldest cardinals (by restricting voting rights to those under eighty years of age), making the top foreign-service jobs five-year renewable appointments, and appointing new members in order to rejuvenate and internationalize the personnel of both groups. The new rules gave these bodies a new vitality and ensured that the papal conclave after his death would be heavily loaded with appointees of his own choosing. The mandatory retirement age for bishops being seventy-five years and that of cardinals eighty years, it seems that Paul VI had no intention of retiring himself, since he died at the age of eighty-one. By refusing to retire, he laid himself open to the criticism of Pius IX by a cardinal who liked to say jokingly that the cardinals had elected a Holy Father and had ended up with an Eternal Father.

In addition, Paul VI's 1969 revival of Italian Catholic Action was based on a reform which strengthened its centralized character, putting it under closer papal and hierarchical control. In a letter to Archbishop Franco Costa, general ecclesiastical assistant to Italian Catholic Action, Pope Paul approved the changes made that year: "Reading the new statutes, we noted with satisfaction the firm determination of Italian Catholic Action wisely to maintain those characteristics which guarantee its authenticity, because they constitute the reason for its existence and differentiate it from other, quite legitimate forms of apostolate, i.e., its educational finality and its special relationship of direct collaboration with the Hierarchy (cf. Decree *Apostolicam Actuositatem*, 20)."[3]

The major change in this 1969 reform of Italian Catholic Action was the creation, at the national level, of a general council (*consultà*) for the lay Apostolate which included Catholic Action and the organizations, offices, and agencies of the lay apostolate. The aim of the reform was to revitalize Catholic Action and to give it a new lease on life by uniting it with the newer and more dynamic lay-apostolate groups. By integrating all these organizations into a body along the lines of the laity councils suggested by Vatican II,[4] the reform also put Catholic Action in a central position in the lay movement in Italy, since key roles in the *consultà* were given to Catholic Action leaders. Thus the Vatican and the hierarchy used Catholic Action, which they controlled quite securely, to co-opt and coordinate the more autonomous lay movements.

Pius XII had used Catholic Action to canalize the forces of the laity, and had relied on the Christian Democrats as a first wall of defense, whereas John XXIII had more or less rejected both. Montini had always preferred the Christian Democrats to Catholic Action in spite of the fact that they were less tightly controlled by the Vatican. But now, reverting to Pius XII's conservative position on that issue, and being unwilling to put the Church at the mercy of a group as unreliable as the Italian Christian Democratic Party, he chose to revive Catholic Action and to make it a major instrument of his control over the Italian laity.

The new alliance of Pope Paul VI with the conservatives in the Roman Curia against the progressive clergy can also be understood in a similar fashion. Unable to control most of the lay forces, many parts of the clergy, and even some sections of the episcopate, Paul VI decided to revert to Pius XII's type of reliance on the bureaucratic power of the curia to insure his control over the Church. The Synod of Bishops, far from becoming a means for collegial sharing of decision-making between the episcopate and the pope, with the curia as an instrument of that collegial power, became a mere consultative organ for the pope and his new powerful ally, the curia. In modern Catholicism, Catholic Action has been the real political party of Church officials, because the pope and the hierarchy can really control it. Catholic or Christian parties and trade-unions are tactical instruments used in certain contexts when they are judged opportune. When greater advantages can be obtained through surer means, they are abandoned, as was the case under Pius XI when concordats with reactionary regimes in sore need of religious legitimation were used to get the financial arrangements and school reforms desired by Church authorities.

The greater initiative and freedom given to the laity and the clergy, and especially to the theologians and the bishops, under John XXIII, and the split between that pope and his curia, were leading to the ideological and organizational breaking-up of the Church and to the reinforcement of radical and national tendencies among Catholics in many countries. Paul VI did not want to go down in history as the pope who oversaw the dismantlement of the Church. In choosing between the models set up by his immediate predecessors, he first hesitated between pursing John's work or reverting to the conservative line of the Pius popes. In practice, he seemed to prefer the latter alternative, but not in a determined manner. He played both sides against each other, choosing to walk the thin line between the two. Increasingly, he came out with statements that impugned the motives of his leftist critics, but he sometimes had words of mixed praise and understanding for them, words that seemed to represent efforts at recuperation. His actions (e.g. nominations for important positions) were increasingly lopsided toward conservatism, but he managed to come up with enough progressive moves to make it impossible to classify him neatly and definitively as a dyed-in-the-wool conservative. For example, among appointees, the progressive secretary of state, Cardinal Jean Villot, was counterbalanced by the conservative undersecretary for Ordinary (internal) Affairs, Giovanni Benelli, who wielded most of the power but who in turn was held in check by another progressive diplomat, Msgr. Agostino Casaroli, the undersecretary for Extraordinary (foreign) Affairs, who has been mainly responsible for developing the Vatican's *Ostpolitik* of collaboration with Communist regimes. Benelli was made a cardinal and archbishop of Florence by Paul VI, and Casaroli was named secretary of state and made cardinal by John Paul II.

When he was elected pope, Paul VI was called upon to preside over a house divided, polarized between irreconcilable tendencies. He played a holding game, trying to maintain some form of unity in an organization that was increasingly moving toward fragmentation and isolation. Pleading for moderation, he lashed out verbally at those on his left who threatened the stability of the Church's existing structure, and he negotiated with the extreme rightists, like Msgr. Marcel Lefebvre who rejected his innovations and those of Vatican II, siding with the conservatives and the moderates who were relieved that Pope John's revolution had finally come to a stop. He did not dare at first to push any line very resolutely, for fear of occasioning a further breakup of the institution. So he just kept discreetly pushing a centrist line, indecisively, pessimistically, underhandedly. His was a holding operation to avoid hard choices; he refused to move ahead or to resolutely turn back. He reaffirmed some of the ancient truths, leaving the door open for some of the newer viewpoints, torn between the growling reactionaries who yearned for a new authoritarian leader and the shouting radicals who wanted to pursue the unfinished *aggiornamento*. To both of these groups, he seemed to be saying: "Can't you see we are in a bind; we can't satisfy all of you; you are partly right and partly wrong, you exaggerate, you lack moderation." He was at an impasse and he knew it. Lacking the determination, optimism, and courage of John XXIII, he did not dare innovate, and lacking the infatuation and dogmatism of Pius XII, he did not dare dictate. He searched for a way out of his dilemmas, trying to be everything to all men, making a few minor concessions to the more moderate progressives and increasingly greater concessions to acceptable conservatives. After 1968 he seemed to have fewer qualms about favoring conservatives, both religious and political, who saw him as one of their own. This may indicate that he had finally found a way out of his "Hamletic" hesitations and dilemmas. This sophisticated conservatism failed to satisfy the inte-gralists, who seem to have become more demanding in the last few years of his pontificate.

The few progressive gestures of the early part of Paul VI's pontifi-cate, such as his U.N. speech against war (October 4, 1965) and the encyclical *Populorum Progressio* (March 26, 1968), were rapidly superseded by numerous conservative acts. In May 1967 he travelled to Fátima, in Portugal, where he launched a verbal attack on the "excesses of progressivism" and on the "persecution of the Church" in Communist countries. In June he came out with his encyclical *Sacerdotalis Coelibatus*, on priestly celibacy, a document he wrote without consulting the episcopal conferences or the Synod of Bishops. The repeated curial attacks against the Dutch catechism could not have occurred without the approval and encouragement of Paul VI. Not only laymen, but priests, theologians, and bishops were being forced to fall in line. Also in 1967, he decided that 1968 would be a "Year of Faith," and in June 1968, as a discreet answer to and censure of the Dutch catechism, he promulgated a conservatively worded papal "credo." That same year he also increased the central control of the Secretariate of State over the curia itself, retired the left-leaning Cardinal Lercaro of Bologna, attacked revolutionary means for social change during a trip to Bogotá, and initiated a secret investigation of the progressive Dutch theologian Edward Schillebeeckx.

Following the publication in July 1968 of *Humanae Vitae*, his famous encyclical against birth control, a secret letter was sent by the secretary of state, Cardinal Cicognani, to bishops and superiors of religious orders demanding that they support the pope's position in this matter.[5] On September 18, Paul VI lashed out at critics and activists, who had become bolder and more numerous, lumping together very different forms of challenges to religious authority: "A spirit of corrosive critique has become fashionable in certain sectors of Catholic life. . . . And what should we say of certain recent cases of occupations of churches and cathedrals, of inadmissible movies, of collective and concerted protests against our recent encyclical, of propaganda for political violence to attain social goals, of acts of inter-Communion contrary to the correct ecumenical line?"

The July 1968 birth-control encyclical was the decisive and irreversible turning point in Paul VI's emergence as a doctrinal traditionalist. At the last session of Vatican II he had tried, unsuccessfully, to get the bishops to make conservative changes in the section on marriage in schema 13. With *Humanae Vitae* he rejected the majority report of his special commission on birth control, and reaffirmed the conservative doctrine of Pius XI and Pius XII in that area.

The theologian Bernard Häring, who was active among the majority group of the special commission, in an effort to explain this sudden turn to the right without directly attacking the pope, said in an address in 1968:

> We had no possibility to approach the Pope. In my eyes he was
> walled in. And thus it came to this document, which in my eyes is a
> test-case of non-collegial exercise of papal authority. . . . But here is
> on one side the representatives of the laity, the theology of today, the
> bishops, and on the other side is the Curia. It is a test-case in history,
> the post-encyclical era; whether the pope will be rescued, whether he
> will be in touch with all through free channels, or will be walled in
> by a Curia which is more concerned for face-saving in this case than
> for solutions for the future.[6]

We have here a fascinating attempt at interpreting Paul VI's conservative stand: it is blamed on the curia, which supposedly controls his
means of information. This explanation has some elements of truth in
it, but it is unsatisfactory, especially in the light of numerous subsequent decisions and declarations of a similar nature that Paul VI made
during the rest of 1968 and after. The evidence is that Paul VI was
very much his own man, and that the idea of his being controlled by
his curial advisers is without foundation.

What seems much more probable is that there was an alliance
between a conservative curia and a liberal pope turned conservative, an
alliance aimed at ensuring the stability of the Church's apparatus of
power. Centrist, liberal ideology, customarily expressed in the Church
since the time of Benedict XV by the papacy's Jesuit advisers, by the
social doctrine of the Church, and through the Vatican's backing of
Catholic parties, was replaced by a somewhat more conservative orientation, characterized by the political, bureaucratic, and financial
interests of the curialists, and by the Vatican's fear of a loss of the
advantages accruing to it from its privileged position as an independent state. The Vatican bureaucracy, with the pope at its head, once
more led the Church in a conservative direction. This bureaucratic
alliance had become necessary for both the pope and the curia, because
a conflict between them could have spelled the downfall of both. And
both tried to convince the bishops that they too had better join with
them in the alliance, lest the combined challenge of protesting laity
and clergy undermine both the episcopate's and the Vatican's prerogatives. The subdued atmosphere of the five Synods of Bishops held
between 1967 and 1977 seems to indicate that, except for some rare
individual bishops and a few national hierarchies, the bishops concurred. Those who disagreed were ostracized and punished, as in the
case of the Dutch hierarchy. Besides, the rigid curia control over
nominations insured that very few critical spirits were chosen as
bishops.

The manifestations of a turn to the right in the central government of the Catholic Church came as somewhat of a shock to those who had hoped that Paul VI would pursue the course set by John XXIII. It was not long before a strong internal opposition to such papal actions and policies came into quite open expression among priests and laymen, as well as among some bishops and a few cardinals.

2. CHALLENGES TO POPE PAUL VI'S AUTHORITY AND THE RESPONSE OF THE VATICAN

Cardinal Leo Suenens of Malines-Brussels in Belgium took a leading role in the challenge to the anticollegial manner in which decisions on birth control and other issues were being taken in Rome. By attacking the entourage and the system rather than the pope himself, like Bernard Häring, he may have been using a strategy of indirect attack to get wider support for his position. For example, in May 1969, the lay periodical *Informations Catholiques Internationales* published an interview with Cardinal Suenens by its senior editor, José de Broucker. Returning to the theme of a book he had published the year before on co-responsibility in the church, the Cardinal attacked the "essentialist, bureaucratic, static, juridical centralizing tendency" of the Roman Curia, called for a downgrading of the authority of the curia and the college of cardinals, and proposed an increased decentralization so that laymen, priests, and bishops would have a greater say in the affairs of the Church. He declared that the Church and the pope were imprisoned in a rigid authoritarian system, reproved the pope's stand on priestly celibacy and birth control, and called for an upsurge of public opinion which would "liberate everyone, including the pope, from the system."[7]

A year later, on May 5, 1970, in another interview, this time with *Le Monde*'s religious editor, Henri Fesquet, Cardinal Suenens reiterated most of his criticisms, insisting particularly on the questions of celibacy and collegiality. Following the interview, he was firmly rebuked by the Vatican on various occasions, especially through the *Osservatore Romano*, which Suenens had accused of doing a disservice to the papacy with its biased reporting of Church controversies.

By 1969, Pope Paul's authority was being challenged from many directions. Forty internationally recognized Catholic theologians published a manifesto calling for greater freedom of inquiry and expression in the Church. Then there were meetings of protesting Catholic priests at the gathering of European bishops at Chur and at the second Synod of Bishops in Rome. Some of the strongest blows to papal authoritarianism and conservatism came from Italian priests and laymen. The ACLI (Christian Association of Italian Workers), for example, decided to stop supporting the Christian Democrats, and declared itself in favor of socialist reforms, a move which infuriated the Vatican. The Isolotto parish in Florence, with its pastor Don Enzo Mazzi at its head, rebelled against church authorities, and in Rome itself, several priests, Giulio Girardi among them, became celebrities and even heroes for many because of their identification with poor slum-dwellers and their repeated attacks on Vatican involvement in local structures of oppression and exploitation in the housing and construction industries. Groups of radical and socialist Catholics, who refused to be led by Church authorities, became more and more numerous. Catholic publishing houses and bookstores which had often been forced to take certain books out of circulation because of pressures from the Roman Curia during the reign of Pius XII were now finding a very good market for progressive books on religion.

Carlo Falconi, in his 1969 book on protest in the Church, describes this protest movement as it developed between 1966 and 1969 in various countries, among bishops, priests, religious, and the laity. Concerning the laity, he recognizes the importance and the radical implications of the third World Congress for the Lay Apostolate in the development of a lay protest movement in the Catholic church.[8] Because we have sufficiently insisted on this congress and its immediate aftermath in previous chapters, it is not necessary to return to it here, especially since the next section of this chapter will be devoted exclusively to the relationship between Paul VI and the Council on the Laity and the Catholic International Organizations after the third World Congress for the Lay Apostolate.

During 1970 the protests against the conservatism of the pope and his curia continued to erupt, and these led to further authoritarian responses. One could cite the Roman Curia's investigation of progressive Bishop Salvatore Baldassari of Ravenna, the rebuttal (followed by more subtle kinds of retaliation) given to the progressive declaration on divorce by three Jesuit sociologists from the Gregorian University (Emile Pin, Paolo Tufari, and José Diez-Alegria), and the unsuccessful attempt to block the election of a progressive Chilean as head of the international Movement of Christian Workers. Such efforts to control and block progressive developments made it increasingly evident that, in spite of opposition, Pope Paul VI's counterrevolution was being established on a firm basis.

In 1970, Hans Küng, the famous Swiss Catholic theologian, described Pope Paul's decisions on birth control, celibacy, and mixed marriages as ''efforts to restore a pre-conciliar theology.''[9] In response to this and to the theological opinions of Küng, as expressed in a series of controversial articles and books, the curia instituted a long-term investigation of the Swiss theologian which led in July 1973 to the publication by the Congregation for the Doctrine of the Faith (the former Holy Office. successor to the Holy Inquisition) of *Mysterium Ecclesiae*, a document aimed at countering Küng's ideas on papal infallibility, which he rejects. Neither side was willing to make concessions, because the very important issue of papal authority was at stake, and with it the future of Catholicism as it has existed for centuries. Faced with a serious challenge to the very basis of its authority, the papacy reacted with the only means at its disposal, namely, social and normative power. At an earlier time, a theological rebel like Küng would have been condemned, excommunicated, perhaps even burned at the stake. That time being past, the Vatican maneuvered secretly to have his ideas refuted by his peers. It was suggested to theological colleagues and northern European bishops that Küng be persuaded to come to Rome to participate in a sort of kangaroo court set up to try to get him to retract and repent. Since Küng was a diocesan priest employed by a secular university, he was much less vulnerable than many others to Vatican pressures on his means of subsistence. Besides, his scholarly reputation and the ecumenical importance of the controversy raised by him made it difficult for the Vatican to intervene with more severity. Furthermore, Küng was too shrewd a Church politician to let himself be caught in any of the bear traps and rabbit snares that the curialists put in his way. Küng's challenge to papal authority was not just a stand in heavy theological debate. It became a series of practical ecclesiastical skirmishes in which he was trying to shake up the Vatican apparatus of power. He was finally condemned in late 1979 by the Congregation for the Doctrine of the Faith, but he continues to fight on.

Canon law, especially since its codification in 1917, has been one of the favorite means of control by the hierarchy over the rest of the Church. There is widespread agreement that the 1917 codification of canon law is completely inadequate, but there is a lot of disagreement among canon lawyers and others involved on how to reform the code. When the secret draft for the revised section on the laity in the new code of canon law leaked out in December 1971, it immediately received a strong barrage of criticism from many quarters for its ineptness and narrow legalism.[10]

Küng and others have repeatedly pointed to the unjustice of grievance and redress procedures in cases when one is attacked by Church authorities for doctrinal reasons. For example, Küng has asked to have access to the secret dossier his anonymous detractors have built up against him, but canon law does not give him the right to know what precise accusations have been made against him, and by whom. He could not even choose his own defenders. It is not surprising then that he has refused to submit himself to a trial and has continued to attack the autocratic manner in which the power of the papacy and the curia is exercised.

There was another international uproar in 1971 when the Vatican's Secretariate of State requested that its Justice and Peace Commission not intervene in questions of torture in Brazil and in Portuguese colonies in Africa, as some of the members of the commission suggested. In mid-May, three members of the commission resigned in protest, stating that Archbishop Giovanni Benelli of the Secretariate of State was preventing them from taking progressive positions on social issues. The two persons who stepped up to defend Benelli and the Secretariate of State were Cardinal Maurice Roy (president of both the Justice and Peace Commission and the Council on the Laity) and Vittorino Veronese. Cardinal Roy excused the secretariate's effort at control by stating that the commission was an official organ of the Holy See, and that its positions engaged the responsibility of the Holy See, implying thus that it could not and would not do anything so radical and undiplomatic as condemning torture.[11] Less than two weeks later, Veronese also rose to the defense of the secretariate, affirming that the status of the commission had always been purely consultative, and that it was nothing more than an instrument of the pope.[12] In effect, both Cardinal Roy and Veronese, men with liberal credentials, were stating that it was naïve for anyone to expect that the Vatican could let any of its agencies take public stands that ran counter to the official positions determined by the pope and his Secretariate of State. They completely avoided the question of whether the official position on torture was morally acceptable, assuming that Church leaders, i.e. the pope and his advisers, obviously would always know when it was best to speak out on such questions.

During the same year Bishop Loris Capovilla, former private secretary of John XXIII, was demoted from his position as president of the episcopal conference of the Abruzzi province because of his strong stands in favor of social justice in Italy. In addition, some progressive Italian Catholic periodicals—*Il Regno, Rocca, Servizio della Parola, IDOC*—were censored by Italian bishops and by the Vatican. These Church authorities also de-confessionalized the ACLI by taking their chaplains from them because of the socialist leanings of that association of Italian Catholic workers.

During 1971 and 1972 the Vatican pursued its conservative course, while lay demands and protests continued to grow. The forty-first congress of the Italian Federation of Catholic University Students, meeting in Naples in September 1971, called for the separation of church and state in Italy, opposed legal-political guarantees for religious marriages, and talked of an excessive concentration of power at the summit of the Catholic Church. Coming from a group of Catholic actionists which Pope Paul had done so much to inspire when he was its chaplain during the early years of fascism, these statements must have seemed particularly harsh indeed to the beleaguered Vatican, but there was no official condemnation and only discreet bureaucratic harassment was used in retaliation.

There was also a meeting of progressive lay Italian groups in Rome near the end of 1971. The representatives of these grass-roots communities spent much of their time attacking the concordat between Italy and the Vatican, showing again that many Italian Catholics were becoming more and more opposed to the compact between politics and religion that exists in their country.

The third Synod of Bishops, held in October-November 1971, was a well-controlled event which manifested again the Vatican's desire to contain the whole Church, including the bishops, under its narrow tutelage. In April 1972, progressive Italian priests and laymen, disappointed by the fact that the synod had produced so little and had proved so timid vis-à-vis the encroachments of the Vatican, founded the November 7 Movement (in reference to the 1971 Synod of Bishops, which had ended on that date). One of the founders of this group, a young Italian Jesuit named Pietro Brugnoli, was subsequently relieved of his position as teacher of the theology of the laity at the Gregorian University in Rome because of his major leadership role. The movement's first congress, in November 1972, attacked the Vatican for its tendency to use the Italian state as its secular arm.

In December 1972, eleven radical Italian Catholic periodicals (and one Protestant journal) sponsored a meeting in Florence to coordinate their action, deciding on a more activist policy in the working-class struggle for social justice. This developed into a group called Christians for Socialism, which met for a congress in 1973 at Bologna and in 1974 at Naples, to the great consternation of Church authorities. These Christian leftists opposed not only the Christian Democrats but also the Communists' much-discussed "historical compromise," which they saw as a projected alliance between monopoly state capitalism, the Vatican, and Communist party bureaucrats. To this new holy alliance, they opposed a political alliance of various left tendencies among the masses, Christian and non-Christian. The organization of Christians for Socialism was influenced by similar groups founded in other countries. For example, in May 1972 more than 400 revolutionary laymen and priests met in Santiago, Chile, for the first Latin American embodiment of Christians for Socialism. In April 1973, fourteen groups of "critical Christians," as they called themselves, met in Geneva, and in November of the same year another international meeting of "critical Christians" was held at Lyons in France. In April 1975 a similar meeting took place in Quebec.

These organized radical priests and laymen represented a new development in the lay movement in the Catholic Church. Faced with the continuing integration of the Vatican into the international capitalist system and the hierarchy's continuing accomodation to dominant political forces, these groups saw little hope that the institutional church would speak out critically on the important issues of the day. In Italy, Chile, and many other countries these Catholics rejected the papacy's and the hierarchy's involvement with bourgeois parties and with capitalism, and chose a position of solidarity with the interests and struggles of the working class, as expressed in various political parties and movements of the left. For them, the lay-clergy distinction is nothing but a false dichotomy which should be replaced by less obfuscating types of relationships.

Criticism of the recent actions and orientations of the papacy came from many quarters, and was increasingly directed at the pope's deputy secretary of state, Archbishop Giovanni Benelli. In articles in *The Observer* (London) on March 11 and March 18, 1973, the English Jesuit Peter Hebblethwaite, editor of the Catholic periodical *The Month*, accused Benelli, who was then deputy secretary of state and coordinator of various Vatican departments, of having reactionary sympathies and of using his position "to gain control of the central government of the Catholic church." The much heralded rejuvenation and internationalization of the Roman Curia, according to Hebblethwaite, had not brought about any radicalization or even liberalization of its operations. He went on to say that the Secretariate of State had become a more important center of power than had been the case under any previous pope. It has been said that the secretary of state himself, Cardinal Jean Villot of France, who was less conservative than Paul VI and Benelli, tried to resign in 1971, and that the pope refused his resignation. Villot probably was opposed to the more conservative positions of the pope and the curia on married priests and on social issues such as torture in Brazil, but did not dare to speak out publicly. He had refused to accompany Paul VI on his trip around the world in

November-December 1970, because he disapproved of the pompous and political manner in which the trip was organized; he would have preferred less insistence on the political and diplomatic aspects of the papal journey, according to the Vatican experts whom I interviewed during that trip.

In the reorganized Roman Curia, after the reform of 1967, the names of most of the sections were changed and their operations were made more efficient. Many non-Italian cardinals were put in charge, officially, but the structure still remained under the control of Italian monsignors and cardinals like Benelli who had spent their whole lives pursuing careers in the government of the Church. The position of these men had been reinforced rather than weakened by the increasing recruitment of like-minded moderate and conservative priests and bishops from various countries into some leadership positions in the curia apparatus.

Having himself spent most of his adult life in the Roman Curia, and more specifically in the Secretariate of State, Pope Paul realized how powerful these sections of the Church bureaucracy really were. He remained very attached to the Secretariate of State as an instrument of government. He knew that with a curia out of his control or under the collegial control of both the pope and the Synod of Bishops, he would gradually become nothing more than a figurehead leader. Consequently, to keep the papacy in its central position, Paul VI had to use the curia and develop an alliance with it. To fight the curia or to let it fall under the tutelage of the world episcopate would have meant to sign the death warrant of the papacy and of the Church as they had existed until John XXIII came along.

Pope John's innovations had led to a crisis of monumental proportions in the Catholic Church, on questions of both ideology and organization. The movement had to be reversed, otherwise the papacy would have lost most of its power. This reversal could only come about through an alliance between the pope and the curia, because the episcopate was already too radicalized in some countries to become a reliable support group for the papacy. In other words, the pope had to choose between the episcopate and the curia, and he chose the latter. Squeezed between a conservative curia and a relatively unpredictable episcopate, the moderate, centrist Paul VI opted to join forces with his old enemies, because their traditionalist ideology made them his unconditional supporters. The opposite choice would have left him highly vulnerable between an entrenched and intractable curia and increasingly impatient bishops, priests, and laymen.

The fourth international Synod of Bishops, held in Rome in the fall of 1974, was a good illustration of the basic split in the Church between the pope and his curia on the one hand, and the more progressive episcopate, backed by most of the clergy and the laity, on the other. Paul VI came down very hard against revolutionary and violent social change, and against a type of involvement which focuses on political, economic, and social realities rather than on the traditional religious mission of the church.[13] The synod was split on these issues, and Paul VI did not hesitate to show that he agreed with the conservative minority rather than with the progressive majority. This synod, the fourth of a series which began in 1967 at the same time the third World Congress for the Lay Apostolate was taking place, did not accomplish what the synods, in the words of Francis X. Murphy, were created to do, namely, "to extricate the governance of the church from the control of the curia, the Vatican's administrative offices. So far, little power has been transferred to the bishops."[14] As during the time of Pius XII, the pope and the curia reigned supreme over the rest of the Church, over bishops, clergy, and laity. The only difference was that under Paul VI the opposition was not so minuscule, unconditionally loyal, elitist, and silent as it was in those days. The conflict had shifted from a conservative-liberal tension to a situation where the moderate conservatives and liberals had merged, and where the opposition to that new "progressive-conservatism" came from forces farther to the left and to the right. For example, the Christians for Socialism (or Critical Christians, as they are sometimes called) had increased in numbers, particularly in Italy. The question of Christian-Marxist dialogue and cooperation had become a very serious issue since the spectacular gains made by the left in various Latin countries of Europe. Church authorities, afraid that a new political situation would greatly affect their own situation, were reluctant to condemn and anathemize in the uncompromising manner they used during the Pius pontificates. This moderation of Church authorities, and the increasing strength of the radical Catholic forces that want to move beyond the Catholicism of Vatican II as represented by Paul VI, probably brought into the open the strong right-wing backlash exemplified by Msgr. Lefebvre, which had been building up for years.

The charismatic movement had also grown tremendously in recent years, alongside the integralists and the radicals (it even succeeded in getting the support of Paul VI, Cardinal Suenens, and Archbishop Helder de Càmara of Recife, Brazil), but it was the integralists who were attracting most of the publicity and attention, probably because they presented a more striking challenge to papal authority. Lefebvre's and his followers' movement represented a last ditch effort of pre–Vatican II nostalgists who rejected the socioeconomic, political, and ideological changes that followed in the wake of the great revolutions of the late eighteenth century. The challenge from the right made Paul VI seem like a progressive by comparison (somewhat as Ronald Reagan made U.S. President Gerald Ford look less conservative than he really was), but the effect of that challenge also made Paul VI and the hierarchy more sensitive and understanding toward the positions of these integralists. For example, the progressive Italian bishop of Ravenna, Msgr. Baldassari, who had been censured in 1970, was dismissed from his bishopric in 1976, because of his radical stands on various issues.

Paul VI also hit a hard blow at women's equality in the Church by ruling out on scriptural and theological grounds the possibility of the priestly ordination of women. Another telling example of the new conservative mood was the fact that the theme chosen by the Vatican for the 1977 Synod of Bishops was the bland topic "Catechetics," rather than a more controversial one. As he grew older, Paul VI appeared as much more of a conservative than a liberal, even if there were definite limits (he was certainly not a religious reactionary and political fascist like Msgr. Lefebvre) that he would not cross.

Part of Paul VI's "progressive-conservatism" consisted of a return to a dogmatic and bureaucratic mode of operation reminiscent of that of Pius XII (for example, the number of employees of the Roman Curia rose from 2,260 to 3,400 between 1970 and 1976). Another aspect of that "progressive-conservatism," probably as important as the other, was simply that after 1968 the *aggiornamento* nearly completely stopped, which meant that the process of continual change which characterizes a dynamic organization simply did not continue to unfold as during the preceeding ten years. This aspect of Paul VI's pontificate was well captured by Robert Solé, a journalist of *Le Monde*, in a December 1976 article entitled "The Vatican in Slow Motion." Solé noted that the more competent Vatican-watchers were speaking of the motionlessness or stagnation of this "end of a pontificate," and that some members of the newer secretariates and committees said, "Everything is blocked."[15]

The reasons for Paul VI's peculiar kind of conservatism can be partly discovered by an analysis of the political and economic background behind the religious struggles and conflicts. But first one should look closely at his relationship with the official international lay associations, namely the Catholic International Organizations and the

Council on the Laity, a relationship discussed very briefly in chapters 3 and 4 in connection with the three World Congresses for the Lay Apostolate.

3. PAUL VI, THE CIOs, AND THE COUNCIL ON THE LAITY

The pope and the curia's dissatisfaction with the increasingly radical demands and critiques of lay groups, both the officially recognized groups and those independent of clerical control, led them to attempt a greater centralized supervision of the various lay organizations. In October 1968, for example, a year after the third World Congress, Msgr. Benelli of the Secretariate of State asked Ms. Pilar Bellosillo, president of the Conference of the Catholic International Organizations, to cooperate with the secretariate's plan to integrate the CIOs into the Council on the Laity. The Vatican had decided that the funds collected by the secretariate through the Pius XII Foundation and previously given the Conference of the CIOs would be given instead to the Council on the Laity. Since the council was a department of the Roman Curia with three ecclesiastics at its head, and since it did not yet have a permanent status in the central Vatican apparatus, this transfer of funds and the effort at co-optation were resented by many international organizations that did not want to be boxed into such a narrow framework where their autonomy and their freedom of action would be curtailed. Consequently the CIOs refused to be integrated into the Council on the Laity. At its February 1969 meeting in Fribourg, Switzerland, the Conference of the CIOs decided instead to create a committee of cooperation which would function as its consultative body within the laity council. This move was aimed at preserving the autonomy of the CIOs vis-à-vis the laity council and the Vatican while assuring a certain amount of collaboration with the Vatican and its lay agency.[16] Two years earlier, in 1967, the Conference of the CIOs and the Council on the Laity had theoretically agreed to establish such consultative relationships through a cooperation committee, but the decision had not been formally implemented. The Secretariate of State's efforts at encroachment in 1968 helped to prod the Conference of the CIOs into institutionalizing this protective mechanism. In early 1975 the secretariate was still trying to impinge on the autonomy of the CIOs: a CIO-commissioned report on population problems was secretly censored by Archbishop Benelli, undersecretary of state, who demanded that the printed copies of the report be retrieved and destroyed. It was only when the story leaked to the press that the secretariate stopped its "unbelievably petty harassment" and "allowed the publication to go ahead."[17]

The Conference (or administrative body) of the federated CIOs is one of the most powerful Catholic bodies to operate with some degree of independence from the Vatican. Its ramifications in numerous sectors of activity and its partly democratic structure give it a legitimacy and an influence which the Vatican and the Secretariate of State would like to utilize, and which they consider to be a potential source of competition and opposition.

It was more than fifty years ago, in 1927, that a federation of the CIOs was founded by eleven organizations, and a liaison center established in Fribourg. In 1930 that federation created a "continuity committee" to ensure permanence between annual meetings. World War II interrupted most of the activities, but immediately afterward the number of member organizations doubled and the coordination of activities was resumed. Offices were opened in Paris, Geneva, New York, and Rome, and specialized committees were formed. Statutes were drawn up and accepted with the approval of the Vatican in 1951.

The first World Congress for the Lay Apostolate, in 1951, as noted in chapter 3, was partly an effort by the Vatican to bring the CIOs into its orbit. In March 1955, Pius XII urged the Conference of the CIOs to collaborate with the episcopate and with the Holy See.[18] Each of the factions that were struggling for hegemony inside Italian Catholicism was hoping to see its own position strengthened by the entry of the CIOs into the picture in Rome. At first, the Conference of the CIOs was somewhat flattered by all this attention, and was generally happy to collaborate with the Vatican, but little by little some of the organizations in the conference became more sensitive about their freedom of action and their autonomy. They began to manifest their opposition to the Vatican's encroachment policy.

The most far-reaching attempt to date by the Vatican to subordinate the Conference of the CIOs was the official publication in 1971 of "Guidelines for the Definition of Catholic International Organizations."[19] These guidelines, the writing of which was officially attributed to the Council on the Laity, indicated that to be recognized by the Holy See as being part of the CIOs an association would thenceforth have to meet certain conditions, such as the approval by the Secretariate of State of the association's statutes, its chaplains, and the candidates for its presidency. Furthermore, not only would all the leaders of the association have to be Catholics, but also they would have to take care to maintain the necessary reserve as regards taking a stand or engaging in public activity in the field of politics or trade-unionism. Abstention in these fields will normally be the best attitude for them to adopt during their term of office. . . . Needless to say, as in the past, the organizations will always find a ready interlocutor in the secretariate of state, which is ultimately competent to evaluate how far the church is committed by the activity of any Catholic body at the international level.[20]

The guidelines constituted an effort on the part of the Secretariate of State to solidify its control over the Conference of the CIOs indirectly, through its docile (and more presentable) arm, the Council on the Laity. But even if it was the council which "indicate[d] in these guidelines the criteria for a definition of Catholic International Organizations,"[21] everyone knew that it was the Secretariate of State which was behind the move to cut down the CIOs to size. In spite of the fact that the council praised the CIOs for being democratic and based on the spontaneous initiative of the faithful, it remained obvious that the subordination of the CIOs to the council would probably lead to the suppression of whatever aspects of democratic initiative existed in them. The Vatican could not tolerate real grass-roots autonomy, because any form of autonomy and participation on the part of an independent laity was seen as leading to the gradual disintegration of the Church as an ideological and organizational force and as an apparatus of social and political reproduction.

Thus, the "ultimately competent" Secretariate of State used the Council on the Laity as an instrument to co-opt the relatively freer Catholic International Organizations, in much the same way that COPECIAL and its congresses were used during the 1950s. With the help of some of the influential elements within the CIOs (Pax Romana and some branches of Catholic Action such as the JOC-International), the secretariate reinforced the council with authoritative lay personnel. Nevertheless the council still lacked the grass-roots base that might have been furnished by closer ties with the Conference of the CIOs, which is made up of large federations, many of which arose from the lay initiative.

The Council on the Laity and the CIOs fill the same function, respectively, at the international level that Italian Catholic Action and the Italian Christian Democratic party played after World War II in Italy, the first being a tightly controlled religious organization and the other an indirectly controlled and more secular one. The Conference of the CIOs made efforts to maintain its independence, and it continued to send separate representatives, distinct from Vatican representatives, to various agencies of the United Nations and to certain international gatherings. The Vatican, anxious to bring the grass-roots organizations into its own orbit, resented such "wasteful" duplications of efforts. But what the Vatican really feared was that the CIOs would be identified with radical political causes and contradict its own moderate stands dictated by diplomatic considerations.

In the protracted struggle between the Secretariate of State and the Conference of the CIOs, the Council on the Laity has played a very ambiguous role. For example, in 1973 the council published a special issue (no. 13–14) of its official bulletin, *The Laity Today*, on the CIOs, supposedly to support and strengthen these various associations, but then it let the same issue be used by the secretariate in the publication of the guidelines. The council's ambiguity was further manifested by its own efforts to maintain a certain distance vis-à-vis the more conservative positions of the Secretariate of State and of Paul VI himself. For example, on November 30, 1968, it presented to the pope a report on various responses (including its own, which was not very enthusiastic) to the birth-control encyclical, but it also set up a commission on family life to promote and encourage the study of the encyclical. Similarly, in late 1971 the council organized a symposium in Rome on dialogue within the Church, a theme dear to Paul VI, and then the participants openly urged the Vatican to make its financial statements public, and to employ understanding rather than "severe authority" in its dealings with protesters within the Church.[22]

In spite of the council's efforts to avoid causing embarrassment to the pope, the Vatican was not satisfied. For the Vatican, the council existed to bring in information about the laity, information that would permit a better control over the laity and over modern society. The council tried to give the laity the impression that this knowledge would bring about desired changes, and that it was not a spying agency but a "think tank" which could help transform the curia. All this, however, seemed to indicate that the council was only engaged in careful maneuvers to keep its legitimacy with its lay base without losing the official support of its Vatican masters.

In June 1972, Paul VI extended, for a new experimental period of three years, the life of the Council on the Laity, which had been created for five years in 1967. The officers and thirteen other members were reconfirmed in their functions temporarily, and twelve new members and advisers were named for the same period. The Vatican press release affirmed that these nominations were "the expression of the Holy Father's desire to ensure as balanced a representation as possible between various continents, various life situations, various social categories, and various competences."[23] The three-year renewal, instead of a five-year renewal or a definitive acceptance of the experience, was an indication that the Vatican was uneasy about the council's moderate freedom of expression. Such a procedure exemplifies one of the Vatican's favorite control mechanisms: an organization is created on a trial basis and if all goes well and the members are submissive, the mandate is extended; if not, the organization is suppressed or transformed. Often the mere threat of nonrenewal of the mandate assures conformity. In the case of the Council on the Laity an intermediate solution—a short-term renewal—was found which manifested dissatisfaction without occasioning a complete break. Useful for the projection of a liberal image, the council could not be disbanded without greater damage being caused. Anyway, its operations were low key, well supervised, and rather innocuous. Its main activities were to publish a bulletin four times a year, to organize regional meetings, and to establish contacts with various religious bodies inside and outside the church.

The Council on the Laity had not openly attacked Paul VI and his conservative stands, but it had not shown the expected and desired zeal in defending him. With its credibility at a very low point already among lay activists, the council hesitated to defend such controversial and unpopular official positions as those expressed in *Humanae Vitae* on birth control, in *Sacerdotium Coelibatus* on priestly celibacy, and in the new papal *Credo*. Forced to walk the tightrope between acceptance and rejection of papal authority, in these and other matters, the council took middle positions to avoid papal repression or lay repudiation. Its efforts to maintain credibility on both sides expressed themselves mostly in a series of discussions or conferences which have produced lots of printed words but little original and innovative thought.[24]

Even so, Pope Paul's turn toward conservatism after 1968 was so drastic that even the Council on the Laity, composed largely of his allies and friends from the fifties, preferred to put some distance between itself and the pope's positions. Neither supporting him strongly nor contradicting him openly, it took refuge in bland jargon. Like COPECIAL during the fifties, it seemed to be waiting out the situation, hoping for better or different times, trying to avoid at least the danger of suppression of condemnation by the pope. When the three-year experimental period ended in 1975, the council fell into a sort of legal limbo in which it continued to live de facto from day to day without official and juridical recognition. Clearly, the pope was not happy with the less than complete support he had been getting from the council. Unwilling to suppress it, he opted for the other conservative solution; that is, he tightened the Roman Curia's control over the council, while giving the impression that he was increasing the importance of the laity in the Church.

The denouement came on December 16, 1976. The pope decided then to turn the council into a permanent curial body called the Pontifical Council for the Laity. The new permanent status was a mixed blessing for the laity. Since then the council has been not a consultative body any more, but a branch of the curia with real powers. Cardinal Opilo Rossi has been named as its head. Unlike Cardinal Roy before him, Cardinal Rossi does not preside also over the Justice and Peace Commission. The two bodies are now more separate and more permanent than before, and thus have more weight inside the curia. On the other hand, the two top lay posts held by Rosemary Goldie and Mieczyslaw de Habitch have been abolished since only clerics can be undersecretaries in the branches of the curia that exercise real powers of order and jurisdiction.

Even more significant as an indication of the Vatican's desire for tight control of the new Council was the creation of a presidential committee of cardinals, on top of the existing structure, to represent it in the various interlocking meetings that are held by the cardinals in charge of the different branches of the Roman Curia. Consequently, the Pontifical Council for the Laity is now a Vatican organ in which the laity is more dependent and subjugated than before, when the Council on the Laity was less permanent and less integrated into the curia.

4. THE CHURCH AND ITALIAN POLITICS

Chapter 6 has shown that the problems encountered in the study of papal control and lay demands for change in the Catholic Church cannot be understood independently of the political and socioeconomic problems of our time, especially those that emerge in the Italian context. In remaining sections of this chapter, I shall try to show how this approach is particularly applicable to the pontificate of Paul VI. The Vatican's and the Italian church's political and financial interests must be examined if there is to be a balanced explanation of the continuing efforts by the papacy to maintain control over the laity, amid the increasing challenges to its authority.

John XXIII, as we have seen in chapter 6, repudiated Gedda's Civic Committees and blocked the development of Italian Catholic Action. Carlo Falconi notes:

> During John XXIII's pontificate, the Church abandoned what had been until then the instruments of an indirect but nonetheless abusive control: the pressures of the Secretariate of State, the protectionism of the bishops, the pseudo-religious crusades of Catholic Action and the pseudo-civic crusades of the Civic Committees, the compromising alliances with the so-called Catholic party, etc.[25]

Between 1960 and 1970, in good part because of Pope John's downgrading of Catholic Action, that organization lost about a million members. Although Paul VI was more favorable than John XXIII toward Catholic Action, its decrease in power and popularity was not substantially slowed, and his pontificate saw Catholic Italy become more divided politically than at any time since 1948. Politicking by Church authorities was open and active, as the pope and the pro–Christian Democrat hierarchy maneuvered to maintain Church interests amid a series of political crises.

A study of Italian government by a British political analyst, describing the role of the Church in politics since the death of John XXIII, concludes:

> For my part, I would put the dyarchy of the Roman Catholic hierarchy and the big economic groups at the center of the Italian ruling class, and the political administrative leaders behind them as their agents, but with a wide area for maneuver. The power of the church is logical in a predominantly Catholic country which is the home of its temporal seat and in which the Catholic party has been in power for close on thirty years, largely thanks to the Church's electoral influence.[26]

Paul VI and Pius XII, by career, class origin, and the political involvement of their own families, were both predisposed to become political popes, but Paul perhaps proved a more astute conservative politician than the last of the Pius popes. In contrast, John XXIII, with his very different background and Church career, was not an Italian politician, and his perspectives can be said to have been oriented more toward religion and the international scene rather than toward the specific Italian political struggles.

Giovanni-Battista Montini had been close to the Christian Democratic party since its birth. His father had been a founder of its forerunner, the Popular Party. Montini himself, as shown in the previous chapter, was one of the party's early backers, along with his brother Ludovico and friends in the FUCI.

As Paul VI, Montini saw, unlike Pius XII, that a careful move of the Christian Democrats toward the left might strengthen the party's influence. Thus, he strongly backed this Catholic centrist party while encouraging reforms and alliances with moderate Socialists when they became necessary. Pius XII pushed the Christian Democrats toward alliances with rightists against the left, a strategy which, had it succeeded, might have undermined the party and the political influence of the Church. As it was, his policies tended to weaken the Christian Democratic appeal among progressive Italian intellectuals and workers. Pope John, in making friendly gestures toward socialism and withholding massive Church support from the Christian Democrats, made it easier for Catholics to vote for nonreligious parties of both the left and the right. On the other hand, to counteract the growing weakness of the Christian Democrats, Paul VI made use of Catholic Action, the Civic Committees, and episcopal intervention, just as Pius XII had done after World War II. In short, he was less conservative than Pius XII, and less progressive than John XXIII.

Generally, Paul VI preferred to let the Italian bishops take care of the Italian situation, although on becoming pope he had encouraged the right-wing Christian Democrats, to get them to support Moro's coalition government with Nenni's Socialists. A pastoral letter published in the fall of 1963 by the Conference of Italian Bishops (with the obvious approval of Paul VI) pushed a very hard line against communism, but did not oppose the center-left coalition which was under way. The major reason for the coalition was to integrate the Socialists in a strengthened anti-Communist government that would be favorable to the Atlantic alliance and would introduce measures to rationalize the economy, control the unions, stabilize incomes, and keep the powerful Communist Party at bay.

The Italian episcopate was not unanimous in its support of Pope Paul's politics and of the Christian Democratic programs, so the Vatican created various kinds of difficulties to thwart the more outspoken among the progressive bishops. For example, Cardinal Giacomo Lercaro was relieved of his seat as archbishop of Bologna, Cardinal Michele Pellegrino of Turin was surrounded in his Piedmont province by new conservative bishops selected from inside the Roman Curia, and Bishop Loris Capovilla, former secretary of John XXIII, was transferred from Chieti to the small diocese of Loreto and removed from the permanent committee of the Conference of Italian

Bishops. The most extreme case of the kind was that of Don Giovanni Franzoni, abbot of St-Paul-Outside-the-Walls, in Rome; he was driven out of office (1972), suspended *a divinis* (1974) and reduced to the lay state (1976) because of his radicalism.

Paul VI and the Italian episcopate took a certain amount of time to revert to the blatant and outspoken support of Christian Democracy that had been current under Pius XII. But this came in January 1968, when the Conference of Italian Bishops published a statement on "Christians and Political Life" in which they returned to their old habit of asking Catholics to vote for the political party which expressed their unity. According to various sources, it was Paul VI himself who encouraged the bishops to thus intervene in the 1968 elections in Italy and to insist on the necessity for all Catholics to support the Christian Democrats.[27]

This intervention in politics, and the forced resignation of progressive layman Raniero La Valle as editor of the Catholic daily *L'Avvenire d'Italia*, sparked a series of protests from numerous groups of progressive Catholics. Prior to the election, some lay leaders openly manifested their decision to stop backing the Christian Democrats and to participate in the new resistance against the government with the left forces outside that party.

For the May 1972 national elections (called fourteen months ahead of time because of the recurring political crises), the Christian Democrats received the massive backing of the Civic Committees, after the Vatican and the Italian episcopate made it clear that an all-out effort should be made to elect the Catholic party's candidates. The bishops made a common statement alluding to "liberty," the official motto of the Christian Democrats, and everyone knew who they were campaigning for.

In these May 1972 elections, Livio Labor, former president of the ACLI (and a lay national delegate at the third World Congress for the Lay Apostolate in 1967), presented a new leftist party of Catholics to oppose the procapitalist orientation of the Christian Democrats. After the failure of the new party at the polls, most of these radical Catholics joined the Socialist Party (some joined the Communists), and the ACLI itself returned to a slightly less radical position that before. The long period of radicalization which the ACLI had gone through under Livio Labor's leadership had brought about a split on the part of its conservative wing. By late 1972, the Italian bishops and the Vatican had succeeded in getting these conservative secessionists to create a new Catholic workers' association, the Christian Workers' Movement, because of the ACLI's determination to remain independent of the Christian Democrats and the hierarchy and to support union solidarity between Catholics, Socialists, and Communists. In the context of the Vatican's tremendous influence over Italian society and the Italian state, this decision of the ACLI to start acting like an autonomous association was a momentous one, because the ACLI numbered about 700,000 members, all salaried workers, and represented the Christian Democrats' reservoir of working-class votes. A shift of only part of these votes away from the Christian Democratic Party would mean a strengthening of the power of the parties of the left, especially of the Communists.

In 1974, after trying for more than twenty-five years to break the unity of the Christian Democrats and to form a common front with the Socialists, the Communists started seriously to push a different strategy. Using the example of the defeat of Allende in Chile as an argument for the necessity of an alliance of Christian Democrats and leftists to avoid the destruction of democracy, the Communists put forward the claim that they should have a share in the political power at all levels, and that a "historical compromise" should be made between themselves and the Catholic party. The Christian Democrats and the Vatican vehemently opposed the idea of accommodation that the Communist leader Enrico Berlinguer was proposing as an alternative to the endemic stalemate which had become the major characteristic of the Italian political system. Because of the impasse of the center-left coalition, such an arrangement was probably the only one that could put Italy back on its feet. Such a coalition functioned after the fall of Mussolini, but the Christian Democrats' smashing electoral victory in 1948 gave complete control to the Vatican- and United States-supported party and thus eliminated the possibility of a sharing of power—between Socialists, Communists, and Christian Democrats —which could in the long run have brought about more serious and profound societal and political changes.

In the partial regional elections of 1975, the Communists made spectacular gains. With 33.7 percent of the votes (5 percent more than in the previous elections), the Communists came close to surpassing the Christian Democrats' 35 percent, which was a 5 percent drop from the preceding contest. In early 1976 the Socialists, who have been the Christian Democrats' major partners in the various center-left governments that have ruled Italy almost continuously since 1963, signified to them that they must accept Communist representation in the cabinet. An acute crisis followed, which observers predicted would lead to anticipated national elections.

In March, the Christian Democrats' national congress was marred by an open split between the right and the left wings of the party. The left-leaning Benigno Zaccagnini was reelected secretary-general of the party by a thin margin (51.5 percent against 48.5 percent) over Arnaldo Forlani, the minister of defense, in a burlesque atmosphere of insults and fist fights. Less than a month later, the right wing made a comeback with the election of its leader, Amintore Fanfani, as president of the national council of the party. On April 30, the government of Prime Minister Aldo Moro was finally forced to resign. Thus the referendum on abortion was avoided, in which the Vatican and the Christian Democrats risked losing face as they had done in the 1974 divorce referendum. Elections were called for June 20, to fill the 630 seats in the Chamber of Deputies and the 315 seats in the Senate.

The May-June 1976 campaign resembled in many ways the electoral battle of 1948. The specter of communism was again brandished, and liberty again became the Christian Democrats' major issue. They made it clear that they would not let the Communists participate in the government with them, although they let it be known that they might govern with the help of the fascists of the Movimento Sociale Italiano.

The Catholic bishops, collectively through the Conference of Italian Bishops and individually in their dioceses, intervened directly in the campaign, threatening with excommunication those Catholics who would vote Communist or appear as candidates on the Communist lists. Pope Paul reechoed these warnings several times, especially as regards the six famous Catholic laymen who chose to run as independents on the Communist Party lists. On May 12, the pope labeled as traitors these six Catholics (one of them was La Valle, the former editor of *L'Avvenire*), who had been left-wing Christian Democrats. As in 1948, the alternative between Christ and freedom on the one hand, and godless materialism and slavery on the other was brandished by Church authorities. On May 21, Pope Paul told the Conference of Italian Bishops that it was "intolerable" that Catholics should back a party that was "radically opposed ideologically and historically to a Christian viewpoint." According to him, Catholics had the duty to support the Christian Democratic Party, in spite of its shortcomings, because that party respected Christian values.

The party indeed had many shortcomings. In recent years, it had been plagued with numerous scandals involving many of its high-ranking members. The Lockheed affair, for example, was not completely aired out because the Christian Democrats succeeded in having the inquest pushed back and substantially hushed up. What is known, however, is that some of the top leaders of the party had received funds totaling millions of dollars to give contracts for the Hercules C–130 to Lockheed. Similarly, it was revealed by the Italian newspaper *La Stampa* that between 1948 and 1976 huge sums of money were given by the CIA to anti-Communist parties, unions, and associations. In October 1975, William Colby of the CIA revealed the existence of a secret six-million-dollar aid program to Italian political parties. In February 1976 a report by a House of Representatives' commission revealed that secret American gifts totaling $65 million were given to Italian political parties between 1948 and 1965, and that an additional $10 million was granted in 1972. Even the Vatican, it seems, had benefitted from the largesse of the United States government because of its dedication to the fight against communism in Italy.

The pope, his curia, and the Italian bishops gave ideological legitimation to a party and to a system which brought them many advantages, economic or otherwise. The fact that their Party's alignment with the United States was greater than the Communist party's alignment with the USSR did not stop Church authorities from speaking of the Christian Democratic Party as the defender of liberty and the Communist Party as a totalitarian force. The massive intervention of Church authorities in partisan politics in favor of a conservative party which was ready to make a coalition with the neo-fascists but not with the Communists was certainly indicative that earthly interests rather than gospel values were at stake. Before the June 1976 elections, hundreds of Catholic intellectuals and labor leaders signed a declaration saying that, although they did not necessarily agree with the six laymen's decision to run on the Communist lists, they found it was a decision which compensated for the confusion between the Gospels and politics created by politicians and prelates. The results of the June national elections in both the Chamber of Deputies and the Senate represented a substantial increase for the Communists, a corresponding decrease for the small parties of the right, and essentially an unchanged number of seats for the Christian Democrats. The bishops' and the pope's warnings undoubtedly had some effect (the expected debacle of the Christian Democrats did not materialize) but did not succeed in holding back a trend which had been developing with an increased tempo in recent years, namely, the rise in popularity of the

Communist Party in elections at every level. Table 12 illustrates the long-term trend in the percentages of votes in national elections in the Chamber of Deputies between 1946 and 1976. Although the 1976 campaign in many ways resembled that of 1948, the results looked more like those of 1946, the left (Communists and Socialists) having a higher percentage of the votes than the Christian Democrats but not enough to form a government.

Table 12 is instructive in many ways. The gradual rise in popularity of the Communists is most striking, especially the leap made in the 1976 elections. Some of the additional 1976 votes for the Communists obviously came from the other parties of the left, but they probably came mostly from the Christian Democratic Party, which maintained its strength by dipping in the reservoir of right-wingers outside the

TABLE 12   *Percentages of Votes in Italian National Elections for the Chamber of Deputies, by Political Party, 1946–1976*

Party	1946	1948	1953	1958	1963	1968	1972	1976
Communist	18.9		22.6	22.7	25.3	26.9	27.2	34.4
Proletarian	20.7		—	—	—	4.5	1.9	1.5[b]
Socialist	—	31[a]	12.8	14.2	13.8		9.6	9.6
Social Democratic	[c]	7.1	4.5	4.5	6.1	14.5[d]	5.1	3.4
Christian Democratic	35.2	48.5	40.1	42.4	38.3	39.1	38.8	38.7
Republican	4.4	2.5	1.6	1.4	1.4	2.0	2.9	3.1
Liberal	6.8	3.8	3.0	3.5	7.0	5.8	3.9	1.3
Monarchist or Neo-Fascist	8.1	4.8	12.7	9.6	6.8	5.7	8.7	6.1
Other[e]	5.6	2.4	2.7	1.7	1.3	1.5	1.5	2.6

SOURCES: Italian Government, *Italy: Documents and Notes*, no. 6, 1971, pp. 419ff. and no. 3, 1972, pp. 198–199; P. A. Allum, *Republic without Government* (New York: Norton, 1973), pp. 64–65; and André Béliveau, "Les Démo-chrétiens en quête d'alliés," *La Presse* (Montréal), June 23, 1976, p. A 16.
[a] In 1948, the Socialists presented joint lists of candidates with the Communists.
[b] The Socialist Party for Proletarian Unity presented candidates in 1946, 1968, and 1972. In 1976 a new party of the left, the Proletarian Democrats, got 1.5 percent of the vote. That party was made up of the "Lotta Continua" and "Manifesto" people.
[c] In 1946, the Social Democrats formed a bloc with the Liberals.
[d] In 1968, the Socialists joined forces with the Social Democrats.
[e] Others include small regional or ephemeral parties. A few of the small ephemeral parties are lumped together with Social Democrats, Liberals, and Monarchists or Neo-Fascists.

party. These latter conservative voters, fearful of a Communist victory, probably switched to the Christian Democrats and thus contributed to the near collapse of the small center and right-wing parties.

The Socialist Party, in spite of the fact that it had only 9.6 percent of the votes, effectively held the balance of power, thanks to the refusal of the Communists and the Christian Democrats to work together. The Christian Democrats could not run the country without the support of the Socialists (or the Communists), and the Socialists refused to continue in a center-left coalition unless the Communists participated also. Figure 1, based on table 12, shows the evolution of the percentage of the vote of the Christian Democrats in comparison with the added percentages of the Communist Party and of the Nenni and Proletarian Socialists. The previous ten years' history of Italian politics is expressed in the relationship between these two curves. Their relationship makes us better understand the Christian Democratic–Socialist–Communist coalition of 1946, the 1948 Christian Democratic victory and the consolidation of the party's power which followed, the gradual rise of the left and concomitant decline of the Christian Democrats which led to the 1963 opening to the left, the stalemate between 1963 and 1972, and the real but limited victory of the left in June 1976.

FIGURE 1   *The Christian Democratic Party versus the Left, 1946–1976. Percentage of votes in Italian national elections for the Chamber of Deputies.*

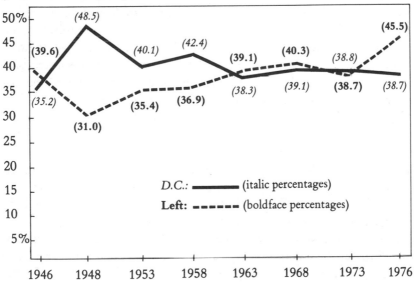

D.C.: ——— (italic percentages)

Left: ▬ ▬ ▬ ▬ (boldface percentages)

The results of the June 1976 elections brought about the possibility of a deadlock of even greater proportions than the one which existed before. The problem was aggravated by the fact that political leaders of the four major Western capitalist countries (the United States, Germany, Great Britain, and France) secretly agreed at a meeting in Puerto Rico that they would cut all credits to Italy if the Communists participated in the new government.

Since another center-left coalition was ruled out by the refusal of the Socialists to pursue that avenue, and since the possibility of the "historical compromise" was also excluded, the Christian Democrats and the Communists worked out a novel solution to the crisis. The Christian Democrats would try to rule all by themselves, without including any Socialists or Communists in the government. In order to get the Communists to give outside support to their *monocolore* cabinet, the Christian Democrats had to make several concessions. First, they agreed to let a Communist, Pietro Ingrao, serve as president of the Chamber of Deputies, keeping for one of their own, Amintore Fanfari, the presidency of the Senate. Furthermore, the chairs of seven of the twenty-eight parliamentary committees were given to the Communists. The Christian Democratic government would be able to survive the vote of confidence test only on condition that the Communists abstained from voting against it. It seems that the six parties that founded the Republic decided to put aside some of their differences in order to work together to try to resolve the pressing economic problems. If the Socialists maintained their refusal to participate in a coalition government (which would not be assured of having a sufficient number of votes anyway), the Communists would have the enviable position of remaining in the opposition while holding at the same time a veto power over the government and its program. It was clear, then, that the battles would be over the content of the government's program, with both the Christian Democrats and the Communists fighting over its orientation and each trying to avoid being held responsible for precipitating a new crisis. The severe shock brought about by the kidnaping and assassination of Aldo Moro by the Red Brigade in the spring of 1978 does not seem to have changed the relative strength of the two parties. What the Communists lost in popular and electoral support in the 1979 elections seems to have been compensated by greater access to the levers of power.

In the long run, because of the inevitable secularization of politics, the Christian Democratic Party seems bound to break up. Already at work under John XXIII were centrifugal forces which Paul VI was barely able to contain. In the next few years, if the left in Italy should work at breaking the unity of the Catholic vote, a good number of Catholic votes would gravitate toward the various parties of the left, and this would leave a left coalition as the only viable political force in the country. Because of possible outside interference in Italian affairs, the Italian left is wary of moving too fast, confident that time is playing in its favor. Because of the strategic position of Italy, its political future is one of the key questions of our time, and that future hinges in good part on the future of the Christian Democratic Party and its relations with the Vatican. The Communists have no intention of letting power slip out of their hands by making precipitous and imprudent moves.

As early as 1921, Antonio Gramsci hit upon the fundamental ambiguity of a Catholic party in Italy. According to him, the Catholic party of that period, the Popular Party, was a mass party composed of heterogeneous elements: a vast rural base lacking class consciousness and manipulated by the old conservative groups who had largely abandoned the direction of the party to the industrialists. Gramsci thought that as the peasants awakened, they would shake off the yoke of those who wanted to maintain the existing order.[28] The crisis envisaged by Gramsci never came about, because Pius XI and Mussolini destroyed the Popular Party before its internal contradictions could break it up. The same kind of ambiguity survives in the Christian Democratic Party, which has a peasant and worker electoral base controlled by the alliance of the bourgeoisie with Church authorities. If the "historical compromise" is to be essentially an integration of the working class in the state apparatus through the co-optation of Communist Party leaders, then it will be a reformist compact between monopoly capitalism and party bureaucrats. But if the left follows Gramsci's suggestion for the creation of a new historical bloc of socialist forces, then it stands the chance of becoming a revolutionary alliance between the working class and the progressive elements of the peasantry and the petty bourgeoisie.

The Christian Democrats' official ideology, like their electoral support, cuts across class lines, but the party is really, and increasingly, a conservative organization defending the interests of the bourgeoisie. The Communist Party would like to govern in coalition with the Christian Democrats, in order to have a government with a strong (albeit politically moderate) working majority, and to avoid seeing Italy become a second Chile. This "historical compromise," according to them, would then lead the country, slowly but surely, to socialism. Other groups and parties more to the left have a different strategy. They think the left should work to split the Christian Democratic

Party and bring its left wing into a narrower, but purer, alliance with itself and the Socialists. Ideally, and in the long run, this seems to me to be the best solution for the left, but such a left government would be in a weaker position than the left-center alliance proposed by the Communist Party. In my opinion, the "historical compromise" just might be the best short-term strategy to bring about later the realignment wished for by many people on the left.

The present stalemate, which permits the Christian Democrats to govern without a majority of seats, thanks to the abstention of Communists on crucial votes and to their support of a limited economic and law-and-order program, is really a new arrangement by which the Communist Party is extending and consolidating its power through limited cooperation at the national level and through direct control of many local and regional governments.

The usual small increase or decrease in the percentage of votes for the different parties, by itself, cannot bring about much change, but can trigger a realignment of party support, and a breaking up of the Christian Democratic Party. In this sense, the next general election in the early eighties could possibly be a critical election and might even lead the way toward the novel form of Western Marxism that has recently been called Eurocommunism. But all this could only come about if Catholics should stop voting as a united bloc. In other words, the Italian political crisis will only be resolved with the breaking up of the Christian Democratic Party. It is to avoid this calamity that Church authorities in Italy stress so strongly the importance of unity among Catholics and use all means of control at their disposal to maintain that unity.

In spite of popular observations to the contrary, the political system of Italy has been relatively stable between 1948 and 1979. There has been a form of stalemate rather than real political instability. The same party has remained in power all this time. The same economic, political, and religious elites have been dominant. Behind the frequent changes of cabinets, the same political leaders of the Christian Democratic Party have kept on reappearing as heads of different ministries. There has also been a remarkable continuity in other branches of government. From 1948 to 1963 the Christian Democrats were in power and required practically no support from minor parties to form the government. Just as the active participation of the Vatican, the episcopate, the clergy, and the organized laity played a crucial role in the impressive Christian Democratic victory of 1948, similarly the lack of such intervention by John XXIII and other Church officials was an important factor in the success of the Socialists and Communists in the 1963 national elections. The return to a policy of intervention under Paul VI in 1968 did not really succeed in halting the erosion of the Christian Democrats' power, although the killing of Aldo Moro by the Red Brigade seems to have succeeded partially in slowing down the process.

After the 1972 elections, a crisis began to unfold which may lead eventually to the breakup of the Christian Democratic Party. One of the clearest signs of the Catholic hierarchy's weakening grip on Italian politics was its inability to obtain a repeal of the divorce law passed in December 1970. The law was attacked publicly by Church officials as a breach of the 1929 concordat. The unsuccessful effort to get the Italian electorate to repudiate it through a referendum (held on Mother's Day, May 12) led to a decrease in papal and hierarchal authority. It also brought a weakening of the power of the Christian Democrats, who in the parliament had only the backing of the neo-fascist party in their effort to repeal the law. The Church's ability to run Italy was dealt a severe blow which was probably the most serious defeat ever for the Christian Democrats and their ecclesiastical sponsors. Fanfani had hoped to break up the Communist vote with the referendum, but it was the vote of the Catholic bloc which turned out to be divided.

Having taken a position contrary to that of Church officials on such a crucial issue, in the national elections of 1976 a portion of the working-class Catholic voters switched from the Christian Democrats to the Communists. Not even Pope Paul's and the bishop's appeals were sufficient to bring them back to the Christian Democrats, although the appeals certainly helped avoid a complete debacle. Although the Communist Party lost some seats in the 1979 general elections, it must be remembered that most of these seats went to the Radical Party, a leftist party with libertarian socialist leanings, and not to the Christian Democratic Party, which remained with nearly the same number of seats.

Paul VI's turn to religious conservatism cannot be understood outside of the context of the recurring Italian political crises. He seemed to fear that a loosening of the grip of the Church on the Italian people, brought about by a decline of religious practices, a relaxation of divorce laws, or future reforms of the outdated clauses of the concordat, would ultimately lead to a breakup of the Christian Party and a subsequent loss of power and privileges for the Church.

Xavier Rynne, in his authoritative report on Vatican II, mentions that some people were saying that the pope's conservative gesturing in late 1963 was "due to concern for the financial assets of the Vatican in Italy—the fear that is, that a further drift toward the left by the Church would give added strength to the Communist vote which had already reached alarming proportions in the spring election of 1963."[29] Rynne rejects this explanation offhand, on the basis of his claim that Paul VI was "determined to carry through his purposes which were still those of Pope John XXIII and the majority of the Council, but of course in his own way and in his own time. There was no need to assume a 'counter-revolution.'"[30] Rynne has proved to be wrong about the "counter-revolution," which did come about between 1963 and 1968, and especially after 1968. And in the light of this, since indeed there was a "counter-revolution," the economic and political reasons rejected by Rynne would seem to have been very plausible ones. Before the election of Montini as pope, and until 1968, it was still possible to speak of him as ambivalent, circumspect, enigmatic, incapable of making decisions.[31] After 1968 there could be no doubt in anybody's mind about the fact of his conservatism, and the only question that remained was why he had thus changed.

Some of Paul VI's critics, like Hans Küng, the progressive Swiss theologian who has challenged papal infallibility, tried to explain the pope's conservatism by referring to the lingering power of traditional institutional teachings. In an interview given to a senior editor of *Look* magazine, Küng is quoted as saying: "The drama of Paul VI is that he has been educated in this very narrow Roman theology. . . . We have this wrong decision on birth control only because the pope is the prisoner of the teachings of previous popes."[32] In 1960, Gaston Fessard, a French philosopher-theologian, strongly criticized some of Paul VI's intellectual mentors, such as Jacques Maritain and Charles Journet. Fessard attributed their inability to cope adequately with problems of the "historical present" to their narrow Neo-Thomist theological and philosophical training.[33]

Any analysis of Paul VI's political conservatism must take into account such factors as intellectual formation and psychological make-up. But it must also, as has been done in this section of the present chapter, look at the political factors involved, since Paul VI was fundamentally a Christian Democratic politician; it must even, as in the next section, delve into the socioeconomic factors influencing papal actions and policies. No matter who the pope is, there are structural and institutional influences that operate because the Vatican is not only a religious institution and a center of political power but also an economic institution with vast financial and real estate holdings, a "fiscal paradise" which ranks alongside Monaco and Hong Kong as a haven for tax evasion. Even if a pope's ideology were such that he really wanted to transform the Catholic Church, the political and economic interests of the Vatican bureaucracy would make a change very difficult, as was the case during Pope John's pontificate. Only the unleashing of the combined power of many lay persons, priests and bishops, in alliance with a progressive pope over a good number of years, could possibly induce a significant transformation. As long as the Vatican remains a relatively rich and powerful state, run by an entrenched bureaucracy comprising hundreds of dedicated conservative men who support the Christian Democrats and who are themselves part of the Italian bourgeoisie, even a progressive pope can do little by himself to bring about significant changes. The conservative bureaucracy of the Roman Curia is very powerful when it can work with a like-minded pope, and it can still wield a lot of power, mainly through the forces of inertia it can muster, when it has to work with a pope whose progressive policies it does not readily accept. That was the case during the pontificate of John XXIII, of whom Cardinal Siri of Genoa is reported to have said during Vatican II something to the effect that it would take the curia forty years to undo the harm the pope had done in four. On the other hand, it seems that Paul VI's pontificate, in spite of the rumblings from the rightists and reactionaries like Msgr. Lefebvre, came a long way toward satisfying the conservative curialists and politicians whose major preoccupation was to maintain the sacred alliance of church, state, and capital in Italy.

5. THE POLITICAL ECONOMY OF THE VATICAN

The political involvement of the pope and of other Church officials is generally quite easy to see, since it has to take place in a fairly open manner in order to have any impact at all. On the other hand, their economic and financial operations are difficult to evaluate, since the greatest discretion and secrecy constitute the most efficient strategy for successful action in this area.

Under Pius XI and Pius XII, and even until recent years, the finances of the Vatican were a very well-kept secret. The rare articles that appeared on the subject (for example the one published in *Oggi*, a Roman magazine, on October 15, 1952) were ignored or vilified by Church authorities.

In 1968 an American financial reporter and former professor of sociology, Nino Lo Bello, published the results of his investigations.[34] Since then, two other important books, one by an American investigative reporter specializing in financial affairs,[35] the other by an Italian journalist and author of many books on the papacy,[36] have filled in some of the gaps in Lo Bello's data. Furthermore, numerous articles have appeared in periodicals such as *The Economist, The Sunday Times, Le Monde, L'Expresso, L'Europeo, Business Week, Forbes, National Catholic Reporter, Dossiers de Vie Ouvrière, Lumière et Vie, Informations Catholiques Internationales, Il Mondo,* and *Concilium.*

Consequently, it is now possible to get a reasonably exact idea of the organizational structure of the Vatican as far as economic matters are concerned, even if we are still somewhat in the dark concerning the actual functioning and the specific operations. Some information is now publicly available in official Vatican documents. It is known, for example, that of the six bureaus that figure in the organigram (see chap. 1, n. 16) of the Roman Curia, two (the General Administration of the Patrimony of the Holy See, and the Prefecture for Economic Affairs) are very powerful economic entities with both local (i.e. Roman and Italian) and international ramifications. The Prefecture for Economic Affairs is entrusted with the general supervision and coordination of the financial empire of the Vatican, and is responsible for making budgets and financial statements. The General Administration of the Patrimony of the Holy See is in charge of collecting the ordinary revenues and managing the financial affairs of the papacy. The General Administration, in sum, administers the bulk of the Vatican's wealth, while the Prefecture for Economic Affairs, the equivalent of a ministry of finance, has the task of overseeing the General Administration and other Vatican entities active in financial matters.

There are other sections of the Vatican bureaucracy that are engaged in economic affairs. The Institute for Religious Works, for example, is the Vatican's bank, created in 1942. It assembles funds from various sources (e.g. religious orders, Roman congregations, cardinals, Vatican citizens) and invests them as would any other bank. It is the only economic body in the Vatican which is not controlled by the Prefecture for Economic Affairs. In late 1978 it was controlled by the pope through a commission of five cardinals: John Wright, Jean Villot, Maximilian de Fürstenberg, Agnelo Rossi, and Umberto Mozzoni. All the others, including the Administration of Vatican City (which among other things is responsible for the sale of Vatican postage stamps, an operation that brings in around $3 million a year), "Cor Unum" (for international aid), the Pius XII Foundation (for lay organizations), and the Roman Congregations (the richest ones being the Congregation for the Evangelization of Peoples and the Congregation for the Clergy), are all directly under the control of the Prefecture for Economic Affairs as far as their financial operations are concerned. These organizations administer substantial budgets and manage the considerable assets that have been entrusted to them over the years. Curia cardinals are officially in charge of all these branches of the financial empire of the Vatican, but the pope himself and his Secretariate of State have the ultimate authority over them, above and beyond the control of the Prefecture for Economic Affairs. In late 1978 the General Administration of the Patrimony was presided over by Cardinal Villot with the assistance of Cardinals Sebastiano Baggio, Pericle Felici, Franjo Seper, and James Knox. In fact, the real boss was the secretary, Msgr. Lorenzo Antonetti, who was helped by Msgr. Luigi Esposito in the Ordinary section (salaries of personnel, real estate) and by Msgr. Benedetto Argentieri in the Extraordinary section (investments). The Prefecture for Economic Affairs was presided over by Cardinal Egidio Vagnozzi, with the collaboration of Cardinals Joseph Hoeffner and Giuseppi-Maria Sensi, and directed by a secretary, Msgr. Giovanni Abbo. After the death of Cardinal Villot, Archbishop Giuseppe Caprio was named president of the General Administration of the Patrimony (and Archbishop Agostino Casaroli was named head of the Secretariate of State and the Council for the Public Affairs of the Church). Both Caprio and Casaroli were named cardinals by John Paul II on June 30, 1979.

The actual operations of these Vatican bodies, and their evolution over the years, are somewhat more difficult to describe than their organizational structure. The information that is made available is scant, but with what the critics and other observers have found out and what the Vatican itself has divulged, it is possible to piece together a fairly accurate, albeit incomplete picture on the functioning of the Vatican in financial affairs during the period already covered above for religious and political matters.

After the Protestant Reformation, which was occasioned to a great extent by opposition to the sale of indulgences and benefices by the pope's representatives, the income of the papacy came chiefly from taxes levied in the papal territories. When these territories were annexed to Italy in 1870, it was mainly thanks to the special collection called Peter's Pence that the Vatican was able to keep afloat financially. Even today, Peter's Pence remains an important source of income, bringing in an estimated $5 million a year.[37]

In 1878 the pope created the Administration of the Patrimony, which had jurisdiction over what was left of papal properties. Each year between the time of the signing of the Law of Guarantees (1871) and the signing of the concordat with Mussolini (1929), the popes refused to accept the annual indemnity of 3,225,000 lire which the government of Italy had granted them in compensation for the lands taken in 1870. This refusal, added to the carefree generosity of Benedict XV, created a situation such that at his death in 1922 the Vatican was on the verge of bankruptcy. Pius IX, his successor, succeeded in resolving this serious financial crisis in 1929, with the financial convention of the Lateran Agreements between the Vatican and Fascist Italy. This agreement brought about a definitive settlement of the Roman Question by giving the Vatican, among other things, the equivalent in Italian money of $40 million in cash, and of $50 million in Italian government bonds paying interest of five percent a year. Furthermore, ecclesiastical corporations were exempted from paying taxes to the Italian state, and all parish priests started receiving a small salary from the state.

That same year, Pius XI created the Special Administration (the present General Administration of the Patrimony of the Holy See comes from a fusion of this Special Administration and the Administration of the Patrimony of 1878), and named an Italian layman, Bernardino Nogara, to administer the $90 million received under the Lateran Agreements. Nogara obtained assurance from the pope that he could invest anywhere in the world and without being importuned over moral or religious considerations. In spite of occasional problems and scandals, he worked with the Fascist government and later with the Christian Democrats, performing skillful takeovers of companies and building the $90 million gift into one of the most impressive portfolios ever assembled.[38] Thanks to tax exemptions, the investments yielded higher returns to the Church than to ordinary investors. Lo Bello estimates that by 1967, thanks to Nogara's astute policies, that sum had grown to $550 million.[39] For example, he reportedly invested $26.8 million in gold bullion at $35 an ounce. Vatican II is said to have been financed in good part by the sale of some of that gold. It is also said that gold worth $22 million (at the old price of $35) was left after Vatican II, which means that the remaining hoard, if kept, would now be worth many times that amount. And gold is only one of the Vatican's many assets. Nogara invested similar large amounts in real estate and in shares in Italian companies.

In 1968, following the controversy concerning the secret tax exemption (given to the Vatican after World War II by its Christian

Democratic friends) on dividends from shares in private Italian companies, the Italian minister of finance, Luigi Preti, put forward certain figures: the Vatican had illegally avoided paying around 3 billion lire a year for dividends from shares worth 100 billion lire (around $160 million). This did not include any bonds, or any shares in non-Italian or Italian semipublic enterprises. The Italian journalist Gianpaolo Di Jorio, nephew of Cardinal Alberto Di Jorio who was for many years the man responsible for the financial affairs of the Vatican, estimated the worth of Vatican investments in the United States alone, around 1968, at about $75 million.[40] Such figures give an idea of the Vatican's wealth, even if they do not reveal the precise dimensions. More important than the exact amount of the papal fortune, in my view, are the scale and type of financial operations engaged in by the pope and his assistants. The Vatican's financial portfolio is administered like any conservative capitalist's wealth, and this leads to Vatican interference in politics. Following the 1948 national elections in Italy, the Christian Democrats voted laws favorable to the Vatican and granted large construction contracts to companies in which the Vatican held substantial interests. One of these companies was the Società Generale Immobiliare, a multinational corporation which the Vatican controlled, thanks to the 15 percent of the shares which it bought in 1949. In 1967 the SGI earned profits of $62 million. Nogara's financial strategy was to buy enough shares of a company to have a substantial influence (but not necessarily the majority control) over its board of directors, through a small pool of trusted Italian laymen he had gotten named to the board, without actually having to bother about managing the enterprise on a day-to-day basis. He would have his lieutenants push for growth for growth's sake.

One of these key laymen in the financial affairs of the Vatican, under Pius XI and Pius XII, was Count Enrico Galeazzi, an engineer who started his Vatican career as a friend of Cardinals Spellman and Pacelli in the 1930s. Pius XII made him acting governor of Vatican City, director-general of Economic Services, and Keeper of the Sacred Fabric of St. Peter. As the man responsible for the maintenance of Church property and a trusted friend of Pius XII, his name appeared on many boards of directors of companies in which the Vatican had major interests. Peter Nichols mentions the role played by such laymen in the growth of the original amount of money received from Mussolini:

> Shrewd administration of this basic capital sum has made the Vatican one of the largest financial powers in the world. No balance sheets

are ever published; no direct indication is ever given of where the Vatican has placed its wealth. It can be surmised however that the presence on the boards of Italian companies of such persons as Count Galeazzi and Prince Carlo Pacelli (one of Pius XII's nephews) means that the Vatican holding therein is large. It seems clear that the Holy See is closely connected with buildings, banking, insurance, public services and largescale public works.[41]

The three Pacelli princes, relatives of Pius XII whose nobility titles were a by-product of the 1929 Lateran Agreements, were also papal agents on the boards of Italian companies. Some say that Msgr. Montini's move to Milan in the mid-fifties was partly occasioned by his discovery and criticism of the self-serving financial dealings of some of these lay protégés of Pius XII.[42] Nino Lo Bello, in the chapter of his book on Vatican wealth which describes "The Pope's Shop," adds to these laymen the name of Luigi Gedda: "Other Vatican names, powers to a lesser or greater degree in papal business affairs, are those of Luigi Gedda (a former president of Catholic Action) . . ."[43] All this points to an obvious fact. For the Vatican, economic interests, political power, and religious organization were intimately interrelated. Gedda's career is an excellent illustration of this. The same can be said of Vittorino Veronese's career in the Church, in politics, and in finance. Under John XXIII and Paul VI this important "lay apostle" emerged as a leading Italian banker and one of the Vatican's key financial experts.

The Vatican is particularly active in the world of banking, real estate, and finance, but it still invests in other areas, both inside and outside Italy. In the late sixties, the Vatican was present in many sectors of the Italian economy. It had substantial interests in Italian multinational corporations such as Montecatini Edison, Italcementi, Manifattura Ceramica Pozzi, Italgas, and SNIA Viscosa, and in dozens more. It was also involved with industrial cartels controlled by the Italian government, for example, IRI (Istituto di Ricostruzione Industriale), a public enterprise which controls 130 companies and has ties to United States Steel, Raytheon, Vitro Corporation, and Dalminter of New York. The Vatican was also linked with the European steel giant Finsinder, and it invested substantially in Alfa Romeo, the second-biggest auto manufacturer in Italy. It was also involved with Finmeccanica, the most important industrial network in Italy, and with Finmare, one of the largest passenger transporters in the world. The Vatican's interests extended to STET, the largest Italian telephone company, which itself controlled and participated in dozens of other enterprises. As a general rule, the Vatican preferred bonds to shares as far as state enterprises were concerned, a policy which minimized Vatican control over the company while tending to put Vatican funds at the service of rather conservative managers and directors working more or less openly for the Christian Democrats.

In 1968 the Vatican let go of its control of the SGI, selling a block of 15 million shares to an American conglomerate called Gulf and Western. The Vatican's idea was to divest itself of much of its shares in Italian companies, in order to be less vulnerable to critics accusing it of controlling too much of the Italian economy, and in retaliation against the Italian government's decision finally to collect some taxes from the Vatican's investments in Italy. With the funds from this sale of Italian shares, the Vatican moved into the more lucrative European and American economic and financial networks, where its presence would be less conspicuous and in less danger of being hit by taxes and controls.

The Vatican at last began to carry out its long-standing threat to the Italian government, that it would get rid of its shares in Italian companies, but this was done without fanfare and little by little. A leading Catholic expert on the Vatican wrote in 1970:

> The plan seems to be to shift Vatican shares out of relatively stable Italian industries into more profitable American concerns. Another advantage is that it will be less easy to trace Vatican interests within the permutations and combinations possible in large corporations. . . .
>
> The Vatican has widened its range of consultants on financial affairs. Previously Vittorino Veronese, prominent in the lay apostolate and also president of the bank of Rome, was a leading consultant; but the Vatican has recently turned to American investment consultants.[44]

By 1970, Pope Paul had succeeded in centralizing the various economic services of the Vatican. It was possible for him to know how much the Vatican owned and to make public the budget of the Holy See. That the Vatican continued to refuse to shed any real light on its financial and real-estate holdings can only serve to confirm in people's minds the rather high estimates of some Vaticanologists as to the papacy's wealth.

Because of his past experience in financial affairs in the Secretariate of State (at one time he was in charge of bequests made to the Vatican), Paul VI had a better grasp of the economic affairs of the Vatican than any other recent pope. In June 1970 he attacked critics by saying that although certain persons attributed ''fabulous wealth'' to the Church, there was not even enough money to meet the many demands made upon it: a statement which could mean anything, depending on what might be regarded as demands. In July, the *Osservatore Romano* tried to refute Lo Bello's claims about the Vatican's wealth with blanket details.[45] That probably did not convince many people that the Vatican was poor. As long as the budgets and balance sheets are not made public, the presumption of truth will have to go to the serious investigators.

Paul VI replaced some of the lay Vatican fiduciaries (including Galeazzi, Gedda, and the Pacellis, who had survived through John XXIII's pontificate) with other laymen, and tended to rely more on members of the clergy. Msgr. Paul Marcinkus, secretary of the Institute for Religious Works, and Cardinal Vagnozzi, head of the Prefecture for Economic Affairs, became two of the most powerful men in Vatican financial affairs. As the Vatican switched from Italian to other European and especially to American investments, it preferred to make less use of active Italian laymen such as Veronese, and to have trusted clerics deal directly with the business world instead. Vagnozzi, who had previously been apostolic delegate to the United States, expressed in an interview to the journalist Paul Horne the new investment policy of the Vatican:

> We have decided to avoid attempting to maintain control of the companies in which we invest, as was done in the past. The financial responsibility of the Holy See for such companies has to be reduced. We are thus diversifying our investments over a larger number of companies, while reducing our holdings to minority positions. This means getting away from the traditional practice of lay Vatican fiduciaries sitting on the board of companies in which we invested. The Vatican simply cannot afford primary responsibility for business failures requiring transfusions of capital. We do not want to commit the Church to only a few companies, nor to a single investment field, nor even a single national economy. We are reducing our real estate holdings and increasing securities investments. The Vatican's investment policy remains basically conservative, although the Church's increasing needs mean that the balance between conservation and the need to increase income has been moving toward the need to increase income. We are, to put it simply, more performance minded now.[46]

In this interview, Vagnozzi lifted part of the veil from the Vatican's actions in the world of finance. It can be seen that the basic strategy was to increase revenues through security investments (stocks and bonds, essentially) at the international level, and to have a minimum of active participation in management of companies and even in their boards of directors. In other words, the Vatican would act as a sort of rentier-capitalist, as a big conservative investment fund. The sale of two-thirds of its SGI stock is a good example of this new orientation. The money obtained was used to buy shares in companies outside Italy and also to move from shares to bonds. For these operations Paul VI used the services of Michele Sindona, the banker and speculator who later fled from Italy, where he was wanted on charges of financial fraud and embezzlement, to the United States. Sindona was using some of the pope's money for his own speculative ventures. His sand castle collapsed with the resounding bankruptcy of his banks in various countries. The Watergate revelations indicated that he had offered a million dollars to Maurice Stans as a contribution to Richard Nixon's 1972 campaign for the American Presidency. Estimates of the Vatican's losses in the Sindona affair have ranged from $40 million to $240 million.[47] The amount was put at 10 percent of the Vatican's total worth in the estimate of Massimo Spada, another Italian banker close to the Vatican who has also been in trouble with the Italian government.[48]

Because of the recession and inflation which hit Italy in recent years, and because of rising taxes, new construction, and other increasing costs of operation (salaries and raises for the 3,400 curial employees, whose number had tripled in fifteen years) and a decrease in the amount of gifts received, the financial situation of the Vatican indeed became temporarily precarious. The Holy Year 1975 was a financial disaster, as far as revenues accruing from the pilgrims to the Vatican were concerned. The year started with an announcement that the Vatican might be forced to fire many employees, since financial difficulties had forced the Council of Ministers of the Vatican (i.e. the cardinals at the head of the various branches of the curia) to reject the budget submitted for 1975.[49] Budget cuts of about 25 percent were introduced across the board in every section of the curia, no new hirings were made, and some positions were eliminated in order to arrive at a healthier position. The newer and more progressive sections of the curia (the three secretariates, the Justice and Peace Commission, and the Council on the Laity) were the most affected. The Vatican was forced in 1975 to use special funds to cover nearly half of its expenses for the government of the Church and for the administration of the diocese of Rome and of Vatican City. The deficit in 1975 is believed to have been around $6 million, in a budget that slightly exceeded $20 million. In 1979, it was between $12 and $18 million, in a budget of $36 million.[50]

It is not only the entanglement of the Vatican in dubious operations like the Sindona affair, but also the day-to-day functioning of the pope's financial empire, which has attracted criticism from Catholics and non-Catholics alike. Many problems and scandals probably would not have arisen if Church funds had been administered more openly and by competent people instead of being entrusted in secret to dishonest or incompetent people. In many organizations, such errors of judgment on the part of top leaders would bring about their dismissal or resignation, and a demand for detailed public accounts of all financial operations.

The new policies of the Vatican, seen in the light of the Church's own ethical standards, actually represent a backward rather than a forward step. Vatican funds now serve international and especially American capitalism, without any possibility that the Church, as a bondholder or small stockholder in many companies, will have much influence on their policies. Before 1968, the Vatican, theoretically at least, could have intervened to ensure that the companies it controlled did not engage in unethical practices. It is practically impossible, if you are a minority stockholder in numerous multinational conglomerates, to know all that these companies are doing or to do anything about it if you do know, and that is the situation of the Vatican now.

It is not sufficient to suggest, as James Gollin does in the chapter entitled ''Manage What Thou Hads't'' which closes his book, that the clergy be given a better administrative training, that research and short-term planning be improved, that there be a better sharing of resources at the international level, and that religious authorities open their accounts to the laity.[51] There must also be a more humane, less capitalistic use of funds. The Vatican could use its economic power to help transform the capitalist and imperialist economic and political system, instead of trying to profit from it. It could start by using its influence to make companies more socially responsible, working to eliminate exploitation, discrimination, and oppression. It could favor workers' self-management and the creation of workers' production cooperatives. It could actively encourage small scale selfhelp projects to alleviate hunger and suffering in the poorer countries of the world. How can a church seriously condemn the socioeconomic injustices manifested in economic concentration, worker exploitation, and the looting of resources when it participates unabashedly in all of this, when its concrete economic operations so patently contradict the message that it preaches? As long as the financial institutions of the Vatican function partly as means to evade taxes (i.e. to avoid paying to the state its fair share of taxes that are used in part by the state to bring about some degree of justice and equality in the distribution of wealth and in the distribution of social services), the Vatican will continue to be viewed by many as a fiscal paradise for profiteers and speculators like Sindona.

The only way to ensure a reorientation of the use of the economic assets of the Vatican is to struggle for a grass-roots control over these assets. Also, the sheer size of these resources is undoubtedly one of the major roots of the problem. If the pope and the Vatican were truly poor, the pressure to legitimate and support the capitalist system would surely not be so great. To be taken seriously as being a church of the poor and the oppressed, the pope would have to divest himself of much of the Vatican's wealth.

Paul VI's great fear of the Italian left and his increasing conservatism in religious and political matters in the last years of his reign were certainly linked to his manifest desire to protect the political privileges and economic assets of the Vatican. He was well aware that economic and political interests were often invoked as motives of the papacy's policies, since in the letter written in defense of Pius XII's memory, just before his own election as pope, he defensively said that it was not true that Pius XII was guided by opportunistic calculations of temporal politics or by motives of economic nature.[52] It is one thing to deny such allegations, and another to show clearly that they have no basis in fact.

Religious, sometimes psychological, and even political motives are put forward by critics of the papacy and other Church authorities in order to explain Vatican conservatism, but in recent years an increasing number of people have been looking at the economic side of the picture also. Carl Boggs, Jr., in an article on the Italian left, has said about the political and economic importance of the Catholic Church in Italy:

> To perhaps an even greater extent than most other capitalist societies, Italy is dominated by a small handful of corporate enterprises, many of which are partly owned and controlled by American business. . . . An almost equally powerful force is that spiritual order known as the Catholic Church, which itself is the second largest business enterprise in Italy (behind Fiat), which owns mammoth real estate interests of all sorts, and which of course exercises, directly and indirectly, a controlling influence in the Christian Democratic Party.[53]

Nino Lo Bello is more explicit about the importance of economic factors. The last chapter of his book *The Vatican Empire* gives the following explanation for the Vatican's anticommunism and conservatism:

> The contemporary decline of religious belief in many parts of the globe, a phenomenon that has followed in the wake of industrialization, political sophistication and scientific and educational progress, spells trouble for the Vatican as a religious institution. And the Vatican knows it. But the Vatican is more than a religious institution, more than a political institution. It is a solid economic entity firmly entrenched in the world of business and finance.
>
> As a "big business," the Vatican considers Communism its great enemy. . . .[54]

The various efforts made by the Vatican to avoid paying taxes on its income from dividends were a clear indication of the importance of economic interests in explaining its political and organizational activities. It has become rather obvious that the renewed support of the Christian Democrats by the Italian episcopate and the Vatican under Paul VI was in good part due to the fact that the Church received numerous financial advantages from them in Italy, especially in the areas of salaries for priests, tax exemption, and funds for Catholic schools and other institutions. Paul VI and other Church officials in Italy feared an abrogation or a radical revision of the 1929 concordat which would eliminate many privileges enjoyed by the Italian clergy and by the Vatican itself.

6. BETWEEN RENEWAL AND RESTORATION

The road traveled by Montini in less than thirty years was a long and difficult one. The 1951 Congress for the Lay Apostolate was not only a religious consultation, it was also, as has been shown, a political maneuver and even, ultimately, an episode in a struggle over economic resources. Montini and Veronese did not agree with Pius XII and Gedda that the Vatican's assets, the Christian Democrats' power, and the Church's position could be maintained by reverting to a right-wing political orientation after the fall of fascism. For them, only a centrist alternative, leaning if necessary on moderate left support, could ensure that. In 1951, by trying to use the pressure of the organized international laity to bolster their own uncertain influence in the Church and promote the centrist line of the Christian Democratic Party, they laid the groundwork for a religious and political ideology which would prove to be helpful to legitimate state monopoly capitalism in Italy and elsewhere in the late sixties and in the seventies.

At first, Paul VI was more discreet than Pius XII in his relations with the Christian Democrats. He tried to give the impression that he was above politics. His pseudoneutrality only partly succeeded in veiling his endorsement of existing forms of socioeconomic and political domination and control, and of cultural manipulation. Although there were progressive-sounding passages in some of his speeches, the major directions taken concretely by the Vatican during his pontificate were generally quite conservative, especially near the end of his life. In 1976, all pretenses of neutrality were abandoned, with Paul VI and the Italian bishops intervening in electoral politics as Pius XII would never have dared to do.

Before becoming pope, and in spite of a few temporary setbacks, Montini had maintained his position against the more conservative forces in the curia, thanks to the help of the laity, just as Gregory VII in the eleventh century had moved toward an absolute papal power in the church, using lay support against the seigniorial church.[55] But a few years after his election as pope, Paul VI started trying to use Catholic Action, the Council on the Laity, and other sectors of the Vatican bureaucracy to impede further transformations and to support the Christian Democratic Party. Montini, Veronese, and the Italian Democrats of the Dorotei line (the left-of-center faction at that time) had realized that it was only by taking a reformist line that capitalism and Christian Democracy would survive, and that is why the problem of the control of Italian Catholic Action was so crucial in the late forties and early fifties.[56] Their disagreement with Pius XII and Gedda was not a conflict over ends but over means. They thought that in the long run their way of meeting the challenges of the day was more reliable than the outmoded antics of their conservative adversaries, and that they must carefully reverse some of the conservative policies of the Pacelli era, in the same way that Leo XIII had come to reverse most of the reactionary positions of Pius IX. In their view, the stakes were too high, both politically and economically, to be lost because of inept leadership. They probably thought that a Christian Democratic pope, well integrated in the perspectives of the new ruling class of Italy, although not quite as conservative as Pius XII, was needed to ensure a harmonious relationship between the Italian ruling class, the government of Italy, and the Vatican.

As Paul VI, Montini implemented his ideas, but his strategy rapidly became obsolete when the center-left coalition proved to be no solution to Italy's political and socioeconomic woes. Paul VI had the choice between moving resolutely to the left or turning to the right. After trying to avoid the issue for a while, he opted for a conservative restoration, which, like most restorations, fostered the very trends it endeavored to defeat. Paul VI, like many of his predecessors, was worried about the decrease of papal power and authority. Temporal power in the form of the papal state was defended as being the best means of ensuring the independence of the papacy and the Church, rather than being seen as something that was in contradiction with its religious role.

As the pontificate of Paul VI went on, he proved to be considerably more conservative than had been expected. This was especially true in moral, ecclesiastical, and theological questions, but in time the new pope began to reveal a greater political conservatism as well. The grass-roots thrust for change inside the Church, however, was not broken. The rumblings of protest became more profound as Rome reemerged as a symbol of stability and conservatism, and as even reactionaries like Lefebvre started rearing their heads again, clamoring for a complete return to pre–Vatican II Catholicism.

Pope Paul's conservative positions on birth control, collegiality, dogma, and Italian politics blocked the modernization of the Church that was initiated during the pontificate of John XXIII. Although some observers regard the entire period of post–Pius XII Catholicism as an era of progressive developments in the Church, an increasing number now see Paul VI's pontificate as representing a partial restoration of the old order, rather than an extension and a consolidation of Pope John's and Vatican II's newer orientations. For them, Paul VI's pontificate represents a conservative middle way between the reactionary stands of Pius XII and the progressive positions of John XXIII. The choice of the name John Paul by Paul VI's two immediate successors, rather than names such as Pius XIII, John XXIV, or Paul VII, indicated their intention of striking a middle road between the progressiveness of John XXIII and the moderate conservatism of Paul VI.

The return to a conservative papacy under Paul VI was aptly treated in the political testament of Palmiro Togliatti, leader of the Italian Communist Party, as early as 1964. Togliatti was one of the first to see what nearly everyone else was to admit in 1968. Togliatti was careful to distinguish between the "center" and the "base" in the Church because, under Paul VI, the difference between the two was clearly noticeable:

> In the organized Catholic world and among the mass of the Catholics there was a clear move to the left during the time of Pope John. There has now been a swing back to the right of the center. At the

base, however, there persists the conditions and the pressure for a move to the left.[57]

Pope Paul VI was never a religious radical; it was only in contrast with Pius XII and with the reactionaries in the curia that he appeared, at times, to be a progressive prelate. When Montini and his lay Christian Democratic companions questioned the conservative orientation of the Vatican, they differed with Pius XII about means rather than goals; they only represented a type of token loyal liberal opposition inside the Vatican. When their time to be in power in the Church finally came, they showed themselves for what they really were: a more modern and adapted type of conservatism, a new conservatism more attuned to contemporary capitalism. The means of control were more sophisticated, the use of power was less abrasive, but the fundamental reality remained the same: religious control under various guises was still used to protect and legitimate socioeconomic and political interests.

In other words, what I have been saying is that the use of power in a religious organization like the Catholic Church is determined in good part by political and socioeconomic pressures as they are mediated through the ideology and the interests of the top leadership and especially the central bureaucracy of that organization.

Section 4 of the present chapter has stressed the importance of the political factors involved. Section 5 has sought to show that the return to a more conservative type of social control on the part of Paul VI and the Roman Curia vis-à-vis the laity and the rest of the Catholic Church had some of its roots in the economic realm. In evaluating the relative importance of economic and political factors, let us keep in mind, however, the judicious comment made by Berger and Luckmann on the growth of religious bureaucracies: "Bureaucracies end up being dominated by principles of an economic rather than of a political nature, even when they deal with the State. Their policies, their organization, and their personnel make them look like economic organizations, in contrast with ancient bureaucracies which looked much more like their government counterparts."[58]

The importance given here to political and especially to economic factors should not be construed as an effort to discount totally the weight of ideological, cultural, and specifically religious factors that operate both inside the Church and in its immediate environment. Much attention is given here to an examination of the Vatican, both as a political and as an economic structure, and to an examination of political and economic factors operating in the Church's environment, but that does not mean that I do not concede any importance to internal organizational imperatives. In this, I am in agreement with Antonio Gramsci, who had this to say about the interplay of organizational, political, and economic factors in the genesis of ideological struggles in the Catholic Church:

> We do not consider enough that many political acts are due to internal necessities of an organizational character, which means that they are linked to the need to give coherence to a party, to a group, to a society. . . . If we wanted to find for each ideological struggle inside the Church an immediate primary explanation in the structure we would never succeed: many politico-economic novels have been written with this intention. It is evidently clear, on the contrary, that the major part of these discussions are linked to the sectarian necessities of organization.[59]

Weber says something similar when he shows that it is on the basis of internal religious charisma that the Church moves in on political power. Weber indicates how the Church transforms its internal control into conservative political legitimation: "The Church advances its demands toward the political power on the basis of its claims to office charisma."[60] On the basis of its office charisma, the Church obtains certain privileges from the state, like tax exemptions, special subsidies, and protection from disrespect and even from secular jurisdiction:

> In particular, the Church establishes a distinctive way of life for its officials. This requires a specific course of training and hence a regular hierocratic education. Once it has created the latter, it also gains control over lay education and, through it, provides the political authorities with officials and subjects who have been properly brought up in the hierocratic spirit.[61]

From parochial schools to Catholic colleges, from minor seminaries to the pontifical universities in Rome, the Catholic educational system, with few exceptions, was organized under the central control of the Catholic hierarchy and the Vatican. Pius XI and Pius XII even centralized the education of the higher-echelon clergy in Rome, so that most candidates for high Church offices would have at least one year of studies there. Building on all these educational institutions, with the help of a private taxation system and important investments, the Church developed a far-reaching system of socialization and controls which ultimately functioned to block threats to the established secular system. This ecclesiastical system of controls included, besides the various educational facilities, a whole network of mass media and meeting places for retreats, meetings, and various other kinds of sessions and congresses of groups and organizations, the most important of which have been examined in some of the preceding chapters.[62]

The relative independence of the Catholic Church bureaucracy vis-à-vis political and socioeconomic forces permits it to fulfill better the role of agent of ideological control which the ruling class assigns to it, and which it willingly assumes because of its links with that ruling class. Conservative Church officials do not have to receive direct orders from businessmen and from politicians to act in accordance with ruling-class interests, since their own interests coincide with those of the ruling class. The exercise of power in the Church is generally a structural phenomenon, not a personal one. It is based on the bureaucratic apparatus of the curia, which stands for a conservative social class and helps reproduce the class system. Anyone, including a pope, who does not function inside the formal and informal parameters set by the curial apparatus finds it difficult, if not impossible, to operate at the higher levels of the Church organization. It is much easier for a pope to work with his curia than to try to transform it, because pope and curia always form a winning coalition in the Church.

The fact that I have insisted on the political and economic roots of Paul's turn to manipulative and conservative techniques of control should not be construed as an effort on my part to completely reduce religious and psychological phenomena to their infrastructural underpinnings. I have chosen to insist on these factors because I feel their importance is usually underestimated in studies of the papacy and of the Catholic Church. It may also seem that in chapters 6 and 7, I have switched too frequently from the organizational to the personal (i.e. papal) level. To this, I answer that the analyses of the importance of political and economic factors have been tempered with a constant preoccupation with what C. W. Mills calls "biography and history." In this respect, the following remarks by James A. Beckford in his essay "Religious Organization" appear very much to the point:

> The influence of contextual or environmental factors can never be ascertained with complete accuracy, nor is it useful to conceive of the environment-organization relationship in deterministic terms. Rather, the role of leaders or decision-makers is crucial in mediating the relationship in accordance with the situational evaluation of . . . the organization's "dominant coalition," i.e. those who are in a position to impose their will on the organization of a given time.[63]

VIII

Conclusion

This book is intended as a contribution to the study of conflicts of power in religious organizations. Through its focus on papal control and lay demands, it seeks to analyze the processes by which a well-established religious organization functions to maintain control over its constituency, when cultural, political, and socioeconomic changes in the environment are undermining the traditional foundations of its authority and power. Although I have made extensive use of historical material, my primary goal was not to write a history of laity-papacy relations in the Catholic Church, but rather to describe analytically the techniques of control used by top officials in a highly centralized and hierarchical religious bureaucracy, one that Kaufmann, following Weber, sees as "the historical prototype of all the present forms of bureaucratic organization."[1]

Up to now, the approach has been historical and critical. In this concluding chapter, I wish to raise the theoretical sights a little, endeavoring to summarize in a somewhat more abstract and sociological manner what the preceding chapters have conveyed about the manner in which the pope and his curia exercise their authority over the rest of the Church, and particularly over the lay movement. First, I shall try to develop a new typology of means of control, one that is more useful than the existing ones for the analysis of religious and other similar organizations. Then I shall briefly review some of the conclusions of the various chapters, using that typology as a tool for analysis of changes in the style of papal control over the laity through the centuries, especially during the past hundred years. Particular attention will be given to Italian Catholic Action, to Christian Democracy, and to the international structure of the lay apostolate, as it manifested itself in COPECIAL and its congresses and in the Council on the Laity, during Paul VI's pontificate. In the third section, I shall examine a few of the specific techniques of control (e.g. secrecy) used by the Vatican, in order to show how my typology is helpful in analyzing them. In a fourth and final section, I shall give a glimpse of what I think my findings mean, both for the future of the Catholic Church in contemporary society, and for the future of sociological research on the Catholic Church.

1. TYPES OF MEANS OF CONTROL
USED BY CHURCH AUTHORITIES

In each chapter I have shown with numerous examples how Church officials, especially the successive popes, have maneuvered to maintain and extend their control over their constituents, specifically the lay elites that participate in the organizational life of the Church at the supradiocesan level. I have tried to explain and interpret various aspects of the internal struggle for hegemony and autonomy between different sectors of the Catholic ecclesiastical institution, taking into account, as much as possible, the pressures for change that operate both inside the Church and in its environment.

The Catholic Church is a powerful bureaucracy which is increasingly being forced to become once more a voluntary association. Generally, in almost any religious organization, attempts to use coercive or remunerative means of control lead to alienation, aggressiveness, and loss of commitment on the part of the membership. If purely normative means are used, especially the nonmanipulative normative means that respect the members' freedom, then the officials tend to lose their importance in the organization, because of the renewed interest in participation that this strategy brings forth. There are then also fewer, but more committed members. For officials who want to keep their grip over an organization but who cannot openly use coercion and remuneration to do so, the tendency is to use the more manipulative of the normative means of control, those which Weber characterizes as "psychic" or "hierocratic" coercion.[2] This is what has happened in recent years in the Catholic Church. In order to avoid the grass-roots autonomy and the internal democratization that numerous Catholics are pressing for, Church authorities have updated their manipulative control mechanisms, making them more efficient and more in tune with prevailing norms and values.

For classifying these means of control and for understanding changes of strategy and tactics, Weber's concepts of psychic and hierocratic coercion and Etzioni's tridimensional (remunerative, coercive, normative) classification of means of organizational control are useful, but not entirely adequate.

Contemporary Marxists have not really produced any classification sufficiently distinctive from or more refined than the one put forward by Etzioni. For example, two French sociologists of religion, influenced by Althusser's Marxist structuralism, in an article on the challenge to hierarchical authority in the Catholic Church, distinguish the same three kinds of power as Etzioni, which they call financial, authoritarian, and ideological:

> After the financial power which is practically uncontrolled, the ecclesiastical hierarchy exercises an authoritarian power. The accession to the episcopacy comes through a system of aristocratic co-optation. The people of God, the faithful, have no controlling power. The bishops' power, once acquired, is nearly absolute, as long as one respects the supreme norms of orthodoxy that the ruling stratum itself has established. Without elections, without parties, without unions, ecclesiastical power rules according to the model of absolute monarchy. . . . In its relationship with political power, ecclesiastical power is in perfect symbiosis, as long as there is no mutual disagreement. . . . The financial basis and the power of the church condition its doctrine and its ideology.[3]

This convergence between Etzioni and neo-Marxism is not at all surprising since it is well known that Etzioni's classification is inspired by Weber, who himself borrows a lot from the Hegelian-Marxist tradition. What the Marxists and Weberians call economic, political-repressive, and political-ideological can be taken to mean, in Etzioni's scheme, remunerative, coercive, and normative.[4]

For my purposes Etzioni's model serves as a good theoretical point of departure, even if it does need to be refined and extended, especially as far as various subtypes of normative control are concerned. Weber's psychic coercion is one example of an additional kind of normative power. It is what Etzioni might call normative-coercive power.

Etzioni himself talks of normative social power and social power as two extra types of power, in the section of his book on modern organizations where he gives his tridimensional typology of the means of control, but he seems to limit a little too narrowly the meaning of these two expressions, using them to signify two kinds of indirect normative control that operate through one's peers only.[5]

One logical way of refining Etzioni's concept of normative power is to look at Weber's three types of authority (traditional, charismatic, rational-legal) as three forms of normative power. Since authority is simply legitimate power, then we could say that officials who use normative power to maintain their control can do it by appealing to tradition, charisma, or rationality-legality. This is particularly true in the case of certain religious organizations, where tradition and charisma are very important phenomena.

There actually exists a classificatory model of the bases of social power which can be considered as a partial synthesis of both Etzioni's and Weber's famous tridimensional classifications, especially if we keep in mind that organizational analysis research during the fifties and sixties, following Chester Barnard's distinction between authority of position and authority of leadership and Talcott Parsons' challenge to the identification of hierarchical position and superior knowledge, frequently dichotomized Weber's rational-legal ideal type into its two dimensions, namely, legality and rationality, or positional or line authority and professional or staff expertise. This model, created by French and Raven, distinguishes five types of bases of social power:

1. Reward power (which corresponds to Etzioni's remunerative power)
2. Coercive power (which corresponds to Etzioni's coercive power)
3. Referent power (a subtype of Etzioni's normative power which corresponds more or less to Weber's charismatic authority)
4. Expert power (another subtype of Etzioni's normative power, grossly corresponding to one aspect of Weber's rational-legal authority, i.e. professional or staff expertise)
5. Legitimate power (another subtype of Etzioni's normative power, roughly corresponding to the other aspect of Weber's rational-legal authority, i.e. positional or line authority)[6]

Keeping in mind the various techniques of control already encountered in our study of the papacy in its relationship with the laity, and using Weber, Etzioni, French and Raven, and other authors who have written on the questions of authority, power, and means of control, I have built a model that should help classify the kinds of control used by upper-echelon officials in the Catholic Church.[7]

There is nothing sacred about this classification. It is just a useful, perfectible, temporary instrument which I shall use to order some of the things I have dealt with at length in previous chapters, and to make certain generalizations. With the further refinements of additional empirical research, such a classificatory model might prove to be useful for the study of other, similar organizations. My eight types are ordered roughly along a material-ideal continuum:

1. *Ecological power*, based on the physical control of material environmental conditions. An example of this is the use of territory, buildings, or real estate to control people through the domination of their environment. For example, convent walls, or the grouping together of the Council for the Laity and the more progressive branches of the curia in San Callisto Palace, away from the Vatican, are instances of the use of ecological power.

2. *Remunerative power*, based on material or nonmaterial rewards or compensations. An example of this is the way the Pius XII Foundation uses its funds to support some lay activities and not others.

3. *Coercive power*, based on physical or psychic violence. Examples of this are burning at the stake, torture, imprisonment, banishment, blackmail, removal from office, denouncement.

4. *Social power*, based on the use of structural-organizational or psycho-sociological mechanisms such as Catholic Action congresses, peer-group pressures, rumors, co-optation, social ostracism, socialization, use of mass media, nepotism, and selective recruitment. An example of social power is "conditioning," as discussed by Louis Bernaert.[8]

5. *Legal power*, juridically founded, or simply based on bureaucratic and administrative norms, procedures and maneuvers. An example of this is the rule of secrecy which affects, under the pain of "grievous sin," the affairs of the Secretariate of the Pope and the Council for the Public Affairs of the Church in their relations with Vatican diplomats and other high-ranking prelates. Another example is censorship, through the *nihil obstat* and the *imprimatur*.

6. *Traditional power*, based on the use of traditional symbols, rituals, ideas, and sentiments. The cementing of loyalty through a mass or a torch-lit procession during a congress would be an example of this kind of power. Appeals to practices (e.g. speaking Latin) and documents popular or prevalent in previous times are also instances of the use of traditional power.

7. *Expert power*, based on professional, technical, or scientific or

purely rational arguments. An example of this is the recourse to commissions of experts in theology or the social sciences to bolster one's position. Pius XII's speeches to numerous groups on a multitude of topics was also an effort to control through expert power.

8. *Charismatic power*, based on exemplary or ethical prophecy. Examples of this are calls for social justice and equality, or the giving away of some of the Church's possessions for certain causes. In a less prophetic vein, the replacement of personal charisma by charisma of office, and the routinization of charisma, are other examples of the use of this kind of power and of the tendency to link it up with or transform it into the more predictable kinds of power, namely, legal, traditional, and expert power.

Types 1, 2, and 3 tend to be what is often referred to as raw power, as the carrot-and-stick approach. Types 4, 5, 6, 7, and 8 are more normative in nature; they are often referred to as authority rather than power because of the greater degree of legitimacy which they connotate. Types 4, 5, and 6 lend themselves more easily to a manipulative approach, whereas types 8 and 9 leave more room for persuasion, for rational, ethical, and exemplary appeals to man's intelligence, freedom, and initiative.

Even if an instance of papal or hierarchical power can often be classified in more than one of these eight categories, and in more than one of the three general groups of categories just mentioned, these two classifications still have some value, at least for analytical purposes. This is due to the fact that in any complex classification there are loose ends and an imperfect fit of the categories when they are applied to reality. Nevertheless, the main classificatory model encompasses most of the possibilities that I encountered in my study of papal control over the laity in the Catholic Church, and it is thus quite useful in helping to go beyond concrete historical description. The threefold division I have just introduced into the model has even greater drawbacks, but it should also prove useful to indicate the orientations that Church officials have used in the past, are using now, and could use in the future, when they operate with these means of control.

2. PAPAL CONTROL OVER THE LAITY: A SUMMARY

In the first decades of the Church, when Christianity was just a small sectarian movement growing among the weak and despised Jewish ethnic group and among the lower classes of the Roman Empire, charismatic power and, to a lesser degree, expert, traditional, and social power were the only means that Church leaders could effectively use for control of the membership and for the recruitment of new members. We have seen that authority in the early Church manifested itself mainly through exemplary and ethical prophecy, consisting of a charismatic announcement of the ''good news'' and exemplary service to the community. The quarrels between the Judaizers and the Hellenizers were centered over the relative importance of legal, traditional, and social-ethnic means of control versus expert and charismatic means of control, but the gradual identification of Church officials with Rome reintroduced legal, traditional, and social-ethnic (albeit Roman rather than Jewish) means of control. At first, there was no question of using property or money to buttress religious authority, since the early Christians were quite poor both individually and collectively. There was no possibility of using coercive power either, since the state was an enemy that monopolized force for its own ends and would not permit the use of coercion by the Church. In time, however, when an alliance developed between Church and state, Church officials became richer and more powerful, more able to use ecological, remunerative, and coercive power in order to obtain compliance and conformity from the people. A clear-cut administrative-legal structure was developed with the pope at the top and the laity at the bottom. The material wealth and the political power of the hierarchy went hand in hand with the disappearance of internal democracy and the increasing use of authoritarian, repressive, and manipulative methods of control. The whole process of change in the Catholic Church from very early times on has been one of the routinization and traditionalization of charisma, that is, the replacement of charismatic and expert power by social, legal, and traditional power. Lay prophets and apostles, and scholarly experts and theologians (e.g. the Fathers of the Church) were replaced in positions of authority by upper-class careerists. The episcopacy followed the same route of routinization, centralization, traditionalization as the clergy and the laity; all this ended up with the absolute power of the pope and his court over the rest of the Church.

Feudalism in Europe was a socioeconomic and political system in which the bishops of large urban centers, particularly the pope, succeeded in exercising the major ideological role: the legitimating function. The princes of the Church, as they were often called, were not only allies of the feudal lords; they themselves became feudal lords, acquiring wealth and property which allowed them to use remunerative and ecological power as well as social, legal, and traditional power. Church officials were so powerful that they in fact did not need to use their formidable coercive power until the social order started to show signs of instability. As soon as their interests and privileges were threatened, they began using their material resources (through simony, nepotism) and the more violent kinds of physical coercion to protect themselves against the deviants (schismatics, heretics, and reformers).

In summary, Church officials moved from their position as charismatic leaders of oppressed classes and ethnic groups in the Roman Empire, to a position of ideological legitimators of the empire, to a final position of religious substitutes for the officials of the empire. The pope came to function as the religious equivalent of the emperor, using some of the techniques of control developed by the Empire. Roman law and Roman administrative procedures, for example, served as the models for the development of the Catholic Church's canon law and administrative organization. The Church became dominant under feudalism in the form it had acquired of a religious equivalent of the Roman Empire's bureaucracy after the fall of the empire. In certain aspects, the Church also resembled the mode of production known as oriental despotism, since an absolute ruler (the pope) governed with the help of a bureaucracy (the Roman Curia) centered in the imperial city (the Vatican) but having local ramifications (bishops and pastors). That despot was not served by a hereditary nobility, but by educated eunuchs (the clergy) co-opted by a complex system of socialization and favoritism legitimated by canon law and tradition.

The Holy Inquisition's burning of heretics and the Crusaders' holy wars against the schismatics and the infidels were but two of the more extreme forms that hierocratic coercion took during the late feudal period. The Church was often just as oppressive as the state, because there was little restraint, popular or otherwise, on the arbitrary whims of hierarchs invested with all of God's power. The pattern of authority was often despotic and authoritarian. Church leaders did not always need to make deals with the state in order to be able to maintain their control, since they often dominated the state outright. As for the pope, he had a separate state, with an army and with serfs who worked his land. At times he was so powerful that he could even depose temporal rulers.

The crisis of Catholicism started with the disintegration of the religious legitimation of medieval society, and reached a first breaking point during the period that extended between Luther's Reformation and the French Revolution.

As the bourgeoisie rose to supplant the aristocracy, it often forged alliances with monarchs who were also interested in building the nation-state, and it inevitably entered into conflict with the conservative Church, which was wedded to the feudal order. As it became increasingly difficult (because of the close identification with feudalism) to use violence or muster the support of the state to maintain ideological hegemony over the masses, Church authorities started to build intricate normative means of control. The suppression or co-optation of lay protest movements, the upgrading of the training of the clergy, the formalization of Church laws, the proliferation of disciplined religious orders, the centralization of all power in the hand of a bureaucratized Roman Curia, the negotiation of concordats with political leaders—all were techniques that the papacy developed to enhance its authority as it was increasingly being challenged by a changed order all over Europe.

No longer able to use the repressive power of the state, Church authorities became more and more interested in using the legal and ideological power of the state through the laws enshrined in the concordats, through education of youth in schools and universities, and through welfare services such as hospitals and charity organizations. In fact, the Church increasingly became an ideological apparatus which fulfilled for the state and for the ruling class the functions necessary for their own growth and reproduction.

Inside the Church, the bishops and priests became functionaries of the central organization, with little individual freedom of their own. An awakening laity was itself turned into a pawn in the papacy's frantic efforts to retain its position of absolute power in Europe and especially in Italy. After the crisis of the Catholic-feudal alliance and the ensuing breakup of the hegemony of Church officials at the end of the eighteenth century, lay Catholic associations like those that eventually comprised Catholic Action and Catholic political parties gradually became choice instruments of the waning papal and episcopal control, when it became clear that concordats would not suffice to maintain Church officials in their privileged position.

What happened at those highest levels of the organization of the Church in the late nineteenth and early twentieth centuries cannot be understood if we neglect to consider recent Italian history, especially the situation since the unification of that country. Richard A. Webster concludes his book of the relationship between fascism and Christian Democracy in Italy with the following comments, which summarize very well what happened in the last few centuries:

> The history of the Italian Catholic movement throws light upon one of the great problems of world history, that of the relationship of the Roman Catholic church and the pontiff to the modern State and to civil society in general. From the promulgation of *Unum Sanctum* through the eras of Counter Reformation, Absolutism, Revolution and Restoration, the direct, political power of the pope waned, and the age of Liberalism put an end to it, except for the Vatican itself. The Papacy has come to depend on alliances with rulers, from Francis I to Mussolini, which assured it a substantial indirect power. However in our own time this method has been visibly failing, and the Church has begun to exert its indirect power in complex new ways. The Catholic lay militant has been pressed into service as a twofold intermediary between the Papacy and the modern State: as a member of Catholic Action he responds to the Hierarchy and assists it but as a Christian Democrat he assumes direct political responsibilities that the Hierarchy must shun. Through him, a new figure in the history of the Church, the Papacy learns much about the modern world and how it can be influenced. But in sponsoring or at least permitting lay Catholic parties with some degree of political autonomy, the Papacy has renounced no part of its claim to a rightful empire over the minds of men, but has rather chosen a new method in harmony with the mass organization of the modern world.[9]

Catholic Action was a social means of control which Church authorities used to transform some of the more involved and obedient laity into what Gianfranco Poggi has called a "clero di reserva," a reserve clergy. Because of the advancing secularization and anticlericalism, an effort was made to "clergify" part of the laity. This was considered to be less of a risk for hierarchical authority than the laicization of the clergy which was already starting. On their own volition and in response to forces outside the hierarchy, the lower clergy were starting to alter the nature of their worldly involvement, notably in politics. The hierarchy feared such a development, because the clergy represented a greater immediate threat to its authority than the laity. Priests are normally more dependent on church authorities than are laymen, but once that dependence is broken, they are potentially much more dangerous, because of their influence over their constituents, even when they are at odds with higher authorities, and because they are insiders and not peripheral members like the laity.

The question of control of the laity became a key issue, because any initiative of the faithful at the grass-roots level which was not tightly controlled was seen by many Church officials as leading to the ideological and organizational breaking up of the Church.

Italian Catholic Action has been torn between various positions. Under Pius IX and Leo XIII, it was a kind of Catholic spiritual militia or secular arm of the papacy created for the defense of the traditional territorial and political prerogatives of the church. Pius X and Pius XI (and Benedict XV and John XXIII, but for different reasons) stressed the internal religious and apostolic dimensions of the movement and consequently worried less about the problem of control. Pius XII and Paul VI both insisted on strict control by the hierarchy and the Vatican and, more than any of their predecessors, used Italian Catholic Action as the political arm of the papacy in an effort to dominate Italy.

The creation of lay organizations such as Catholic Action and the convocation of congresses for lay elites are themselves excellent examples of the use of social power by the supreme authorities of the Church. It is not surprising, then, that these organizations and congresses started being used just after the coercive and ecological means of control (i.e. the temporal power and the control of territories) of the papacy had disappeared. The Lateran Agreements of 1929 were also a way to replace the lost ecological (and coercive) power by remunerative and legal power. The conflicts which erupted shortly thereafter concerned the sharing of social, legal, traditional, and charismatic power between the Fascist state and the papacy.

Catholic Action was created in an effort to reach lay Catholics as members of age, sex, and occupational groups rather than simply as inhabitants of a territorial community, since the parish and the diocese, as ecological units, were losing their capacity to control. Catholic Action became a sort of lay religious order, a congregation inside the Church. It actually became the true permanent party of the Catholic Church in many countries. By its insistence on the training of its members, and on involvement in social issues where the interests of Church authorities were at stake, it nevertheless had a somewhat liberating effect on laymen conditioned by centuries of passivity. Church authorities wanted to reactivate laymen in order to enlist them as subordinate collaborators, as extensions of and substitutes for themselves, but laymen often went beyond these boundaries. People trained in Catholic Action, and those involved in Catholic parties, often became progressive political activists and even at times appeared to be quite critical of conservative clerical interference in the political arena.

It was as though their past interaction with members of the clergy had made them less awestruck by the sacred authority of ecclesiastical officials, especially when these officials attempted to interfere in secular politics.

Catholic Action and Catholic parties, as instruments for maintaining the prerogatives of the Church, thus came to appear to the papacy as less effective than concordats with political rulers. Pius XI, because of his great fear of socialism, tried to revive the treaty-making techniques popular with popes a century before. In the 1920s and 1930s, with the help of the young and ambitious Msgr. Pacelli, among others, he negotiated a total of eighteen concordats, a record for any pope. He even bragged once that he would be willing to make deals with the devil himself if it was for the good of the Church. Although he later drastically reversed his attitude on Mussolini and Hitler, at first he saw them as great men because of their anticommunism, and because they were willing to sign a concordat that was advantageous to the Church. Pius XI and his successor Pius XII were conservative men who were hoping (before Hitler's racism and genocidal policies ruined their dream) for the eventual creation of a mosaic of authoritarian Catholic states in southern Europe.[10] They were counting on traditional forces and on the coercive and legal power of the state to help them keep control of the laity.

After World War II, when the chances of such a dream coming true had vanished, Pius XII decided to return to the Catholic party strategy. Since concordats were now frowned upon by most governments, he encouraged the creation of the Christian Democratic Party, which would be securely held back from radicalism by a tightly centralized Catholic Action movement. No longer an alternative to Catholic Action, as had been the case in the first quarter of the century, the Catholic party was now dominated by it.

By reverting to a moderate, centrist political position, the Vatican could give the appearance of being neutral, nonpartisan, above politics. Its practical option in favor of privileged elites and classes, its backing of Italian neo-capitalism and American imperialism, was partly veiled by occasional progressive-sounding declarations.

Italian Catholic Action had been, before and during World War II, a growing force of opposition to fascism. But after the war, when anti-Fascist Catholic Action leaders moved directly into politics, they left the lay organization in the hands of those who, like Luigi Gedda, had been less critical of fascism. Catholic Action was strong because it could get the vote out. During Pius XII's pontificate, the Vatican's control over the Christian Democratic Party was not a direct one. It was mediated by Catholic Action and by Gedda's Civic Committees. The long chain of command was intended to give the impression of clerical noninterference in politics, and to circumvent the concordat's prohibition of direct involvement in Italian politics by Catholic Action and the clergy.

In the interviews that he conducted in order to evaluate the relative power of various pressure groups in Italy, Joseph La Palombara found that many of his informants considered Catholic Action to be the "most powerful organized group in the Italian polity."[11] One of these informants explained how both Catholic Action and its Civic Committees operated as vote-getting machines through which the Vatican and the clergy kept a tight hand on the Catholic party:

> . . . Catholic organizations are in a key position to influence the outcome of elections. For example, a Christian Democrat deputy who clearly runs into the opposition of the Civic Committees runs the risk of being surpassed (in number of preferential votes) by those other Christian Democrats, in good standing with Catholic Action and its civil committees, for whom the greatest amount of campaign activity will be exerted. The electoral power of Catholic Action is one of the major weapons it uses in disciplining those deputies who are not members of Catholic Action or of other Catholic organizations.[12]

Participation in state power, in a period of state monopoly capitalism, is an ideal way for a religious bureaucracy to recoup lost or dwindling ecological, remunerative, coercive, social, legal, and traditional power. With the advantages accruing from such an alliance, the papacy touched up its fading public image, firmed up its shaky financial base, and even succeeded in strengthening the authority it enjoyed through charisma and expertise.

Between 1948 and 1958, Gedda's Civic Committees and Catholic Action (which Gedda gradually took over around 1950) exercised a great deal of influence over the Christian Democrats, thanks to the support Pius XII gave to these two lay organizations. After 1958, however, during John XXIII's pontificate, the Christian Democrats' party secretary, Amintore Fanfani, was able to break the power of Catholic Action over his party, as La Palombara[13] and many others have ascertained. But in the early seventies, because of Paul VI's return to conservatism, Catholic Action once more became involved in Italian politics, and the temporary extrication which Pope John had succeeded in bringing about was reversed. Paul VI did not abandon the centuries-old tradition of making direct deals with various governments (in fact he extended this strategy of concordats to socialist countries), he continued to rely, as Pius XII had done, on intervention by Catholic Action and the episcopate in order to help the Christian Democrats remain in power. The creation of the Council on the Laity represented a further step, beyond Catholic Action and Christian Democracy, by which the Vatican was trying to maintain its hold over the laity. The international lay apostles often were the Papacy's new Zouaves, who defended the economic and political privileges of the Vatican, both in Italy and internationally, and helped maintain the authoritarian, hierarchical structure inside Catholicism. There was a trade-off involved, in the sense that, in return, Church authorities legitimated the class privileges of the moderately conservative laymen who were predominantly active in these movements. Church authorities, for example, helped them keep Catholic workers and peasants outside of the radical workers' movements by stressing class collaboration and acceptance of the God-given order of things.

Catholic Action was the first effective substitute for the lost coercive and ecological power of the clergy. It was also a means for the clergy to maintain its existence as a separate caste in the Church, as Ralph C. Beals has shown in the conclusion of his dissertation on Mexican Catholic Action:

> . . . The informal or "latent function" of the Catholic Action movement, far from seeking a radical transformation of the social order, was to create and maintain a stable basis for priestly survival in a modernizing society.[14]

Catholic parties are even more effective than Catholic Action as instruments of control. Using the votes of the laity as a political power base, Church officials try to build up their various bases of control. Ecological power, remunerative power, social power, legal power, traditional power are all reinforced when a Catholic party is strong in a country. Catholic parties, world wide, have chiefly developed as parties of the privileged classes, even when they publicly flirt with social-democratic reforms in order to attract working-class votes. That these parties have often helped create quite conservative regimes (e.g. in Chile and Western Germany) is hardly surprising.

The conflicts inside Italian Catholic Action and the Italian Christian Democratic party and, at the international level, the Vatican's effort to coordinate Catholic International Organizations and other forms of lay apostolate manifested themselves at the first World Congress for the Lay Apostolate. As early as 1951, the Vatican tried to further its influence in the modern world through the leaders of international and national lay Catholic organizations. At that time, most Catholic Action organizations outside Italy were well under the control of local bishops, who themselves were treated as mere representatives of the central authorities in Rome. But the Vatican conservatives wanted to have a more direct control over the national Catholic Action organizations, and also to curtail the budding autonomy of the rapidly expanding Catholic International Organizations, since the national hierarchies had practically no power over these latter associations. It was not so much that these Vatican conservatives resented the actual policies and activities of the CIOs, as that they wanted to make sure future developments would take place under definite Vatican supervision. The international congress movement, which was sponsored by the Vatican during the fifties, was started in an effort to coordinate lay associations administratively under the auspices of the Secretariate of State. Msgr. Montini and Vittorino Veronese, representing a moderately progressive orientation, hoped that this effort at Vatican centralization and control would weaken the conservative orientation of Italian Catholic Action and reinforce Christian Democracy, whereas Pius XII was mostly preoccupied with the advantages accruing from greater Vatican control over the international and national lay movements. As long as Veronese and other Montinians ran COPECIAL, that organization was not much more than an office with a Roman address, so neither tendency really succeeded in attaining its goals. The stalemate ended under John XXIII, when COPECIAL became much more important as the Vatican center for lay affairs. The question of control, however, was overshadowed by Vatican II and the impending conflict between the Roman Curia and the world episcopate. It was only when Paul VI created the Council on the Laity, as Vatican II had suggested, that the issue of Vatican control came back to the fore. Instead of letting the Conference of the CIOs have a central role in the newly founded Council on the Laity, Paul VI preferred to rely more heavily on COPECIAL, where Vatican control was more dependable. The CIOs were given a role in the Council on the Laity only insofar as they were willing to abandon much of their already limited autonomy. The council itself was created some months before the third World Congress for the Lay Apostolate, because the pope thought that this fait accompli would forestall the demand by the congress for a new, democratically selected, and progressive structure.

The Vatican tried to give the impression that the CIOs had an important role in the Council on the Laity by nominating as one of the two assistant secretaries of that new organization the permanent secretary of the Conference of the CIOs. In fact, that was an effort at personal and institutional co-optation much more than anything else. Far from giving participatory power to the CIOs as such, this action nudged them under the narrow administrative and social control of the Vatican. Later attempts by the Secretariate of State to dominate the choice of leaders, the financing, and even the existence itself of the CIOs, further manifested the efforts of co-optation of this relatively independent lay federation and accentuated the alienation felt by many lay leaders. In other words, the effort to put the CIOs under the control of the Secretariate of State and the submissive Council on the Laity amounted to an attempt to use social, legal, and even remunerative power to dominate the lay movement.

Because there had been lay congresses in 1951 and 1957, it would have been rather difficult not to have another one after Vatican II without replacing it by something equivalent. The third congress, in 1967, was organized and controlled by friends and protégés of the former Msgr. Montini (now become Pope Paul VI) who had been the main instigators, as well as the liberal and loyal opposition, at the first two meetings. The first lay congresses came about, as we have seen in chapters 3 and 6, in the post–World War II context of the struggle in Italy, both in the Church and in the Christian Democratic Party, between a conservative and a liberal tendency. The second, near the end of Pius XII's pontificate, was similar in many ways to the first, except that the conservatives were even more strongly in control. The third one, however, was quite different, because between 1957 and 1967 Montini and his like-minded friends had gained control of the Vatican. In 1967, Paul VI was starting to set aside the progressivism of John XXIII to return to a conservatism reminiscent of that of the Pius popes.

The 1967 Congress for the Lay Apostolate, which has been discussed at length in chapters 4 and 5, presented numerous instances of the use of various types of papal power to control the lay movement. The fact that it was held in Vatican buildings in Rome, rather than elsewhere in Europe, for example, shows how ecological power was used to impede autonomy. The grants for paying travel expenses of African and Asian delegates constituted an effective use of remunerative power. The congress itself was held in check through a mixture of social, legal, traditional, expert, and charismatic means of control.

Manipulation of the delegates was not involved in each instance of the use of these kinds of power, but it definitely was in certain cases, for example in Cardinal Maurice Roy's unsuccessful attempt to influence the resolution-making process. The various techniques suggested by Cardinal Roy or used by the organizers consisted of a mixture of social and legal power. There was an effort to mask the use of these means of control behind a façade of expertise and charisma. For example, there was a plenary session which consisted entirely of "personal witnessing" by such Catholics as the British economist Barbara Ward, the Italian Jesuit Roberto Tucci, the American astronaut James McDivitt, and the black American lay leader Stanley Hebert. Furthermore, there was an entire category of congress participants, with no voting rights, who were classified not as delegates or as observers (a category restricted to non-Catholics), but as experts.

When the first gross efforts at manipulation failed, more subtle means were instituted, as was apparent in Cardinal Roy's frantic (and largely successful) efforts to cover his tracks concerning his secret speech to the bishops, and in the Vatican's efforts to pressure the COPECIAL secretariate into giving credence to its unfounded reinterpretations of the resolution concerning birth control. These instances of manipulative social control exemplify the kinds of power frequently used by the Vatican, that is, by the pope and his close collaborators in the Roman Curia, from late 1967 to late 1978. They also illustrate quite well what I mean by the expressions papal power and Vatican control over the laity.

3. BEYOND DESCRIPTION AND ANALYSIS
TO EXPLANATION AND INTERPRETATION

It is not sufficient, in a study such as this one, to describe and analyze in some detail a particular phenomenon as it developed historically. One should also, I think, show how the situations under study can be explained and interpreted, if not in a completely satisfactory manner, at least in a preliminary and tentative way.

The autumn of 1967 was an important landmark in the retraditionalization and rebureaucratization of the office of the papacy. Progressive Catholics had pinned high hopes on the first Synod of Bishops and the third World Congress for the Lay Apostolate, held simultaneously in Rome in October 1967. Some were expecting these meetings to open up new vistas which Vatican II had not been able to reach, but the meetings, in fact, had just the opposite effect. The conclusions of these meetings clearly indicated that the charismatic and progressive period of Pope John and Vatican II had come to a close, as far as the

Vatican was concerned. By and large, the five bishops' synods held between 1967 and 1977 accepted Paul VI's symbolic closing of the "windows" opened by John XXIII. The laymen present at the third World Congress for the Lay Apostolate openly challenged some of Pope Paul's conservative ideas, at a time when his flirtations with progressive ideas and movements were coming to an end. The charismatic period of Pope John had thus been replaced by a moderately conservative restoration era. Following an almost regular pattern of papal succession for the previous hundred and fifty years, a conservative pope had once more succeeded a progressive one.

Some sociologists have looked at these major transformations of contemporary Catholicism since the death of Pius XII and have tried to explain them in various ways. E. A. Tiryakian, for example, sees these changes as a somewhat belated effort at Protestantization:

> The very upheaval of the Catholic Church today involved in its protestantization within one generation is one of the most far reaching cultural events of world history, structurally identical to the Protestant Reformation of the Sixteenth century.[15]

This might have been true, up to a certain point, of some of the changes that led up to Vatican II, but Tiryakian's analysis does not adequately describe or explain the whole transformation inside Catholicism up to and including the seventies. The post–Vatican II period in the Church resembles the Counter-Reformation as much as the Reformation, especially when attention is focused on the Vatican's efforts to control the forces for change in and around it. If the evaluation of the change includes Pope Paul's entire pontificate, it could be as exact (and finally as untrue) to speak of an "Orthodoxification" of Catholicism as to speak of Protestantization. A picture of the present crisis as a kind of belated "Protestantization," or as some other form of past religious reform is not an entirely adequate interpretation. Although the present situation may have certain similarities with past religious changes, an understanding of the current confrontation between laity and papacy cannot be properly reached through historical analogies alone.

Furthermore, the situation cannot be understood and explained by making reference to purely ideal factors, such as theological opinions and beliefs or psychological hang-ups, as some commentators are often inclined to do. For example, T. L. Westow writes: "The stirring within the Church is most certainly due to the work of such men as Rahner, Schillbeeckx, Congar, Küng, Metz, Schoonenberg and many others of that caliber."[16] Similarly, James F. Andrews, editor of a book on Paul VI, tries to explain "Paul's frequent strictures against institutional change in the church" by his inability to "bring himself to accept the risk of insecurity in the church itself."[17] Interpretations which stress the interplay of theological, psychological, and organizational factors are much more satisfying than such purely idealist explanations which attempt to explain everything in terms of theology or psychology. But we must go even beyond that to look at the wider cultural and institutional factors and especially at the political and infrastructural context. The present changes have to be examined in their own right, and in the context of the breakdown of certain patterns and structures, as has been done in the study of the Church by the French sociologist Renaud Dulong.[18] Such an analysis, with its mixture of historical, empirical, and theoretical perspectives, and its emphasis on cultural and institutional factors (including political and socioeconomic aspects), can permit a deeper probing into the issue of Church transformation. This kind of approach is quite similar in many respects to that of Thomas O'Dea.[19]

O'Dea's analysis, in *The Catholic Crisis*, is made primarily, but not exclusively, in terms of culture and institutions. He emphasizes the causal influence of a crisis of authority and, more deeply, a crisis of meaning and direction, themselves part and consequence of a social, political, philosophical, and intellectual revolution. O'Dea's reliance on content analysis of theological documents makes his study one which gives a great deal of importance to ideas without entirely neglecting structural and material factors.[20]

Even more satisfying are the explanations which insist first on socioeconomic and political factors without rejecting the importance of cultural and ideological ones. The theologian Robert Adolfs[21] and sociologists such as François Houtart and Emile Pin,[22] René Lourau,[23] and Antoine Casanova[24] have analyzed current changes in the Church or in Paul VI's pontificate, using that kind of approach.

The American lay Catholic writer Gary McEoin takes a similar view of the relative importance of ideal and material factors in his evaluation of Paul VI's style of leadership.[25] He mentions psychological factors— "Paul VI's somewhat hesitant and diffident temperament," "the pope's temperamental hesitancy and distrust"—but considers them to be of marginal significance.[26] For him it is the system that is determinant and not the persons involved, whose "options are immediately reduced to what it [the system] permits."[27] He goes on to say that "structures based on the concepts and practices of medieval autocracy" were responsible for Paul VI's opposition to change. The sociologist Gordon Zahn explains Paul VI's failure to take a clear stand on controversial issues by stressing political and institutional realities rather than personal idiosyncracies.[28]

Carlo Falconi similiarly thinks that the 1968 turn to the right was practically inevitable and in many ways independent of Pope Paul's personality: "In a similar situation John XXIII would not have acted differently . . . unless he had been ready to accept the reduction of the papacy to what for centuries had been the role of the western patriarch of Rome, namely an office and a charge with only a primacy of honor and not of effective juristiction over the whole church."[29] The promulgation of Paul VI's conservative *Credo* on June 30, 1968, constituted a watershed of sorts in his reign. For Falconi, the inevitable process of desacralization and secularization was fundamentally responsible for Paul's *svolta*. "It is thus obvious that Paul VI decided that the change of direction . . . was necessary in order to save the Church from self-annihilation—annihilation that seemed to him to be possible inasmuch as the ultimate bastion of the Church, the papacy, was then seriously menaced."[30] In other words, the turn to the right was due to the need to save the papacy and the Church from the destruction coming from the assaults which Vatican II itself helped to unleash. If the Vatican did not pursue the *aggiornamento* launched by John XXIII, it was because it could not do so without negating and destroying itself.

My approach is, broadly speaking, a neo-Marxian one, where religion is viewed as a part of the superstructure of society, considerably but not entirely dependent on what is happening at other levels of the social structure. This perspective is compatible with that of Weber, Durkheim, and the functionalists, in that it does not see religion as a mere reflection of political orientations and socioeconomic phenomena such as class, mode of production, or economic interests. On the other hand, it gives considerable, and even primary, attention to these important and often neglected structural and infrastructural roots of ideological phenomena.

Although the point of departure of my study was an international congress of the laity, held in 1967, rather than the Italian lay movement, the papacy, and the Italian state in their reciprocal relationship, I was inevitably led to look at that relationship and to investigate the historical background of that relationship, in order to understand the contemporary situation of the laity and the demands it makes on hierarchical leaders.

It was not sufficient to ask: Who were these lay persons present in Rome in October 1967, what did they do, and what were their attitudes and opinions? I had to ask: Why were they chosen, and how did the two previous congresses set the scene for the one studied? Going beyond what happened during the 1967 congress itself, I had to find out who had organized that congress, and why, and also who were the real protagonists, and what were the fundamental issues at stake. A meeting, a congress especially, cannot be understood if we do not look at its social and historical context, if we ignore the conflicts and oppositions that exist in the organizations that sponsor and constitute it, if we neglect the total environment of the meeting and of the organizations that participate in it.

Concerning the various means of control used by different popes and by Paul VI in particular, which I have described at length in this study, I had to go beyond the ecclesiastical façade to look at some of the political and economic factors which have played an important role in the promotion of the autocratic and manipulative style of papal control. I have dealt extensively with the relationship between the Vatican and Italian politics, showing that Church authorities have let themselves be used by political and economic elites as ideological legitimators of capitalism and conservatism, in return for economic advantages and political favors.

There is also a close relationship between the Vatican and American imperialism, which was cemented mostly during the last years of World War II and in the late forties. Money from CIA conduit foundations was important, not only to fight elections and split the working class parties and unions in Italy, but also to help build Church-controlled recreation and welfare facilities and manipulate Catholic youth and intellectual organizations, as Victor Marchetti revealed in an interview given to the Italian magazine *Panorama* in April 1974.[31]

In spite of the purely religious image that it endeavors to put forward, the Vatican is deeply involved in Italian and international politics and finance, promoting conservatism and capitalism while professing a Christian approach to democratic reforms. The Vatican is constantly intervening in Italian politics to protect its interests, including its economic interests. The Vatican is not only a political and a religious entity; it is also an important financial enterprise. This has been documented, for example, in two articles in the *Financial Times* of London on Vatican finances which were subsequently reproduced in the *National Catholic Reporter* along with two original articles by

Vatican expert Desmond O'Grady. These articles also revealed that Pope Paul's advisers' mishandling of Church funds, following the decision to move from Italian to international financial dealings after 1969, had led to very serious losses.[32]

In summary, then, the papacy gives religious legitimation to the socioeconomic and political status quo in Italy in exchange for political and economic advantages. It is itself controlled partly by the remunerative power of the ruling class, and in return it uses various kinds of normative and social control mechanisms to keep the laity loyal to itself and to the socioeconomic and political system that supports it. It helps reproduce the monopoly capitalist system and is in part determined in its own internal control activities by economic and political imperatives.[33]

4. SPECIFIC TECHNIQUES OF PAPAL CONTROL OVER THE LAITY

As is the case for most religions, the Catholic Church is an organization in which various types of mechanisms of control are used to ensure compliance. When the level of consensus is high it is not necessary for ecclesiastical authorities to make use of the whole battery of means of control, especially not the more repressive ones which only tend to create greater alienation. Even manipulation is not absolutely necessary then, since people willingly conform. Normative means, especially those I have called expert and charismatic power, are most commonly used when commitment is high, and they contribute to further enhancing commitment. But when there is disagreement and conflict, and when the environmental conditions permit it, voluntary commitment is often replaced by or complemented with more authoritarian and manipulative types of control, including physical and psychic coercion. Threats of punishment, including excommunication and hell-fire, for example, are some of the methods used when socialization to shared values and beliefs does not suffice.

Since the middle of the last century, these durable means of control have lost some of their appeal because of changes in the Church's social, political, and cultural environment. In recent decades, Church authorities have relied extensively on more subtle control mechanisms. Such mechanisms are sometimes so complex that it is difficult to classify them neatly with the categories I have been using. Consequently, in this section, I shall look at some concrete examples of control mechanisms, and, using my classification, try to see in which of the categories they fit, in order to test the usefulness of that classification.

Let us start off by looking at a famous open letter presented to the pope in 1968 by dissatisfied Catholics from France and elsewhere. The letter severely criticized the Vatican's excessive attachment to wealth and power, stressing the idea that Church authorities are too repressive and manipulative:

> The whole Church apparatus is organized for control: the Roman Curia controls the bishops, the bishops control the clergy, the clergy controls the laity . . . and the lay Christians control (what an illusion!) mankind. Hence, a multiplication of secretariates, commissions, structures, etc., with their programs and rules. . . . Underhand influences have suffocated the openness which had manifested itself at the lay congress in Rome, a congress which had very little communication with the bishops who were then meeting in a synod.[34]

After this attack on the abuses of social and legal power by church authorities, the letter goes on to describe three of the favorite techniques of control used by the Vatican: secrecy (there are secret files even against bishops), spying and informing, and repression (used even against some of the most respected theologians).

Secrecy can be classified as either a legal or a social method of control, depending on whether it is used as an administrative-legal procedure or a simple social defense-mechanism. Spying and informing would clearly be instances of social power, since they entail the use of social processes. Finally, repression, as discussed in the open letter, refers to a mixture of legal, coercive, and even remunerative power. Concretely, it includes the habitual recourse by Church officials to excommunications, censures, condemnations, demotions, and the removal or firing of offenders from their ecclesiastical jobs.

This brief analysis seems to indicate that my classification permits us to deal with the complexity of reality. The test can be pursued by a closer examination of some of the control mechanisms mentioned in previous chapters.

A religious organization, like any other normative organization that has limited resources and that functions in a relatively pluralistic world, must of necessity operate mostly with social and normative power. Economic assets or violent means are used mostly in circumstances when the environment of the organization permits the use of those kinds of raw power.

One of the most ironic aspects of manipulative methods of control like the social and legal mechanism of secrecy is that they often hide themselves behind an ideology of dialogue, communication, and participation. The leadership remains bureaucratic and secretive, while it veils its manipulation behind a screen of words. Appeals for lay involvement do not go beyond a mere token consultation that rarely influences the outcome of decision. Officials maintain a monopoly over the decision-making process, often trying to give the impression that the ideas and desires at the grass-roots are being taken into account when such is rarely the case. It is rather obvious that in such a context, keeping as much vital information secret as possible, while at the same time producing a deluge of irrelevant information, constitutes a combination of social, legal, and expert power.

Very little is known about the inner workings of the Vatican, because top-level officials are sworn to what is called pontifical or papal secrecy, a secrecy which encompasses all sorts of information, ranging from office information concerning nominations and preparation of documents to accusations of errors and crimes.[35] A March 1974 press conference given by the head of the Vatican press office revealed that new norms of pontifical secrecy had recently been issued. These instructions only diminished the sanctions against those who violated a secret, making few substantial changes in the norms themselves. Before the issuance of these new instructions, a violator was excommunicated, and only a few confessors named by the pope could give the absolution. Now, Church officials who are bound by pontifical secrecy and who fail to observe it can be suspended for a time or fired from their job. They are guilty of a ''serious'' sin, which can now be absolved by any confessor.

As far as laymen are concerned, except for trusted men like Bernardino Nogara under Pius XI, Count Enrico Galeazzi, the Pacelli brothers, and Luigi Gedda under Pius XII, and Vittorino Veronese under John XXIII and Paul VI, none of the lay leaders are really informed about what actually goes on at higher levels of the Church organization. The lay leaders who work in Rome (for example, in various branches of the Roman Curia, especially in the Pontifical Council for the Laity, and who might be in a position to know a little more than the others, are kept loyal by the Vatican's control of their careers, and by a careful screening process. Their selection in the first place was due to their loyalty, and they have so internalized the norms of the curia that they have themselves become major instruments of control over the rest of the laity. The Vatican is very cautious in the choice of lay officials. Unreliable people are simply not permitted to hold positions of authority. Only those who give assurances of being obedient are nominated and promoted. Those who prove to be unreliable are isolated and forced to resign before they succeed in establishing a following.

In the case of the laity, the resocialization and segregation processes are not as rigid as for the top clerical officials of the Catholic bureaucracy (there are no special costumes, no assigned residences, no changes of name as is the case in many religious orders), but they are still quite strong. Some lay leaders are members of secular institutes, organizations in which there are certain requirements of obedience, perpetual celibacy, and personal poverty like those in the traditional religious orders. This makes them especially vulnerable to pressures coming from Church authorities, who are inclined to favor them when they are selecting "representative" lay leaders.

Another key mechanism of Vatican control is the use of probationary periods for new organizations. The Council on the Laity, for example, was created in January 1967 by Paul VI, but it only acquired permanent status in December 1976. With its permanent status came tighter controls, through the inclusion of more cardinals, bishops, and priests in the leadership positions of the organization, and through the addition of the word "Pontifical" to its name. The Pontifical Council for the Laity is now nothing more than a traditional Vatican congregation, a disciplinary body which has the task of "seeing that the church's laws regarding the laity are strictly observed and examining by administrative means disputes involving lay people," according to the papal decree of December 15, 1976.[36]

This tightening of the reins had been in the works for years. Just over a year earlier, the World Consultation of the Laity, organized by the Council on the Laity, had been a firmly controlled affair, where most of the time had been spent in praying and in listening to preselected speakers. The calls for involvement in the struggles for liberation and for solidarity with the oppressed, which managed to arise at that meeting in spite of everything, were very few. One dissatisfied but subdued lay leader said it all when he privately confided to a journalist: "We are waiting the end of a papacy."[37]

The Pontifical Commission for Justice and Peace, which achieved permanent status in December 1976 along with the Council on the Laity (both after nine years of probation and a period of economic and administrative uncertainty during 1976 since the third temporary mandate had not been followed by a fourth when it expired in

January), had undergone an important crisis in 1971 when two priests and a lay woman resigned from top positions in it because of strict limitations imposed by the Secretariate of State's Archbishop Giovanni Benelli on the commission's declarations against torture in Brazil. Rumors circulated in the Vatican that one of the priests was resigning because he wanted to get married, but all three persons said they were resigning because they could not continue working in a system which placed diplomacy and political interests over the necessity to denounce injustice.[38] That there were few such protests and resignations at high levels of lay leadership was an indication of the effectiveness of selection and co-optation processes, and of the fear that exists among lay leaders. Control over jobs and probationary periods for organization, given the consequences that usually ensue, thus appear to be a mixture of remunerative, social, and legal means of control.

Essentially, the lay leaders' nearly complete isolation from any decision-making position is the principal means by which they are kept under control, except at the lowest levels and for secondary issues. The absolute centralization of power in the hands of the pope and the Roman Curia has transformed the bishops, the priests, and, especially the laity into simple agents of Vatican decisions. Vatican II tried to initiate a certain decentralization when it decided to make the central government of the Church a more collegial affair, at least as far as the bishops were concerned. However, the curia gradually regained control after the close of that meeting. Slightly modernized (as far as its methods of operation were concerned) and somewhat de-Italianized (at least at the upper level of the bureaucracy), it became once again all-powerful and extremely resentful of local initiatives. Instead of weakening it, Paul VI extended its power and kept the Synod of Bishops in a purely consultative role. Of course, no laymen participate in these synods, whose role in the Church remains practically null. It is well known that many bishops were dissatisfied, but few dared say so publicly. A few men in the immediate entourage of Paul VI, Archbishop Giovanni Benelli, Msgr. Pasquale Machi, Msgr. Paul Marcinkus, Cardinal Sergio Guerri, Cardinal Jean Villot, Cardinal Sebastiano Baggio, Msgr. Lorenzo Antonetti, Msgr. Giovanni Abbo, Cardinal Egidio Vagnozzi, and Cardinal John Cody, for example, the supervisors of the political and financial affairs of the Vatican, became the new men of power in the curia. During Paul VI's most important trip outside Italy, which took him in late 1970 to Australia and Hong Kong, among other places, it was Machi, Marcinkus, and, especially, Benelli who ran the show, as most of the journalists and Vatican experts in the rear of the plane were able to ascertain. Paul VI's trusted advisers and collaborators, often referred to as the "Milan Mafia," actually included also a few conservatives from the United States, among them Cody and Marcinkus; along with the Italian prelates, they held the remunerative and social power in the Vatican.

Decisions on important issues, such as Vatican finances and the participation of Church authorities in Italian politics and international affairs, were taken by the pope himself in consultation with a few very close curial collaborators. In Catholicism, there are no checks and balances to counter the absolute power of the pope and his collaborators in the curia except "ecumenical" councils, which have occurred less often than once every hundred years. The Synod of Bishops could do something, but it is so dependent on the pope and the curia that it has practically no possibility of acting autonomously and radically, as recent experience has shown.

As in many patrimonial bureaucracies, there are some individuals and groups that want to challenge the holders of power, but this opposition is too weak to effect significant changes. The sacred character traditionally attributed to the head of the Catholic Church, the legal and administrative trappings that accompany it, and the fact that the bureaucratic officials in the curia hide behind the traditional and legal power of the pope make it difficult for any far-reaching changes to take hold.

A rational-legal type of bureaucratization might actually restrain Vatican officials somewhat and make them more accountable to bishops, priests, and layman than the present spoils-system of patrimonial rule, but it would not bring about a substantial reorientation of the way power is exercised. Such a reorientation might come about if a challenge arose among a significant number of bishops, priests, and laymen and got some support from a few cardinals.[39] This reform movement might have to use much of the charismatic, expert, social, and remunerative (and even traditional and legal) power at its disposal. A first step might be to push for collegiality and decentralization, even if such a move should bring problems of its own. Such reforms, however, are practically unfeasible without an anticurial pope such as John XXIII, since the curia plays a crucial role in the selection of bishops and also effectively runs the Church in the name of the pope.

After Pius XII's illness in 1954, the curia became as powerful as the pope himself. Pope John and Vatican II reversed that trend a little, but Paul VI put the curia in a central position of power once again. Only in a few of the sections of the curia (those created by John XXIII and

Vatican II and housed in the San Callisto Palace) was there a little bit of opposition to the dominant conservatism of the older branches.

The Council on the Laity, for example, did not give strong support to Paul VI and the rest of the curia on the questions of birth control, democratic participation of laymen, and Church intervention in social issues, but neither was its inclination toward autonomy very effective. Its power base was too weak, and it was too dependent economically and administratively on the more established and conservative branches of the curia to be able to assert itself. It was in the awkward position of being too radical for the pope and the curia, and too conservative for almost everybody else (except, understandably, for the reactionary sector of the clergy and laity that considered Paul VI himself to be too progressive).

When we speak of the power of the curia, we must keep in mind the fact that inside the curia, there has been in recent years a switch in power from the heads of congregations to the Secretariate of State. Under Pius XII and John XXIII, the old Italian cardinals who supervised the work of the various congregations were very powerful. Paul VI changed that, transforming the Secretariate of State into a real ministry of the interior, with absolute power over all other branches of the curia. In the secretariate there were special sections which corresponded to each of the congregations of the curia, and which supervised their activities. It is as if Paul VI, who under Pius XII held the position of undersecretary of state, had decided to implement for his undersecretary, Benelli, the same type of curia reform that he would have liked Pius XII to make for him before 1954. As a matter of fact, Paul VI's reform of the curia, according to Desmond O'Grady, was described in the Vatican as ''an undersecretary's reform designed for an undersecretary.''[40] Paul VI even subsequently made Benelli archbishop of Florence, an important northern Italian see, naming him cardinal immediately, thus probably indicating that he would like Benelli to be his successor as pope, since he himself had followed a very similar administrative-pastoral career pattern before becoming pope, although he had not been named cardinal in 1954 by Pius XII but by John XXIII in 1958.

At the conclave following Paul VI's death, it was clearly Benelli who put together the coalition of cardinals which elected Cardinal Albino Luciani of Venice as the new pope.[41] It had become clear that neither the reactionary Siri, nor the conservative Bertoli, nor the centrist Baggio, nor the left-leaning Sergi Pignedoli would be able to muster the 75 necessary votes rapidly enough. Cardinal Siri of Genoa, the curia's perennial candidate, was in the lead with around 25 of the 111 votes on the first ballot. But on the second ballot these votes switched en masse to the compromise candidate, Luciani (whom Benelli had been backing even before entering the conclave), in order to block Pignedoli, who was emerging as the candidate of the more progressive cardinals. On the third ballot, it seems that Luciani received more than 90 votes, that Pignedoli received 17, and that Cardinal Aloísio Lorscheider, archbishop of Santo Angelo in Brazil, got one (Luciani's). There was a fourth ballot, a confirming one, that made the vote for Luciani overwhelming enough to silence the dissident Archbishop Lefebvre, who had previously announced he would not accept the decision of a conclave that did not include the 16 cardinals over eighty whom Paul VI's rules had kept from participating in the voting. Since 75 out of 111 votes was the minimum required for election, the final vote of well over 90 was deemed useful in order to leave no doubt whatsoever as to the validity of the election of Luciani, who became Pope John Paul I.

The conclave following the new pope's death, less than two months later, elected Cardinal Karol Wojtyla of Poland as his successor. There were, it seems, eight ballots. On the first ballot, Siri and Benelli himself were the two who led the vote, with around 25 to 30 votes each, while Wojtyla got five. On the second ballot, Benelli was nearly elected, but not quite. In the following ballots, electors from both ends of the spectrum refused to back Benelli and there was no Italian compromise candidate who could rally any substantial number of votes. Benelli started losing votes to moderate and progressive Italians and to Wojtyla, who had received some support in the early votes of the preceding conclave. After four ballots, the conclave seemed to be deadlocked and Wojtyla's chances started picking up, thanks to the North and East European, the North and South American, and the Third World cardinals. Even Benelli and a few Italians finally joined them, so that on the sixth ballot he was ahead. On the eighth and last ballot, he was elected with a good majority, though without the support of Siri or any large number of the Italian cardinals. The Church now had a Polish pope, the first ever, and the first non-Italian pope in 455 years. Wojtyla, who took the name John Paul II, at the age of fifty-eight, was the youngest pope in 132 years. He inherited many problems which Paul VI had left unresolved.

Judging by his performance in the first year or so of his pontificate, John Paul II will try to follow in Paul VI's footsteps, but he will also gradually have to take positions on these problems and put his own imprint on Vatican affairs. The fact that he is not an Italian and did not receive major support from the Italians in the conclave will have a tremendous influence on his relationship with the Roman Curia, and will affect his position vis-à-vis the Italian political situation. It is still much too early to attempt any description and evaluation of his pontificate, but one thing seems certain: his election to the papacy marks the end of an era and the beginning of another for Catholicism, no matter how hard he may try to follow into Paul VI's footsteps. John XXIII and Paul VI both tried to curtail the power of the curia, but John XXIII in the five years of his pontificate did more to revamp the structure and teachings of the Church, in spite of old age and thanks mainly to Vatican II. Paul VI started off as a reformer, but his reforms bogged down in curial intrigues because he refused to share his power with the episcopate, the clergy, and the laity, preferring to try to use the Secretariate of State to renew the curia from the inside. Paul VI's strategy failed because the curia was too solidly entrenched, and he finally ended up like Pius XII, a lonely and powerful autocrat arbitrating power struggles between the curia and an increasingly weakened secretariate. If John Paul II succeeds, like John XXIII, in going for support to the episcopate, the clergy, and the laity (for example, through more direct contact with them and through the Synod of Bishops—in Cracow, he was reputed to be a listener, and a man of collegiality), he will become a real innovator rather than just a Polish pope doing his best to be accepted by Italians and Romans and fighting outdated skirmishes with an Italy-centered Roman Curia. Because of his background and present stamina, and because he is prudent, attractive, and popular, he will probably be a very influential and authoritative pope, a strong and charismatic leader. In spite of this, there are certain movements and developments which he will not be able to stop or deflect. In any eventuality, it is still much too early in his pontificate to pass any serious judgement on the orientation that he will give to the Church.

The fact that the real struggle for power remains inside the curia and has not really progressed much since the time of Pius XII has made many Catholics, including many priests and some bishops, quite cynical about the possibility of a more democratic sharing of power in the Church. What happens outside the curia—for example, in Catholic Action—does not have as much importance as what happens inside, since that is where the power is lodged. Many lay Catholics have written off not only the official Catholic Action type of activity, but other forms of hierarchy- and clergy-controlled organizations as well.

Mostly because of the increasing conservatism of Paul VI during and after 1968, the Vatican and the local bishops have lost their strong control over the lay movement. Catholic Action has become very weak in most countries, and efforts to revive it have not met with success. Since 1968 there has been an increasing development in the Catholic Church of many autonomous, loosely organized groups of various religious and political tendencies, made up of clergy and laity who refuse to be controlled by the gerontocratic caste which has been reproducing itself in the government of the Church for many centuries. The hierarchy and the papacy are being challenged from the right and from the left, and there does not seem to be much possibility that they can regain control of the situation. This movement is linked to an emerging situation of pluralism which affects the clergy and the laity in every country and even touches some members of the hierarchy.

5. THE FUTURE OF THE PAPACY

From the time of Pius IX to the pontificate of Paul VI (and except for a minor radical breakthrough during the pontificate of John XXIII), Catholic authorities, from the papacy down, oscillated between conservatism and liberalism. The pope's orientation more or less determined the orientation of the rest of the Church, at least as far as public positions were concerned. But now pluralism is increasing. The latent party structure of Catholicism has clearly come to the fore, and it will have to be tolerated as such by Church officials. There will probably develop, as in Judaism and in other branches of Christianity, various tendencies extending from the right to the left, on both religious and political issues. It seems unlikely that Catholicism can ever return to a state of stability and consensus. The divergences are too deep, the convictions too strongly anchored, the forces of change too numerous and strong. The most probable outcome is more conflict and crisis, a protracted struggle like the one between the "Hellenizers" and the "Judaizers" in the primitive Christian church.

Many categories of lay Catholics are just not willing to continue putting up with the present order of things. Women, for example, are now starting to challenge the de facto discrimination to which they are subjected in the daily life of the Church. There can be an increasing internal polarization and a continued loss of members, but there can also be tolerance and stalemates if the cleavages are cross-cutting, as is the case now, rather than overlapping. On the other side of the spectrum, traditionalists (for example, the followers of Archbishop

Lefebvre) are once more rearing their heads in an effort to return to the most conservative practices and beliefs of the pre-Vatican II period. The Catholic charismatic movement, which started off as quite otherworldly and conservative, has recently manifested some radical proclivities, attracting progressive figures like Archbishop Helder Càmara of Recife in Brazil.

The Catholic crisis and the deep stirrings which occurred during the fifties and sixties among the Catholic laity were intimately tied to the transformations simultaneously taking place in the social, political, and economic spheres. The challenges were rather muted in the three World Congresses for the Lay Apostolate, because the delegates chosen to participate were largely moderate leaders of "safe" organizations. But the recurring crisis in the youth, student, and worker sectors of Catholic Action have shown very well that the desire for liberation and emancipation which characterizes our times has reached out to include even the religious sphere. Many Catholic laymen want more autonomy, freedom, and power in all aspects of their lives. They refuse to be passive and obedient members of the clerically dominated Church and to function as ideological Zouaves for the papacy.

It is not authority as such which is rejected, but authority exercised as domination rather than as service and love. There is no need for economic and political power if this orientation is to be implemented, and insofar as there would be any control, it could be vested in the Church membership as a whole rather than in the hands of office-holders and day-to-day decision-takers.

It seems likely that the clergy-laity division as it has continued for centuries is on the way out. Already, just with the disappearance of certain costumes, the lay-clergy dichotomy has suffered a severe blow. Married deacons and priests are already being introduced, and it is highly improbable that any ecclesiastical authority will be able to undo this blurring of roles.

There are also tremendous pressures building up on the question of democratization at various levels of the Church structure. The present system of nomination to positions of authority, which (except in the case of the election of the pope) functions entirely by co-optation from above (with some occasional possibilities for limited consultation), is increasingly being challenged and criticized by lower clergy and laymen.

It is nearly impossible for Church officials to cope with the challenges to their authority and to their compromises with ruling elites, because most of their critics remain in an ambiguous and marginal position vis-à-vis the organization, which makes it difficult to chastise or co-opt them. Vacillating between building counter-institutions, working patiently through the institution, or just leaving the institution, these critics are neither clearly inside nor clearly outside the Church. They use expert and charismatic power to counter the legal and traditional power of Church officials, but they are not really certain whether it is worth the effort.

The Vatican tries to co-opt competent and charismatic people, but since the latter often lack loyalty toward Church authorities or are less reliable over the long run, the temptation is strong to revert to administrative and bureaucratic managerialism, and to reliance on traditional and manipulative means of control.

With the election of a non-Italian pope, there is now a new awareness of the fact that the pope is really, above all, the resident bishop of Rome rather than just a super-patriarch towering over the whole Church. The fact that the bishop of Rome is not a Roman, an Italian by origin, does not really matter much, as John Paul II has often noted, since Peter himself was not a Roman. This marks the universality of the Church, and it also gives less warrant for intervention by the pope (and his curia) in Italian politics and in the affairs of other dioceses.

The realization of this fact by the present pope could reinforce his desire to give more attention to his own diocese of Rome than try to run every diocese in the world in a bureaucratic and centralized manner. Already, John Paul II has started visiting Roman parishes, he addresses people as "brothers and sisters" rather than as "sons and daughters," and he has started speaking up for individual rights and against oppressive structures of domination and exploitation. He could go even further and move from the Vatican to the Lateran, and really involve himself in the pastoral problems of his diocese, rather than in international and Italian politics and finance.[42] He could also become a new Pius IX, if he bosses rather than serves.

This type of decentralization and debureaucratization would go a long way to meet the critiques made of the papacy over the centuries, especially if the political sovereignty of the Church over the Vatican state were to be abandoned. Since it is the accommodation of the Catholic Church with the realm of socioeconomic and political power that has led it to replace coercive power by social and normative means of control, and since that accommodation has been greatly facilitated by the existence of the particular political-spiritual setup that is the Vatican, a dismantlement of that setup would most probably make the

Church less authoritarian and more responsive to progressive forces. Vatican officials have for centuries put forward the claim that the Vatican state is necessary to the Church in order to give it a certain degree of independence in announcing its message, but it seems rather obvious that the entanglement of the pope and his curia with the trappings of wealth and power have been among the major factors leading them to dominate and manipulate the laity rather than put all their efforts into serving the people in a prophetic manner.

Very little research has been done on the Vatican, on the pope and his curia, from a sociological point of view. Much of the existing research on Catholicism has centered on priests and laymen, on parishes or on dioceses. It seems that if we really want to analyze what is going on in a highly centralized organization like the Catholic Church, our efforts should be concentrated on studying the levels of the structure where the decisions of importance are being taken, where the ultimate power lies. Even if access is difficult, we should try to discover and explain what is happening in the various branches of the central bureaucracy of the Church and at the supra-diocesan level.

There should be studies of the careers of Church officials and of the struggles between various religious leaders and organizations, analyses of the relations between religious ideology and economic reality and between internal organizational arrangements and legal-political structures. Using historical documents, it should be possible to reconstruct developments in many sectors where religion and society meet, cooperate, and clash. Not only a sociology, but a political economy of the Vatican remains to be developed. Even religious ideology, including theology, has to be analyzed in its relationship with the cultural, political, and socioeconomic reality of the Vatican and of contemporary society.[43] Another fruitful area of research would be the parallel between social classes in society and the hierarchical structure of the Church through an analysis of the social background, ideology, financial investments, and social interactions of holders of authority in the Church.

There is much more information publicly available or obtainable through interviews with well-placed informants and through investigative documentary analysis than many researchers imagine. Although I have tried here to orient my research in such a direction, I am conscious of the fact that much remains to be done before we can unravel the mysteries of the control that religious organizations and their leaders exercise over the lives of contemporary man.

If many of the important and interesting developments in the economic sector of society gravitate around the question of workers' control as opposed to the corporate control exercised by the owners of capital, it might very well be that the issue of lay control versus authoritarian control by Church bureaucrats will prove just as fruitful an area of study and research for the religious sphere.[44]

Notes

CHAPTER I

1. See, for example: Thomas O'Dea, *The Catholic Crisis* (Boston, 1968); François Houtart, *L'Eclatement d'une église* (Paris, 1969); Carlo Falconi, *La contestazione nella Chiesa* (Milan, 1969); Renaud Dulong, *Une Eglise cassée* (Paris, 1971); Jacques Guichard, *Eglise, lutte de classes et stratégies politiques* (Paris, 1972); Peter Hebblethwaite, *The Runaway Church* (London: Collins, 1975).

2. Franz X. Kaufmann, "Religion et bureaucratie—Le Problème de l'organisation religieuse," *Social Compass* (Louvain–La Neuve), 22, no. 1 (1974):101–107. See also François Houtart, "Réflexions sociologiques sur le service diplomatique du Saint-Siege," *Concilium* (London), 91 (January 1974):155–165; and Ivan Vallier, "The Roman Catholic Church: A Transnational Actor," *International Organizations* 25, no. 3 (1971):479–502.

3. Amitai Etzioni, *The Active Society* (New York: Free Press, 1968), p. 314. Or, as Weber has it, power is the likelihood of getting obeyed (*The Theory of Social and Economic Organization* [New York: Free Press, 1947], p. 324).

4. Etzioni, op. cit., p. 361.

5. Amitai Etzioni, "Social Control: Organizational Aspects," in David L. Sills, ed., *International Encyclopedia of the Social Sciences* (New York: Macmillan and the Free Press, 1968), 14:396–402.

6. Op. cit., p. 154.

7. *The Sociology of Religion* (Boston, 1963), pp. 235–236.

8. "Images of God, Images of Man, and the Organization of Social Life," *Journal for the Scientific Study of Religion* 11, no. 1 (March 1972):1–15. Richard T. LaPiere (*Theory of Social Control* [New York: McGraw-Hill, 1954]) similarly distinguishes between psychological, physical, and economic techniques of social control; these can be positive or negative, formal or informal.

9. Kenneth A. Briggs, "Questions for Church Authority," *New York Times*, July 3, 1977, p. E5.

10. Henri Fesquet, *Rome s'est-elle convertie?* (Paris: Grasset, 1966); idem, *Une Eglise en état de péché mortel* (Paris, 1968); Carlo Falconi, *La svolta di Paolo VI* (Rome, 1968).

11. "Religious Organization," in Sills, op. cit., 13:433. Wilson puts the invested wealth of the Church at $5 billion, but compare the lower estimates cited in chap. 7, sect. 5.

12. As a curial official put it at the time: "Milan is Montini's Siberia."

13. *Catholic Action in Italy* (Stanford, Calif., 1967).

14. *Presidential Power: The Politics of Leadership* (New York: Wiley, 1960), p. 195.

15. More specific information on the methodology used for that survey will be given in Chap. V, which analyzes the data obtained from the questionnaires.

16. In *Models of the Church* (New York, 1974), the noted Jesuit theologian Avery Dulles describes five basic models of the Church that theologians identify: The Church as institution, as mystical communion, as sacrament, as herald, and as servant. The first of these models is the one that pictures society as a stratified, hierarchically structured organization. The last, the Church as servant, corresponds to the third model mentioned above as being the form that Christian church probably took in the first and second centuries. That this form had long been abandoned was evident long before Vatican II unsuccessfully tried to revive it.

Theological talk about various "models" hides a much more prosaic bureaucratic setup. F. X. Kaufmann ("L'Eglise, organisation religieuse," *Concilium* 91 [January 1974]:69) points to the danger of accepting such self-definitions at face value.

The government of the Church, the Roman Curia, is a complex organization which can be represented in the accompanying organigram.

The pope runs the organization, with the help of the Secretariate of State, which has two branches: the Secretariate of the Pope (previously, Ordinary [i.e. internal] Affairs) and the Council for the Public Affairs of the Church, (previously, Extraordinary [i.e. external or political] Affairs). Then come the nine congregations, each with a cardinal as president and a high-ranking prelate as secretary. Among these, the Congregation for the Doctrine of the Faith oversees the others on questions of doctrinal orthodoxy. There are also the three secretariates. The Pontifical Council for the Laity and the Justice and Peace Commission are actually secretariates also.

POPE

SECRETARIATE OF STATE

SECRETARIATE OF THE POPE	COUNCIL FOR THE PUBLIC AFFAIRS OF THE CHURCH
Congregations	Diplomatic service of the Vatican
Doctrine of the Faith	(nuncios, apostolic delegates, etc.)
Bishops	
Oriental Churches	
Sacraments and Liturgy	
Clergy	
Religious	
Catholic Education	
Evangelization of Peoples	
Causes of Saints	
Secretariates	
Christian Unity	
Non-Christians	
Non-Believers	
Pontifical Council for the Laity	
Justice and Peace Commission	
Tribunals	
Rota	
Apostolic Signature	
Penitenciary	
Bureaus	
General Administration of the Patrimony of the Holy See	
Apostolic Chancellery	
Apostolic Chamber	
Statistical Bureau	
Prefecture of the Apostolic Palace	
Prefecture for Economic Affairs	

17. "Bureaucratic organization has played a major role in the Catholic Church. It is well illustrated by the administrative role of the priesthood (Kaplanokratie) in the modern church, which has expropriated almost all of the old church benefices, which were in former days to a large extent subject to private appropriation. It is also illustrated by the conception of the universal Episcopate, which is thought of as formally constituting a universal legal competence in religious matters. Similarly, the doctrine of papal infallibility is thought of as in fact involving a universal competence, but one which functions 'ex cathedra' in the sphere of the office, thus implying the

typical distinction between the sphere of office and that of the private affairs of the incumbent.'' (*The Theory of Social and Economic Organization*, p. 334.)

I agree with Graham M. S. Dann (''Religious Belonging in a Changing Catholic Church,'' *Sociological Analysis* (DeKalb, Ill.), 37, no. 4 [Winter 1976]:283–297) that this uniform Weberian bureaucratic model should be replaced by a model capable of encompassing sociologically varied phenomena (such as decentralization, interest groups, parties, and conflict) which are emerging or reappearing in the Church. On the other hand, the pluriform model of religious belonging, based on Parsons's ideas, which Dann offers as an alternative to the Weberian model seems to me to have many shortcomings also.

18. See, for example, Louis Althusser, ''Idéologie et appareils idéologiques d'état,'' *La Pensée* (Paris), no. 151 (June 1970); see also Yves Barel, *La Reproduction sociale* (Paris: Anthropos, 1973).

19. See Marx and Engels, *On Religion* (Moscow, 1957), and Kautsky, *Foundations of Christianity* (London, 1925), passim.

20. *To Comfort and to Challenge* (Berkeley and Los Angeles, 1967), p. 203.

21. Renaud Dulong, for example, in his book *Une Eglise cassée* (Paris, 1971) shows how certain cultural-institutional changes are breaking up the Catholic Church as we have known it for centuries, and are bringing about a serious crisis of authority. The laity-clergy distinction, solidly established during the Middle Ages, became the fundamental model of the Church, and succeeded in maintaining the Church as a going concern, as long as the clergy was able to hold on to power, knowledge, prestige, and other desirable resources. When the Renaissance ushered in a new culture, the clergy was able to keep the old model afloat, but gradually Catholic laymen had to be taken into account. From listener and spectator, the upper-class layman became an actor and collaborator. Moreover, political and socioeconomic factors operating outside became much more important for the life of the Church. Being unable to maintain the internal structure with the time-tested religious control mechanisms, the upper clergy tried to muster support from the sociopolitical order. When this course ended mostly in failure, Vatican centralization and appeals to the laity were used to prop up the old system. By trying to find alliances with the declining feudal and monarchical regimes, and then with the rising bourgeoisies, Church leaders were exchanging legitimation for the political and socioeconomic maintenance of clerical privileges and prerogatives. The minor crises which hit the Church before 1960 were usually skirmishes over tactical details on how to apply this major strategy of compromise. Dulong sees Pope John's pontificate as representing an effort at liberating Catholicism from the stranglehold of feudal-capitalist legitimation. This process might have continued with Paul VI, had there not erupted, around 1968, a world-wide cultural and sociopolitical crisis challenging the clerical and hierarchical nature not only of the Catholic Church but of many contemporary institutions, including schools and universities,

political parties and governments, and corporations and trade unions. Consequently, the basic laity-clergy model of Church organization—which Vatican II had not really altered—was being challenged as energetically as was the Church's conservative legitimizing function. Thus, despite compromises on the political front, extending even to détente with East European Communists, the internal position of Church hierarchs was losing the solid support of its members, according to Dulong, so they decided to put a brake on further developments lest the whole structure crumble.

22. *Méthodes des sciences sociales* (Paris: Dalloz, 1972), p. 383.

23. "The Oversocialized Conception of Man in Modern Sociology," *American Sociological Review* 26 (April 1961):184. C. Wright Mills also argues the point forcefully:

"The sociological imagination enables us to grasp history and biography and the relations between the two in society. . . . No social study that does not come back to the problems of biography, of history and of their interaction within a society has completed its intellectual journey. . . . Every well-considered social study requires an historical scope of conception and a full use of historical materials." (*The Sociological Imagination*, [New York: Grove Press, 1959], pp. 6, 145.)

24. *Rethinking Sociology* (New York: Appleton-Century-Crofts, 1973), p. 14.

25. Two contemporary French sociologists of religion, Renaud Dulong and Emile Poulat, express this same idea in discussions of studies in their own areas of specialization. In *Une Eglise cassée* (p. 87), Dulong writes;

"Most sociologists, even when they declare that they are doing synchronic studies, cannot avoid presenting their materials according to a diachronic development scheme of presentation. It is as if the public—or the researchers themselves—were incapable of explaining the phenomena of contemporary society without reference to a historical development which very often finally constitutes the explanation of these phenomena."

Poulat, in an article entitled "La société religieuse et le problème du changement" (*Revue française de sociologie* 7, no. 3 [July–September 1966]: 305), is even more explicit:

"A sociology of the future of Christianity might be possible (and personally I think it is possible): it does not dispense with the need for doing a sociology of its history. Many contemporary events remain unintelligible, incomprehensible, if we do not go back to the debates and the struggles of the beginning of this century, and even of the last century."

26. "L'Eglise, organisation religieuse," p. 69.

27. See Philip Selznick, *The Organizational Weapon* (New York: Free Press of Glencoe, 1960).

28. *Modern Organizations* (Englewood Cliffs, N.J.: Prentice-Hall, 1964), p. 74.

CHAPTER II

1. "The constitution regulates the duties and rights of the religious functionary (clergy) and the laity, and it defines the order of the clergy" (*The Comparative Study of Religion* [New York, 1958], p. 134).

2. Joachim Wach, *The Sociology of Religion* (Chicago, 1962), p. 336.

3. *Ancient Judaism* (Glencoe, Ill., 1952), p. 380.

4. Salo Wittmayer Baron, *A Social and Religious History of the Jews*, (New York: Columbia University Press, 1937), 1:71.

5. E.g. Exodus 19:4; Deuteronomy 7:6–12.

6. E.g. 1 Peter 2:9–10; Acts 15:14.

7. In his study of the New Testament roots of Church authority, a noted Catholic biblical scholar thus summarizes his findings:

"Church authority is not a dominant theme in the New Testament. . . . The New Testament is anti-authoritarian in a proper sense. It abhors that type of domination which in the New Testament world was seen in secular power or in religious autocracy. It is anti-authoritarian in the sense that it permits no member of the Church to occupy a position of dignity and eminence; the first in the Church must be the lackey and the slave of others, and may strive for no dignity and eminence except in dedication to service in love.

"Authority in the New Testament is conceived in a way which must be called democratic rather than absolute. Authority in the Church belongs to the whole Church and not to particular officers. The New Testament is strangely silent both on commissions to command and on exhortations to obedience and submissiveness to Church authority. If exhortations to submissiveness are addressed to anyone in particular, they are addressed to the officers of the Church. Both the idea and the use of authority in the New Testament show no signs of rigorous control of the members by authority. Since the mission of the Church is the responsibility of all the members of the Church, all members have a concern in the exercise of authority." (John L. McKenzie, *Authority in the Church* [New York: Sheed and Ward, 1966], pp. 84–85.)

8. E.g. Jeremiah 26:7–11 and 34:19; Isaiah 24:2.

9. Pierre Nautin, "L'origine des structures actuelles de l'Eglise," *La Lettre*, no. 188 (April 1974), pp. 20–24.

10. Wach, *Sociology of Religion*, p. 152.

11. *A History of Christianity* (New York, 1953), p. 133.

12. Ibid., pp. 286–287.

13. (New York, 1931), 1:99.

14. *Foundations of Christianity* (New York, 1953), p. 384.

15. Ibid., pp. 286–287.

16. "Religion, Wirtschaft und Gesellschaft," in *Aufsätze zur Geistesgeschichte und Religionssoziologie* (Tübingen, 1925), p. 2, as quoted in Norman Birnbaum and Gertrud Lenzer, *Sociology and Religion* (Englewood Cliffs,

N.J.: Prentice-Hall, 1969), p. 198.

17. Bryan R. Wilson, "Religious Organization," in Sills, *International Encyclopedia of the Social Sciences* (New York: Free Press, 1968), 13:430.

18. *The Social Teachings of the Christian Churches* (New York, 1931), 1:100.

19. See Hugues Portelli, *Gramsci et la question religieuse* (Paris: Editions Anthropos, 1974), pp. 61–62.

20. (New York: Herder and Herder, 1973), p. 129.

21. *The Organization of the Early Christian Churches* (New York, 1972), p. 141.

22. Ibid., p. 151.

23. On the relationship between the pope and bishops see, for example, William Telfer, *The Office of a Bishop* (London: Darton, 1962).

24. The title Supreme Pontiff (Pontifex Maximus) was passed over from the emperor to the pope during the last half of the fourth century.

25. Augustin Fliche and Victor Martin, eds., *Histoire de l'Eglise*, vol. 7 (Paris: Jean Leflon, 1951).

26. *Selected Writings in Sociology and Social Philosophy*, ed., T. B. Bottomore (New York: McGraw-Hill, 1964), p. 190.

27. *Economy and Society* (New York, 1968), 3:985–986.

28. *The Democratic and the Authoritarian State* (New York: Free Press, 1957), p. 243.

29. *The Modern Prince and Other Writings* (New York, 1957), p. 66.

30. Troeltsch, op. cit., p. 353.

31. *The Modern Prince*, p. 358.

32. Antonio Gramsci, *Il materialismo storico e la filosofia di Benedetto Croce*, p. 85, and *Il Risorgimento*, p. 24 (both, Turin: Einaudi, 1966).

33. *The Civilization of the Renaissance in Italy* (New York: Modern Library, 1954), p. 98.

34. *IDOC* (Information-Documentation on the Conciliar Church) (Rome), October 9, 1967, p. 3

35. Cardinal Newman anticipated this new lay awakening in his 1859 essay *On Consulting the Faithful in Matters of Doctrine*, for which he was denounced in Rome.

36. Adrien Dansette, *Histoire religieuse de la France contemporaine* (Paris, 1948). 1:326–327.

37. *Interest Groups in Italian Politics* (Princeton, N.J., 1964), p. 426.

38. *Actes du premier Congrès Mondial pour L'Apostolat des Laïques* (Rome: COPECIAL, 1952), 1:45.

39. Quoted in Giorgio Candeloro, *Il movimento cattolico in Italia* (Rome, 1955), p. 152.

40. Giuseppe De Rosa, *L'Azione Cattolica* (Bari, 1953), 1:98, 135, 155.

41. Giovanni Spadolini, *L'opposizione cattolica* (Florence, 1955), p. 178.

42. Gianfranco Poggi, *Catholic Action in Italy* (Stanford, Calif., 1967), p. 16.

43. A speech made in San Marino in August 1902 by Don Romolo Murri shocked many members of the Italian hierarchy because it asked for freedom for the Catholic laity to break with the past, condemned "clerical" social politics as conservative, and rejected the bishops' right to give political direction to the political movement for renewal. See Michele Ranchetti, *The Catholic Modernists: A Study of the Religious Reform Movement, 1864–1907* (London: Oxford University Press, 1969), p. 102.

44. Daniel Callahan, *The Mind of the Catholic Layman* (New York, 1963), pp. 66–67.

45. Alongside these, the Society for Catholic Youth (predecessor of Italian Youth Catholic Action) and the Italian Federation of Catholic University Students were already thriving. Other clerically-controlled conservative lay Catholic organizations were created subsequently, including the Italian Women's Union, and the Italian Catholic Young Women's Association.

46. Carlo Falconi, *The Popes in the Twentieth Century* (Boston, 1967), p. 97. In sections 8–10 of this chapter I have made considerable use of Falconi's and Gabriele De Rosa's works. I have also consulted Giancarlo Zizola's *Quale papa?* (Rome, 1977) during final revisions.

47. Benedict was responsible for calling to Rome the young priest Angelo Roncalli, the future John XXIII, as head of the central council (for Italy) of the "Pontificie Opere Missionarie." This was done at the suggestion of Roncalli's progressive bishop, Giacomo Maria Radini-Tedeschi, who was a friend of the pope; and although Pius XI later promoted Roncalli away from Rome, Benedict XV's original appointment was instrumental in opening up his Vatican career.

Benedict also encouraged the founding, in 1921, of Pax Romana, a lay association of students from the Netherlands, Switzerland, and Spain that gradually developed into an influential international federation of Catholic students and intellectuals. Leaders in Pax Romana became, in the postwar lay movement, the new leadership of the official laity that sponsored, through their active participation in COPECIAL and the Council on the Laity, the three twentieth-century lay congresses that we shall examine in chaps. 3–5.

48. Even as late as August 25, 1937, the *Osservatore Romano* said that members of Catholic Action could also be members of the Fascist Party of Italy.

49. Antonio Gramsci, *Note sul Machiavelli, sulla politica e sullo stato moderno* (Turin: Einaudi, 1964), chap. 3, quoted by Poggi, op. cit., p. 165.

50. Carlo Falconi, *La Chiesa e le organizzazioni cattoliche in Italia (1945–1955)* (Turin, 1956), p. 258.

51. Quoted in Alfonso Prandi, *Chiesa e politica* (Bologna, 1968), p. 27.

52. Quoted, ibid., p. 29.

53. Quoted in Falconi, op. cit., p. 381.

54. Ibid.

55. "Such dependence is most strict for Catholic Action: for Catholic Action, indeed, represents the official lay apostolate" (*Actes du premier Congrès Mondial pour l'Apostolat des Laïques*, 1:48).

56. Eva Maria Jung, "The Third Lay Congress," *Catholic World* (Ramsey, N.J.), February 1968, p. 203.

CHAPTER III

1. Jean-Pierre Dubois-Dumée, "Pour la première fois, les catholiques de 74 pays ont établi les conditions de leur apostolat," *Témoignage Chrétien* (Paris), no. 380 (1951), p. 1.

2. *Actes du premier Congrès Mondial pour l'Apostolat des Laïques*, 2 vols. (Rome: COPECIAL, 1952), 1:139.

3. Ibid., p. 144.

4. Ibid., p. 136.

5. Desmond O'Grady, "Vittorino Veronese," *U.S. Catholic* (Chicago), February 1968, p. 44.

6. *Memorie* (Milan, 1965), p. 148.

7. Quoted in *Laymen Face the World* (*Texts of the Second World Congress for the Lay Apostolate*, vol. 2 [Rome: COPECIAL, 1958]), p. 275.

8. *Actes du premier Congrès Mondial . . .*, 1:357.

9. It is only at the third World Congress in 1967 that there were delegations from various socialist countries.

10. In 1967 the equivalent documents took up only 11 pages of the first volume of the *Proceedings*.

11. "The Apostolate of the Laity," *Cross Currents* (Dobbs Ferry, N.Y.), 2, no. 3 (Spring 1952):30–31.

12. *Actes du premier Congrès Mondial . . .*, 1:144.

13. Ibid., p. 109.

14. Alden Hatch, *Pope Paul VI* (London: W. H. Allen, 1965), p. 92.

15. *The Popes in the Twentieth Century* (Boston, 1967), p. 243.

16. *Vatican Council II* (New York, 1968), p. 144. The best explanation of the Montini exile to Milan can be found in Giancarlo Zizola, *Quale papa?* (Rome: Borla, 1977), pp. 152–154. Zizola insists on Italian politics, Italian Catholic Action, and priest-workers as the reasons for the exile.

17. See especially *Il Pentagono Vaticano* (Bari: Laterza, 1958).

18. Gianfranco Poggi, *Catholic Action in Italy* (Stanford, Calif., 1967), p. 120. See Mario Rossi, *I giorni dell'omnipotenza* (Rome, 1975), for the best description of these events.

19. *La Chiesa e le organizazione cattoliche in Italia (1945–1955)* (Turin, 1956), pp. 399–400.

20. Ibid., p. 207–211.

21. *Jalons pour une théologie du laïcat* (Paris, 1953).

22. *Laymen in the Church* (*Texts of the Second World Congress for the Lay Apostolate*, vol. 1 [Rome: COPECIAL, 1958]), pp. 43–44.

23. *Panorama of the Organized Lay Apostolate in the World* (Rome: COPECIAL, 1963).

24. "A Foretaste of Things to Come: Impressions of an Observer-Consultant," in *God's People on Man's Journey (Proceedings of the Third World Congress for the Lay Apostolate,* vol. 1 [Rome: COPECIAL, 1966]), p. 139.

25. "Rome and the Lay Apostolate," *Ecumenical Review* (Geneva), 1958, pp. 322–323.

26. As quoted in Peter Nichols, *The Politics of the Vatican* (London, 1968), p. 109. Zizola, in *Quale papa?* (pp. 147–160), attempts a lengthy and fascinating reconstruction of the victory of Roncalli over Cardinal Pietro Agaganian in the 1958 conclave.

27. Pope John XXIII, *Journal of a Soul* (New York: Signet, 1966), p. 353.

28. *The Popes in the Twentieth Century,* p. 329.

29. Letter, Cardinal Tardini, secretary of state, to Msgr. Alberto Castelli, vice-president of the Ecclesiastical Commission of COPECIAL, August 6, 1959.

30. *Panorama of the Organized Lay Apostolate in the World.* There were editions in various languages.

31. Reported in Rynne, *Vatican Council II,* p. 165.

32. *La Croix,* September 25, 1965, p. 5.

33. *La Documentation Catholique* (Paris), no. 1436 (November 15, 1964), col. 1456.

34. Ibid., no. 1436 (November 15, 1964), col. 1474.

35. Ibid., no. 1436 (November 15, 1964), cols. 1456–1479, *passim.*

36. Ibid., no. 1412 (November 17, 1963), col. 1512, and no. 1413 (December 1, 1963), col. 1577.

37. Rynne, *Vatican Council II,* p. 325.

38. Ibid., p. 328.

39. Troeltsch, *The Social Teachings of the Christian Churches* (New York, 1931), 1:349.

40. Walter M. Abbott, S. J., ed., *The Documents of Vatican II* (New York, 1966), p. 100.

41. *Vatican II et l'évolution de l'Eglise* (Paris, 1969), p. 211.

42. Rocco Caporale, "The Dynamics of Hierarchy: Processes of Continuity in Change of the Roman Catholic System during Vatican II," *Sociological Analysis* 28, no. 2 (Summer 1967):68.

43. Casanova, op. cit. (in n. 41 above), pp. 119–121.

CHAPTER IV

1. Yves Congar, *Lay People in the Church: A Study for a Theology of Laity,* (Westminster, Md.: Newman Press, 1957).

2. "Regulations," in *Lay Apostolate,* Bulletin of the COPECIAL, 1967, no. 2, pp. 5–8.

3. "Le Troisième Congrès Mondial de l'Apopstolat des Laïcs et le renouveau de l'Eglise," *Le Devoir* (Montreal), November 9, 1967, p. 5; my translation.

4. James O'Gara, "The Two Churches," *Commonweal* (New York), November 3, 1967, pp. 138–139.

5. Ibid., p. 139.

6. *Catholic Voice* (Oakland, Calif., November 8, 1967), p. 10.

7. "Legfolkets Oktoberrevolusjon," *St. Olav* (Oslo), no. 21 (1967), pp. 328–329.

8. Quoted and translated in *The Laity Today*, Bulletin of the Consilium de Laicis (Rome), December 1969, no. 4–5, p. 120.

9. *U.S. Catholic*, February 1968, p. 44.

10. *God's People on Man's Journey* (Proceedings of the Third World Congress for the Lay Apostolate, vol. 1 [Rome: COPECIAL, 1968]) p. 59.

11. "Towards the Future," ibid., pp. 165–166.

12. Ibid., p. 162–163.

13. *Man Today* (Proceedings of the Third World Congress for the Lay Apostolate, vol. 2 [Rome: COPECIAL, 1968]) p. 224.

14. Ibid., p. 228.

15. Ibid., p. 117.

16. Ibid., p. 118.

17. "Regulations," in *Lay Apostolate*, no. 2, 1967, p. 8.

18. *La Croix* (Paris), October 17, 1967, p. 4, col. 4.

19. *Lay Apostolate*, no. 3, 1967, p. 29.

20. Robert C. Doty, "The Laity Jolts the Church," *New York Times*, October 22, 1967, p. 6E.

21. "We now strongly assert it to you again: Give the world of today, the energies which will enable it to advance on the paths of progress and freedom, and to solve its great problems: hunger, international justice, peace" (*God's People on Man's Journey*, p. 26).

22. Ibid., p. 24.

23. *National Catholic Reporter*, October 25, 1967, pp. 1, 10.

24. October 16, 1967.

25. October 30, 1967, p. 57.

26. *God's People on Man's Journey*, p. 123.

27. Ibid., p. 127.

28. Ibid., p. 25.

29. Ibid., p. 132.

30. *Man Today*, p. 224.

31. *National Catholic Reporter*, November 1, 1967: *La Croix* (Paris), December 7; *Informations Catholiques Internationales* (Paris), December 1; *L'Astrolabio* (Rome), December 3.

32. In *Twin Circle* (Los Angeles), November 26, 1967, p. 2.

33. *Man Today*, pp. 230, 235–236.

34. Ibid., p. 225–26.

35. Ibid., p. 228.

36. Ibid., p. 231.

37. *The Laity in the Renewal of the Church* (*Proceedings of the Third World Congress for the Lay Apostolate.* vol. 3 [Rome: COPECIAL, 1968]), p. 25.

38. Ibid., p. 98.

39. Ibid., p. 105.

40. Ibid., p. 106.

41. Ibid., p. 5.

42. "The Two Churches," *Commonweal*, November 3, 1967, p. 139.

43. *The Roman Catholic Church* (New York: Doubleday, 1971), p. 120.

44. *The Times* (London), October 19, 1967.

45. *Man Today*, p. 228; see also *Lay Apostolate*, no. 3, 1967, p. 15.

46. Ibid., p. 118.

47. *National Catholic Reporter*, November 1, 1967, p. 1, and November 15, p. 9; also *New York Times*, August 11, 1968, p. 32.

48. Quoted in *Lay Apostolate*, no. 3, 1967, p. 19.

49. Carlo Falconi, *La contestazione nella Chiesa* (Milan, 1969).

50. *Le Monde*, weekly edition, November 9–15, 1967, p. 11.

51. Letter from Cardinal Villot, secretary of state, in the name of the Delegated Presidents of the Synod of Bishops, to Cardinal Roy, president of the Council on the Laity, quoted in "The Lay Congress and the Synod of Bishops," *The Laity Today* (Vatican City), no. 4–5, December 1969, p. 103.

52. Arthur J. Moore, "Bishops and Laity in Rome," *Christianity and Crisis* 27, no. 50 (November 27, 1967):280.

53. Dr. Hans-Ruedi Weber, "A Foretaste of Things to Come: Impressions of an Observer-Consultant," in *God's People on Man's Journey*, p. 144.

54. *La Croix*, 20 October 1967, quoted in *The Laity Today*, no. 4–5, December 1969, p. 125. One of the best evaluations of the congress was published in another French daily a year later:

> "More than 3,000 lay people went to the congress, to say what they thought of 'man today.' Chosen by their bishops among the leaders of Catholic Action, these faithful sons of the Church were to bring her, after the *aggiornamento* of their council, their assent and their gratitude.
>
> "At least, that is what was expected of them. In fact, they immediately got involved in heated disagreements. To the benevolent clergies who, under new and well-intentioned forms, reaffirmed their paternity, they replied with a proclamation of brotherhood; to the dictates of authority, they wanted to substitute a common research of truth.
>
> "Coming from 'specialized movements,' they asked for the breaking up of these forms and for the multiplication of small groups of reflection and experimentation more attuned to the realities of social life and to cultural specialities. The old conception of obedience was shattered by the discovery of full responsibility, of the equality of people in each and every social cell . . .
>
> "The shock of such a challenge was immediately smothered, by reflex much

more than by a deliberate decision. An ecclesiastical society which had not been prepared for such a challenge was inclined to see it only as the modern symptom of an old disease, anti-Roman epidermic irritation. Unable to grasp the meaning of the internal debates of the congress, the members of this ecclesiastical society failed to understand that what these distinguished laymen were saying was, essentially: 'If Rome does not listen to us, we shall go forward by ourselves, without Rome.'" (J. Nobécourt, "La Crise de l'Eglise romaine, "*Le Monde*, December 15–16, 1968, p. 9; my translation.)

CHAPTER V

1. My interviews in France in 1966 with more than 100 lay leaders (Ivan Vallier and Jean-Guy Vaillancourt, "Catholicism, Laity, and Industrial Society: A Cross National Study of Religious Change," *Archives de Sociologie des Religions*, vol. 23 [January–June 1967], pp. 99–102) helped considerably in the elaboration of the questionnaire by indicating centers of interest of some members of the Catholic laity. A pretest of the questionnaire to be used in Rome was made at the April 1967 Congress of the National Council of Catholic Men, in Pittsburgh; this pretest helped me eliminate or change some questions which were not operative, and add a few more which were required to get a better-working instrument.

2. Kish, *Sample Survey* (New York: Wiley, 1965), pp. 20–21.

3. The other 2 percent left the spaces blank, since for this type of question there were only four possible answers, two positive (definitely agree and agree somewhat) and two negative (disagree somewhat and definitely disagree). I collapsed the four categories into two, positive and negative, i.e. agree and disagree.

4. Charles Y. Glock and Rodney Stark, *Christian Beliefs and Anti-Semitism* (New York, 1966).

5. Ibid., p. 5.

6. Ibid., p. 190.

7. Ibid., p. 7.

8. "The Roman Catholic Laity in France, Chile and the United States: Cleavages and Developments—Part I," *IDOC*, no. 68–7 (February 18, 1968), p. 5. I was responsible for the interviews that took place in France for this study, during the summer of 1966, and Caporale for the subsequent interviews in Chile and the United States.

9. In my 1967 Rome survey, I used the following question which approximated as much as possible the wording of the question put to the informants in the Vallier-Caporale study:

Here are three kinds of demands of laymen. Write in the number 1 near the one you consider most important of the three. Write 2 near the second most important and write 3 near the least important of the three. (This question is different in structure from the others; instead of checking once, you write in three numbers).

(a)_____demand for participation in the power structure and decision making of the Church organization

(b)_____demand for more specific definitions of the lay action roles especially those having to do with the relation between Church and society (e.g. problems of mandate vs. autonomy, humanization vs. evangelization).

(c)_____demand for more meaningful forms of interpersonal association especially in the liturgical and social sphere.

Another of my questions permitted a further step by helping specify the kind of participation desired. Here 24 percent indicated that participation in decisions about liturgy and cult was important whereas 65 percent indicated that participation in administrative and policy decisions was of the utmost importance. It is interesting to note that only 2 percent stated that laymen should not participate in decision making in the Church. For the lay national delegates, at least, the era of "pray and pay" was over.

10. G. Poggi, *Catholic Action in Italy* (Stanford, Calif., 1967), pp. 109–124.

11. René Didier shares this conclusion, as can be seen from his report on the congress: "The problem of participation is much more a question of a clear definition of roles and of functions, than an impatient questioning of authority itself" Troisième ("Le Congrès mondial des laïcs et le renouveau de l'église," *Le Devoir*, December 10, 1967, p. 4).

12. The use of geocultural regions as important variables in the sociology of religion has been developed, albeit for much smaller regional units, by Fernand Boulard and Jean Rémy in *Pratique religieuse urbaine et régions culturelles* (Paris: Editions Ouvrières, 1968), chap. 3, "La Région socio-culturelle comme variable explicative fondamentale," pp. 57–91. In *Bilan du monde: Encyclopédie catholique du monde chrétien*, 2 vols. (Paris: Casterman, 1964), a similar regrouping of countries is used, and the groups of countries are called "geographico-cultural" groups.

13. Andrew Greeley and Peter Rossi, *The Education of Catholic Americans* (Chicago: Aldine, 1966), p. 79.

14. René Didier, in an interview given me on October 26, 1968, mentioned his stupefaction when he realized that the delegates from French-speaking African countries, which he knows quite well, were not at all representative of the lay movements there. "Unknown people chosen by the nuncios," he called them.

15. The representation, in this study, of older people as being more orthodox than younger people does not necessarily mean that orthodoxy increases because people get older. The indicated difference between old and young might be simply due to the very different socialization process that the present younger generation has undergone, as Rodney Stark has shown ("Age and Faith," *Sociological Analysis* 29, no. 1 [Spring 1968]:1–10). In fact, a decrease in orthodoxy might be occurring with age, but difference in the socialization process of various generations could be large enough to veil

that fact to those who imagine that today's old people were in the past like today's youth. As is the case for the geocultural region, age cannot really be considered to be a variable with a real causal influence per se. As Travis Hirshi and Hanan Selvin note, age is a measure of time dimension during which certain events have the opportunity to occur, i.e. it indicates length of exposure to causal variables, just as the geocultural region could indicate place of exposure (*Delinquency Research* [New York: Free Press, 1967], p. 86).

16. Leo Goodman and William Kruskal, "Measures of Association for Cross Classification, I," Journal of the American Statistical Association 49 (December 1954). W. Allen Wallis and Harry Roberts in their book *Statistics: A New Approach* (Glencoe, Ill.: Free Press, 1956), p. 599, have another name for this same measure; instead of calling it gamma, they call it "h."

17. This type of correlation matrix is sometimes used as a starting point for factor analysis, or for simpler techniques called "cluster analysis" and "smallest space analysis," to uncover new dimensions among a group of variables (independent or dependent). Here, however, the use of the correlation matrix is entirely different. I consider the variables on the left, representing elements of the religious ideology of the delegates, as being dependent variables, and those on top as independent variables. This does not exclude the possibility of interdependence. In some cases, for example in the relationship between orthodoxy and ritualism, it is even highly probable that orthodoxy would be the independent variable and ritualism the dependent variable. In any eventuality the variables on the left are nearly all in a different time order from the variables on top and consequently we are in the domain of explanatory analysis and not in the area of index construction.

18. *Synod '67: A New Sound in Rome* (Milwaukee, 1968). That new sound, for these two authors, was the congress just as much as, and maybe even more than, the Synod of Bishops which took place at the same time.

19. *T.V.A. and the Grass-Roots* (New York: Harper and Row, 1966).

20. These two chapters are partly influenced by Marx's critical view of institutional religion, which is expressed succinctly in the following passage: "Every history of religion even, that fails to take account of this material basis, is uncritical" (*Capital: A Critical Analysis of Capitalist Production*, 3 vols. [Moscow: Progress Publishers, 1965–1967], 1:372). Although I do not agree with the materialism and the economic reductionism prevalent in much of Marxist thought (political and ideological factors having in my opinion a certain consistency and a reality of their own), I still think that socioeconomic variables are extremely important and that they are often neglected or purposely hidden from view. Catholicism, like all other religions, systems of thought, and elements of the superstructure of society, can gain in being subjected to a Marxist type of analysis, even if such a critique cannot exhaust all aspects of the phenomenon under study. I think that a religion that really cares about man and that refuses to buttress injustices in the social order can

become an ally of an open type of humanist Marxism that functions as a method of analysis of socioeconomic, political, and ideological reality rather than as a vulgar materialist and antireligious creed that functions as the official ideology of bureaucratic parties and states.

CHAPTER VI

1. A Dutch sociologist, in an important document on the problems of the laity in the Catholic Church written just before the third World Congress for the Lay Apostolate, remarks that one must look at what goes on in Italy to understand the place of the organized lay apostolate in the Church: "If one day it is wished to make an inventory of the organized lay apostolate in the Catholic Church, it would be necessary to take greater account of the *Italian situation*" (emphasis in original). Jan Grootaers, "Structures and Living Communities in the Conciliar Church," *IDOC*, no. 15–16, (May 15, 1967), p. 6.

2. *Une Eglise cassée* (Paris, 1971), p. 172.

3. Arturo Carlo Jemolo, *L'Eglise et l'état en Italie du Risorgimento à nos jours* (Paris: Seuil, 1960), pp. 82–83.

4. Pius X sent one of the progressive directors of the Opera dei Congressi, Msgr. Radini-Tedeschi, to be bishop of the diocese of Bergamo, a nomination that was intended as a demotion much more than as a promotion. Radini-Tedeschi chose the newly ordained Angelo Roncalli (the future John XXIII) as his personal secretary. During his first years as a priest, Roncalli was strongly influenced by this bishop's progressive ideas. In a book he later wrote on Radini-Tedeschi, he recalls the two books that his bishop often had on his table: the New Testament and Leo XIII's social encyclical *Rerum Novarum*. In 1909, Roncalli and his bishop supported a textile workers' strike in Ranica near Bergamo. (Vittorio Gorresio, *The New Mission of Pope John XXIII* [New York, 1970].) Roncalli also did considerable organizational work with Catholic Action groups both before and after World War I. Thus we see that his progressive stances as pope were not exactly without any experimental basis.

5. *Economy and Society* (New York, 1968) 3:985.

6. At his priestly ordination, Roncalli had asked to be assisted by Ernesto Buonaiuti, later to be excommunicated as a modernist. The Holy Office kept a file on Roncalli because of this youthful request.

7. Antonio Gramsci, in an article published anonymously in *L'Ordine Nuovo* on February 22, 1922, unveiled the significance of this alliance with Giolitti: "The Gentiloni Pact signifies the passage of the ecclesiastical hierarchy from the service of the conservative party, i.e. of Sonnino and the agrarians, to the service of the democratic party, i.e. of the bankers and industrialists and Giolitti" ("Socialismo e facismo," reprinted in his *"L'Ordine Nuovo," 1921–1922* [Turin: Einaudi, 1967], p. 459; my translation).

8. *Il Partito Popolare e la questione romana* (Florence, 1922), p. 45.

9. *"L'Ordine Nuovo," 1919–1920* (Turin: Einaudi, 1970), p. 284: "The 'popolari' are to the [Italian] Socialists what Kerensky was to Lenin . . .''

10. Carlo Falconi, *La Chiesa e le organizazioni cattoliche in Italia (1945–1955)* (Turin, 1956), pp. 63–64.

11. "I Popolari," in *Opere di Antonio Gramsci* 9 (Turin, 1954):284–286; see also Paolo Alatri, ed., *L'Antifacismo italiano* (Rome: Riuniti, 1961), pp. 421–425.

12. *Storia di quattri anni* (Turin: Einaudi, 1946), p. 49.

13. Op. cit., pp. 24ff.

14. *Politica comunista* (Rome, 1945), p. 85; my translation.

15. *La costruzione del Partito Comunista, 1923–1924* (Turin: Einaudi, 1971), p. 524; my translation.

16. *Sotto la mole, 1916–1920* (Turin: Einaudi, 1960), p. 390.

17. D. A. Binchy, *Church and State in Fascist Italy* (London, 1941), p. 158.

18. See Msgr. Guido Anichini, *Cinquant 'anni de vita della F.U.C.I.* (Rome: Studium, 1947).

19. Avro Manhattan, *The Vatican in World Politics* (New York: Gaer Associates, 1949), pp. 121–126. In spite of some exaggerations, Manhattan's book contains some useful remarks and information.

20. Ibid., pp. 174–175.

21. Quoted in *The Popes in the Twentieth Century* (Boston, 1967), p. 194.

22. Franz von Papen, *Memoirs* (New York: Dutton, 1953), p. 279.

23. *Actes et documents du Saint-Siège relatifs à la guerre mondiale*, vol. 4, *Le Saint Siège et la guerre en Europe, Juin 1940–Juin 1941* (Vatican City: Libreria Editrice Vaticana, 1967), p. 148.

24. Harry Kessler, *Tagebücher 1918–1937* (Frankfurt-am-Main, 1961), as quoted in the historical appendix of Rolf Hochhuth, *The Deputy* (New York: Grove Press, 1964), p. 296.

25. *National Catholic Reporter*, December 15, 1972, p. 13.

26. Ibid., December 22, 1972, p. 3.

27. Falconi, *The Popes in the Twentieth Century*, p. 233.

28. Letter in *The Tablet*, June 1963, p. 2.

29. Carlo Falconi, *The Silence of Pius XII* (Boston, 1970), pp. 85–98.

30. Quoted in *Actes et documents* 4:11. According to the diary of Joseph Goebbels, in 1943 Pius XII tried through an Austrian prelate to convince the Nazis to reactivate the concordat, to free the priests from Dachau, to stop anti-Semitic prosecutions, and to unite with England and the United States against the U.S.S.R. In a recent article (Robert A. Graham, S.J., "Goebbels e il Vaticano nel 1943: Un enigma risolto," *La Civiltà Cattolica*, no. 2984 [October 19, 1974]), a major expert on Vatican diplomacy tries to minimize the importance of that revelation.

31. Hochhuth, *The Deputy*, p. 352.

32. *National Catholic Reporter*, April 20, 1973, p. 6, and *New York Times*, April 5, 1973, pp. 1, 5.

33. Joseph L. Lichten, *A Question of Judgement: Pius XII and the Jews* (Washington, D.C., 1963).

34. Guenther Lewy, "Pius XII, the Jews and the German Catholic Church," in Eric Bentley, ed., *The Storm over "The Deputy"* (New York, 1964), p. 216.

35. *Italy—Republic without Government?* (New York, 1973), p. 50.

36. *Politica comunista*, p. 251.

37. "After three years of maneuvering against the Italian left, the U.S. assumed a direct role in the 1948 parliamentary elections. . . . Millions of dollars were covertly poured into the Christian Democratic coffers. . . . All in all, the C.I.A. funneled some $75 million to the Christian Democrats and other center and right parties between 1948 and 1972, $10 million in 1972 alone." (Joanne Barkan, "Democracy Italian Style," *Seven Days* [New York], June 16, 1978, p. 21.) See also Philip Agee and Louis Wolf, *Dirty Work: The CIA in Western Europe* (Secaucus, N.J.: Lyle Stuart, 1978).

38. Joseph La Palombara, *Interest Groups in Italian Politics* (Princeton, N.J., 1964), p. 30.

39. Ibid., p. 9.

40. Peter Nichols, *The Politics of the Vatican* (London, 1968). This information concerning the "Sturzo Operation" originates from two basic sources: a biography of De Gasperi written by his daughter, who had access to numerous documents including the unpublished diary of Emilio Bonomelli (Maria Romana de Gasperi, *De Gasperi, uomo solo* [Milan, 1964), and an article and a book written during the pontificate of John XXIII by a leading conservative Roman Christian Democrat, Giulio Andreotti.

41. Francis X. Murphy, *Pope John Comes to the Vatican* (New York: Robert M. McBride, 1959), pp. 195–196.

42. Chap. 2, n. 47.

CHAPTER VII

1. *Three Popes and the Cardinal* (New York, 1972), p. xiii. It must be pointed out, however, that Paul VI was more conservative on theological and, even more so, political issues than on social issues.

2. Quoted in Carlo Falconi, *La svolta di Paolo VI* (Rome, 1968), p. 25; my translation.

3. Quoted in Msgr. Pino Scabini, "Renewal of the Lay Apostolate Structures in Italy," *The Laity Today*, 1970, no. 6, p. 54.

4. Ibid., pp. 65–69.

5. On this particular means of control see *Le Monde*, October 6, 1968, p. 8.

6. *The Tablet* (London), August 31, 1968, pp. 878–879.

7. Reprinted in *National Catholic Reporter*, May 28, 1969, p. 1.

8. *La contestazione nella Chiesa* (Milan, 1969), pp. 210–214.

9. *Le Monde*, June 1, 1970, and *Informations Catholiques Internationales*, no. 363, (July 1970), p. 11.

10. *National Catholic Reporter*, December 17, 1971, pp. 1, 14, 15.

11. *Le Devoir*, May 20, 1971, p. 7.

12. Ibid., June 1, 1973, p. 16.

13. Desmond O'Grady, "Pope Opens Synod, Condemns Violence," *National Catholic Reporter*, October 4, 1974, p. 3.

14. Francis X. Murphy, "The Question in Rome is One of Bishop-Power," *New York Times*, September 29, 1974, p. 10E. The only sign of independence manifested by the bishops was their refusal to accept a document prepared by conservative curialists.

15. "Le Vatican au ralenti," *Le Monde*, weekly edition, December 16–22, 1976, p. 9.

16. *Informations Catholiques Internationales*, no. 326 (December 15, 1968), p. 12, and no. 331 (March 1, 1969), p. 15.

17. Michael Duggan, "Vatican Reserves Stand on Banning Population Book," *National Catholic Reporter*, March 14, 1975, pp. 1–2.

18. "Three Popes Speak to the CIO," *The Laity Today*, special issue on the CIOs, 1973, no. 13–14, p. 43.

19. *Acta Apostolicae Sedis* (Vatican City), 63 (1971):948–956 (English translation in *The Laity Today*, 1973, no. 13–14).

20. *The Laity Today*, 1973, no. 13–14, pp. 100–101.

21. Ibid., p. 95.

22. *National Catholic Reporter*, March 17, 1972, p. 2.

23. *Informations Catholiques Internationales*, no. 411 (July 1, 1972).

24. See, for example, the report "Family Life" in *The Laity Today*, special issue, 1970, no. 7–8; the texts from the Panafricano-Malagasy Laity Seminar, ibid., special issue, 1972, no. 11–12; and the texts in the study sessions on "The Christian in the University," ibid., 1973, no. 15–16. See also Paul VI's speech to the lay members and clerical "moderators" of the Council on the Laity, October 2, 1974, in *Acta Apostolicae Sedis* 66, no. 19 (October 31, 1974), in which he stressed the need for unity and communion with the hierarchy and approvingly quoted Ignatius of Antioch's famous "Let nothing be done outside the bishop," a dictum which had been stigmatized publicly at Vatican II by Bishop D'Souza, of Bhopal, India, as smacking of "clerical totalitarianism."

25. *La svolta di Paolo VI*, p. 189; my translation.

26. P. A. Allum, *Italy—Republic without Government?* (New York, 1973), p. 244.

27. See, for example, the article "Unita politica della Chiesa," *Il Regno* (Bologna), March 1, 1968, pp. 98–99, and the editorial "Per la chiarezza," *L'Osservatore Romano*, February 16, 1968, p. 2.

28. *Socialismo e facismo: "L'Ordine nuovo," 1921–1922* (Turin: Einaudi, 1967), p. 18–19.

29. *Vatican Council II* (New York, 1968), p. 274.

30. Ibid., pp. 274–275.

31. Pope John himself, in early 1963, had referred to Montini as a Hamlet-like figure, in a talk to priests from the diocese of Milan.

32. Quoted in Joseph Roddy, "The Vatican: The Power and the Glory are Passing," *Look* 35, no. 21 (October 19, 1971):24. The Catholic sociologist Gordon Zahn, although he gives less importance to economic factors and more to political ones, seems to substantially agree with my evaluation when he writes, in an essay on Paul VI's peace platform:

"The restraint which robs his words of any really productive impact is probably more institutional than personal, though as we shall see the latter is an important factor too. As long as the papacy jealously guards the fiction of 'Temporal sovereignty,' it will continue to feel bound by the rules of the diplomatic game with the almost inescapable result that, in any apparent clash between the two, papal concern for diplomatic formalities and procedures will take precedence over concerns of the moral order that may be involved. As a result when the pope does choose to speak his voice is likely to be muted and uncertain." ("Pilgrim for Peace," in James F. Andrews, ed., *Paul VI: Critical Appraisals* [New York, 1970], p. 73.)

33. *De l'actualité historique* (Paris, 1958), vol. 1.

34. *The Vatican Empire* (New York: Trident Press, 1968). See also, for example, Giovanni Grilli, *La finanza vaticana in Italia* (Rome, 1961); the series of articles by Desmond O'Grady in the weekly *National Catholic Reporter*, February 14–March 21, 1975; and Giancarlo Zizola, *Quale papa?* (Rome, 1977), pp. 238–261.

35. James Gollin, *Worldly Goods—The Wealth and Power of the American Catholic Church: The Vatican and the Men Who Control the Money* (New York: Random House, 1971).

36. Corrado Pallenberg, *Vatican Finances* (London: Penguin, 1973).

37. Ibid., pp. 26–27. Robert Hutchison, in an article on Vatican banking in the *Financial Post* (September 2, 1978, pp. 1, 4), says: "Under John XXIII, Peter's Pence averaged $11.5 million a year. But in the last years of Paul VI's reign it was said to have slipped to $2.3 million." Giovanni Cereti, in an article in *Concilium* (no. 137 [1978]) mentions similar figures: from $13 to $15 millions under John XXIII, and around $4 millions in recent years under Paul VI. Pallenberg says that the United States is the major contributor to Peter's Pence, with around a half million dollars or more a year. Cereti also mentions that $63 million netted in special pontifical collections for missionaries was distributed in 1975.

38. Pallenberg (p. 67) estimates the amount of that "gift" at U.S. $81 million, while Giancarlo Zizola, ("Les Comptes du Vatican," *Lumière et Vie*, nos. 129–130 [1976], pp. 127–147) talks of a billion lire in bonds and 740 million lire in cash. Zizola adds that Nogara bought gold, transferred capital to the United States before the war, and invested heavily in Italy after the war.

39. According to *The Economist* of London, March 27, 1965 the Vatican had investments valued at $4.8 billion. Some Vatican watchers put forward the sum of $12–15 billion, but this is clearly exaggerated, unless one includes in that amount the value of the Vatican's holdings in real estate, art, old books, etc. Gollin (see n. 35) does not agree with Le Bello on the extent of the Vatican's control over the Italian economy, but puts forth a similar figure for the total of Vatican investments around $500 million. Zizola, in his 1977 book (pp. 255–256) estimates the total productive capital of the Vatican at over $825 million. In my view, the wide discrepancies in the estimates result in good part because the various critics of the Vatican have very little secure information to draw from and because their terminology (e.g. "wealth," "assets," "investments," and "productive capital") can include very different things. My impression is that those who mention a $5 billion figure are talking more in terms of total wealth or assets (including real estate) and that those who talk of $500 million to $1 billion are talking of investments or productive capital only.

40. Reported in Pallenberg, p. 182. Gollin, on the other hand, estimates the amount in the United States to be close to $80 million and the total of Vatican investments in Italian companies to be around $300 million.

41. *The Politics of the Vatican* (London, 1968), p. 168.

42. Malachi Martin, *Three Popes and a Cardinal* (New York, 1972), p. 8.

43. *The Vatican Empire*, p. 36.

44. Desmond O'Grady, "Vatican to Make Financial Changes," *National Catholic Reporter*, July 10, 1970, p. 5.

45. Issue of July 21, 1970, p. 1.

46. Quoted in Pallenberg, *Vatican Finances*, p. 195.

47. Desmond O'Grady, "The Vatican Purse," pt. 1, *National Catholic Reporter*, February 21, 1975, p. 3. *L'Europeo* estimated the loss at $750 million, which seems a bit exaggerated.

48. Desmond O'Grady, "The Vatican Purse," pt. 2, ibid., February 28, 1975, p. 15. See also *Business Week*, March 3, 1975, p. 53, and *Financial Post*, September 2, 1978, p. 4.

49. On January 16 the secretary of state announced that the Holy See was in a desperate financial situation because of the raise given to curia employees by Paul VI on January 1. Villot did not mention the fall of stock market prices and bad investments as other reasons, although Professor Federico Allessandrini had authoritatively confirmed earlier in the *Osservatore Romano* that the Vatican had lost a lot of money in the crash of Michele Sindona's Unione Bank. See, for example, the article in *Le Jour* (Montreal), January 23, 1975, p. 5.

50. Desmond O'Grady, "$: Vatican Flap Again?" *National Catholic Reporter*, June 4, 1976, p. 6. See also *Business Week*, December 24, 1979.

51. Op. cit. (see n. 35), pp. 489–497.

52. *The Tablet* June 21, 1963, quoted in Jacques Nobécourt, *Le Vicaire et l'histoire* (Paris, 1964), p. 338.

53. Carl Boggs, Jr., "The Italian Left: A New Political Synthesis," *Socialist Revolution* 2, no. 3 (May–June 1972):92–93.

54. Pp. 181–182.

55. Ernst Troeltsch, *The Social Teachings of the Christian Churches* (New York, 1931), 1:349.

56. Lo Bello notes: "To understand in part, how the Christian Democrats have managed to retain control for a quarter of a century, one must examine the role of Catholic Action in Italy" (op. cit., p. 150).

57. "On International Working-Class Unity," *Political Affairs*, 43, no. 10 (October 1964):44–45.

58. Peter L. Berger and Thomas Luckmann, "Aspects sociologiques du pluralisme religieux," *Archives de Sociologie des Religions* 23 (1967):120.

59. *Oeuvres choisies* (Paris: Editions Sociales, 1959), p. 205; my translation.

60. *Economy and Society* (New York, 1968), 3:1165.

61. Ibid.

62. Alain Touraine, one of the outstanding contemporary French sociologists, expresses this view of the Church in the following way: "In the West, the Catholic Church was a large organization both centralized and diversified, with its study centers, its production services, its mechanisms of social control, its methods of socialisation" (*Pour la sociologie* [Paris, Seuil, 1974], p. 136; my translation).

63. *Current Sociology* 21, no. 2 (1973):35.

CHAPTER VIII

1. Franz X. Kaufmann, "L'Eglise, organisation religieuse," *Concilium* 91 (January 1974):70.

2. Max Weber, *The Theory of Social and Economic Organization* (New York: Free Press, 1947), p. 154.

3. David Gabriel and David Larche, "La Contestation dans l'Eglise," *L'Homme et la société*, no. 16 (April–June 1970), pp. 340–341.

4. Even Talcott Parsons, when he placed his four categories of values as media in a similar hierarchy of control (money = *A*, power = *G*, influence = *I*, commitments = *L*), gets his inspiration from the Marxian-Weberian conceptual scheme, itself based on the Hegelian scheme and sharing with it the fundamental distinction between the economic infrastructure on the one hand, and the political-repressive, normative-ideological superstructure on the other. See his "The Political Aspects of Social Structure and Process," in David Easton, ed., *Varieties of Political Theory* (Englewood Cliffs, N.J.: Prentice-Hall, 1966), p. 111. See also his *The System of Modern Society* (Englewood Cliffs: Prentice-Hall, 1971), p. 1, where he refers to his intellectual roots: "Perhaps the most influential is German idealism, as it passed from Hegel through Marx to Weber."

5. A. Etzioni, *Modern Organizations* (Englewood Cliffs, N.J.: Prentice-Hall, 1964), p. 59.

6. John R. P. French and Bertram Raven, "The Bases of Social Power," in Dorwin Cartwright and Alvin Zander, eds., *Group Dynamics* (Evanston, Ill.: Row, Peterson, 1960), pp. 607–623. All that is missing here for a perfect synthesis of Weber and Etzioni is the mention of a sixth possibility, traditional power, which is particularly important in organizations which have a long history, like the Catholic Church.

7. One of these other authors is Gaston Fessard (*Autorité et bien commun* [Paris, 1969], p. 12), who gives three major meanings for the word *authority*: (1) juridical power, (2) de facto (i.e. social-structural) power, and (3) the power of values. See also Gene W. Dalton, Louis B. Barnes, and Abraham Zaleznik, *The Distribution of Authority in Formal Organizations* (Boston: Division of Research, Harvard Business School, 1968), Appendix: "The Concept of Authority and Organizational Change," pp. 199–212.

8. "The Problem of Conditioning in the Church," *Cross Currents*, Fall 1962, pp. 433–444. Similarly, a good example of traditional power is the use of "dramaturgy" as analyzed by T. R. Young and Garth Massey, "The Dramaturgical Society: A Micro-Analytic Approach to Dramaturgical Analysis," a mimeographed paper (Red Feather, Colo.: The Red Feather Institute, 1978).

9. *The Cross and the Fasces* (Stanford, Calif., 1960), pp. 184–185.

10. "One of the solutions of this general crisis of capitalist imperialism (and favored especially by the Vatican) was a federation of the Catholic states in southern Europe which would be a homeland for world Catholicism, provide the Vatican with a broad geographical basis, and serve as a bulwark against communist intrusion and intervention" (Scott Nearing, *The Making of a Radical* [New York: Harper, 1972], p. 182).

Today the Vatican pursues its ideal in a slightly different way. It seems to be trying to establish a sort of social-democratic third way between capitalism and socialism, between the United States and the USSR. It sees European unity as one of the best vehicles for attaining that goal since, in a united Europe, a strong Catholic bloc could help preserve Church influence. The preoccupation with ecological and remunerative power remains, but there is also an interest in the legal and social power that cooperation with the state can furnish.

11. *Interest Groups in Italian Politics* (Princeton, N.J., 1964), p. 354.

12. Ibid., pp. 333–334.

13. Ibid., pp. 337, 362–363.

14. "Bureaucratic Change in the Mexican Catholic Church, 1926 to 1950" (Ph.D. diss., University of California, Berkeley, 1966), p. 138.

15. "Structural Sociology," in J. C. McKinney and E. A. Tiryakian, *Theoretical Sociology: Perspectives and Developments* (New York: Appleton-Century-Crofts, 1970), p. 135.

16. "The Heart of Unity," in Michael de la Bédoyère, ed., *The Future of Catholic Christianity* (Philadelphia: Lippincott, 1970), pp. 144.

17. "The Pope in an Age of Insecurity," in James F. Andrews, ed., *Paul VI: Critical Appraisals* (New York, 1970).

18. *Une Eglise cassée* (Paris, 1971).

19. *The Catholic Crisis* (Boston, 1969).

20. Ibid., pp. 2, 244–247.

21. *The Grave of God* (New York, 1967), chap. 1.

22. *L'Eglise à l'heure de l'Amérique latine* (Tournai: Casterman, 1965), chap. 5.

23. *Les Analyseurs de l'Eglise* (Paris, 1972), p. 57.

24. *Vatican II et l'évolution de l'Eglise* (Paris, 1969), chap. 1.

25. "The Style of Paul's Leadership," in Andrews, op. cit.

26. Ibid., p. 130.

27. Ibid.

28. "Pilgrim for Peace," ibid., p. 73.

29. *La svolta di Paolo VI* (Rome, 1968), p. 312; my translation.

30. Ibid., p. 303; my translation.

31. English translation, "The CIA in Italy: An Interview with Victor Marchetti," in Philip Agee and Louis Wolf, eds., *Dirty Work: The CIA in Western Europe* (Secaucus, N.J.: Lyle, Stuart, 1978). See also Philip Agee, *Inside the Company: A CIA Diary* (London: Penguin, 1975). Agee indicates that Pax Romana and the International Catholic Youth Federation were indirectly used by the CIA for student and youth operations. *Time* magazine, September 11, 1973, revealed that the CIA had used the Christian Democratic parties of various European countries, including Italy, to channel funds secretly to the Chilean Christian Democrats to help overturn Allende's government. Both Marchetti and Agee are former CIA agents with an excellent knowledge of CIA ways of doing things.

32. Desmond O'Grady, "The Vatican Purse," pts. 1 and 2, *National Catholic Reporter*, February 21 and 28, 1975. O'Grady's first article reported that Swiss banking authorities in Geneva, where the last of Sidona's banks closed its doors in January 1975, estimated that when the full losses on Sidona's empire are finally computed, "The Vatican share could well exceed $240 million."

33. In *Catholicism, Social Control and Modernization in Latin America* (Englewood Cliffs, N.J.: Prentice-Hall, 1970), Ivan Vallier shows that the Church's potential for social control varies with the kind of relationship the Church entertains with political powers and civil society.

34. IDOC-France, *"Se Cristo Vedesse": Si le Christ voyait cela. Des Chrétiens écrivent au pape* (Paris: Editions de l'Epi, 1968), pp. 20–21; my translation.

35. *Le Devoir*, March 15, 1974, p. 18, and *National Catholic Reporter*, March 22, 1974, p. 6.

36. Reported in the *San Diego Union*, December 17, 1976, p. A-19,

"Pope Tightens Grip on Two Lay Forums," and *Los Angeles Times,* December 18, pt. 1, p. 32, "Pope Establishes Two Watchdog Agencies." See also Desmond O'Grady, "Bodies in Limbo," *National Catholic Reporter,* October 15, 1976, p. 2.

37. Robert Delany, "Holy See to Laity: Listen, Pray, Don't Think," *National Catholic Reporter,* November 21, 1975, p. 18. The December 1976 degree stipulated that the Pontifical Commission for Justice and Peace could take no declaration or initiative without the approval of the Secretariate of State.

38. *Le Devoir,* May 20, 1971, p. 6.

39. In an evaluation of Paul VI's pontificate, Desmond O'Grady stated: "Paul has protected papal authority so well from the threat the bishops might have presented that the synod is emasculated. And if he is worried about bishops, there is no chance of another world congress of the laity." ("Pope Paul VI: Priest and Pontiff," pt. 1, *National Catholic Reporter,* October 10, 1975, p. 13.)

40. Ibid., p. 13.

41. The following reconstruction of what seems to have happened during the two conclaves of 1978 is based on the reports of Vatican experts Peter Hebblethwaite, Andrew Greeley, Francis X. Murphy, Alain Woodrow, Kenneth L. Woodward, and Giancarlo Zizola which appeared in the *National Catholic Reporter, La Presse, Le Monde, Newsweek,* and *Il Giorno* in the first few weeks afterward. These experts based their reports on leaks and, especially, on public remarks of many cardinals who did not realize that the limited information they were giving, added to that of the others, finally permitted the well-guarded secrecy of the conclaves to be pierced. Hebblethwaite and Greeley each published a book in 1979 on the double conclave of 1978. Francis X. Murphy wrote a devastating critique of Greeley's book in the *National Catholic Reporter,* June 15, 1979 (pp. 17, 21), calling its accounts and evaluations "far from accurate," "far from factual," "calumnious," and "in bad taste," and stigmatizing the book as being "yellow journalism," "riddled with error," "unworthy," and "one of the least authentic books written about the papacy in ages." In contrast, Hebblethwaite's book was said to be "dignified and factual" (see also the favorable review, ibid., March 16, 1979).

42. Giancarlo Zizola, "Le Diocèse de Rome," *Informations Catholiques Internationales,* no. 367 (September 1, 1970), pp. 20–29. See also Falconi, *La svolta di Paolo VI,* p. 96, and H. Küng's article in *Le Monde,* October 17, 1979.

43. In a brief but important article in which he discusses the question of research on religious organizations, F. X. Kaufmann shows that the sociology of religion has neglected to study the organizational aspects of religious phenomena, and that problems in that area have been further compounded by a tendency, especially in Catholicism, to dissimulate problems of organization behind a theological façade. According to him, the bureaucratic

character of the Church, the forms of hierocratic power used by its top leaders, and the legitimating veil of sacralization have developed over a long period of time in response to the emergence of various political forms. Kaufmann thinks that because of the current general disaffection toward bureaucracy, organized religion will be increasingly unable to remain the object of positive affective identification on the part of its members. ("Religion et bureaucratie: Le Problème de l'organisation religieuse," *Social Compass* 21, no. 1 [1974]:101–107.)

44. René Lourau, one of the sociologists of the new French school of institutional analysis, seems to think along these lines, as we can see from his book on the Catholic Church: "Déclergification et autogestion dans l'église: qu'on le veuille ou non, et que le socianalyste le veuille ou non, c'est dans cette double stratégie que l'analyse institutionnelle sur le terrain est impliquée politiquement" (*Les Analyseurs de l'Eglise* [Paris, 1972], p. 295).

In a somewhat similar vein, Michel Carrouges concludes his book on the laity by saying that the problem of the laity is "above all the problem of the emancipation of salaried workers in the Church, a problem that is inseparable from their emancipation in society." For Carrouges, the emancipation of laymen and the emancipation of workers are problems that are intimately linked. The higher clergy have wanted to make use of an active laity to promote the Church's alliance with conservative forces in society, but active Catholic laymen are reluctant to play that role because they are often linked to sectors of society struggling for equality and liberation. That is the root of the dilemma. Church authorities need the layman and want to control him, but very few laymen are willing to function as docile sheep under the guidance of conservative ecclesiastical shepherds. We have here a fundamental opposition between the needs of grass-roots Catholics and the requirements of the top officials of the Church. (See Carrouges, *Le Laïcat: Mythes et réalités* [Paris, 1964], p. 221.)

Selected Bibliography

Abbot, Walter M., S. J., ed. *The Documents of Vatican II.* New York: Guild Press, 1966.

Actes et documents du Saint-Siège relatifs à la seconde guerre mondiale. 8 vols. Vatican City: Libreria Editrice Vaticana, 1965–1974.

Acton, Lord. *Essays on Church and State.* London: Hollis and Carter, 1952.

Adolfs, Robert. *The Grave of God.* New York: Harper and Row, 1966.

Algisi, Leone. *John the Twenty-third.* London: Longman and Todd, 1963.

Alix, Christine. *Le Saint-Siège et les nationalismes en Europe: 1870–1960.* Paris: Sirey, 1962.

Allum, P. A. *Politics and Society in Post-War Naples.* Cambridge: Cambridge University Press, 1973.

———. *Italy—Republic without Government?* New York: Norton, 1973.

Ambrosoli, Luigi. "Interpretazioni e studi sul movimento cattolico italiano." *Movimento operaio,* 7 (January–February 1955): 135–150.

Andreotti, G. *De Gasperi e il suo tempo.* Milan: Mondadori, 1965.

Andrews, James F., ed. *Paul VI: Critical Appraisals.* New York: Bruce Publishing Co., 1970.

Annuario Pontificio. Vatican City. Published annually since 1943.

Atti e documenti della Democrazia Cristiana, 1943–1967. Rome: Cinque Lune, 1968.

Balducci, Ernesto. *John "The Transitional Pope."* London: Burns and Oates, 1965.

Basso, Lelio. *Due totalitarismi: Facismo e Democrazia Cristiana.* Milan: Nuova Academia, 1951.

Bazelaire, D. *Les Laïcs aussi sont l'Eglise.* Paris: Fayard, 1958.

Beales, A. C. F. *The Catholic Church and International Order.* London: Penguin, 1941.

Beals, Ralph Carleton. "Bureaucratic Change in the Mexican Catholic Church, 1926 to 1950." Ph.D. dissertation, University of California, 1966.

Bentley, Eric, ed. *The Storm over "The Deputy."* New York: Grove Press, 1964.

Berger, Peter L. *The Noise of Solemn Assemblies.* Garden City, N.Y.: Doubleday, 1961.

———. *The Precarious Vision.* Garden City, N.Y.: Doubleday, 1961.

———. *The Sacred Canopy: Elements of a Sociological Theory of Religion.* New York: Doubleday, 1967.

Binchy, D. A. *Church and State in Fascist Italy.* London: Oxford University Press, 1941.

Blanshard, Paul. *American Freedom and Catholic Power.* Boston: Beacon Press, 1958.

———. *Paul Blanshard On Vatican II.* Boston: Beacon Press, 1966.

Bosworth, William. *Catholicism and Crisis in Modern France: French Catholic Groups at the Threshold of the Fifth Republic.* Princeton, N.J.: Princeton University Press, 1962.

Breines, A. R. "The Catholic Layman in Time of Crisis: A Study in Sociology of Religion." Microfilmed. Ann Arbor: University of Michigan, 1959.

Bright, Laurence O. P., ed. *The People of God.* London: Sheed and Ward, 1965.

———, and Clements, Simon, eds. *The Committed Church.* London: Darton, Longman and Todd, 1966.

Brown, Robert McAfee. *Observer in Rome.* New York: Doubleday, 1964.

Bull, George. *Vatican Politics at the Second Vatican Council, 1962-1965.* Oxford: Oxford University Press, 1966.

Bury, John Bagnell. *History of the Papacy in the Nineteenth Century (1864-1878).* London: Macmillan, 1930.

Cadet, Jean. *Le Laïcat et le droit de l'Eglise.* Paris: Vie Nouvelle, 1960.

Callahan, Daniel. *The Mind of the Catholic Layman.* New York: Scribner's, 1963.

Camp, Richard L. *The Papal Ideology of Social Reform: A Study in Historical Development, 1878-1967.* Leiden: Brill, 1969.

Candeloro, Giorgio. *L'Azione Cattolica in Italia.* Rome: Edizioni di Cultura Sociale, 1950.

———. *Il movimento cattolico in Italia.* Rome: Edizioni Rinascita, 1955.

———. *Storia dell'Italia moderna.* 4 vols. Milan: Feltrinelli, 1956-1964.

Caporale, Rocco. "The Dynamics of Hierarchy: A Study of Continuity-

Change of a Religious System. The Second Vatican Council of the Roman Catholic Church.'' Ph.D. dissertation, Dept. of Sociology, Columbia University, New York, 1965.

Caporale, Rock. *Vatican II: Last of the Councils.* Baltimore: Helicon Press, 1964.

Capovilla, Loris. *The Heart and Mind of John XXIII.* London: Corgi Books, 1964.

Carrier, Hervé, and Pin, E. *Sociology of Christianity: International Bibliography.* Rome: Gregorian University Press, 1964.

Carrouges, Michel. *Le Laïcat: Mythes et réalités. Le Peuple a-t-il sa place dans l'Eglise?* Paris: Editions du Centurion, 1964.

Casanova, Antoine. *Vatican II et l'évolution de l'Eglise.* Paris: Editions Sociales, 1969.

Cassidy, Sally Whelan. "Some Aspects of Lay Leadership." Ph.D. dissertation, University of Chicago, 1959.

Cavallari, Alberto. *The Changing Vatican.* New York: Doubleday, 1967.

Cervelli, I. *I cattolici dall'unità alla fondazione del Partito Popolare.* Bologna: Universale Coppelli, 1969.

Cianfarra, C. M. *The War and the Vatican.* London: Burns and Oates, 1945.

Civardi, Luigi. *Compendio di storia della Azione Cattolica Italiana.* Rome: Coletti Editore, 1956.

Charles-Roux, François. *Huit ans au Vatican, 1932–1940.* Paris: Flammarion, 1947.

Chasseriaud, J. P. *Le Parti Démocrate-Chrétien en Italie.* Paris: Armand Colin, 1965.

Chevalier, Jean. *La Politique du Vatican.* Paris: S.G.P.P., 1969.

Clough, Shepard B., and Saladino, Salvatore. *A History of Modern Italy.* New York: Columbia University Press, 1968.

Congar, Yves. *La Crise dans l'Eglise et Mgr. Lefebvre.* Paris: Editions du Cerf, 1977.

———. *Jalons pour une théologie du laïcat.* Paris: Editions du Cerf, 1964.

———. *Laity, Church and World.* Baltimore: Helicon Press, 1961.

———. *Lay People in the Church: A Study for a Theology of the Laity.* Westminster, Md.: Newman Press, 1957.

Conti-Guglia, C. "La pia lega dell'apostolato," *Studi sociali* 1, no. 4 (July–August 1961): 224–241.

Corghi, Corrado. *Dalla Democrazia Cristiana alla "Nuova Sinistra."* Florence: Cultura, 1969.

Coutrot, Aline. *Un Courant de la pensée catholique: L'Hebdomadaire Sept (1934–1937).* Paris: Editions du Cerf, 1961.

———, and Dreyfus, François G. *Les Forces religieuses dans la société française.* Paris: Armand Colin, 1966.

Cross, Robert D. *The Emergence of Liberal Catholicism in America.* Cambridge, Mass.: Harvard University Press, 1958.

Dalton, Gene W., Barnes, Louis B., and Zaleznik, Abraham. *The Distribution of Authority in Formal Organizations.* Boston: Division of Research, Harvard Business School, 1968.

Dansette, Adrien. *Destin du catholicisme français, 1926-1956.* Paris: Flammarion, 1957.

―――. *Histoire religieuse de la France contemporaine.* 2 vols. Paris: Flammarion, 1948-1951.

Davidson, A. "The Tendencies towards Reformism in the Italian Communist Party, 1921-1963," *Australian Journal of Politics and History,* no. 3 (December 1965): 335-349.

De Gasperi, Maria Romana. *De Gasperi, uomo solo.* Milan, 1964.

De Kadt, E. J. *Catholic Radicals in Brazil.* London: Oxford University Press, 1970.

De La Bédoyère, M. *The Future of Catholic Christianity.* Philadelphia: Lippincott, 1966.

―――. *The Layman in the Church.* London: Burns and Oates, 1954.

Della Torre, G. *Memorie.* Milan: Mondadori, 1965.

De Lubac, Henri. *Catholicism: A Study of Dogma in Relation to the Corporate Destiny of Mankind.* New York: Menton Omega, 1964.

De Rosa, Gabriele. *L'Azione Cattolica: Storia politica dal 1874 al 1904.* Bari: Editori Laterza, 1953.

―――. *L'Azione Cattolica: Storia politica dal 1905 al 1919.* Bari: Editori Laterza, 1954.

―――. *Il movimento cattolico in Italia dalla restaurazione all'eta giolittiana.* Bari: Laterza, 1970.

―――. *Il Partito Popolare.* Bari: Laterza, 1969.

De Rossi, G. *Il Partito Popolare Italiano dalla fondazione al 1920.* Rome: Ferrari, 1920.

Desroches, Henri. *Marxisme et religion.* Paris: P.U.F., 1962.

Domenach, J. M., and De Montalvon, R. *The Catholic Avant-Garde: French Catholicism since World War II.* New York: Holt, Rinehart and Winston, 1967.

Dulles, Avery. *Models of the Church.* New York: Doubleday, 1974.

Dulong, Renaud. *Une Eglise cassée: Essai sociologique sur la crise de l'Eglise catholique.* Paris: Editions Ouvrières, 1971.

Durkheim, Emile. *Les Formes élémentaires de la vie religieuse.* Paris: Alcan, 1912.

Eagleton, Terry. *The New Left Church.* London: Sheed and Ward, 1966.

Edwards, David L. *Priests and Workers: An Anglo-French Discussion.* London: SCM Press, 1961.

Einaudi, Mario, and Goguel, François. *Christian Democracy in Italy and France.* Notre Dame, Ind.: Notre Dame University Press, 1952.

Ellis, John T. *American Catholicism.* Chicago: University of Chicago Press, 1955.

Falconi, Carlo. *La Chiesa e le organizzazioni cattoliche in Europa.* Milan: Edizioni di Communità, 1950.

————. *La Chiesa e le organizzazioni cattoliche in Italia (1945–1955).* Turin: Einaudi, 1956.

————. *La contestazione nella Chiesa.* Milan: Feltrinelli, 1969.

————. *Luizi Gedda e l'Azione Cattolica.* Florence: Parenti Editore, 1958.

————. *El Pentagono Vaticano.* Bari: Laterza, 1958.

————. *The Popes in the Twentieth Century.* Boston: Little, Brown, 1967.

————. *The Silence of Pius XII.* Boston: Little, Brown, 1970.

————. *La svolta di Paolo VI: Valutazione critica del suo pontificato.* Rome: Ubaldini, 1968.

Ferrari, Francesco Luigi. *L'Azione Cattolica e il "regime."* Florence: Parenti Editore, 1957.

Fesquet, Henri. *The Drama of Vatican II: The Ecumenical Council, June 1962–December 1965.* New York: Random House, 1967.

————. *Une Eglise en état de péché mortel.* Paris: Grasset, 1968.

————. *Le Journal du premier synode catholique.* Paris: Robert Morel, 1968.

Fessard, Gaston. *Autorité et bien commun.* Paris: Aubier-Montaigne, 1969.

————. *De l'actualité historique.* 2 vols. Paris: Desclée de Brouver, 1960.

Fisher, Desmond. *The Church in Transition.* London: Geoffrey Chapman, 1967.

Fitzsimons, Mathew A., et al., eds. *The Catholic Church in the Twentieth Century: A Study of the Church throughout the World.* 6 vols. Notre Dame, Ind.: University of Notre Dame Press, 1970.

Fogarty, M. *Christian Democracy in Western Europe: 1820–1953.* London: Routledge and Kegan Paul, 1957.

Franck, Frederick. *Exploding Church: From Catholicism to catholicism.* New York: Delacorte Press, 1968.

Freemantle, Anne, ed. *The Papal Encyclicals in their Historical Context.* New York: New American Library, 1963.

French, John P. R., and Raven, Bertram. "The Bases of the Social Power." In *Group Dynamics,* edited by Darwin Cartwright and Alvin Zander. 3d ed. New York: Harper and Row, 1968.

Friedlander, Saul. *Pius XII and The Third Reich.* New York: Knopf, 1966.

Galeazzi-Lisi. *Dans l'ombre et la lumière de Pie XII.* Paris: Flammarion, 1960.

Galli, G., and Prandi, A. *Patterns of Political Participation in Italy.* New Haven: Yale University Press, 1970.

Garrone, C. *L'Action Catholique: Son histoire, sa doctrine, son panorama.* Paris: Fayard, 1958.

Giovanetti, Alberto. *Il Vaticano e la guerra (1939–1940).* Vatican City: Libreria Editrice Vaticana, 1960.

Glock, Charles Y., Ringer, Benjamin R., and Babbie, Earl R. *To Comfort and to Challenge: The Dilemma of the Contemporary Church.* Berkeley and Los Angeles: University of California Press, 1967.

————, and Stark, Rodney. *Christian Beliefs and Anti-Semitism.* New York: Harper and Row, 1966.

————, ————. *Religion and Society in Tension.* Chicago: Rand McNally, 1965.

Gorresio, Vittorio. *The New Mission of Pope John XXIII.* New York: Funk and Wagnalls, 1970.

————, ed. *Stato e chiesa.* Bari: Laterza, 1957.

Gouldner, Alvin W. *Patterns of Industrial Bureaucracy.* New York: Free Press, Macmillan, 1954.

Graham, Robert. *Vatican Diplomacy: A Study of Church and State on the International Plane.* Princeton, N.J.: Princeton University Press, 1959.

Gramsci, Antonio, *The Modern Prince and Other Writings.* New York: International Publishers, 1957.

————. *Opere di Antonio Gramsci.* 11 vols. Turin: Einaudi, 1947–1960.

————. *Selections from the Prison Notebooks.* London: Laurence and Wishart, 1971.

Grilli, Giovanni. *La finanza vaticana in Italia.* Rome, 1961.

Grisoni, D., and Maggiori, R. *Lire Gramsci.* Paris: Editions Universitaires, 1973.

Group 2000, eds. *The Church Today: Commentaries on the Pastoral Constitution on the Church in the Modern World.* Westminster, Md.: Newman Press, 1968.

Gruppo-Praesenza. *Crisi a l'Avvenire d'Italia.* Florence: Cultura, 1970.

Guichard, Jacques. *Eglise, lutte de classes et stratégies politiques.* Paris: Editions du Cerf, 1972.

Guilmot, Paul. *Fin d'une église cléricale? Le débat en France de 1945 à nos jours.* Paris: Editions du Cerf, 1969.

Guitton, Jean. *The Pope Speaks: Dialogues of Paul VI with Jean Guitton.* New York: Meredith Press, 1968.

Hales, E. E. Y. *The Catholic Church in the Modern World.* New York: Doubleday, 1960.

————. *Revolution and Papacy.* Notre Dame, Ind.: University of Notre Dame Press, 1966.

Harrison, Paul M. *Authority and Power in the Free Church Tradition: A Social Case Study of the American Baptist Convention.* Princeton, N.J.: Princeton University Press, 1959.

Hatch, Edwin. *The Organization of the Early Christian Churches.* New York: Burt Franklin, 1972.

Hebblethwaite, Peter. *"Inside" the Synod: Rome, 1967.* New York: Paulist Press, 1968.

Hervieu-Léger, Danièle. *De la mission à la protestation: L'Evolution des étudiants chrétiens en France (1965–1970).* Paris: Editions du Cerf, 1973.

Hobsbawn, E. J. *The Age of Revolution: 1789–1848.* Cleveland: World, 1962.

Houtart, François. *The Challenge to Change: The Church Confronts the Future.* New York: Sheed and Ward, 1964.

————. *L'éclatement d'une église.* Paris: Mame, 1969.

————. *The Eleventh Hour.* New York: Sheed and Ward, 1968.

Hoyt, Robert G., ed. *Issues That Divide the Church.* New York: Macmillan, 1967.

Hughes, H. Stuart. "Pope John's Revolution: Secular or Religious?" *Commonweal* 83, 10 (December 1965): 301–303.

————. *The United States and Italy.* Cambridge, Mass.: Harvard University Press, 1965.

Jacini, A. *Storia del Partito Popolare Italiano.* Milan: Garzanti, 1951.

Jemolo, Arturo Carlo. *Chiesa e stato in Italia negli ultimi cento anni.* Turin: Einaudi, 1958.

Katz, Fred E. *Autonomy and Organization: The Limits of Social Control.* New York: Random House, 1968.

Kautsky, Karl. *Foundations of Christianity: A Study of Christian Origins.* New York: Russell and Russell, 1953.

Keating, Edward. *The Scandal of Silence: A Powerful Lay Critique of the Catholic Church in the United States.* New York: Random House, 1965.

Kogan, N. *A Political History of Postwar Italy.* New York: Praeger, 1966.

Küng, Hans. *The Church.* New York: Sheed and Ward, 1967.

————. *The Council in Action: Theological Reflections on the Second Vatican Council.* New York: Sheed and Ward, 1963.

————. *The Council, Reform and Reunion.* New York: Sheed and Ward, 1961.

La Malfa, U. *La politica economica in Italia, 1946–1962.* Milan: Communità, 1962.

La Palombara, Joseph. *Interest Groups in Italian Politics.* Princeton, N.J.: Princeton University Press, 1964.

————. *Italy: The Politics of Planning.* Syracuse, N.Y.: Syracuse University Press, 1966.

Larson, Martin A. *Church Wealth and Business Income.* New York: Philosophical Library, 1965.

Latourette, Kenneth Scott. *A History of Christianity.* New York: Harper and Row, 1953.

Latreille, André, and Remond, René. *Histoire du catholicisme en France.* Vol. 3. *La Période contemporaine.* Paris: Spes, 1962.

Laurentin, René. *Le premier synode: histoire et bilan.* Paris: Le Seuil, 1968.

The Lay Apostolate: Papal Teachings Selected and Arranged by the Benedictine Monks of Solesmes. Boston: St. Paul Editions, 1961.

Lewy, Guenther. *The Catholic Church and Nazi Germany.* New York: McGraw-Hill, 1964.

Lichten, Joseph L. *A Question of Judgment: Pius XII and the Jews.* Washington, D.C.: National Catholic Welfare Conference, 1963.

Lo Bello, Nino. *The Vatican Empire.* New York: Trident Press, 1968.

Lourau, René. *Les analyseurs de l'Eglise: analyse institutionnelle en milieu chrétien.* Paris: Editions Anthropos, 1972.

Luckmann, Thomas. *The Invisible Religion.* New York: Macmillan, 1967.

Maccarone, Michele. *Il nazionalsocialismo e la Santa Sede.* Rome: Editrice Studium, 1947.

Macciochi, M. A. *Pour Gramsci.* Paris: Le Seuil, 1974.

MacEoin, Gary. *What Happened at the Council and Its Implications for the Modern World.* New York: Holt, Rinehart and Winston, 1967.

———, and the Committee for the Responsible Election of the Pope. *The Inner Elite: Dossiers of Papal Candidates.* Kansas City: Sheed, Andrews and McMeer, 1978.

MacGregor, Geddes. *The Vatican Revolution.* Boston: Beacon Press, 1957.

Mack-Smith, D. *Italy: A Modern History.* Ann Arbor: University of Michigan Press, 1959.

McKenzie, John L. *Authority in the Church.* New York: Sheed and Ward, 1966.

———. *The Roman Catholic Church.* New York: Doubleday, 1971.

Magri, F. *La DC in Italia.* 2 vols. Milan: La Fiaccola, 1954–1955.

Maier, Hans. *Revolution and Church: The Early History of Christian Democracy, 1789–1901.* Notre Dame, Ind.: University of Notre Dame Press, 1969.

Mammaulla, Giuseppe. *Italy after Fascism: A Political History, 1943–1965.* Notre Dame, Ind.: University of Notre Dame Press, 1966.

Markmann, Charles Lam. *Mussolini's Italy.* New York: Macmillan, 1973.

Martin, Malachi. *Three Popes and the Cardinal.* New York: Farrar, Straus and Giroux, 1972.

——— [pseud. Michael Serafian]. *The Pilgrim.* New York: Farrar, Straus and Giroux, 1964.

Martini, A. "Gli ultimi giorni di Pio XI." *La Civiltà Cattolica,* no. 4, 1959, pp. 236–250.

Marx, Karl, and Engels, Friedrich. *On Religion.* Moscow: Foreign Languages Publishing House, 1957.

Mathes, Joachim, ed. *International Yearbooks for the Sociology of Religion.* Vol. 1. *Religious Pluralism and Social Structure.* Stuttgart: Westdeutscher Verlag Köhn und Opladen, 1965.

Metz, René, and Schlick, Jean. *Les groupes informels dans l'Eglise.* Deuxième colloque du Cerdic, Strasbourg, May 13–15, 1971. Strasbourg: Cerdic-Publications, 1971.

Meynaud, Jean. *Rapport sur la classe dirigeante italienne.* Lausanne: E.S.O., 1968.

Michels, Roberto. *Political Parties: A Sociological Study of the Oligarchical Tendencies of Modern Democracy.* New York: Collin Books, 1962.

———. *Il proletariato e la borghesia nel movimento socialista italiano.* Turin: Fratelli Bocca, 1908.

Middleton, Neil. *Catholics and the Left.* Springfield, Ill.: Templegate, 1966.

Miliband, Ralph. *The State in Capitalist Society*. London: Weidenfeld and Nicholson, 1969.

Molette, Charles. *L'Association Catholique de la Jeunesse Française (1886–1907): une prise de conscience du laïcat catholique*. Paris: Librairie Armand Colin, 1968.

Moltmann, Jurgen. *Religion, Revolution and the Future*. New York: Scribners, 1969.

Montuclard, M. *Conscience religieuse et démocratie*. Paris: Le Seuil, 1965.

———. "Aux origines de la démocratie chrétienne." *Archives de Sociologie des Religions* 3, no. 6 (July–December 1958): 47–89.

Murphy, Francis X., C.S.S.R. [pseud. Xavier Rynne]. *Vatican Council II*. New York: Farrar, Straus and Giroux, 1968.

———, and MacEoin, Gary. *Synod '67: A New Sound in Rome*. Montreal: Palm Publishers, 1968.

Mutchler, David E. *The Church as a Political Factor in Latin America*. New York: Praeger, 1971.

Nautin, Pierre. "L'origine des structures actuelles de l'Eglise." *La Lettre*, no. 188 (April 1974), pp. 20–24.

Naville, Robert. *The World of the Vatican*. New York: Harper and Row, 1962.

Neuvecelle, Jean. *The Vatican: Its Organization, Customs and Way of Life*. New York: Criterion Books, 1955.

Newman, Jeremiah. *Change and the Catholic Church*. Baltimore: Helicon Press, 1966.

Nichols, Peter. *The Politics of the Vatican*. London: Pall Mall Press, 1968.

Nobecourt, Jacques. "Le Vicaire" et l'histoire. Paris: Le Seuil, 1964.

Nobis, Enrico. *Il governo invisibile*. Rome: Edizioni di Cultura Sociale, 1955.

O'Dea, Thomas. *American Catholic Dilemma: An Inquiry into the Intellectual Life*. New York: Sheed and Ward, 1958.

———. *The Catholic Crisis*. Boston: Beacon Press, 1968.

d'Ormesson, Wladimir. *Pie XII tel que je l'ai connu*. Paris: Pedone, 1968.

Otten, C. Michael. *University Authority and the Student: The Berkeley Experience*. Berkeley and Los Angeles: University of California Press, 1970.

Pallenberg, Corrado. *Inside the Vatican*. New York: Hawthorn Books, 1960.

———. *Paul VI: The Making of a Pope*. New York: Macfadden-Bartell Corporation, 1964.

Paris, Robert. *Histoire du fascisme en Italie: des origines à la prise de pouvoir*. Paris: Maspéro, 1962.

Pastor, Ludwig. *The History of the Popes, from the Close of the Middle Ages*. 40 vols. London: Routledge and Kegan Paul, 1928–1953.

Pernot, M. *Le Saint-Siège, l'Eglise catholique et la politique mondiale*. Paris: A. Colin, 1924.

Philip, Gerard. *The Role of the Laity in the Church*. Chicago: Fides Publications, 1956.

Pierantozzi, Libero. *I cattolici nella storia d'Italia (1870–1970).* Milan: Edizioni del Calendario, 1970.

Pin, E., and Houtard, François. *The Church and the Latin American Revolution.* New York: Sheed and Ward, 1965.

Poggi, Gianfranco. *Catholic Action in Italy: The Sociology of a Sponsored Organization.* Stanford, Calif.: Stanford University Press, 1967.

Portelli, Hugues. *Gramsci et la question religieuse.* Paris: Anthropos, 1974.

Poulain, Claude, and Wagnon, Claude. *L'Eglise: essai de critique radicale.* Paris: Editions de l'Epi, 1969.

Poulat, Emile. *Catholicisme, démocratie et socialisme: Le Mouvement catholique et Mgr Benigni de la naissance du socialisme à la victoire du fascisme.* Paris: Casterman, 1977.

———. *Eglise contre bourgeoisie: Introduction au devenir du catholicisme actuel.* Paris: Casterman, 1977.

———. *Histoire, dogme et critique dans la crise moderniste.* Paris: Casterman, 1962.

———. *Intégrisme et catholicisme intégral: un réseau secret international anti-moderniste. La "Sapinière" (1909–1921).* Paris: Casterman, 1969.

———. *Naissance des prêtres ouvriers.* Paris: Casterman, 1965.

Prandi, Alfonso. *Chiesa e politica: La gerarchia e l'impegno politico dei catholici in Italia.* Bologna: Il Mulino, 1968.

Prudy, W. A. *The Church on the Move: The Characters and Policies of Pius XII and John XXIII.* New York: John Day, 1966.

Rahner, Paul. *The Christian of the Future.* New York: Herder and Herder, 1967.

———. *The Church after the Council.* New York: Herder and Herder, 1967.

Rémond, René. *Forces religieuses et attitudes politiques dans la France contemporaine.* Paris: Armand Colin, 1965.

Roche, Douglas J. *The Catholic Revolution.* New York: David McKay, 1968.

Rossi, Ernesto. *Pagine anticlericali.* Rome: Samonà e Savelli, 1966.

———. *Dal Partito Popolare alla Democrazia Cristiana.* Bologna: Universale Cappeli, 1969.

Rossi, Mario. *Laïcs pour des temps nouveaux.* Paris: Editions de l'Epi, 1965.

Rossini, G. *Il movimento cattolico nel periodo facista.* Rome: Cinque Lune, 1966.

Rouquette, Robert. *Une nouvelle chrétienté.* Paris: Editions du Cerf, 1968.

Ruether, Rosemary Radford. *The Radical Kingdom: The Western Experience of Messianic Hope.* New York: Harper and Row, 1970.

Rynne, Xavier. See Francis X. Murphy.

Salamone, W. A. *Italy in the Giolittan Era—Italian Democracy in the Making, 1900–1914.* Philadelphia: University of Pennsylvania Press, 1960.

Salvatorelli, Luigi. *Chiesa e stato dalla rivoluzione francese ai nostri giorni.* Florence: Nuovo Italia, 1955.

———, and Giovanni, Mira. *Storia d'Italia nel periodo facista.* Turin: Einaudi, 1957.

Sánchez, José M. *Anticlericalism: A Brief History.* Notre Dame, Ind.: University of Notre Dame Press, 1972.

Sartori, G., et al. *Il parlamento Italiano 1946–1963.* Naples: Edizioni Scientifiche Italiane, 1963.

Sassoli, D. *La destra in Italia.* Rome: Cinque Lune, 1957.

Scalfari, E. *L'autumno della Repubblica, la mappa del potere in Italia.* Milan: Etas Kimpass, 1969.

Scanù, L. *Il cardinale Mercelle Mimmi: L'uomo dell'essenziale.* Naples: Fiorentino, 1964.

Schillebeeckx, Edward. *The Layman in the Church.* New York: Alba House, 1963.

Scoppola, Pietro. *Crisi modernista e rinnovamento cattolico in Italia.* Bologna: Il Mulino, 1969.

Selznick, Philip. *Law, Society and Industrial Justice.* New York: Russell Sage Foundation, 1969.

———. *The Organization Weapon: A Study of Bolshevik Strategy and Tactics.* New York: Free Press of Glencoe, 1960.

Serafian, Michael. See Malachi Martin.

Seton-Watson, C. *Italy from Liberalism to Fascism.* London: Methuen, 1967.

Siefer, Gregor. *The Church and Industrial Society.* London: Darton, Longman and Todd, 1964.

Smith, Denis Mack. *Italy: A Modern History.* Ann Arbor: University of Michigan Press, 1959.

Spadolini, Giovanni. *Gioletti e i cattolica.* Florence: Vallechi, 1960.

———. *Le due Rome: Chiesa e stato fra '800 e '900.* Florence: Le Mounier, 1973.

———. *L'opposizione cattolica.* Florence: Vallechi, 1955.

Stark, Rodney, and Glock, Charles Y. *American Piety: The Nature of Religious Commitment.* Berkeley and Los Angeles: University of California Press, 1968.

Stéphane, André, *L'Univers contestationnaire ou les nouveaux chrétiens: Etudes psychanalytiques.* Paris: Payot, 1969.

Sturzo, Luigi. *Il Partito Popolare italiano.* 3 vols. Bologna: Zanichelli, 1956–1957.

———. *Popolarismo e facismo: Saggi e testimonianze.* Rome: Civitas, 1960.

Suffert, Georges. *Les Catholiques et la gauche.* Paris: Maspéro, 1960.

Swanson, Guy E. *Religion and Regime: A Sociological Account of the Reformation.* Ann Arbor: University of Michigan Press, 1967.

Tardini, Domenico. *Memories of Pius XII.* Westminster, Md.: Newman Press, 1961.

Thompson, K. A. *Bureaucracy and Church Reform: The Organizational Response of the Church of England to Social Change.* London: Oxford University Press, 1970.

Togliatti, Palmiro. "Facisti e popolari nel 1922–1923." *Rinascita* 20, no. 12 (March 23, 1963): 17–19.

Troeltsch, Ernst. *The Social Teachings of the Christian Churches.* 2 vols. New York: Macmillan, 1931.

Truman, Tom. *Catholic Action and Politics.* London: Merlin Press, 1960.

Ullman, Walter. *The Growth of Papal Government in the Middle Ages: A Study of the Ideological Relations of Clerical to Lay Power.* London: Methuen, 1955.

Underwood, Kenneth. *Protestant and Catholic.* Boston: Beacon Press, 1957.

Vallier, Ivan. "Religious Specialists." In David L. Sills, ed., *International Encyclopedia of the Social Sciences.* New York: Macmillan and the Free Press, 1968.

———. "Roman Catholicism in Transition." In Ivan Vallier et al. *Anglican Opportunities in South America.* New York: Columbia University Press, 1963.

Van Lierde, Peter Canisius. *The Holy See at Work: How the Catholic Church Is Governed.* New York: Hawthorn Press, 1962.

Vaussard, Maurice. *Histoire de la Démocratie Chrétienne.* Paris: Seuil, 1956.

Vercesi, E. *Storia del movimento cattolico in Italia (1870–1922).* Florence: La Voce, 1923.

Wach, Joachim. *A Comparative Study of Religion.* New York: Columbia University Press, 1958.

———. *Sociology of Religion.* Chicago: University of Chicago Press, 1962.

Weber, Max. *Ancient Judaism.* Glencoe, Ill.: Free Press, 1952.

———. *Economy and Society.* Edited by Guenther Roth and Claus Wittich. New York: Bedminster Press, 1968.

———. *The Sociology of Religion.* Boston: Beacon Press, 1963.

Webster, Richard A. *The Cross and the Fasces: Christian Democracy and Fascism in Italy.* Stanford: Stanford University Press, 1960.

Woodrow, Alain. *L'Eglise déchirée.* Paris: Editions Ramsay, 1978.

Yinger, J. M. *Religion in the Struggle for Power: A Study of the Sociology of Religion.* Durham, N.C.: Duke University Press, 1946.

Zahn, Gordon. *German Catholics and Hitler's War: A Study in Social Control.* New York: Sheed and Ward, 1962.

Zizola, Giancarlo. *Quale papa?* Rome: Borla, 1977.

———. *L'Utopie du pape Jean XXIII.* Paris: Seuil, 1978.

Index

Abbo, Giovanni, 288

Abortion referendum, 236

ACLI. *See* Christian Association of Italian Workers

Action Catholique de la Jeunesse Française (ACJF), 42

Action Française, 42; papal condemnation absolved, 50

Adenauer, Konrad, 62, 206

Adesso, suppressed by the Holy Office, 210–211

Administration of Vatican City, 246

Adolfs, Robert, 281

Adzhubei, Aleksei, 206

Africa, 103; liberal bishop from, 100; and preparation for the second World Congress for the Lay Apostolate, 71; torture in, 220

African delegates at the third World Congress, 99, 104; geocultural classification of, 134, 152, 156, 157, 158, 161, 162–163, 167; grants for travel expenses, 99, 278

Age: and attitudes on Church authority, 164; correlated with orthodoxy and Church authority, 163–164, 166–167; divisions in Catholic Action, 47, 69; of lay national delegates, 99, 135, 152, 156, 163–164, 166–167

Aggiornamento, 125, 209, 214, 225; initiated by John XXIII, 282

Alexandria, 26

Allum, P.A., 197

Amichia, Joseph, 115

Andreotti, Giulio, 189

Andrews, James F., 281

Anglo-Saxon lay national delegates, 152, 156, 157, 161, 162

Anticlericalism, 34, 39, 272

Anticommunism, 58; of Hitler and Mussolini, 274; of the Vatican and the papacy, 51, 53, 73, 190, 191, 194, 196–197, 199, 201, 203, 256

Anti-modernist purges by Pius X, 42, 179

Antioch, 26

Antonetti, Lorenzo, Msgr., 247, 288; encyclical drafted by, 38

Lay Congress of Mainz, 37, 38

Lay demands, 6, 7, 85; for change in
birth control, 110–113; for participation in decision-making, 118–119,
124, 131, 149, 151; for participation
in Church affairs, 36–37, 84–91, 103,
118–119, 120–121, 128–129, 147–
151; for representative structures and
elections, 120–121, 128–129; at the
third World Congress, 120–126

Lay leaders, 104–105; development of
organized activity by, 36–41; emerging from the first World Congress,
63; interaction with Vatican officials,
9, 62, 96–97, 114–117; obtaining
data on, 10–11; organizational control
by Church authorities, 15; papal and
Vatican control over, 9, 166–170,
286–287; role in organizing the third
World Congress, 102–103; selection
of representative, 287. *See also* Lay
national delegates

Lay movement: auditors and guests at
Vatican II, 80–84; conservatives vs.
progressives in, 42–43, 45, 58, 98,
99–101, 105, 106; financial support
of, 67–68; and first World Congress
for the Lay Apostolate, 60–67; influenced by media coverage of politics at
Vatican II, 92; and lay members on
the board of directors for COPECIAL,
78; legitimation of lay organizations,
72; moderate opposition to the Roman
Curia, 66; organizations classified by
COPECIAL, 79–80; power struggles
in Italian Catholicism, 67–70

Lay movement, origins of, 19–59; and
the Counter-Reformation, 33; development of the clergy-laity distinction,
21–22, 25–26, 27, 33, 35; development of organized activity, 36–41;
during the French Revolution and
nationalism, 34–36; during the Middle Ages, 29–32; during the Renaissance, 32–33; in the eleventh century,
27–28; elimination of the autonomy
of the laity, 31–32; influence of Benedict XV's policies, 44–45

Lay national delegates, 130–170; attitudes toward racism, 137, 154–155;
correlates of religious ideology of,
163–166; Church authority and power
viewed by, 144–145; episcopal and
priestly authority viewed by, 145–147;
geocultural categories of, 6, 134, 151–
163; homogeneity among, 157; lay
power and participation viewed by,
147–151; moderate liberal orientation
of, 138, 143, 147, 151, 166; religious
activities and beliefs of, 138–141, 157–
163; selection process for, 162, 167;
social and political backgrounds of, 134–
138, 154–157; sociological survey of,
132–170; travel grants for, 99, 154,
162, 278; and Vatican control of lay
groups, 166–170

Lay participation in Church affairs, 103;
debated at Vatican II, 84–91; lay demands for, 36–37, 84–91, 103, 118–
119, 120–121; opinions of lay national
delegates on, 147–151; papal opposition to, 118–119, via representative
structures and elections, 120–121,
128–129

Lazzati, Giuseppe, 52, 54

Lebanese delegates at the third World
Congress, 123

Lebret, Louis-Joseph, 71

Ledochowski, Count Wladimir, 192

Lefebvre, Marcel, Archbishop, 294; and
election of John Paul I, 291; rightist
reactionary position of, 8, 214, 224,
245, 258

Left: Catholic party of, 178, 234; Catholic vote for, 198, 241; Christian
Democrats, 196, 197; formation of
Christians for Socialism, 221–222;
gains in national Italian elections, 238;
and Pope John XXIII, 204–208. *See
also* Communist Party; Socialist Party

Legal power, 267, 278, 279; attack on
the abuses of, 285

Legion of Mary, 72

Legitimation, 92; and concessions from
conservative governments, 190; of the
Fascist regime, 186, 187, 188; during

tinction between international and national delegates at, 63–64; evolution of, 57–58; goal of, 61; lay leaders emerging from, 63, 72; liberals vs. conservatives at, 57, 65–66, 67; as a political maneuver, 57, 256; published proceedings of, 64, 66, 71; representatives at, 63, 70; resolutions at, 66–67; speech by Pius XII at, 39, 66, 117; topics discussed at, 62–63, 64; Vatican control of, 64–65

World Congress for the Lay Apostolate, second, 7, 10, 70–74; Catholic Action discussed at, 72; delegates at, 70; liberals vs. conservatives at, 72–74; non-Catholic observer at, 72; published proceedings of, 74; role of the Italian laity at, 70; themes of, 71, 72

World Congress for the Lay Apostolate, third xiii, 7, 9–10, 95–170, 282–283; birth control issue at, 109–113, 117, 123, 126; bishops vs. freedom and demands of the laity at, 113–117, 120–121, 128; conservatives vs. progressives and liberals at, 98, 99–101, 105, 106; control mechanisms used by the Vatican and the hierarchy at, 95–96, 97, 100–101, 110, 114–119 *passim;* 126, 278–279; democratization of the Church discussed at, 120–121, 124–126; documents of, 97–98, 113–115; expectations of, 103–104; experts at, 97, 98, 102, 109, 133, 279; grants for travel expenses, 99, 154, 162, 278; hierarchical and papal reaction to, 126–131; influenced by Vatican II, 92, 103; and international protests against the Church, 218; lay demands at,

120–126; lay obedience stressed by Pope Paul VI at, 118, 120; "mandated" and "sponsored" groups at, 98, 103; moderate leaders at, 106; national and international delegates at, 97, 98, 99–100, 133 (*see also* Lay national delegates); non-Catholics at, 131; opening day of, 104–105; organizers and participants of, 96–101, 167; power of the Steering Committee for, 97, 98, 106, 108, 115, 120; preparation for, 79, 101–104; published proceedings of, 108, 124, 127; questionnaire survey used at, xiv, 7, 11, 14, 133, 134, 311; resolutions of, 97, 98, 108, 109, 112, 115, 121–126; themes of, 96, 104, 109, 121. *See also* Lay national delegates

World Consultation of the Laity, Vatican control of, 287

World Movement of Christian Workers, 102

Wright, John, 246

Wrong, Dennis, 14

Wu, John C.H., 72

Young Catholic Workers. *See* Jeunesse Ouvrière Catholique (JOC)

Young Men's Catholic Action, 69

Youth, 98

Youth Catholic Action, 48, 50, 54; crises in, 85

Zaccagnini, Benigno, 236

Zahn, Gordon, 282

Zeitlin, Irving M., 14–15

Zoa, Jean, 100

Zouaves, 174, 175, 276, 294

Designer:	Eric Jungerman
Compositor:	Freedmen's Organization
Printer:	Publishers Press
Binder:	Mountain States Bindery
Text:	Compugraphic Bem
Display:	Weiss Series II initials
Cloth:	Holliston Roxite B
Paper:	50 lb. P&S Offset